Riches
and
Regrets

Betting on Gambling in
Two Colorado Mountain Towns

Patricia A. Stokowski

UNIVERSITY PRESS OF COLORADO

© 1996 by the University Press of Colorado
Published by the University Press of Colorado
P. O. Box 849
Niwot, Colorado 80544
Tel. (303) 530-5337

The University Press of Colorado is a cooperative publishing enterprise supported, in part, by Adams State College, Colorado State University, Fort Lewis College, Mesa State College, Metropolitan State College of Denver, University of Colorado, University of Northern Colorado, University of Southern Colorado, and Western State College of Colorado.

Library of Congress Cataloging-in-Publication Data

Stokowski, Patricia A.
    Riches and regrets: betting on gambling in two Colorado mountain
towns / Patricia A. Stokowski.
        p.   cm.
    Includes bibliographical references and index.
    ISBN 0-87081-428-1
    1. Gambling—Economic aspects—Colorado—Gilpin County.
    2. Gambling—Social aspects—Colorado—Gilpin County. 3. Community
development—Colorado—Gilpin County. 4. Tourist trade—Colorado—
Gilpin County. 5. Blackhawk (Colo.) 6. Central City (Colo.)
I. Title.
HV6721.G55S76 1996
338.4'7795'0978862—dc20   96-10138
                                                CIP

This book was set in Adobe Caslon and Adobe AG Oldface.

The paper used in this publication meets the minimum requirements of the American National Standard for Information Sciences—Permanence of Paper for Printed Library Materials. ANSI Z39.48–1948
∞

10   9   8   7   6   5   4   3   2   1

ACKNOWLEDGMENTS

I could not have conducted the research described in this book, or completed the writing, without the generous assistance and encouragement of many people. Much of the data collection, analysis, and early draft writing occurred between 1991 and 1994, while I was a research associate with the Environment and Behavior Program, Institute of Behavioral Science, University of Colorado, Boulder. I am grateful to Dr. Charles W. Howe, E&B Director, who provided technical resources, timely financial support, and continuous positive reinforcement for my work. My E&B colleagues were wonderfully stimulating, and several provided extraordinary assistance at critical moments. In particular, Dr. Warren Hern, Jeri and Bob Carruthers, Marcia and Dr. Bob Davis, Joanne Dunnebecke and Dr. John Wiener, Mary Fran Myers, Dr. Brigitte Desaigues and Dr. Ari Rabl, and Joanne Howe and Dr. Chuck Howe all provided accommodations when I returned to Boulder on research trips in 1995 and 1996, and each also contributed substantial doses of emotional support throughout the entire research and writing process. Many other members of the IBS staff clipped news articles, helped fix computer problems, and kept me informed about gambling-related matters; I very much appreciate their assistance.

Most of the book was written in 1994 and 1995, after I had taken a faculty position with the Department of Recreation, Park and Tourism Sciences and the Texas Agricultural Experiment Station at Texas A&M University, College Station. I appreciate the support of my new institution, department, and colleagues in facilitating the completion of this book. Dr. John Crompton and his wife, Liz, were especially helpful. John was always willing to review my writing, and he offered scholarly guidance as well as motivational talks to smooth my way. Liz contributed her sensitive listening skills and home-cooked meals to sustain me through the difficult parts. I am privileged to have such compassionate, caring friends. I also appreciate the skilled computer help of our graduate student, J. Ethan Beeson, who produced the two figures used in the book.

Many residents and community leaders in Central City, Black Hawk, and Gilpin County generously shared their time, thoughts, and feelings with me in both formal interviews and informal conversations. Because I promised confidentiality to most, I cannot reveal their names. I do hope, though, that each person who spoke with me knows how very much I value their comments and time; I am honored by their trust. I would like to publicly acknowledge the assistance of Roger Baker, formerly librarian at the Gilpin County Public Library, and then administrator at the Gilpin County Chamber of Commerce. Roger provided extensive and continuous assistance throughout the project, proving that the best friend one can have in conducting this kind of community research is a librarian-historian-journalist who shares materials and knowledge! His willingness to check references, keep me posted on the latest local news, and read drafts of my articles and book saved me from numerous embarrassing errors. I am grateful for all his help and for his friendship.

Many government agencies, voluntary organizations, and casino managers in Black Hawk, Central City, and Gilpin County discussed their operations with me. Again, because I promised confidentiality in interviews, I am unable to name specific individuals; I remain grateful for their input and willingness to share their ideas and time with me. In addition, several local residents were especially generous in providing access to special kinds of organizational data or in facilitating contacts with other persons. I would like to thank Diane Rittenhouse, Columbine Family Health Center; John Rittenhouse, Gilpin County Search and Rescue; Bruce Hartman, Gilpin County Sheriff; Jeannie Nicholson, formerly Gilpin County Nurse; Pat Carr and his staff, Gilpin County Social Services; Lew Cady, *The Little Kingdom Come;* and Pat Wendleton, formerly Central City's information officer.

I am indebted to officials in various divisions of Colorado's state government and the federal government, as well as many private organizations, for providing information and for sharing reports containing historical and contemporary data. Most of the organizations are credited in the tables, but I would especially like to acknowledge the courtesy and helpfulness shown to me by Tom Kitts, Division of Gaming; David Chapman, Mike Rose, and others at the Colorado Department of Labor and Employment; staff at the Colorado Department of Transportation, Department of Education, and the State Auditor's Office; Jack Kirtland, Colorado Department of Local Affairs; Richard D. Lamm, former Colorado governor; and staff at the National Park Service and Environmental Protection Agency. Likewise, the library staff of

CONTENTS

TABLES AND FIGURES

TABLES

FIGURES

PREFACE

I first visited Central City and Black Hawk in early spring 1989 when, on holiday, a friend and I drove into the mountains in search of a gold mine to tour. We eventually found ourselves in Central City, where a stiff March wind chased dried sage around historic Main Street buildings. When I unexpectedly moved to Colorado several months later to accept a position at the University of Colorado at Boulder, I renewed my acquaintance with Gilpin County. As in my first visit, I was struck by the tangible sense of history and the feeling of remoteness present in these towns. The granite buildings remembered older, more glorious, gold rush times, and mine tailings dumps scattered across the hillsides were testimony to the hard work and hopefulness of early miners. Carved from the mountains, Black Hawk and Central City seemed lost in time.

The proposal to introduce limited stakes gambling to Black Hawk, Central City, and Cripple Creek, emerging in fall 1989, was particularly interesting to me, as I had been teaching and conducting research about issues related to social and cultural impacts of tourism and rural, resource-dependent communities for several years. I was especially intrigued by the overwhelmingly positive claims of gambling proponents, and by how readily citizens apparently accepted their claims as "the truth." I began to follow with more than passing interest the progress of the gambling campaign, expanding my interest into full-scale research work. To the best of my knowledge, I am the only researcher who initiated research projects in the community prior to the actual operation of casinos; I have subsequently continued my research work for six years.

Though I never intended to write a book about the gaming developments, I found in my research that issues related to community economic development and gambling tourism were complex as well as socially and politically meaningful. I was particularly interested in three issues:

1. How did local history and culture influence the process of gambling development?
2. To what extent is gaming development similar to or different from other types of boomtown experience?
3. What can other communities interested in gaming development, especially rural communities, learn from the process and outcomes of the developments in Central City and Black Hawk?

As my scholarly journal articles about these topics became more and more lengthy, a book began to take shape.

I focussed my research and writing primarily on the Gilpin County towns of Central City and Black Hawk, Colorado, providing data from Cripple Creek (Colorado's third gaming town) and other gaming places only when it illustrated something important about the situation in the Gilpin County towns. Confining my attention to Central City and Black Hawk allowed me to evaluate the shared geographical, historical, economic, political, and social circumstances that simultaneously formed these towns and persistently influences their futures. My research took the form of a multimethod, longitudinal case study extending across the entirety of the gambling tourism development process: from the historical conditions that allowed the idea of gambling to achieve public acceptability, through the predevelopment activities of discussion and negotiation, into the construction phase prior to and including Opening Day, and over the next five years of impacts and community adaptation. Throughout, my focus was not on individuals but on community, and on the processes by which gaming tourism development affects community well-being, coordination, power, and meaning.

For those interested in the methodological details, I provide the following list of research activities. Living just an hour from Gilpin County, I visited Black Hawk and Central City regularly, often weekly, over the first several years of gaming development to observe and record community transformations. I reviewed primary and secondary historical and contemporary materials, including census documents, literary works, writings and photographs, and news accounts of the early gold rush days and more recent events. I documented quantitative changes in the communities using statistical data provided by local, county, and state agencies; these data included information about population trends, business activity, criminal and police reports, traffic, social and health services, the gaming industry, and other variables. I conducted several hundred formal and informal interviews with community leaders, residents, and gaming industry officials. (In this book, all the quotations attributed to "a resident" or "a community leader" are drawn from the transcripts of these interviews. Because I promised confidentiality, I cannot identify respondents by name.) I collected and content-analyzed newspaper articles and opinion letters about the gaming developments from the major county newspaper and from several metropolitan newspapers. In conjunction with a mail survey for the Gilpin County Library, I was able to ask several questions about interorganizational linkages among community agencies. In addition, I documented in photographs and slides the physical changes to the community, shooting more than 1,500 images across all stages of the development process (all the photographs in this book are from my own collection). In the process of writing this book, I also did extensive literature reviews of scholarly and public writing about gambling and gaming development, community impacts of tourism growth, rural and resource-dependent communities, and boomtown growth and decline. Taken together, these methods are typical research procedures used by sociologists to understand communities in transition.

Several technical issues are important to how one reads this book. First, though Central City and Black Hawk are, strictly speaking, "cities" (many gold rush towns adopted that term to make it seem that life on the frontier was more civilized), I refer to them throughout this book as *towns,* perhaps more fitting given their small populations. I reserve the term *cities* for the major metropolitan areas near the gaming towns — Denver, Boulder, Golden, and others. I hope the residents of Gilpin County will forgive this slight manipulation; I think it makes the text easier to understand for people who are not familiar with the area. Likewise, though the "City of Central" is often called just "Central" by locals, this usage can be confusing, so I simply settled on calling it "Central City" throughout the book.

In addition, I have included many primary and secondary citations about local history in the first two chapters, and have given numerous references to newspaper articles about the gaming developments in chapters 3 through 10, in part to provide an organized documentation of community events. Many fictions have been written about Gilpin County history in general, and gaming development in particular, and I felt it was important to provide precise documentary evidence about the chronology and events under study. Moreover, in addition to clarification of this historic record, newspaper articles in particular serve as a source of community information and rhetoric, providing an additional type of data archive for social researchers. Though some of the more prominent authors of articles or opinion columns have been identified, most newspaper citations are referenced under the newspaper name. (In the interests of brevity and reader convenience, the parenthetical references to the *Weekly Register-Call* and *The Little Kingdom Come* have been abbreviated as *WRC* and *LKC*, respectively.)

This book includes both quantitative and qualitative data because there is far too little of either in contemporary debates about the merits of gaming development. Given the political nature and emotionalism of debates about gaming across the United States, and the inclinations of some people to level charges of bias against anyone who disagrees with their viewpoints, I have worked especially diligently to present all sides of the story. Throughout, my primary emphasis has been to provide data-based social analyses so that other communities may be well informed about issues that arise when gaming is considered as a local development strategy.

Government Publications and the Western History Collection, both at Norlin Library, University of Colorado, Boulder, were always willing to help me find and interpret materials.

Several academic colleagues were absolutely central to the development of the research and the completion of the book. Dr. William R. Freudenburg, University of Wisconsin, Madison, was my companion in tours of Gilpin County gold mines and ghost towns. He generously shared his own work on western boomtowns, and offered scholarly criticism, advice, reprints, and encouragement over the entire period of research and writing. Despite other demands on his time, he reviewed the book manuscript in 1995, making substantial, detailed comments that improved the final presentation immeasurably. Kristi Branch, Battelle Memorial Institute, Seattle, was also helpful in early stages of the research, joining me in several data-gathering excursions to the towns and discussing issues relevant to the substance and conduct of the research. At the University of Colorado, Dr. Charles Goeldner (College of Business and Administration, Boulder) and Dr. Rudi Hartmann (Department of Geography, Denver) each gave me opportunities to try out my ideas on their respective tourism and geography classes, a process that helped shaped my own ideas more fully. Rudi also invited me to participate in several events with groups of visiting international geographers, stimulating contacts that have been important for my work. Dr. Bernie Jones (Colorado Center for Community Development, Denver) was kind enough to share results of his Gilpin County research with me. In 1994, Dr. Leanne Sander (Department of History, University of Colorado, Boulder) generously arranged for me to listen to audiotapes of her interviews with Gilpin County old-timers. I am also grateful to my students in organizational communication classes and independent studies at the University of Colorado, Boulder, who challenged my thinking through their own research and writing.

Although my research began primarily as an interesting personal project, it assumed a very visible public life because of the energetic efforts of staff in the University of Colorado, Boulder, Public Relations Office. They understood earlier than I that my work had significant public interest and policy implications, and they accepted the challenge of teaching a confirmed academic how to work with the mass media. I am especially grateful to Peter Caughey for his unfailing good humor and his diligent efforts in publicizing my work and coordinating the public distribution of my research findings. Additionally, Jeannine Malmsbury, Danielle Zieg, J. Martin Natvig, and others in the Public Relations offices were instrumental in bringing my work to the attention of the print and broadcast media, and I remain appreciative of their interest and professionalism.

As a result of the media attention, I was invited to speak with many interest groups in Colorado and elsewhere. I would like to express my thanks to the organizations that were interested in hearing about my research work; the speaking opportunities were helpful in stimulating my ideas about community research, gambling tourism, and western rural places. I also appreciate the work of the fine publishing and editing staff at the University Press of Colorado. Luther Wilson, director, and his staff have been uniformly helpful and congenial, and I feel honored that they have chosen to publish this book. An anonymous reviewer who read my book manuscript in 1995 provided a very useful critical analysis. Whatever errors remain are, of course, my own responsibility.

I am writing the last few sentences of these acknowledgments in Boulder, Colorado, on a winter day of exquisite beauty following a storm that blanketed the area with fresh powdery snow. As I enjoy the brilliant blue sky expanding over our white-mantled Flatirons, I remember fondly all those whose lives have intersected with mine in Gilpin County and in Boulder. Though I have now moved away, landscape and people remain intertwined in my memory of these special places. Consequently, I dedicate this book to my cherished colleagues from the Environment and Behavior Program of the Institute of Behavioral Science at the University of Colorado, Boulder, and to the mountainous landscapes that have filled our spirits, energized our scholarly work, and framed our joyous friendships.

INTRODUCTION

I wondered what the Spirit of the Mountain was thinking, and looked up
and saw jackpines in the moon, and saw ghosts of old miners, and wondered
about it. In the whole eastern dark wall of the Divide this night there was
silence and the whisper of the wind, except in the ravine where we roared.
                                                    — Jack Kerouac (1955: 47)

In the history of Central City and Black Hawk, Colorado, there have been
three unexpectedly great moments exceeding all capacity for imagination and
prediction. The first of these was the 1859 discovery that gold blossomed on
the hillsides and washed down local streams in quantities large enough to
make some miners rich and some communities profitable. The mystique of
the elusive golden mineral, and the challenge of obtaining gold against the
forces of nature, reinforced a notion of power through subjugation, a theme
that can be traced through much of Western American history. Moreover, the
adventurous setting along unexplored frontier territory stimulated a mythology of place that invigorated generations of people who later settled across
these rich landscapes.

The second significant moment in the history of the area was the restoration of the Central City Opera House and the revival of opera performances
in 1932. Music festivals and theatrical presentations had always been popular
in the community, but it took special vision among a small group of people—
heirs of Gilpin County and Colorado pioneer leaders—to transform a crumbling opera house in a remote mountain town into an intimate theater that
attracted society folk from Denver and elsewhere. The successful renovation
of the Opera House redefined Central City and Black Hawk as tourist attractions, but opera restoration highlighted the power of local symbols while
simultaneously producing conflicts over the interpretation of past history.
Restoration also quietly reinforced a model of external support and financing
for local affairs, a situation that was prevalent during the mining times when
eastern and midwestern entrepreneurs and speculators funded much of the
exploration and processing of gold (King 1977).

The mythology of a special Western place, and the model of external financing, were invoked again during the third defining moment in the history of Central City and Black Hawk: the institutionalization in 1991 of limited stakes gambling as a form of local economic development. Gambling development, like mining and opera, uses history and geography to support various representations of reality, some of which are truthful and some of which are not. Like mining and opera, gaming is speculative, mythical, and romantic, enticing dreamers to participate in fantasies of unlimited futures. Whereas mining created community, and opera reaffirmed community spirit, gambling may be the mechanism by which community is replaced with an "attraction" that attends primarily to the interests of tourists, rather than residents.

Each of these three extraordinary events—mining, opera, and gambling—triggered widespread changes in the built and natural environments of Central City, Black Hawk, and surrounding regions of Gilpin County. Each event produced significant social, political, and economic consequences for both local residents and regional populations. Each of these events, unique for its time, placed the local area squarely in the national spotlight of public interest. Of the three, however, gaming development may be the most confrontational and unsettling for the community. From the initial proposals by gaming promoters, beginning in late 1988, and the vote to allow gambling in 1989, through the construction period up to Opening Day on October 1, 1991, and during several years of postopening operation and impacts, the development process has been anything but smooth. Central City and Black Hawk are certainly unusual and extraordinary places, but the outcomes emerging in Gilpin County replicate patterns of gaming development visible in other locales, revealing lessons for other communities that seek their own golden dreams at the slot machines and casino tables.

THE SETTING

The process and rationale for choosing gambling as a development strategy originated in the geography, history, and spirit of place in the Gilpin County mountain communities. Central City (elevation 8,496 ft.) and Black Hawk (elevation 8,042 ft.) are situated only one mile apart in the mountainous terrain of Gilpin County, Colorado (Figure I.1).

Only 150 square miles in size (U.S. Department of Commerce 1994), and bounded by the 14,000-foot-high mountains of the Continental Divide on the western border, Gilpin County is the smallest rural county in Colorado. Located about an hour west of Denver in the foothills of the Rocky Mountains, Black Hawk and Central City are approached from the north or south via the two-lane state Highway 119, also known as the Peak to Peak Scenic

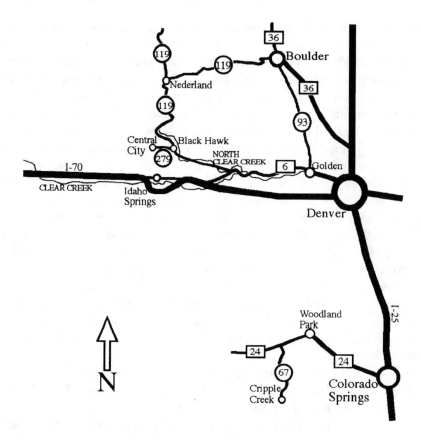

Figure I.1   Gilpin County, Colorado and Surrounding Area

Highway. Along this narrow, winding road are rocky hillsides dotted with mines and mine tailings, wandering herds of bighorn sheep, and the mineral-stained waters of Clear Creek. Currently the only two incorporated places in the county, Central City and Black Hawk were once the focal communities of a network of gold camps and towns scattered throughout the region.

Gilpin County is a place of breathtaking beauty, an area once described as the "Switzerland of America" by visitors (Bowles 1869a). Pine, spruce, and cedar forests meander over the hillsides, connected by patches of wild grasses and mine tailings dumps. In the autumn, stands of aspen spread golden color across the gulches. About 48 percent of the land in the county is privately owned; remaining parcels are managed by the U.S. Department of Agriculture's Forest Service, the Department of Interior's Bureau of Land Management, the Colorado State Parks agency, and the state school lands agency.

Amenities in Gilpin County and the surrounding area include several forest campgrounds, a state park, numerous ghost towns and historic cemeteries, and the Eldora ski resort just north of the county border in Boulder County.

Geography created a complex interdependency between Central City and Black Hawk; history reinforced it. The first significant gold strike in the region that would later become Colorado was made in the canyon about halfway between Central City and Black Hawk. Mine owners, bankers, business owners, and politicians gravitated to the top of the canyon to build a cosmopolitan, commercial, cultured, "Central City," while mine and mill workers were distributed around the area in other townsites. Black Hawk, at the bottom of the canyon, and adjacent to the streambed of North Clear Creek, developed into a working-class town that earned the nickname "City of Mills." It was for a time the terminus of the railroad, the site of large gold crushing and milling operations, and the distribution center for minerals transported down the canyons to Golden, Denver, and elsewhere. The wealth of minerals taken from these hills encouraged miners to acclaim this area as "the richest square mile on earth," and more than 4,300 people once lived in the towns. During the height of the gold rush, houses climbed over one another up the steeply terraced hillsides around and between Black Hawk and Central City.

The entire Gilpin County area, but especially the historic townsites of Central City and Black Hawk, have captured the imagination of people since the beginnings of the gold rush. Visitors did not always have kind words for the area, though. Acclaimed journalist Horace Greeley said at his first view of the gold diggings and towns in 1859, "Mining is a necessary art, but it does not tend to beautify the face of nature" (Greeley 1860: 292). Eastern traveller Samuel Bowles, who toured the valleys of Clear Creek and visited Central City, Black Hawk, and other local mining centers on his summer vacation in 1868, echoed Greeley's sentiments. Glowing with praise for the beauty of Colorado, he was somewhat unfavorably impressed with the mining areas of Gilpin County (Bowles 1869a: 53), writing, "Black Hawk and Central City may be very good places to get gold in, but there can be no genuine homes there. The valley is too narrow, a mere ravine, and all beauty is sacrificed to . . . the mere use of washing out gold." He may have been right: mining eventually declined, and by 1990, fewer than 600 people resided in the two former gold camps.

Bowles may have been overly harsh about the prospects for habitation, as others found the mountainous place evocative. Over time, popular and scholarly writings, and numerous books, theses, and dissertations, have been written to confirm the historical importance of Gilpin County, Central City, and

Black Hawk. The area has also been popularized in movies and television shows: episodes of *Perry Mason* and *Route 66,* and scenes for *The Duchess and the Dirtwater Fox* (a 1970s movie) and the 1980s *Dream West* television miniseries about the life of John Fremont were filmed in the area. Black Hawk and Central City and other parts of the local landscape have also been portrayed in a variety of fictional writings, too. A romance novel (Kramer 1990) recalled the glory days and difficulties of life in the 1871 mining towns; a murder mystery was solved by a cognac-drinking investigator attempting to enjoy a holiday at the Central City Play Festival (Halliday 1943); and a psychoanalyst investigating crimes had spectacular adventures on the roads of Gilpin County (White 1993). Jack Kerouac even described a short 1947 visit to Central City in his 1955 beat generation novel, *On the Road,* though he manipulated the details a bit (Central City was said to be a famous silver mining town situated at an elevation of two miles, for example).[1]

THE WESTERN HERITAGE

Equal in importance to their special geographic and historic characteristics are Central City's and Black Hawk's archetypal qualities as rural Western places. The Western frontier was a place far removed from civilized life in cities and towns of the eastern and midwestern states. The frontier in Colorado was also distinguished by the presence of the visible, magnificent Rocky Mountains, of which Cronin and Loevy (1993: 7) wrote, "The mountains . . . leave a psychological impact on Coloradans. They are rugged and rocky. They test one's independence as well as one's character . . . [encouraging] a sense of freedom, space, and separateness." Pioneers who followed the trails across the plains to the frontier wrote about the extraordinary moment when the mountains rose up from the prairie to touch the sky, rewarding and confirming the independent, adventuresome spirit that motivated emigration. The Rocky Mountains thus became a lasting reminder of the Colorado frontier experience.

Along the frontier, life was hard, nature was unpredictable and often extreme, and only the sturdiest and most hopeful of settlers stayed to forge communities from the wilderness. As explained by Gressley (1994: 12), this was "a West of progress, full of rugged individualism that melded with a democratic spirit, which in turn flowed along with civilization across a hostile land." The challenge of conquering this forbidding land (Limerick 1987) gave rise to a mythology of place and people that supported images of the West as a center of pioneer spirit, burgeoning independence, and progress. For example, journalist A. D. Richardson, who travelled throughout the West during the 1860s and 1870s, wrote (1873: 327, 333): "There is a permanent westerly current in our social and political atmosphere. . . . Western emigration makes men larger and riper, more liberal and fraternal." This illusion achieved status as a national myth, according to White (1991: 621), who explained, "Late-nineteenth-century Americans imagined the West ... as the premodern world they had lost. In it life was primitive but also simple, real, and basic. ... Life in the West could restore authenticity, moral order, and masculinity." Such sentiments are notable for their exclusive views, their idealism, and their disregard for entire social groups of participants in the Western drama, an issue documented most vividly by "New West" historians.[2] Yet the persistence of frontier images is evident even today in much popular discourse, including, as will be seen later, in the rhetoric and presentation of gambling development in Central City and Black Hawk.

The frontier gold mining town, in particular, persists in American culture as a monument to Western individualism and progress. Scarred landscapes of Western gold mining towns are reminders of what is seen to be an imaginative and unlimited past. Mine tailings littering the hillsides attest to past successes, and lure newcomers with subtle messages: "No true vein has ever been known to give out. Gold is beautiful. Gold is indestructible. Gold is the substance of dreams" (Pettem 1980: 120). Gold mining towns were the most romantic of the Western frontier towns, but as Marks (1994: 376) pointed out, "The gold frontier was only a slight exaggeration of the nineteenth-century American frontier in general in being a place of high hopes and dashed expectations." If enthusiasm alone could have sustained the Western gold rush, everyone would have struck it rich in Colorado's mountains and streams. But successful gold mining depended on any number of factors beyond the control of individual miners, a lesson that was learned the hard way by those who returned home penniless from the frontier.

Gold mining towns, and other rural communities that formed around the possibilities for natural resource extraction, were typically unstable places in which to live. Patterns of settlement depended on resource availability, but when resources were depleted or when external influences reversed the climate of good fortune, towns crumbled and people moved away. Limerick (1987: 100) explained that "mining set a mood that has never disappeared from the West: the attitude of extractive industry—get in, get rich, get out." As a result, many Western mining towns suffered repetitive cycles of boom and bust. These cycles were often characterized by rapid growth and unlimited hopes, followed by technological limitations, reduced levels of mineral extraction, community out-migration, and, in some cases, local economic failure. Impacts from boom-and-bust cycles have been felt in varying degrees throughout the intermountain region of the West, and though some generations coped better than others, many former mining communities, including those in Gilpin County, faded after the mineral strikes played out.

Despite the difficulties of boom-and-bust economies, gold mining towns remain as some of the most spectacularly scenic places in the West. Mining towns are usually located in magnificent mountainous landscapes that evoke a strong sense of place among residents and visitors. Englishwoman Emily Faithfull's 1884 account of a visit to the mountains and mining towns of Colorado, for example, described the pull of the landscape echoed by many later travelers. She wrote, "Nature obtained a hold over me in those Rocky Mountains. . . . The very sense of *living* was an absolute delight which cannot be realized by those who have never experienced the buoyancy of this electric air" (Faithfull, in Rinehart 1984: 115). People come to know themselves and others as a result of their participation in meaningful landscapes (Tuan 1977), and these relationships extend to encompass direct ties between persons and nature, as Conover (1991: 93) so aptly illustrated in his description of an interview situation: "Throughout the conversation, both of us had occasionally glanced out the window. . . . So striking was the view that it had almost seemed like a participant in the conversation."

Places are not only meaningful individually or interpersonally, but also are remembered and elevated across communities of people. "The relationship between community and place," according to Relph (1976: 34), "is indeed a very powerful one in which each reinforces the identity of the other, and in which the landscape is very much an expression of communally held beliefs and values and of interpersonal involvements." Artifacts produced in the relationships between community and place become visible reminders of important symbols and meanings in local culture. "No place is a place until things that have happened in it are remembered in history, ballads, yarns, legends, or monuments," wrote Wallace Stegner (1992: 202), and people come to understand who they are as a community by fortifying themselves with the history and images of place that are passed from one generation to the next. Greider and Garkovich (1994: 2) explained this process by linking culture with identity; they wrote, "Our understanding of nature and of human relationships with the environment are really cultural expressions used to define who *we* were, who *we* are, and who *we* hope to be at this place and in this space. . . . [W]hen events or technological innovations challenge the meanings of these landscapes, it is our conceptions of ourselves that change through a process of negotiating new symbols and meanings." The legacy of frontier mining days in early Colorado, then, can be found in the cultures people enact and the stories people tell about who they are, were, and hope to be, in relation to a particular place. In Gilpin County, these stories and myths were invoked both during the pro-gambling campaign and after, as the new gaming industry challenged deeply held images about place and a critical reevaluation of both community and individual identity ensued.

FROM RESOURCE DEPENDENCY TO TOURISM DEVELOPMENT

Once the potential for resource extraction faded, the mountain scenery of mining towns often became simply a backdrop to the daily life of frontier communities. Yet social and economic trends in the last several decades of the twentieth century have encouraged a new view of nature: mountain scenery has assumed value as a "commodity." The commodity view of scenery (the concept has been expanded by scholars to include natural scenery as well as historic and cultural amenities) assumes that scenic places can be defined and marketed as tourist attractions. The redefinition of scenery allows rural communities to consider new strategies for local economic development, especially proposals that are primarily based on fostering tourism growth.

The move from natural resource dependency to tourism development is often a simple progression for traditional resource-based communities. Tourism is viewed as a clean, nonintrusive industry expected to provide a year-round, stable economy compatible with rural community goals, lifestyles, and resources. In rural communities, tourism developers claim that tourism growth strategies will encourage local enterprise and attractions, maintain indigenous culture and history, and protect significant resources. Whether tourism actually accomplishes such goals depends on the abilities of local residents to collectively define acceptable futures, control the influence of outsiders who wish to introduce new tourism-based industry into the local setting, and manage the processes and impacts of community growth.

The often-uncritical acceptance of tourism as a replacement for resource extraction is an economic development model visible in a variety of mountain settings. Tourism projects take many forms, including ski resort developments, retirement or arts communities, community festival programming, gateway towns to parks or forests, and, most recently, gambling development. In too many of these places, though, the natural, historic, and cultural scenery often becomes merely a setting for sophisticated, mass-produced tourist experiences. The rationale supporting such developments is the hope of substantial economic gains with little revision in local life, but it is more common that the new mountain tourist locales—fragile environments even without the added pressures of increased populations of visitors or residents—become stretched to the limit as they are "discovered" by those with the time, money, and ability to travel, as well as by those without financial resources who become the new marginally employed workers in local tourism businesses.

It would be very easy to blame the tourism industry, in general, for fostering and supporting these types of social disruption. An alternative or supplemental explanation, though, suggests that something about rural mountain places or resource-dependent communities gives rise to particular habits of response, regardless of the type of development strategy adopted. As the gambling developments in Central City and Black Hawk illustrate, certain consistencies in the manner of community response to proposed development schemes seems to be apparent. Erikson (1976) called these community predilections "axes of variation," and they influence processes of community transformation just as much as do pressures exerted by external forces.

In Gilpin County, for example, tendencies to replicate the past were evident in the pervasive rhetoric of boom-and-bust imagery. Although lengthy and persistent bust periods were typical, the favored solution to resolving economic decline seemed to be, during all time periods, the potential for a new boom. Boom times were the most vivid and exciting times in local history. Because residents shared a strong sense of ownership in the history and meanings of place, the boom-and-bust rhetoric reinforced mythical values of Gilpin County life: individualism, privacy, frontier living, closeness to nature, and appreciation for theatricality. The sense of ownership carried into all facets of social, cultural, and political life, appearing in the hesitancy to trust outsiders, in the saloon culture of Central City and Black Hawk, and in the confirmed habits of informality and resistance to change in local governance.

The commitment to local history, though, tended to be expressed primarily in terms of personal freedoms rather than by collective participation in community projects or civic improvements. People lived in Gilpin County because it offered a peaceful mountain environment away from the city, escape from the social conventions and laws of other places, and few constraints on individualism. Remembrances of the mining history and summer opera season fueled fantasies that this was a place out of time; correspondingly, residents also came to feel that they were unique and extraordinary for living in this place. As gaming development eventually showed, though, expression of ownership through individualism was not enough to protect valued community symbols and place meanings from external threats once gaming was adopted.

In addition to the power of boomtown rhetoric, structural conditions also stimulated patterned responses when alternative futures were considered. Because mountain environments are often perceived as harsh, difficult places in which to live, claims of scarcity (in terms of resource availability, population stability, and linkages with the external world) were often used to reinforce a sense of desperation in local life. As a consequence, residents fatalistically relied on external forces ("experts," or "the market," or government, for example) to solve local problems. A psychological comfort with the uncertainties of the future, seen most vividly in the gamble with nature to mine gold, also favored individualism above communality. Given their doubts about the future, people generally relied most heavily on others they could trust, which is why jobs and positions in local government appeared to be distributed based on "who knows whom," or who was related by family ties.

Patterns of community-based economic minimalization and social nonparticipation, then, may be firmly entrenched in the passivity of local governance, the reliance on individual initiative and personal freedom, and a nearly religious belief in the return of boom times. In Gilpin County, these conditions applied to all segments of local society, including former miners or their descendants; those who moved to the county to live in a scenic place away from the stresses of urban areas; and those who, marginally employed, felt a sense of freedom in the area that could not be obtained in other places. Each group was equally protective of its own freedoms, and until gambling was introduced, people were rarely challenged in their chosen lifestyles or cultural myths.

THE ECONOMIC SOLUTION: GAMBLING

The notion of *gambling* in Central City, Black Hawk, and Gilpin County refers to more than simply playing games of chance. Throughout all historic periods, a gambling attitude was also the defining characteristic of lifestyle in the mountain environments of Gilpin County. From the early gold rush days, when miners sifted rock from streambeds and dug riches from the hills, to the renovation of the Central City Opera House for summer opera festivals, the goal of all entrepreneurs has been to modify the natural and cultural landscape to capitalize on its riches. As Brown (1979: 45) observed, "In a society where everyone gambled with nature, anything seemed possible." Efforts to develop the new gaming tourism industry in Central City and Black Hawk extended the sentiment to the activity of gambling, marking another phase in efforts to control the destiny and image of those towns.

The 1988 proposal to initiate gambling in Black Hawk and Central City was not without local precedent. In the early days of the Territory of Colorado, gambling was common in all the mining camps that sprang up along the frontier, including those around Central City and Black Hawk. Indeed, most "popular accounts place gamblers in wild and unsettled moments in certain economies—particularly frontier economies in extractive industries—where labor was not yet fully governed by the industry, sobriety, and frugality that molded daily life to the rhythms of industrial production" (Fabian 1990: 6).

Although the Gilpin County towns were not as wild as some Western places, the nearby city of Denver had a reputation as a center of wicked pleasures. Barney (1959: 90), wrote from Denver City, on July 9, 1860, "But of all the evidence that this is a fast town, in a wicked way, gambling stands pre-eminently, barefacedly and unimpeachedly the best. . . . Scarcely a hotel, saloon or low groggery throughout [Denver City] is exempt from . . . the worship of this hell-born devil." Controlling, if not eradicating, the evil of gambling was thus a moral cause taken up by the territorial legislature.

During the formation of the territorial government in Colorado, several laws were passed to control or restrict gambling. An act regulating all forms of community licenses was passed at the First Session of the Legislative Assembly in 1861. It cautioned that "no lawful gaming or riotous conduct" would be permitted in saloons, hotels, or groceries of the new Territory (First Session *General Laws* 1861: 70). Although gaming was not outlawed, specific games "where fraud or cheating is practised" were limited (First Session *Practice of Law* 1861: 313). By the Third Session of the Legislative Assembly, public opinion had apparently changed, and an "Act to Suppress Gambling and Gambling Houses" was enacted. Approved March 2, 1864, this law was probably vigorously applied: it promised to fine both gambling houses and gamblers, and to give half of the revenues collected to the person making the public complaint! It may have been this process that encouraged the City of Denver to apply for and receive approval from the House of Representatives to be exempt from the gaming suppression law (Fourth Session of the Legislative Assembly 1865: 72). By 1866, though, public opinion had turned against gambling once more. Superseding all previous legislation, the January 1866 "Act to Suppress Gambling and Gambling Houses" made all gambling activities and houses illegal in the Territory of Colorado, and outlined procedures for prosecuting those who continued to encourage or take part in gambling activities (Fifth Session of the Legislative Assembly 1866).

Though there were notable local controversies surrounding gambling in some Colorado towns (the intrigues related to gambling during the Central City Opera and Play Festivals are presented in chapter 2), other statewide gambling initiatives began to be discussed again in the mid-1900s. Betting on horse and dog track races was legalized as early as 1949 (Colorado Racing Commission 1949), and Colorado citizens voted in favor of a state lottery in 1983. Discussions about casino-style gaming arose in 1980 when gambling proponents living near Pueblo, Colorado, attempted to place a pro-gambling amendment on the state ballot. More than 45,000 citizen signatures supporting the idea were submitted to the secretary of state. When challenged, though, it became apparent that "petition supporters and circulators had ties to certain unsavory characters—including illegal gamblers—and it was charged that the petition drive was financed by Las Vegas interests" (Dombrink and Thompson 1990: 153). More than half of the signatures were eventually discarded, and the initiative never made it onto the ballot.

The next attempt at gaining casino-style gambling came in 1982. It also originated in Pueblo, and was presented as a countermeasure to elevated levels of city unemployment resulting from the declining steel industry. The petition allowed for casinos to be developed in all high-unemployment Colorado counties, as well as in ski resorts across the state. Again, the required numbers of signatures were collected, but a coalition of community and state leaders opposed to casino gaming, organized by then-Governor Richard Lamm, challenged the submissions. Just as in the previous effort, "the opponents found flagrant evidence of forgeries, improper addresses, and illegal petition circulation practices" (Dombrink and Thompson 1990: 154). The casino gambling initiative was again removed from the ballot.

In 1984, another effort was made to convince voters to allow casino gambling in Colorado. That proposal called for a single entertainment-casino-leisure resort complex to be built outside the city of Pueblo; proponents claimed it would provide up to 30,000 direct and secondary jobs. Although moral concerns and social issues were raised by opponents, this campaign appeared to be untainted by corrupt or unsavory promoters. However, Governor Lamm, the media, and many Pueblo residents voiced opposition to the amendment; eventually, the citizens of Colorado also voted it down (Dombrink and Thompson 1990). In later reflection, Lamm (1994) commented, "In 1984, we were able to get moral indignation working for us."

Though unsuccessful, the early attempts to obtain casino gambling in Colorado prepared citizens with an understanding of the process required to place gambling measures on the state ballot. The spread of lotteries and other forms of betting nationwide during the 1980s also signalled an increasing acceptance of gambling as recreation activity (Eadington 1976; Eadington and Frey 1984). Although lotteries had been accepted as sources of revenue for public construction projects even in the early American colonies, moral uncertainty had plagued many debates about gaming development, particularly those related to casino gaming (Fabian 1990). Nevertheless, recessionary periods in the 1980s encouraged a reevaluation of gambling as an appropriate revenue-stimulating mechanism for communities said to be suffering decline or instability. Indeed, contemporary arguments in favor of gaming development are almost always economic, with proponents claiming that gambling development will increase tourism, bolster governmental revenues, reduce local taxes, provide supplemental funds for capital or service programs that have been shortchanged, and stimulate new investment for community revitalization. The arguments appear to be effective: by 1990, all states except Utah and Hawaii had some form of legal betting or casino operations.

Despite the broad claims of extensive community benefits, the merits of gambling continue to be debated, though often without extensive scholarly research providing a basis for understanding. In the scientific literature, historic and ethnographic accounts of gambling and gamblers predominate (Longstreet 1977; DeArment 1982; Rosecrance 1988), and gambling research has focused primarily on individuals, considering how people become compulsive gamblers (Lesieur 1977) or why people engage in gambling speculation (Brenner with Brenner 1990). The tension between moral uncertainties about gambling and the economic and historic conditions facilitating recent promotion of gaming has been analyzed by researchers (Abt, Smith, and Christiansen 1985; Fabian 1990; Dombrink and Thompson 1990; Johnston 1992), but there has been relatively little research evaluating specific economic, social, political, and cultural impacts of gambling development in different contexts.

ROMANTICISM AND REALITY

The importance of Central City and Black Hawk, their central role in creating the state of Colorado, and their imagined qualities as idealized Western gold mining towns cannot be overestimated. Gold mining was the stimulus for initial community growth on the Western frontier. Opera reconstruction, about seventy years after the boom and bust of mining, reclaimed the depressed community and the decayed Opera House. About sixty years after the return of opera performances to Central City, the local economy was flat and community leaders were searching for a new economic development option. Unable to solve the problems of a declining infrastructure and a static tourist economy with small residential populations, a limited business environment, and meager governmental budgets, the Gilpin County towns turned to limited stakes gaming as the preferred method of economic growth.

The process of promoting and legalizing gambling was conceived as a novel solution to addressing the economic problems of unique communities. Beginning in 1989, local business and governmental leaders organized and managed a campaign to obtain citizen approval for initiating gambling as a tourist attraction in Black Hawk, Central City, and Cripple Creek, three former gold rush towns in Colorado. Their efforts were successful, and after a planning and construction period of about a year, casinos opened in October 1991.

The gambling proposal reinforced images associated with boomtown situations. It presented the potential for substantial gain and an immediate release from the rhetoric of despair that pervaded local life. Moreover, gambling was (as promoters continually reminded listeners) consistent with the "Western" history of the mining region. Shortly after gambling was approved in 1990, in fact, "boom buttons" containing the message "The Boom is Back in Gilpin County!" went on sale in local shops. Gambling seemed to be internally consistent with other cultural myths accepted in a community steeped in boomtown mythology. In addition, claims by proponents that gaming development might singlehandedly produce renewed economic vigor for slumbering communities were simplistic, but paralleled the passionate claims of pioneer miners who faced wilderness and frontier challenges with a belief that riches were just another hillside away. Likewise, the reincarnation of mountain-town opera from the crumbling brick remains of a dilapidated theater constituted an effort in commitment to an ideal, not necessarily a reasoned evaluation of benefits and costs. In mining, opera reconstruction, and gambling development, feverish anticipation and idealism tended to substitute for detailed planning or thoughtful evaluation of the consequences.

The proposal to institutionalize gambling capitalized on the myths and images of place already held as true by local people: these were Western places, pioneering people, who embodied the frontier spirit. Given their assumed uniqueness, few parallels were drawn between the three Colorado towns and other, more established gaming centers. To be sure, there were few obvious parallels between the Colorado mountain towns and Nevada's gaming cities of Las Vegas and Reno, or New Jersey's Atlantic City. The only similar model was that of Deadwood, South Dakota, another rural, historic gold-mining-turned-gaming town. Gambling had been approved for Deadwood in 1988, and the new industry had opened for business only in 1989. So, at the time the Colorado communities were debating the merits of gaming, the results from Deadwood were only preliminary.

This book documents and analyzes the impacts of gaming development in two of Colorado's three initial gaming towns, Central City and Black Hawk. The intent is to bring scholarly research to bear on the gambling issue, one of the most contentious and politically sensitive issues for both rural and urban American communities today (Arland-Fye and Pellin 1992; Pizam and Pokela 1985; Stubbles 1990; Canedy and Zeiger 1991; Stokowski 1992; Long, Clark, and Liston 1994; Hartmann forthcoming). The focus in this book is on rural community casino-style gambling, as many small, rural communities currently are drafting proposals to adopt gambling measures without adequate study of the potential outcomes for their communities or their economies. The story of gambling in Black Hawk and Central City elaborates paradoxes of tourism development in rural mountain communities, and cautions observers that gambling is not necessarily the economic salvation touted by promoters.

Romanticism about Central City and Black Hawk produces many reinterpretations of local history, and has consequences for the shape and design of each new development imposed on the natural and cultural landscape of Gilpin County. The hopes of achieving wealth through gold mining, the sentimental restoration of opera, and the newly contrived performances of casino employees, and the gaming industry at large, are all variants on the theme of conquering the Western frontier. As lasting reminders of a bygone era in frontier America, Central. City and Black Hawk display the paradoxes and extremes of the West. Mining uncovered potential wealth, but produced a slashed and polluted environment. Opera brought culture and refinement, but attempted to impose the imagery and meanings of upper-class society on the populace of a rustic and faded setting. Tourists are the lifeblood of the towns, yet are seen as interlopers in the communities. Newcomers move to Gilpin County in search of expansive personal freedoms and to escape urban congestion and big-city problems, but they complain that development levels and services are inadequate in the county, and desire an economic stability that is unlikely to be provided without broader governmental financing and coordination. Long-standing antagonisms remain unresolved, though few community members lived during the times that gave rise to the confrontations. Indeed, the very paradoxes that define this place and these people have set the stage for participants in gaming development to offer competing claims about reality in this community.

Gaming development was supposed to bring riches to the small communities of Black Hawk, Central City, and Gilpin County, but it was not long after gambling was approved that residents began expressing regrets over what they had lost in the transformation of the community. The prevalence of strong collective imagery, drawn from unique historical conditions and skillfully manipulated during the gambling campaign, left local people unprepared for the extensive and disruptive development that ensued once gaming was approved. Some leaders said during the construction and early operation stages of the development process that, because development was being confined to the commercial areas of the towns, local residents would experience few negative impacts. Time has proven these assessments incorrect. Tangible impacts, such as traffic, light pollution, and visual changes to the landscape, extended far beyond city limits, and emotional impacts were widespread across the community. Traffic and congestion problems seem likely to persist, but intangible effects, such as the loss of some areas of the towns as centers for community interactions, may be more important, and may or may not eventually be overcome as new community meeting places emerge. One can only hope that somewhere in local memory there remains a place for the real history of the past, and that this history will be protected and fostered by a civic consciousness that also prepares for the future.

The solution proposed in this book for creating more coherent, saner tourism developments—that of encouraging a more civic society based on people's meaningful participation in community—will be read by some as a plea for a return to an idealized, romanticized past. This is not what I have in mind, especially as I believe that the cultural problems made evident by the dispersion of tourism (especially gambling tourism) across the United States are more serious and dangerous than we might imagine. Instead, I agree with Meštrović, who, in his shattering, brilliant analysis of the Balkan War and western responses to it, wrote, "[O]ne cannot retrieve the past, and one cannot use social engineering to solve a cultural problem. . . . [T]he habits of the heart of the past have already been replaced by contemporary habits of the mind" (1994: 140). Meštrović proposed, as a solution to the postmodern conditions that stimulate worldwide Balkanization, that contemporary economies must be intimately linked with cultures that promote civic religion, a moral conscience, and a democratic spirit. His Durkheimian solution also contains many lessons for communities and states that choose to promote gambling for economic development and, in the process, run the risk of repeating one of history's mistakes: that of elevating corporate self-interest above compassion.

NOTES

1. The development of gaming also stimulated a 1993 play. Written by Steven Dietz and commissioned by the Denver Center Theatre Company, "Boomtown" has been produced in theaters in Chicago, Illinois, and Fairfax, Virginia.

2. The New West historians challenge traditional interpretations of the Western frontier hypothesis. Patricia Nelson Limerick, as one of the key spokespersons for the New West perspective, wrote, in her groundbreaking 1987 book, *The Legacy of Conquest,* "A belief in progress has been a driving force in the modern world; as a depository of enormous hopes for progress, the American West may well be the best place in which to observe the complex and contradictory outcome of that faith" (p. 29). Limerick's efforts, and those of other New West historians, to critique more traditional perspectives of American history have stimulated often angry and abrasive debates. For example, Nash (1993: 4) claimed that "Western historians should be aware that the [New West historians] represent not merely another phase of historical revisionism but are

attempting proselytization for what in essence are totalitarian ideologies." In response, Nash's arguments were disclaimed by other scholars: "To suppose that the categories of race, class, and gender have no relevance west of the Mississippi strains credulity" (Armitage, Jameson, and Jensen 1993: 5); "The traditional view of the frontier west as one primarily of hearty white men conflicting with wild nature and human opponents retarded more probing pictures" (Etulain 1993: 4).

PART ONE
PRELUDE TO GAMBLING

The idea of gambling, and the subsequent development of a gaming industry in the Gilpin County towns of Black Hawk and Central City, did not emerge without substantial preparation and historical seasoning. Geography and history provided an initial orientation and the conditions that structured possibilities for gambling, while social, political, and economic contexts of local cultures contributed significant traditions, habits, and myths to influence the process and outcomes of gaming development. The four chapters in Part I of this book are arranged in chronological fashion, placing the development of gambling within the broader framework of community history. Themes presented in these four chapters repeat throughout all historic periods, providing substance and rationale for future community choices and decisions.

Chapter 1 presents a historical review of the conditions surrounding the 1879 discovery of gold in the area, life in the early mining camps, stabilization of the gold mining industry, development of independent towns, and the subsequent decline of both the industry and the community during the early decades of the twentieth century. The story is continued in chapter 2, which traces the development of a new local tourism economy in the former mining towns based on the renovation and 1932 reopening of the Central City Opera House. Opera revival stimulated the creation of summer pioneer festivals in which recreational gambling played a prominent, though controversial, role. The efforts to establish opera also produced new interpretations of local history, foreshadowing the activities of the future gaming industry.

Chapter 3 analyzes the process, structure, and effects of the pro-gambling campaign in 1989 and 1990, identifying instances in which a rhetoric of despair was used to skillfully manipulate public opinion. Rhetorical features of tourism campaigns are often ignored by scholars, but community rhetoric, reflecting power relationships and elaborating shared cultural meanings, is critical to the success of tourism projects. In addition to tourism campaign rhetoric, construction phase impacts—impacts that arise even prior to the official opening of the new industry—are also often overlooked by tourism researchers. Because these are nevertheless critical components of the community tourism experience, they are considered separately in chapter 4. Data from the 1990–1991 construction period in Central City and Black Hawk showed that development impacts emerging in the period prior to casino opening were measurable and significant for community well-being. Inconsistencies in local control and coordination of the development agenda during this time period, however, revealed the prevalence of "growth-machine politics" that structured future outcomes of casino industry growth, discussed in Part II of this book.

1

GOLDEN DREAMS ON THE WESTERN FRONTIER

> The nervousness and excitability of our people on the gold subject is truly astonishing. Every report of a new strike . . . travels from mouth to mouth . . . producing a feverish restlessness and an increased thirst for gold.
> — Denver City Correspondence, August 12, 1859
> (in Hafen and Hafen 1961: 150)

The search for gold has seduced generations of explorers, lured to remote frontiers with dreams of riches, fame, and power. The craving for excitement, the fever of the rush to gold country, the euphoria of a strike, and then lifelong nostalgia for that meaningful adventure are themes repeated in all gold rush tales. For those who participated, living in wild, unexplored places, chiseling out a living far from the comforts and familiarities of home, and working in a potentially dangerous occupation provided the grandest expression of freedom and self-determination imaginable (Brown 1979). In addition to the personal experiences of the gold seekers, though, community social and political freedoms were perfected in the westward expansion. The gold rushes to California, Colorado, and other mountainous territories "provided *the* major impetus for the initial development of western regions [and] served as a 'safety valve' for restless dreamers and a laboratory for the American democratic experiment" (Marks 1994: 14). This was particularly true in the far reaches of the

Kansas Territory, where the 1859 discovery of gold in an area later known as Gilpin County gave rise to the "Centennial State" of Colorado.

THE PIKES PEAK GOLD RUSH

The search for golden riches in Colorado's Rocky Mountains can be traced back to the gold fields of Lumpkin County, Georgia, where gold was discovered by Cherokee Indians in the late 1820s and 1830s. It was in and around Cherokee and Lumpkin Counties that John H. Gregory and William Green Russell, two men destined to achieve fame in the Colorado gold rush, grew up. Living near the towns of Dahlonega and Auraria (the names mean "golden" and "gold region"), both learned mining skills at an early age. Along with others from that region, Gregory and Russell independently followed the gold rushes to the western parts of the country when they were young men.

Russell and others travelled westward with the "49ers" to participate in the California gold rush (Dorset 1970), passing through what was called the "Pikes Peak country." At that time, Pikes Peak was the only named landmark along the Front Range of the Rocky Mountains (Brown 1985: 4) and served as a guidepost for all mountain travellers. Though they had only marginal success in California, the Russell party did observe that the Colorado Rocky Mountains were similar to the California Sierras in the types and formations of visible quartz rocks. By the spring of 1858, a large party of Cherokees and Georgians led by William Green Russell had returned to the Pikes Peak country to explore for gold. Their first efforts were not promising, and by winter most of the group had returned to the East. Those who stayed eventually did wash out some gold from Ralston Creek, and reports of their find spread along the frontier.

Gregory apparently did not go west with the 49ers but set off later for the British Columbia gold fields (Dorset 1970). Reaching Fort Laramie, Wyoming, in 1858, he heard reports that Russell's party and others had found traces of gold in the South Platte River region of the Pikes Peak area. Revising his plans, Gregory worked south along the foothills of the Rocky Mountains, panning for gold in streams between Laramie and the area around the South Platte River. History does not reveal whether Gregory and Russell met that year, but it is likely that both wintered over near the confluence of Cherry Creek and the South Platte River in 1858. There, the first white settlement in the far western reaches of the Arapahoe County, Territory of Kansas, was organized (Hafen 1941; Hafen and Hafen 1961; Spencer 1966). The names proposed for the community were Dahlonega and Auraria, recalling the riches of the Georgian mines. Auraria, home to the Russell family, was chosen, though this settlement was absorbed in 1860 into nearby "Denver City," named after the governor of the Kansas Territory (Hafen 1941; Brown 1985; Smith 1973).

In the winter of 1858, about 600 miners were engaged in washing gold from local streams and trying to raise "color" in the area around Auraria and other small Cherry Creek settlements (Jewett, in Hafen 1941: 163). Prospectors had only limited success, though, recovering small amounts of placer gold for their efforts. *Placer gold* was a combination of flakes and nuggets obtained by hand-washing rock and soil in pans along streams (placer gold is sometimes also called *float gold;* see Stout (1858), reprinted in Hafen 1941: 143). For all the time and backbreaking labor spent bending over streams, shovelling sand and gravel, and sifting and washing the mixture, placer mining yielded depressingly small amounts of gold. A more desirable solution was to find a *lode*, a vein of gold ore assumed to be located high in the mountains from which placer minerals were carried downstream.

On May 6, 1859, this dream became reality: a rich gold vein was discovered in a narrow, mile-long canyon in the mountains about 40 miles west of the Cherry Creek settlements. The man who made the strike was Georgia native John H. Gregory, who, along with several companions, had prospected along the North Fork of Clear Creek to the burnt-colored rock outcroppings that signalled a gold vein. There, in the "Cradle of Colorado," Gregory "panned dirt from the first lode found in the Colorado mountains and secured an untouchable niche in Colorado history" (Cox 1989: 7). Gregory worked his vein for a few weeks, sold it for the then-exorbitant sum of $21,000 (Greeley, Richardson, and Villard, reprinted in Hafen 1941: 379), and became a special consultant for other gold seekers (Bancroft 1943). William Green Russell also made a productive strike several days later just a few miles south of Gregory's find (Spencer 1966), and other lodes were soon discovered in areas surrounding the Gregory Diggings.

Gregory's strike set in motion a frenzied exodus from the Auraria and Cherry Creek settlements to the mountains, and reports of the gold strikes seemingly flew eastward (Marshall 1920; Hafen and Hafen 1961). Suffering the effects of economic depression after the Panic of 1857, thousands of people in "the States" were heartened by reports of golden riches apparently available to anyone with a miner's pick (Brown 1985). Eager prospectors gathered in the gateway cities of Leavenworth, St. Joseph, and Kansas City, Missouri, and Council Bluffs, Iowa, preparing for the westward journey to the gold fields (Hafen 1941). Following guidebooks written by men who had travelled with early frontiersmen (see, for example, Tierney, Oakes, and Smith 1859, reprinted in Hafen 1941; also see Hafen 1974), about 100,000 people left the States by summer 1859 to search for gold in the Pikes Peak region.

The enormous risks taken by the Rocky Mountain argonauts can be understood only in historical perspective. In 1850, the United States stretched from the East Coast only as far west as Missouri, Iowa, and Wisconsin. Minnesota, New Mexico, Utah, and Oregon, with a combined population of about 90,000, had been organized as western territories by then, according to the 1850 U.S. Census of Population, and the new states of Louisiana, Texas, and California provided a southern route to the Pacific Ocean. West of the Mississippi and Missouri Rivers, however, in the center of the continent, were vast expanses of unmapped wilderness, populated primarily by a few Army outposts, solitary trappers and explorers, various friendly or dangerous Indian tribes, and extensive herds of buffalo. To venture out onto these plains and mountains (organized by 1860 into the Kansas, Dakota, Nebraska, Nevada, New Mexico, Utah, and Washington Territories) required money, wagon trains, horses, mules, oxen, provisions, firearms, sponsors, and companions. Several weeks after leaving Missouri or Iowa, a man might reach the Pikes Peak gold fields of the Kansas Territory—or he might perish on the plains. The risks were tremendous, but the expectation of golden riches at the end of the dangerous trip were, for many, worth the price.

Only a month after Gregory's strike, the "first mass meeting [of miners] ever held in the Rocky Mountains, assembled at the Gregory Diggings, on Tuesday evening the 8th" of June 1859 (Greeley, Richardson, and Villard, printed originally in the *Rocky Mountain News,* June 18, 1859, and reprinted in Marshall 1920: 1). Between 2,000 and 3,000 miners and gold seekers attended the meeting to discuss miner's rights and the staking of mining claims. The event was documented by three journalists touring the western gold regions and territories. Horace Greeley, founder and editor of the *New York Tribune,* addressed the gathering of miners that June night, and he and two other newspapermen—Henry Villard, sent by the *Cincinnati Daily Commercial* to witness the gold rush, and Albert D. Richardson of the *Boston Journal*—wrote a joint account of their observations that was widely reproduced in eastern newspapers. The writers spoke favorably of the extensive gold strikes in the vicinity of the Gregory Diggings, but cautioned that travel conditions and accommodations in the gold camps were primitive. In addition, they noted that the mountainous terrain and elevation of the mining camps suggested a severe climate: "probably by the middle of October, this whole Alpine region will be snowed under and frozen up, so as to put a stop to the working of sluices if not mining altogether. . . . Great disappointment, great suffering, are inevitable" (Greeley, Richardson, and Villard, printed originally in the *Rocky Mountain News,* June 18, 1859, and reprinted in Marshall 1920: 10).

The cautious words of the eminent journalists were not enough to suppress gold fever, though. All estimates of population in the gold regions must be considered suspect, because census-taking was difficult during the continuous east-west migrations, and the mining camps were remote and dispersed in the valleys and mountains. Nevertheless, personal journals, even with their limitations, give some idea of life in the early gold camps. Horace Greeley wrote in his travel journal in early June 1859, for example, that a blacksmith, a butcher shop, about 100 log houses, and a volunteer post office had already been established for the approximately 4,000 inhabitants of the Gregory area (Greeley 1860). He predicted that grocery and provisions stores, along with a hotel, would not be far behind. Those population figures were confirmed in the journal of E.H.N. Patterson, another journalist and frontier traveler who also mined near the Gregory Diggings in 1859 (Patterson, reprinted in Hafen 1974: 191). By July 4, 1859, the population of the area had grown substantially, so that "[w]ithin the area of six miles square ... from 3000 to 5000 claims worked mostly profitable ... and at least ten thousand men at work in the mines" (Garrison, in Hafen and Hafen 1961: 110). Other sources reported anywhere from a few thousand to 15,000 or 20,000 miners spread out across hillsides in the vicinity of the Gregory Diggings during late summer 1859.

Even at the peak of excitement during that first summer, not everyone discovered gold. About half of the 100,000 pioneers who ventured into the Pikes Peak region found the wild stories of available gold a "humbug" and returned to the States by the end of summer (Hafen and Hafen 1961). Reports of hardships were often ignored, though the sentiments were stated clearly enough. Rufus Cable sent a letter home to eastern Kansas in 1859, saying, "Stay where you are and hold on to your farm—'tend to your babies, and you will be better contented than if you were here taking your chance from the hand of the 'fickle goddess'" (Cable, in Hafen and Hafen 1961: 135). A. D. Richardson told of a westward-bound pioneer whose wagon was inscribed with the sentiment "Pike's Peak or Bust." Later, the unlucky man was seen heading back to the States with a new message penned in charcoal below the first: "Busted, by thunder!" (Richardson 1873: 166). Vermont native Libeus Barney (letter of 1860; 1959: 85–86) summarized the potential difficulties of gold mining by describing his own abortive attempt to work a newly purchased $450 half-claim near William Green Russell's strike:

> The water forced itself through our dams, sluices got out of repair, and up to our knees in half frozen mud and water, soon sickened us of mining, and having an offer of fifty dollars in advance for our claim, we at once embraced so favorable an opportunity of extricating ourselves from a bad fix, and bidding farewell to the mountains ... and mining in general, we engaged seats in the first conveyance that left for Denver.

As A. D. Richardson later reflected (1873: 182), "Little time is required to learn the great truth, that digging gold is about the hardest way on earth to obtain it. . . . [S]uccess is very rare."

As the first golden summer passed, early surface-level leads played out, and it became clear that more sophisticated methods were needed to extract gold from the recalcitrant mountains. By August 1859, the combined forces of colder weather in the mountains, the limited mining experience of most pioneers, and inadequate quartz rock drilling and crushing technology produced a temporary retreat from the mining areas (King 1977). A series of reports published in the *Missouri Republican* at that time questioned whether the mining regions around the Gregory strike had "given out," noting that the difficulties of separating gold from the quartz rock without the aid of machinery had sent many of the prospectors packing: "Dozens of idle sluices . . . [and] abandoned cabins . . . could be seen in every direction. . . . [N]ot over seven hundred individuals remain in the valley" (Denver City Correspondence,

August 28, 1859, reprinted in Hafen and Hafen, 1961: 164, 167). Gold fever still gripped the populace, but the capacity of the new western camps to accommodate gold seekers or to provide shelter and food was limited, especially when mining technology and construction equipment were primitive and nature was punishing. Some miners went to Denver City to wait out the winter, while others returned to the States.

CARVING TOWNS FROM THE WILDERNESS

The Gregory and Russell diggings were located in Arapahoe County, the farthest western segment of the Kansas Territory. Kansas included a substantial geographical area (Brown 1985), extending west to the Continental Divide (abutting the Utah Territory), north to the Nebraska Territory (40 degrees

The Pozo Mine shaft house, constructed around 1900 in Nevadaville, still stands near mine tailings dumps, reminding visitors of past glory days in the Gilpin County mining boom.

North latitude, now Baseline Road in Boulder, Colorado, was the dividing line), and south to the Territory of New Mexico (the thirty-eighth parallel was the dividing line). Between winter and spring 1859, gold strikes were made all over the region. George A. Jackson found a rich lode along the South Fork of Clear Creek during the winter; his find, near those of Gregory and Russell, was made public only after theirs had been announced.[1] North of the Gregory mining area, other prospectors struck gold in the vicinity of Nederland, Boulder Creek, and Gold Hill, three areas that were by jurisdiction in the Nebraska Territory and later became part of Boulder County, Colorado (Voynick 1992). A large number of gold seekers were also venturing into the South Park area of the Kansas Territory, finding rich veins in Fairplay, Tarryall, and Breckenridge.

Because the Gregory gold fields were located in the Kansas Territory, the relevant laws were those of Kansas. The populated, eastern part of the Kansas Territory was primarily agricultural, though, and there were no appropriate laws pertaining to the administration of mining claims. Local governments, coordinated and organized by miners, were an organizational alternative to long-distance governance. Miners' meetings were held in the gold camps as early as summer and fall of 1859 to set up the necessary districts, laws, and towns. The large, centrally located Gregory Mining District was organized at the June 8 meeting attended by Greeley and the other journalists; it thus became the first mining district in Colorado. The area immediately surrounding the Gregory Diggings became known as "Mountain City" after the October 29, 1859, miners' meeting (Marshall 1920: 16). The Gregory District also later included the town of "Black Hawk Point" (later Black Hawk), located at the east, or bottom, end of the mile-long canyon Gregory had discovered. Other mining districts were organized around the Gregory District. The three most important of these were the Russell District, which was identified June 18, 1859, and included a town called Russell's (or Russell) Gulch, after William Green Russell; the Eureka District, which was organized July 1859, and included the town of Central City at the top, west end of Gregory Canyon; and the Nevada District, organized January 21, 1860, around the town of Nevadaville, which contained some of the deepest mines in the United States.

Miners' meetings in each of these districts formalized procedures for identifying mining district boundaries and outlined the regulations for staking legal claims, working mines, and registering mining claims and mills, processes later standardized in the 1872 Mining Law. Other civic laws were also outlined, including procedures for conducting ranching activities, settling disputes in miners' court, using and obtaining water rights, cutting timber, keeping public records, voting, owning property, and paying fines. A civic conscience extended to issues of public morality as well. For example, as early as April 28, 1860, a meeting of miners was held in the Nevada District (reported in Marshall 1920: 125) to discuss and codify laws of public behavior. Several paragraphs from the resulting proclamations considered the evils of gambling, drink, and prostitution (the unconventional spelling, punctuation, and sentence structure are consistent with the original):

> Whereas we the Miners of New Nevada District wish to advance the interests and promote peace harmony order and a good understanding between man & man and believing that the allowing Counternancing or encouraging of low Body Houses Grog Shops and gamboling Saloons to be degrading to the Morals detrimental to the sway of peace and order and Disgraceful to the name and character of the District. Resolved that there shall be no Bawdy Houses Grog shops or Gamboling Saloons within the Limits of this District and any person or Company of persons bringing or keeping such nuisances within the limits of this District shall lay himself liable to a fine of $50.00 and be warned to discontinue the Same.

Shortly thereafter, at a miners' meeting on July 23, 1860, in the Eureka District west of Central City, "[i]t was moved, seconded, and carried unanimously that all Gambling houses and Drinking saloons that are open for the carrying on of their business on Sunday be considered, and are hereby declared a nuisance" (Marshall 1920: 84). A miner's column, "News from Nevada Gulch," published in the *Rocky Mountain News* on November 21, 1860, also reported that many of the vices typical to other Western mining towns were under control, at least in some parts of the mining region around the Gregory Diggings: "Gambling, which for a while prevailed in this place, has now almost entirely ceased. The gamblers could not live as we have to on hope and so have cleared out to a man" (Marshall 1920: 136).

The result of these efforts was a civic life that, despite the rigors and harsh conditions of mountain and frontier living, provided a sense of community decency and morality. Whereas the settlement of Denver City had a reputation for wilder entertainments during the early years of the Pikes Peak gold rush (Richardson 1873), the new towns around the Gregory Diggings appeared to be tamer. Visitors to the area wrote about the availability of gambling and saloons in Mountain City, Central City, Black Hawk Point, and surrounding mining settlements (Marshall 1920), but these activities were apparently not as extensive or wicked as those in Denver. The relatively close proximity of Denver City, coupled with short mining seasons in the rugged mountain encampments, and the strong moral convictions of some midwestern pioneers and immigrant miners, probably limited the expansion of more decadent pastimes.

Although mining activity had subsided during the first winter in the Gregory Diggings, the coming of spring 1860 brought a flood of new emigrants willing to take a chance on finding their golden fortunes. With renewed hope, replenished supplies, and new sources of eastern financing (Hogan 1990), newcomers dispersed across the mountainous lands and gold fields of the western part of the Kansas Territory. The 1860 Census[2] indicates that most of the 34,277 pioneer inhabitants of the mining region were men, and most went to the Pikes Peak country seeking gold: more than 22,000 (82.4 percent) of a total of 26,797 persons reported their occupation as "miner" in the 1860 census. Another 1,000 were laborers and carpenters, and 850 others were teamsters and traders. Other entrepreneurs joining the westward migration were those who provisioned and served the new camps, including 216 merchants, 195 farmers, 175 saloon keepers, 163 blacksmiths, 130 butchers, and 115 innkeepers. More specialized emigrants were also counted in the far reaches of the Kansas Territory in 1860. There were 69 bakers, 11 bankers, 11 clergymen, 89 lawyers, 10 teachers, and 27 self-identified gamblers. About 1,500 females (4.6 percent of the total) were counted in the area during the 1860 census; 2 matchmakers also went West.

The census of 1860 reported that about two-thirds of the 34,277 residents of the Kansas Territory's gold region resided in Denver City, the Platte River valley, and the North and South Clear Creek mining areas, including the Gregory Diggings and surrounding settlements. The other third of the populace had settled in the South Park area in the mining camps around the towns of Tarryall and Fairplay. Another 850 people were reported to be living in the Boulder and Gold Hill mining areas of the Nebraska Territory. The prominence of the mining towns near the Gregory Diggings at this time, though, cannot be underestimated. Nearly 4,700 people lived in the mining districts around the Gregory Diggings at the time of the 1860 census, nearly equal to the number reported to be living in Denver City (4,749) at that time.

Despite the potential for striking it rich, one cannot imagine that these towns were easy places in which to live (Bowles 1869a). Mining accidents and other misfortunes, lack of sanitation facilities, the spread of contagious disease and sickness, extremes of mountain weather, the unpredictability of nature (floods, wildfires, snowstorms), and pollution from smelting processes were all documented in letters and newspapers of the time, and all contributed to shortened lives. Graves in the region show that people often died at very young ages; a child's gravestone above Central City, near a large deposit of mine tailings, laments, "Gone too soon."

The extremes of the frontier regions challenged even the hardiest, though miners put a brave face on their situation. A miner's report to the editor of the

Daily Rocky Mountain News in late November 1860 provides an example: "Yesterday snow fell all over the mountains, to the depth of about ten inches. The weather to-day was warm and pleasant. To-night the thermometer is 10 degrees below zero, but it don't feel near as cold as it would in the States at that figure" (Nevadaville miner, in Marshall 1920: 137).

As residents carved towns and mining districts from mountain wilderness, it became clear that their frontier experiences were increasingly and dramatically different from those of most residents of the Kansas Territory. Many of the emigrants felt that "Kansas was too weak, too distant, and too different from the mining county to legislate for it" (Gower 1965: 125). Several efforts were made at establishing an independent regional government (Richardson 1873; Hafen and Hafen 1961; Voynick 1992), and by the autumn of 1859, the "Provisional Government of Jefferson Territory" had been proposed and officials elected. This ineffective, transitional entity was favored in Denver City, but received little support in the mining districts, where the miners had developed workable laws that favored their own interests. Congressional support from the government of the States was also not forthcoming, and the idea of a new Jefferson Territory quietly faded. The growing importance of the western mining areas to the economy and country was acknowledged, however, as the Civil War began to loom in the east (Hogan 1990). Another charter forming the "Territory of Colorado" was drafted and approved by Congress. President James Buchanan, in his last days of office before Abraham Lincoln became president, signed the bill creating the Colorado Territory on February 28, 1861, two years after gold was discovered in Gregory Gulch. President Lincoln subsequently appointed Colonel William

The grave of Lulu, who was born on August 6, 1868, and "Gone Too Soon" on April 23, 1870, rests above Central City; mine tailings are in the background. After gaming was approved, a parking lot was constructed just behind the tailings piles.

Gilpin as the first governor of the new Territory of Colorado (Hafen 1941: 241). The mining towns around the Gregory Diggings joined together in 1861 as Gilpin County, one of seventeen original Colorado counties.

STABILIZING THE INDUSTRY

Despite the difficulties of westward travel in the early 1860s, accounts of the wealth of the Gregory Diggings gold area attracted thousands of gold seekers and visitors. Among the visitors were famous writers, artists, and journalists, and the political and social elite from the States and Europe, who came to view the new western territories and mining operations. George Mortimer Pullman, a young businessman from Chicago, came to speculate in the gold fields (King 1977; Hogan 1990; Leyendecker 1992). Prior to setting out for the Pikes Peak gold rush in spring 1860, he had expanded his father's building-raising business and had also started a business to improve sleeping cars for luxury train travel.[3] In July 1860, he staked a site in Russell Gulch and erected a stamp mill, a steam-powered crushing operation for extracting gold from rock. Later, he opened a store on Lawrence Street in Central City, operated a sawmill, was involved in mining, and had a freighting business (Leyendecker 1992). Like many other entrepreneurs of the time, though, his ventures in the area were speculative, and after making some money, he returned east to Chicago in April 1863, subsequently achieving fame in the railroad sleeping car business.

Also visible in Central City by 1862 was Henry M. Teller, entrepreneur, later to become president of both the Central City bank and the Colorado Central Railroad, financier of the 1872 Teller House hotel, an influential U.S. senator, and Secretary of the Interior under President Chester Arthur (National Park Service 1990). The legendary Horace A. W. Tabor passed through Gilpin County on his way to Leadville, where he earned the title "Silver King" for his successful mining ventures (Smith 1973). Elizabeth McCourt "Baby" Doe, who had lived in both Black Hawk and Central City, divorced her husband Harvey and also moved to Leadville, where she captured the attention and heart of H.A.W. Tabor (Smith 1973; Dorset 1970). Their affair and eventual marriage (the latter occurring prior to his formal divorce from Augusta, his wife of many years) provided substantial material for society gossip, historical writings, and a 1956 opera entitled "The Ballad of Baby Doe." General Ulysses S. Grant visited in 1868 and twice again after he became president, in 1873 and 1875 (Bancroft 1958). During his April 1873 visit, President Grant made a ceremonial entrance into Central City's Teller House hotel, walking across bars of pure silver from a famous silver mine just north of Gilpin County in Caribou, Boulder County (Hollenback 1961: 22).

On March 11, 1864, twelve years before Colorado officially became a state, Black Hawk and Central City were incorporated under territorial charter as two independent towns in the county that honored Governor Gilpin. By that time, the social and economic stratification of the area around Gregory Gulch area was becoming visible. Central City, at the top of the canyon, had emerged as the regional trade and commercial center—the city of bankers, mine owners and managers, and the county seat of governance. Black Hawk, 450 feet lower in elevation, and hugging Clear Creek to take advantage of the water for mill and mining power, had become the city of mills and laborers. Other mining towns radiated around these, giving the impression that "Black-Hawk, Central City and Nevada run into and over each other, and form really but a single town. The clang of mills, the debris of mines, the waste of floods leave nothing that is inviting, except money-making" (Bowles 1869b: 97). A. D. Richardson (1873: 335) described the view on his second trip to the area in 1865:

> Near the old Gregory Diggings we reached the mining settlements of Black Hawk and Central, which thread the narrow valley for three miles, in quaint, crooked, contracted streets ... shut in on both sides by steep, bare mountains. Wood and granite quartz mills, old log-cabins of '59, shops, stables, school-houses, drinking-saloons, handsome brick blocks, newspaper and express offices, side by side crowd each other in the tortuous thoroughfares, while the creek, muddy and turbid from washing out the quartz, tumbles among them.

The growth of mining came at significant environmental cost across Gilpin County. Settlements, mills, and mine structures were all initially constructed of wood, and smelters were wood-fired, so the local hillsides were denuded of trees. By 1865, Richardson saw that "[t]housands of acres, which at my first visit had been covered with stately pines, were now utterly bare. The wood had been consumed for fuel in Denver, and by the mountain quartz mills" (1873: 335). Early photographs show a persistent, thick black smoke from the mills hanging over the mining towns and the hills. Streams, diverted for mining use, were also used for sanitation and as refuse dumps. Even as late as 1880, Central City residents had no water reservoir, but bought drinking water on the street for $0.25 a bucket (Hollenback 1961; National Park Service 1990).

Mining, even in the lucrative gold fields of Gilpin County, was not a predictable venture. Even in the early days of the Colorado gold rush, the mining industry experienced cyclical depressions based on geographic and geologic characteristics, and on external factors such as the availability of new technologies for removing and separating gold ore from rock. By late 1863 and early

1864, several issues combined to push Gilpin County gold mining into a slump (Dorset 1970; Cox 1989). Gold found at deeper levels underground was more difficult to obtain because ore zones were narrower at greater depths, and the physical and chemical makeup of ore changed at different levels. In addition, traditional milling processes were unable to separate ores obtained from deeper mine tunnels. Water was necessary for sifting and crushing ore, but streams went dry by the end of summer; water from a new Consolidated Ditch Company, whose first president was William Green Russell, was expensive (Spencer 1966). Moreover, water had a tendency to seep into and pool in mine tunnels, especially those that were very deep.

Other contextual factors affected the local mining industry, too. Between 1861 and 1865, the Civil War reduced immigrations west, and the financial effects of war were felt in price fluctuations of currency and gold. Also at that time, tensions in the mining camps, which exhibited greater Northern sympathy, resulted in the exodus of some of the early miners of the Pikes Peak gold rush. William Green Russell and some of the other Georgians, for example, attempted to return east with their gold stocks, which were to be used to finance some of the Southern war effort. Indian raids also continued to be problematic, and thieves looted carriages along the stage roads, stealing gold being sent back to the States. This combination of factors produced, by 1866 and 1867, a significant depression in the Gilpin County mining industry (Axford 1976; King 1977).

The most immediate need for reinvigorating the mining industry was an improved system for separating and processing recalcitrant gold ores mined from deeper underground levels. Although a variety of methods were tested, a Rhode Island chemistry professor, Nathaniel P. Hill, developed the most effective technique for efficiently separating and refining ores. Then, using eastern financing and Gilpin County labor, Hill established the Boston & Colorado Smelting Company's first reduction plant in Black Hawk in January 1868 (Cox 1989; King 1977). Although the treated ore initially had to be shipped to Swansea, Wales, for further processing, the opening of Hill's smelter was the single most important event in the revitalization of the gold mining industry in Gilpin County. After Hill's smelter began operation, gold production increased dramatically in the "Little Kingdom of Gilpin."

The ability to attract entrepreneurial capital and maintain a local service economy, despite fluctuations in the gold market and national events, assured the future of Central City and Black Hawk. Other ore separation and processing mills were built, and the railroad soon followed up the canyon from Golden to Black Hawk. In 1871, the most successful twelve-month period in the history of Gilpin County gold mining industry was recorded (Axford

1976), when more than $3,359,000 worth of metals were mined. Indeed, gold mining was once again so lucrative in Gilpin County that the area radiating out from the Gregory Diggings renewed its reputation as "the richest square mile on earth."

INSTITUTIONALIZING COMMUNITY

The social progress of the gold towns can be traced in the rise of stabilizing institutions throughout the 1860s and 1870s (Perrigo 1936). Churches, schools, government, newspapers, and social events flourished, giving the mining towns of Gilpin County a sense of permanence. For example, Methodist missionaries organized a church as early as July 1859; the subsequent construction of the St. James Methodist Church building in Central City, between 1864 and 1872, makes it the oldest Protestant church building still used in Colorado (Hollenback 1961: 81). Other church organizations quickly formed in the area. A Presbyterian church organized in Black Hawk, and a wooden church building was constructed in 1863. Catholic church members met in Central City in local buildings beginning in 1861, and a stone church, St. Mary's of the Assumption (originally called St. Patrick's), was built between 1872 and 1893. Altogether, Gilpin County had eight church organizations, seven church buildings, and 2,050 "sittings" (the number of people attending services), according to the 1870 Census of Population.

Several small private schools opened by 1860 (Brown 1979: 34), but the booming mining towns required expanded, permanent buildings and teachers. By 1862, a public school in Central City had "166 pupils enrolled, but the average attendance was only 40" (Perrigo 1934: 9). Black Hawk residents constructed a frame building that became the first permanent schoolhouse in Colorado; classes were held from April 1870 through May 1960 (Hollenback 1961). Longtime Gilpin County residents can recall riding by horse and wagon into Black Hawk and living with relatives in town to attend school during the week. In time, Central City residents built a granite elementary schoolhouse on First High Street. When the school opened in autumn 1870, 213 students were enrolled. This building later became the high school and, more recently, the Gilpin County Historical Museum (Hollenback 1961).

The first Masonic temple in Colorado was organized in June 1859; its members held meetings in Mountain City (Kemp 1949). By 1887, twenty lodges and fraternal organizations, some of which were secret societies, operated in Central City alone. Kemp (1949) indicated that there were comparable numbers of lodges in Black Hawk and Nevadaville, and somewhat fewer in Russell Gulch. More than twenty-three fraternal orders and fifty individual lodges were meeting in Gilpin County around the turn of the century, according to Carter (1989). Some of the fraternal organizations in the area during the mining days were the Masons, the Knights of Pythias, the Elks, and the International Order of Odd Fellows. These organizations were popular because they encouraged social ties with other members of one's ethnic group and/or trade, by sponsoring dances, dinners, and entertainments (Perrigo 1934). In addition, because miners were rarely covered by insurance, the fraternal organizations also provided death benefits to surviving widows and children if a miner met with a fatal accident on the job (Brown 1979; Carter 1989). Each fraternal organization established a separate cemetery, and these can still be seen on hilltops and in wooded areas around Gilpin County today.

Mountain City had a post office as early as January 17, 1860. As the town expanded up the narrow canyon, it was eventually incorporated into Central City (Bauer, Ozment, and Willard 1990). Black Hawk had its own post office in operation from as early as December 6, 1862. The city was known as "Black Hawk Point" until 1871, then as "Black Hawk" until 1895, and as "Blackhawk" until 1950, when it adopted the current name of "Black Hawk." "Nevada" (also known as "Bald Mountain" and later "Nevadaville") had a post office as early as January 1861 (it operated until 1921), and Russell Gulch had a separate post office for sixty-four years, beginning in 1879.

Newspapers also provided a sense of community permanence. The earliest newspaper in the settlements around Cherry Creek, the *Rocky Mountain News,* distributed its first issue on the streets of Denver in late April 1859. By 1870, Colorado had fourteen newspapers with a combined circulation of 12,750, according to the U.S. Census of Population in 1870. Mining camp papers fulfilled several purposes, including providing news for local prospectors, promoting the camps to outsiders, voicing issues of political or social concern, and giving a voice to local leaders and spokesmen. As Halaas (1981: 2) noted, "A lively town paper was an ideal way of booming the camp and its surroundings, of attracting capitalists, laborers and settlers, of demonstrating to the world that life in the mining West was safe and civilized. The paper also helped to relieve the camp dweller's considerable literary thirst."

The Gilpin County mining camps enjoyed several newspapers of their own (Perrigo 1934; Hafen and Hafen 1961; Hollenback 1961; Halaas 1981), including the weekly *Rocky Mountain Gold Reporter and Mountain City Herald,* published from Mountain City during summer and fall 1859, and the weekly *Colorado Miner,* published in Black Hawk in 1863. Surviving long past the others, the *Miners' Register,* published from Central City beginning in 1862, was at various times a daily, a triweekly, and a weekly. The name was revised several times, but it is best known as the precursor to the current Gilpin County newspaper, the *Weekly Register-Call* (Working 1927; Kemp 1949).

This paper, along with the *Rocky Mountain News,* is one of the two oldest continually published papers in the state of Colorado (Hollenback 1961: 76).[4]

The towns of Gilpin County were populated with European immigrants who had moved to the area to work in the mines. The 1870 census, the first to contain county-level statistics for Colorado, reported that 31.9 percent of the residents of Gilpin County were foreign-born (1,751 persons out of a total of 5,490). By 1880, that number had increased to 41.9 percent (2,717 out of 6,489 residents), and it remained above 35 percent until after the turn of the century. During these decades, the largest numbers of foreign-born were from England and Wales: according to the 1880 census, more than 1,500 Cornish and Welsh emigrants were living in Gilpin County. Large numbers of emigrants also came from Ireland and Germany. The mutual dependence of mine owners and foreign miners was obvious in Gilpin County. Tin miners from Cornwall and Welsh coal miners, experts in hard-rock mining, provided the necessary skills and labor to guarantee productivity for Gilpin County mine owners. As Brown (1979: 8) observed, "The population of the mining frontier was disproportionately foreign in origin, in part because Americans had ... only scattered contact with hard-rock mining."

Cornish miners and their families, in particular, had a significant impact on local culture. Cornish workers in eastern and northern mining areas of the States, as well as those in Britain, were encouraged to move west to Gilpin County to work the deep mines of Nevadaville. Called "Cousin Jacks" because they always claimed to have a cousin back in Cornwall who had the very skills an employer sought (Brown 1979: 5), they were considered the best miners in the world. In addition, they contributed traditions and customs of song, dance, music, festival, and lore to local culture (Carter 1989). One of their beliefs was a reliance on mysterious "little people" who protected them in the mines: "The Cousin Jacks called the wee people tommyknockers, unseen companions who guided them to the good ore and always warned them in time of danger" (Brown 1979: 96).

Other ethnic groups, including Tyrolean, Italian, Slavic, and Scandinavian immigrants who had gained experience in hard-rock mining in other parts of the world, later moved to Gilpin County to work the mines and smelters. There was an air of prosperity to the Gilpin County mining towns; company pay was generally decent; and, unlike in other Colorado mining towns such as Leadville, miners' strikes were generally nonexistent. Miners in Gilpin County achieved some degree of economic independence and autonomy by diversification (King 1977), obtaining multiple sources of income by working a variety of jobs. A Cornish miner, for example, could work for a mining company, lease unworked claims for personal gain, and apply his masonry skills in local building projects. The mortarless stone walls visible in Gilpin County towns even today are the legacy of skilled Cornish masons. In general, people in the Gilpin County mining towns enjoyed "a satisfactory standard of living and general community harmony" (National Park Service 1990: 6, 8).

Although there were clear ethnic groupings and social stratifications among the populace of the Gilpin County mining areas, violent local disturbances were unusual, and the image of the "wild West" cannot be sustained here (Hogan 1990). Even though Cornish miners feuded with Irish immigrants living in Nevadaville and Mountain City, and later the Cornish and Irish joined forces against newly arrived Tyrolean and Italian miners who worked for cheaper wages, "this region was rather unique in its orderliness and freedom from the crime and corruption that typified many gold camps of the West" (Hoffmeister 1940: 99). The notable outlaws who frequented other Western towns possibly found the climate too severe, the terrain too rugged, the lack of a railroad a deterrent to robbery, and the immigrant culture and work ethic too intimidating, for easy lawlessness. Indeed, Dorset (1970: 171) noted that "Central City was the epitome of respectability.... [T]he raw violence that marked other camps was nearly nonexistent in Central." She speculated that the presence of many distinguished and influential lawyers and politicians in Central City created a sense of public order and sophistication. This did not seem to limit the array of available entertainments, however. Numerous saloons, some gambling parlors, and a few small bordellos were available. Black Hawk, whose "rough exterior was an exact representation of its inner character" (Dorset 1970: 186), was nonetheless a town of hardworking miners and families. Together, the cities were blessed by a sense of permanence, civic pride, and optimism for continued economic growth during the 1860s and 1870s.

The most significant event of the stabilization period in Gilpin County was the "Great Fire" of 1874. As in other Western mining towns, wood-frame buildings were the norm, and small fires occasionally broke out in the communities. On May 21, 1874, however, a major conflagration erupted, reportedly in the shop of a Chinese laundryman on Dostal Alley in Central City. Fire raced through the business district of Central City, destroying more than 150 buildings, but fortunately causing no deaths (Hollenback 1961). A belated effort at local planning emerged, and the business district was rebuilt quickly and almost entirely in stone. Indeed, the quality of the stone constructions gave Central City a legacy as one of the finest examples of a late 1800s gold mining town in the western United States. Many years later, in 1961, the U.S. National Park Service designated Central City a National Historic Landmark

District; surrounding mining areas, including Black Hawk and Nevadaville, were later added to the register as well (National Park Service 1990).[5]

The long-term stability of the Gilpin County gold rush communities seemed assured when Colorado achieved statehood on August 1, 1876; the thirty-eighth state became known as the "Centennial State." Soon after that, the completion of the Central City Opera House in 1878 marked the greatest civic achievement in the gold rush community during that decade. Music, plays, and theater had always been important in Central City, perhaps because "Central City's cosmopolitan population, especially the Cornish, Italian, and German contingents . . . had been exposed to classical music and opera in their homelands and thus savored" theatrical performances (Brown 1979: 46). Other authors attribute the strong interest in theater, documented in Mountain City as early as 1859, to the love of folk music and song by the immigrant miners, and to the presence of "circuit rider" theatrical troupes that visited the mining towns of Central City, Georgetown, Cripple Creek, and Leadville during the gold rush days (Sayre 1929; Kemp 1949; Johnson 1980). Whatever the stimulus, music and theatrical performances provided a point of intersection for both the common mine laborers and the sophisticated—sometimes flamboyant—community elite. The result was strong local interest in and support for music and theater (Axford 1976; Young 1903; Bancroft 1958; Perrigo 1936).

Theatrical shows and music festivals were produced in several buildings around the area in the 1870s, and there was strong sentiment for building a permanent structure. An organization supporting the community theater efforts, the Central City/Gilpin County Opera House Association (Perrigo 1934; Johnson 1980), formed to oversee financing and construction efforts. When the Central City Opera House was completed in March 1878, it was regarded as "the best opera house between Missouri and Salt Lake" (Johnson 1980: 10). Seating about 750 people, and made of Gilpin County granite, it was decorated with murals, frescoes, and a gas chandelier (Axford 1976). The structure was the crowning jewel of the mining area, providing a stage for musical and theatrical performances, plays, vaudeville, lectures, and political meetings.

THE DECLINE OF MINING

As the symbolic centerpiece of the gold rush era, the Central City Opera House should have marked the beginning of a new growth period in the Gilpin County mining towns. Instead, it came to signify the end of the pioneer miner's way of life. The Tabor Grand Opera House, financed by silver magnate H.A.W. Tabor, opened in Denver in 1881, and the competition for performance bookings led to the decline of music and theater locally. The Central City Opera House saw limited use for movies, graduations, meetings, and boxing matches, and gradually fell into disrepair, closing finally in 1927 (Johnson 1980). Aging business and mining entrepreneurs also began to seek a more inviting, comfortable lifestyle in the Denver metropolitan area in the 1880s and 1890s. As Hollenback (1961: 14) explained, "Many Central City residents, having made their stake, found they could live in Denver and manage their mining or business interests from there."

The population of Gilpin County peaked around 1900, when 6,690 residents inhabited the mining towns of the area. After that, a combination of circumstances led to a steady decline in both population and the mining industry. In 1877, vast discoveries of silver in Leadville, Colorado, drew attention and investment away from gold mining. Silver was cheaper to mine than gold, and the silver mining industry flourished while gold mining costs escalated. In addition, Gilpin County, which had led all Colorado mining districts in gold production between 1859 and 1893, was surpassed in 1893 by the lucrative Cripple Creek gold mining district in Teller County (National Park Service 1990).

Structural changes in the mining industry also began to affect Gilpin County mining operations by the turn of the century. New technologies were required for cost-efficient hard-rock mining, and there were numerous business

Mine structures and tailings piles high on a hillside above the former town of Mountain City remind visitors of the days when the area was known as "the richest square mile on earth."

consolidations as underground mining became more expensive. By 1917, with falling gold prices on international markets, the local gold mining industry became unprofitable. As the Gilpin County mining industry faded, the historic towns of Central City and Black Hawk also began a steady downward spiral. From about 4,300 total residents in the two towns in 1900, the population dwindled to about 2,450 in 1910, to about 800 in 1930, and to only about 420 by 1960. In December 1913, a big snow totalling about sixty inches cut Central City and Black Hawk off from Denver for two weeks (Kemp 1949), and seemed prophetic of the future.

Over time, the Gilpin County mines produced gold, silver, copper, lead, zinc, and uranium. The exact amounts of gold and other minerals taken from the hills around the old Gregory Diggings is debated, but the wealth of the early mining days is apparent in comparative production figures (Fossett 1879). Between 1859 and 1914, the value of gold produced was $81,998,103; the value of all minerals was $94,856,377 (Bastin and Hill 1917). The 1918 yearbook of the state of Colorado (p. 114) reported $100 million in total Gilpin County mineral production; it also indicated that the Gregory lode and lodes found by Green Russell were still producing in that year. Gold and other mineral extraction continued over the next fifteen years, though at a much slower pace. A historic marker placed in 1932 by the Colorado State Historical Society at the site of Gregory's strike reads, "On this ground, later known as Gregory Diggings, John H. Gregory of Georgia discovered the first lode gold in Colorado on May 6, 1859. This discovery inaugurated the permanent development of Colorado. The district has produced $85,000,000 in gold." By 1988, using the value of metals at the time of production, the mines of Gilpin County had produced ores worth more than $105,125,000 since 1859; using 1988 prices, however, the value of metals produced was more than $2 billion (Cox 1989: 80).

If other mining districts in Colorado are more remarkable for the size or scope of their wealth and technological efforts, or for the outrageous characters who were part of their history, the significance of the Gilpin County mining area for opening the western mountain frontier and stimulating the creation of the state of Colorado is still unparalleled. As Ransome (1917: 13–14) explained,

> Cripple Creek . . . surpassed [Clear Creek, Gilpin, and Boulder counties] in value of annual output, and at Leadville mining operations have been conducted on a larger scale, but in the combined interest that attaches to a long and significant historical record, to number and variety of deposits, and to the place where so much in mining and metallurgic technique had its beginnings, the [Gilpin County and adjacent] region is without peer among the mining districts of the Rocky Mountains.

Old miners still inhabit the towns of Gilpin County, seeking the gold and other minerals that remain hidden in local hills. They continue to hope that the price of gold extraction will someday again be lower than the value of the product. In fact, when gold, sensitive to world political and economic forces, experienced a price increase to more than $850 per ounce in 1980, some Gilpin County mines reopened. Even at those prices, however, the technical challenges of water drainage and deep-rock mining, combined with the new environmental and labor regulations, made few efforts profitable (Cox 1989: 1). Nonetheless, romantics still find happiness dreaming about the old days and panning for color along local streams.

NOTES

1. On a contemporary map, the area of Jackson's strike is just south of Gilpin County near the town of Idaho Springs in Clear Creek County.

2. Interestingly, the Eighth Census of the Population of the United States (1860) reported data under the heading, the "Territory of Colorado," a jurisdiction that had not been approved at the time the census was taken (between June 1, 1860, and January 1, 1861). The relevant jurisdiction for the Pikes Peak gold fields during the enumeration period would have been Arapahoe County, Territory of Kansas. Between the time of enumeration and the 1864 publication, however, the Territory of Colorado was given congressional approval, and a territorial government was put in place. Because the country was changing so rapidly at that time, it is probable that this is an instance of census data being published under the governmental designation current at the time of census printing.

3. Though some popular writers have claimed that Pullman got the idea for his Pullman sleeping car bunks from his experience of miners' bunk beds in Gilpin County, Leyendecker (1992: ix) exposes that notion as myth: "Actually, he already had three sleepers operating in Illinois when he arrived in Denver in July 1860."

4. Although the contemporary *Weekly Register-Call* claims on its front page to be "Colorado's Oldest Continuously Published Newspaper," it is technically second to the *Rocky Mountain News* in terms of initial publishing dates and continuity. The daily *News* was the first paper published in the Pikes Peak region of the Kansas Territory, but when it failed during a blizzard in the 1960s to get a day's issue out on time, the *Weekly Register-Call* stole the motto of the "oldest continually published paper in Colorado."

5. Two frame buildings that survived the fire of 1874 can still be seen in Central City (Granruth 1991). Washington Hall (built and improved

from 1862 to 1864) contained county offices and jail, miners' court, church services, and space for local meetings. The one-story law office of Henry Teller, built in 1862, now located on Eureka Street adjacent to Washington Hall, also survived the fire, protected by the then-new brick Teller House hotel.

2

OPERA, TOURISM, AND THE REVIVAL PERIOD

The bustle and excitement of the thriving mining town has passed, but the glamour and the personality of the former periods will not die. The rugged beauty of the region and the romantic history of the camps that is written in every mine dump and in every weather-beaten structure now act as a magnet to draw thousands of tourists and resorters each year. . . . The gold which was sent out in earlier periods to enrich the East is returning to the mountains to be spent by tourists.

— Hoffmeister (1940: 104)

The glory days of the Gilpin County mining industry were over by about 1917, and the historic gold mining towns of Black Hawk and Central City began a slow but steady decline (Table 2.1).

Of about 6,700 people who had lived in the county in 1900, only 4,100 remained by 1910, and just over 1,350 lived there in 1920. The 1950 census was the last to include separate data for the towns of Nevadaville (the population of which then was reported to be only six hardy souls) and Rollinsville. By 1960, Russell Gulch, Tolland, and Apex had also achieved "ghost town" status, disappearing from the census list of incorporated towns in Gilpin County. Though there were several instances of renewed vigor in the gold mines after 1920, these were usually short-lived. Gilpin County, once the industrial and civic "Cradle of Colorado," became a place lost in time, with mountain scenery replacing gold mining as the primary local attraction.

Table 2.1   Populations of Colorado, Gilpin County, and Gilpin County Places, 1860–1990

Year	Colorado: Territory/State	Gilpin County[a]	Central City	Black Hawk	Nevadaville	Russell(s) Gulch	Other Gilpin County Places
1860	34,277	4,687[b]	598	c	879	480	840 (Mountain City)
1870	39,864	5,490	2,360	1,068	973	d	
1880	194,327	6,489	2,626	1,540	1,084	543	198 (Rollinsville)
1890	413,249	5,867	2,480	1,067	933	673	
1900	539,700	6,690	3,114	1,200	823	728	231 (Rollinsville); 237 (Apex)
1910	799,024	4,131	1,782	668	367	654	353 (Rollinsville); 63 (Apex)
1920	939,629	1,364	552	253	51	153	102 (Rollinsville); 49 (Apex)
1930	1,035,791	1,212	572	253	2	75	150 (Rollinsville); 65 (Tolland)
1940	1,123,296	1,625	706	289	25	168	271 (Rollinsville); 59 (Tolland)
1950	1,325,089	850	371	166	6		201 (Rollinsville)
1960	1,753,947	685	250	171			
1970	2,207,259	1,272	228	217			
1980	2,889,964	2,441	329	232			
1990	3,294,394	3,070	335	227			

Sources: United States Census of Population, from each decade 1860 through 1990.

[a]Gilpin County population includes residents in incorporated and unincorporated areas. The population of Gilpin County places includes only residents living in named places.

[b]The 1860 Census for the Territory of Colorado listed populations for specific mining camps. The total of 4,687 was obtained by summing the populations of camps known to be located in the vicinity of the Gregory Diggings area.

[c]The settlement around Mountain City initially spread up Gregory Canyon toward Central City. Black Hawk was apparently established after the 1860 Census.

[d]Only Central City, Black Hawk, and Nevada(ville) are listed under Gilpin County in the 1870 U.S. Census of Population.

OPERA REVIVAL

During this period of decline, one event stands above all others in charting the course of the postmining community. In summer 1931, a series of serendipitous events led the heirs of Peter McFarlane, former Central City mayor and entrepreneur, and John Evans, the second territorial governor, to undertake a community project that would have historic implications. Ida Kruse McFarlane, along with her close friend, Anne Evans, and several opera and theater aficionados, initiated a campaign to reclaim and restore the crumbling opera building in Central City. The opera house had been in the McFarlane family for several decades, and the effort to transform the granite structure into a functioning performance hall seemed to be a natural extension of the pioneer enthusiasm and hopefulness that so characterized early Gilpin County miners and residents.

The magnitude of the restoration task proved formidable, though, especially during a period of economic instability and depression in the United States. Nevertheless, the planning and restoration group worked tirelessly to achieve its vision. Meeting as a reorganized Central City Opera House Association, and composed primarily of wealthy arts and culture patrons in Denver society circles, the group organized fundraisers, publicity, and restoration activities. To guarantee some measure of permanence, the opera house structure was deeded to the University of Denver as a gift in perpetuity. The McFarlane family had long-standing ties to that institution, and the arrangement allowed the Central City Opera House Association to manage theater productions while placing the building in tax-exempt status with the university. Subsequently, other local properties, including the Teller House, the Bank block, the McFarlane foundry, the Williams' Stables, and various other historic houses and mining properties in Central City were acquired by the Association in conjunction with the university. These additional locations were to provide storage space, practice facilities, and housing for artists and performers in forthcoming years.

The renovated historic Central City Opera House reopened on July 16, 1932, with Lillian Gish starring in *Camille*. The novelty of staging summer theatrical and opera performances in a rural mountain town in a small, 750-seat theater drew patrons from across the country and world. A formal ball was held in the Teller House on opening night, bell-ringers walked the streets of the old mining town announcing the performance, and flower girls from Denver society families distributed nosegays among the audience. National acclaim surrounded both the initial performances and the general concept of mountain opera. An especially enthusiastic newspaper reporter, in evaluating the opening night festivities, wrote, "This slumbering mining ghost town has

The renovation of Central City's famed Opera House initiated a new tourist-based economy for the community in the early 1930s.

awakened to interrupt the mad modern rush of time and to live again the riotous days of the west in its lusty infancy" (Johnson 1980: 47). A new mythology of place was developing.

Celebrities of the day came to watch or to be seen, as the former gold rush town of Central City earned the nickname "the summer theatre capital of the US" (de Chaine 1963). Famed conductor Leopold Stokowski visited in the opening season, and columnists Lucius Beebe and Hedda Hopper, and correspondent Ernie Pyle, reported from Central City (Young 1993). Top entertainers from Broadway, as well as performers from national and continental opera companies and theaters, came to perform. Over the years, Helen Hayes, Beverly Sills, Catherine Malfitano, Howard Keel, Sir Michael Redgrave, William Bendix, Sherrill Milnes, Walter Houston, the D'Oyly Carte Opera Company, and other famous artists performed at the Central City Opera Festival (Gern 1960; de Chaine 1963; Johnson 1980; Johnson 1992). Mae West played *Diamond Lil* in 1949. The original world premiere of *The Ballad of Baby Doe,* which tells the story of "Baby Doe" Tabor, former Central City and Black Hawk resident and wife of millionaire H.A.W. Tabor, was presented in 1956. Lillian Gish made a return engagement in 1971. The season was canceled during World War II and again in 1982, when financial constraints were especially severe. Nevertheless, continually improving management over time and selective artistic choices confirmed the role of the opera as a stable community institution.

The Central City Opera House Association was motivated by a desire to develop cultural resources in a historic mountain setting. But public and community support were also essential for success. Initially, promoters believed that the opera and theatrical performances should form the centerpiece of a new community "Pioneer Revival Festival," in which "a program of activities that presented a real picture of pioneer life, including a production in the Opera House, square dance exhibits, a tintype photo shop, fire hose-cart races, rock drill contests, a pony express race, tours conducted by ushers in early garb, and open gambling would provide atmosphere for the opera festival" (Bancroft 1958: 340). Opera House Association planners asked assistance from interested community members in coordinating some of the activities, though other activities were to be sponsored exclusively by the Opera House Association. The hope was to provide "an environment of the Old West ... [promoting] artistic enterprises ... compatible with the Festival" (de Chaine 1963: 256).

The restoration of the Central City opera house and the development of the summer festival season had important consequences for the local communities. A period of local historic preservation emerged as the Opera House Association and visitors purchased old or abandoned homes and buildings and restored them in Victorian style. Charmed by the history and relics of past mining days, and enjoying the feeling of the town as a quiet retreat from urban living, a summer artist colony and retreat also developed. Census data show that between 1930 and 1940, the populations of Central City and Black Hawk grew. Festival seasons also injected a new optimism among community residents, as well as outsiders who held attachments to the old mining areas. Improving the image of the area also improved the general business climate and stimulated economic development as more tourists visited the towns.

Although the outcomes of the summer opera and play festival were appreciated by community members, efforts to achieve the right mix of appropriate activities eventually created significant community dissension. The first hint of conflict came when people associated with the Opera House Association used the term "American Salzburg" (Bancroft 1958; Johnson 1980) to describe their vision for the future of the mining community. Another supporter proposed that "the entire community ... be renovated as a 19th century historic town like Williamsburg, Virginia" (de Chaine 1963: 256). Reporters and critics quickly adopted these images, applauding the efforts of the Opera House Association, and suggesting that a summer festival would reawaken the romance and spirit of earlier Gilpin County mining times. The opera festival, believed partisan opera supporters, was "an event which exemplifies and perpetuates the love of beauty, of culture, of true Americanism, of the Gilpin County Argonauts" (Kemp 1949: 9).

Romanticism played very well in gaining the support of some cultured audiences, but old-timers and miners living in the Gregory Gulch area were less impressed. They had legitimate concerns about the transformation of their community. Although the Opera House Association did acquire and improve many of the vacant buildings in town, staging opera was a costly business. The Association received tax advantages by deeding its properties to the University of Denver, which had tax-exempt status (Johnson 1992: 43), but what was beneficial to the Association was disadvantageous to Central City and Gilpin County. The tax-free basis of many of the properties used by the Opera House Association created a situation in which the small community's members saw themselves providing significant public services to the Association with little monetary return for their investment (Johnson 1992). Indeed, "The tax free status of the Central City Opera House Association ... estranged the citizens from the ... Association and at one point nearly resulted in the discontinuation of the operations of the Association" (de Chaine 1963: 325).

In addition, local residents felt that wealthy Denver residents were using Gilpin County and Central City as a "society playground," with little effort to support community-driven initiatives or goals. Some residents felt that the culture of Denver society opera patrons did not adequately convey the "real cultural roots" of a mining camp, described in a local newspaper editorial as "liquor and carousing of miners" (de Chaine 1963: 81). The summer opera festival did stimulate tourism, but that came at some cost to the community. The Opera House Association tended to promote Central City as a mining ghost town—an image, locals felt, that was incompatible with the real history and the year-round population of the area (de Chaine 1963). Moreover, by suggesting that the towns were dead except during the summer opera season, the Association adversely affected potential economic growth in both commercial and mining sectors of the economy at other times of the year.

The conflicts over image and community direction eventually flowered into a lively feud. In 1948, Central City residents attempted to recall their mayor, who was said to have made special concessions to the Opera House Association (de Chaine 1963). The recall petition was defeated, but the conflicts did not dissipate. In some circles, feelings of mistrust and strained relations between residents and members of the Central City Opera House Association have persisted for more than fifty years. Even in interviews in 1992, some residents described people linked to the Opera House Association as "snooty," saying "[T]hey lord it over us. . . . [T]hey use our town as a playground and take over the town in the summer . . . [W]hy don't they just go away." In turn, some of the more cosmopolitan opera representatives and patrons describe local residents as provincial and unfriendly. Members of both groups say it is sometimes difficult to work with the other. Opera House Association members claim that some local elected officials look for ways to discriminate against opera people with extensive rules and regulations. Some local leaders claim that the opera people want special privileges but give little back to the community. Such comments do little to resolve the real and imagined conflicts.

THE GAMBLING ISSUE

The fundamental issues in the continuing conflict are the image and representation of Central City and the compatibility between local and Opera House Association goals. Opera supporters saw the community as a cultural center where artistic ideals could be promoted. Originating from the upper classes of Denver society, many members of the Opera House Association had historical ties to Gilpin County. They also had wealth and social status, two ingredients necessary for promoting art, music, opera, and historical reconstruction in Central City. They were well intentioned, and their goals were surely noble, but these were goals imposed by outsiders on a functioning, rural mountain community where residents scraped together a meager living and grew old amid the ruins of past mining glory. In the words of one opera supporter observing the conflict, "local people thought of their town as a mining camp. Dead or alive, they insisted, it was a mining camp and they refused to admit the evidence of *rigor mortis,* long after death had surely set in" (Bancroft 1958: 351).

One of the most contentious issues related to the conduct and goals of the opera festival was that of gambling. In conjunction with the reopening of the opera in 1932, the Central City Opera House Association had proposed to offer entertainment gambling, primarily in the form of slot machines, during the festival season. The intent was to recreate a "mining town atmosphere" (de Chaine 1963; Johnson 1980; Johnson 1992) that would entertain summer tourists and give an Old Western flavor to the Opera Festival. Although gambling was officially illegal in the state of Colorado, enforcement was usually left to local officials, and the Central City town administrators were not averse to the idea of raising a bit of extra revenue themselves in conjunction with opera performances. Gambling was thus allowed in the Teller House, under auspices of the Central City Opera House Association, and slot machines were placed in local shops and saloons in Central City as well.

Though slot machines and games of chance (roulette, poker, craps, and faro) were available during the first and subsequent festivals (de Chaine 1963; Johnson 1992), not everyone favored the idea of gambling. Indeed, the Opera House Association "later deemed gambling incompatible with the artistic dedication of the Festival" (de Chaine 1963: 269), and encouraged elimination of "wide open" gambling. Local businesses, however, continued to offer gambling opportunities for visitors, improving their seasonal revenues in the process. A portion of the proceeds apparently were also collected by the town: longtime residents recall that gambling was common in the summer, and that the monies were used to provide hot lunch programs for Gilpin County students and to improve streets.

In 1934, the Gilpin County sheriff and the district attorney refused to approve a petition to allow gambling during the Opera Festival, but they made no overt efforts to stop the gambling activities that were provided. In 1935, though, a Denver professional was arrested for involving an organized gambling syndicate in management of the Central City entertainments, and local gambling activities were curtailed. By 1941, documented accounts of gambling during the Opera Festival again surfaced. Despite its earlier negative stance, the Opera House Association requested permission in 1947 from the county district attorney for "one gaming establishment . . . to lend historic atmosphere to the Festival" (de Chaine 1963: 270). Permission was denied, but gambling did not disappear from the local scene.

Between 1947 and 1950, despite objections from the district attorney, there were continued disputes about whether gambling could or should be offered locally, and a publicity campaign against gambling arose in the Denver newspapers. Well-publicized "raids" on local businesses were conducted, albeit with appropriate advance warning. Shopkeepers maintained an informal network to publicize such events, and the police—all local boys—somehow seemed unable to discover any gambling machines in the town during the raids. Gaming was again conducted openly during the 1948 Opera Festival, with slot machines readily available in the Teller House and local businesses. There seemed to be little political will among local citizens to enforce the state's anti-gaming laws.

During the 1949 Opera Festival, gambling proceeded on an even larger scale in Central City, and an organized syndicate again became involved. In an effort to stop all gambling operations, the district attorney issued arrest warrants for all local businesses and town government officials involved. Local merchants and citizens were incensed and vowed to retaliate against what they saw as "Denver-sponsored" interference in local affairs. They planned a "Grand Stunt" to publicize their opposition.

As reported by de Chaine (1963: 276) and Johnson (1992: 31), the event involved one Mrs. Alice Ramstetter, an older woman of outstanding character and a pillar of the community. She and her husband owned a Central City grocery store, and she played the organ for Sunday services at the Methodist Church. When officials found a gambling device on the premises of her family's business, she was arrested, and—accompanied by her bed, rocking chair, and radio—was carted off to the county jail. On Sunday mornings, Mrs. Ramstetter was released so that she could meet her religious and musical obligations. In opposition to her incarceration, local residents organized a spectacular torchlight parade down Central City's Main Street and up Eureka Street to the jail. There, they presented Mrs. Ramstetter with a large cake, freshly baked around a shiny new hacksaw.

The local sense of theater produced mixed results. Local and state publicity was extensive. In support of the exciting events, witnesses to the local gambling activities refused to testify in court. Arrest warrants were subsequently canceled, and the local instigators appeared to have won a victory. Nevertheless, gambling devices were removed from the area, and it was clear that a showdown was brewing for the 1950 Opera Festival. That year, a committee of town officials claimed that because Central City's incorporation charter had been signed under the jurisdiction of the Territory of Colorado, which preceded the incorporation of Colorado as a state, Central City was not subject to state anti-gambling laws (Johnson 1992). In concert, other cities with territorial charters instituted gambling activities. Gambling thus became a statewide problem, not merely a local issue. A state court finally ruled against this line of thinking, and threats of prosecution reinforced the ruling. Open gambling finally disappeared from local events. In private moments, however, residents who lived through these times will confirm that behind-the-scenes gambling continued in Gilpin County even past 1950, and some old-timers will happily show off old gambling machines to interested visitors.

LIVING ON SEASONAL TOURISM AND SCENIC BEAUTY

The history of the Opera Festival illustrates the conflict of competing visions and goals between opera promoters and local residents. One cannot blame the Opera House Association for pursuing its vision in the historic setting of Gilpin County, a place so conducive to dreams. Just as surely, one cannot fault the local mining families and descendants of miners for holding on to the only dreams they knew: the hope that mining would one day again be profitable. Bancroft (1958: 351) suggested that "[t]he townspeople reconciled to the idea of a festival when they looked in their cash registers. Tourists were putting money there, not mining." Axford (1976: 132) also waxed eloquent, saying, "[A]nother kind of gold flows into the pockets and cash registers of the citizens of Gilpin County each summer." Yet, to those who believed that mining would return, it was probably little consolation.

The battle was fought over the issue of economics, but this was more than simply a matter of money: it was a contest over the power of symbols. The financial success of the opera provided residents and businesses in the area with a stable source of tourist income, but, because the Opera House Association was viewed as a "colonizing" force, local resistance was inevitable. The miners, after all, had staked first claim in Gilpin County, and they were not about to allow opera newcomers the opportunity to usurp the latest local resource, history.

The gambling issue illustrates the problems associated with controlling the use of symbols. Both local people and opera supporters saw gambling as a legitimate mining-town pastime, but they diverged over the acceptable expression of that history. Opera promoters supported gambling in Association-owned buildings as an addition to the ambience of the festival. Local businesspeople supported gambling across the community as a way to achieve economic independence. As de Chaine (1963: 325) explained, "The feuds and intrigues which were born as a result of illegal gambling ... are historically significant because gambling gave the citizens an economic freedom which, if continued, might have damaged the artistic purposes of the [Opera] Festivals."

Despite the feuds, the Opera Festival succeeded in reinvigorating Gilpin County, and Central City in particular, by stimulating tourism. Between 1940 and 1955, the number of opera performances per season increased, audience attendance rose from 20,250 to about 55,000 opera patrons, and general tourist visits to Central City during the summer festival reached about 450,000 (de Chaine 1963; Johnson 1980). Central City and Black Hawk settled into a pattern of seasonal tourism and off-season slumber. Paving and improvements to Colorado Highway 6, through Clear Creek Canyon, in 1952 made the towns even more accessible, and assured the future of Gilpin County as a summer tourism destination. Hoffmeister's (1940: 104) assertion that "[t]he gold which was sent out in earlier periods to enrich the East is returning to the mountains to be spent by tourists," conveyed the hopefulness of the revival period.

The opera brought tourists and seasonal incomes, especially to Central City and its business district, but the county population began a downward spiral between 1940 and 1960. In 1960, the 685 residents of Gilpin County constituted the smallest number of inhabitants in 100 years. More than 60 percent of those residents lived in the two old mining towns of Central City and Black Hawk. With a median age of 41.9 years, these were the "oldest" group of people ever to inhabit the area. About 300 miners had worked in Gilpin County in 1930 (54.8 percent of all employed persons), but only 31 people (about 10 percent of all employed) were employed in mining in 1950, and only 11 people (4.1 percent of employed county residents) identified themselves as miners in 1960, according to the U.S. Census of Population.

The time period between 1960 and the late 1980s was relatively uneventful in Gilpin County history. Opera performances and summer tourism continued, and fledgling efforts to develop the arts and to reclaim historical structures from the ravages of time were marginally successful (de Chaine 1963), as public and private groups formed to support historic preservation. The 1961 National Park Service designation citing the area as a National Historic Landmark District increased awareness of the historic resources and brought some tax relief for historic properties.

Before gaming development, Central City's Main Street was a place for casual socializing. All of the buildings were constructed after the Great Fire of 1874, and their historic legacy contributed to the designation of the area as a National Historic Landmark District.

Another effort to establish gambling appeared in the form of a 1962 proposal by an outside group wishing to build a $3.5 million casino in Central City (*WRC*, Oct. 2, 1992). They asserted that the town's territorial incorporation charter allowed gambling, but having fought, and lost, that particular battle a decade earlier, the Central City Council tabled the proposal.

Gilpin County experienced a turning point after 1960. According to census data, the number of county residents nearly doubled in the decade between 1960 and 1970, rising to 1,272. It grew again to 2,441 residents by 1980, and continued on an increasing trend to 1990, when 3,070 people were recorded by census enumerators. Most of the newcomers settled in unincorporated areas of the county, though, not in Central City or Black Hawk. As highway access became easier, the county was discovered by people seeking a quiet, peaceful mountain living environment within commuting distance of employment in the Front Range cities of Denver, Boulder, and Golden. The mountainous landscape, the mine tailings and historic structures scattered on the hillsides, and the old Victorian towns provided geographic and psychological barriers to urban life. Whereas Central City, Black Hawk, Russell Gulch, Nevadaville, and the other mining towns had once been the prominent centers of the community, the scenic amenity attractions of the county had become, by 1990, almost more valuable than gold dust.

Since 1970, opera, history, and scenery have been the primary elements of the Gilpin County tourism experience. People who visited Gilpin County during the recent past speak longingly of the joy of summers there. "You cannot imagine what it was like to be there!" said a Denver native who visited the towns in summers. "When friends came to visit, we'd take them for a drive to see the scenery and old mines, and then we'd stop in Central City and have dinner, or maybe go to the opera. After that, we'd walk around the town under the night sky, and stop in the bars to talk and hear the opera singers give impromptu performances!" This was a place that lived in the past (Johnson 1992: 12), much to the delight of visitors and many residents.

As in earlier time periods, Black Hawk and Central City remained the centers of social life in Gilpin County, and functioned as the administrative and business centers as well. Government offices, and about forty to fifty small businesses, were located in the historic buildings along the main streets of the towns. Daily use of the historic buildings reminded residents of the frontier life of the past and kept alive the hope of a new mining boom. The history and charm of the area inspired a type of "local patriotism" (Barthel 1989), a commitment to the symbols, events, and meanings of the past. In expressing that commitment, area residents—a decreasing number of whom were actually miners, or were even descended from the early Colorado pioneers—adopted certain lifestyles based on their images of the past. One distinguishing feature of local life took shape around the saloons.

Saloons had been a mainstay of the local social scene since the early gold rush in Central City and Black Hawk. Carter (1989: 2) reported that between 1897 and 1914, there were about thirty-eight saloons in Gilpin County, more than half of which were in Central City. The proliferation of saloons is not unusual in mining towns, which generally have an extensive young, single, male population. Brown (1979: 45) observed that, historically, "saloons served as a kind of social center. The men discussed their day's labor, talked about local and national politics, and speculated about the future of the mines and their community." Leisure in mining communities usually involved pastimes that demanded little exertion from men who carved a living from the mountains by exhausting manual labor.

The decline of mining in Gilpin County did not produce a corresponding decline in the popularity of local bars. As the towns developed into popular tourist spots, some saloons also became known as perennial party halls. Jack Kerouac wrote about his 1947 visit to Central City saloons; more recently, community events such as the "Jazz Fest" were held in the local watering holes. During the nontourist seasons, community residents maintained the tradition of using local saloons as extended living rooms for neighborly interaction. Drinking beer, playing games with or against one another, and creating tall tales and legends were the primary activities at the local bars, and a saloon culture grew up around these community meeting places.

While the summer opera performances catered to cosmopolitan visitors, the saloons provided the "common opera" and theater for some community residents. The saloon culture celebrates the image of the community as a Western mining camp. It facilitates local affiliations and promotes stories, inside jokes, and meanings particular to participants. Insiders are recognized and given special treatment that elevates their role in the social environment. This is accomplished, in part, through the use of a special language indicating the privileged status of locals. Local people are called *Zekes*, a term drawn from older Gilpin County automobile license plates beginning with the initials "ZK." The term is used to mean a local person, an old-timer, a Gilpinite, an inhabitant of the "pointylands," the mountainous area of Gilpin County. The ability of locals to contrive and maintain a vernacular of their own speaks to the importance of history in shaping local realities, and also to the strength of the bonds supporting the sense of community.

The saloon culture provided a natural environment for the creation of a local newspaper whose name is a play on a phrase meaningful in local history. Founded by two local residents in 1970, the outrageous tabloid known as *The Little Kingdom Come* celebrates local history, events, and personalities, with humor and irreverence. Its name is drawn from the term "Little Kingdom of Gilpin," coined by early miners to refer to the wealth of the gold mining region around the Gregory Diggings. The paper is famous for its motto, "Published Whenever We Damn Well Feel Like It"; for its features, advertisements, and photographs; and for its human interest stories (for example, a miner who lost a limb in a mining accident penned an account entitled "A Farewell to Arm"). With a strong affection for the history and people of Gilpin County, *The Little Kingdom Come* supports and contributes to the spirit of community, and bridges the diverse subcultures of those who have ties to the area. Each summer, for example, the paper prints reviews of that year's operas. These unusual commentaries are always written by an out-of-state critic who has not seen the performance—the assumption being, of course, that if the chosen reviewer actually watched the operas, the reviews might be something less than objective.

In Central City and Black Hawk, the saloon culture and spirit of local fun had a secondary outcome of encouraging a contrary attitude. Local residents played out their own images of living in a Western mining town by engaging in minor lawlessness, or by supporting irreverent or unconventional behaviors. Occasionally, the antics of locals exceeded the bounds of social convention and even the law. As documented in *The Little Kingdom Come*, the determined efforts of a new police officer in 1990 to ticket drunk drivers went unappreciated in the community. In an article (*LKC*, Feb. 16, 1990: 2) entitled "An analysis of the heavy-handed enforcement of the [driving under the influence of alcohol] laws in Gilpin County," the newspaper proposed that "some are more deserving of the horrors of getting a DUI than others. . . . [S]houldn't a cop exercise discretion?" The author suggested that two types of law enforcement exist, "strict . . . and flexible," concluding that "the latter tack has generally worked much better" with the locals. Such examples did much to confirm the idea that "[t]he West was still alive!" (Cady interview 1994) in Gilpin County.

PROBLEMS AND PROSPECTS PRIOR TO GAMBLING DEVELOPMENT

The conditions leading up to the 1989 gambling proposal are relevant for understanding the subsequent processes of community discussion, adoption, and implementation of the development. Basic data provide a general overview of community conditions, but assessments of community character are particularly interesting for later juxtaposition against sentiments related to the gambling issue. Two independent studies conducted in Central City and Gilpin County over the past two decades provide a view of recent community conditions. A series of 1975 planning studies contracted by Central City (Ray and Associates, Inc. 1975) reported that the town had 228 residents, with about 48 percent of all housing units permanently occupied. About 55 percent of the Central City residents worked in that town, whereas 35 percent commuted to work elsewhere (vol. 3). The remaining 10 percent were retired. Many residents were relative newcomers, with just over half of all town residents living in Central City for five or fewer years. At Clark Elementary School in 1975, four teachers and two teachers aides taught eighty-four kindergarten-through-grade-6 students in the 1974–1975 school year; students in grades 7 through 12 attended school in nearby counties.

About 73 percent of all residents said in personal interviews that community growth was desirable. The consultants felt, however, that more than the small population accounted for a lack of community effort and direction. Study authors (Ray and Associates 1975, vol. 3: 5) wrote:

> 59 percent of the residents of the City of Central feel that they are not involved in local government. The relatively short period of residency ... may partially explain this. ... However, apathy and disinterest by the residents must be given credit for much of this attitude. Limited attendance by the citizenry at public meetings, and their absence from work sessions to direct matters of local concern indicates a general malaise toward their participation in community affairs.

The consultants also called for a greater understanding of the importance of historic resources in Central City and the surrounding mining areas of Gilpin County. A general theme in each of their five reports is that any town with a very small population, particularly one that has statewide historic importance, cannot be expected to service a large seasonal tourist population without greater external funding (Ray and Associates 1975, vol. 1: 3, 4). The consultants noted,

> The very preservation and rehabilitation of ... historical attributes invites and encourages seasonal tourism impacts which place an incredible and unrealistic burden on the land, the utilities, the transportation system, the local governmental agencies and on the local public treasury. ... [T]he community is at a critical point in the determination of its destiny.

The Ray and Associates study provides glimpses of life in Central City during the 1970s. A 1990 study of Gilpin County residents provides a broader look at community concerns while reaffirming the findings of the earlier study. Organized by the Gilpin County Revitalization Committee, results must be interpreted with care, as only 267 people returned completed surveys (Colorado Center for Community Development 1991). Notably, the study team found that most respondents were well educated (43 percent with a college degree), commuted to work (about 60 percent worked outside the county), and shopped outside the county for most items except gasoline, which was available at two sites in the county. About 79 percent of the respondents felt that Gilpin County should take steps to improve its economy by encouraging light manufacturing, a grocery store, and recreation. Among this sample, the least desired industries were those related to gambling, gravel quarries, and mining, three issues that had been discussed in local news at the time of the survey.

In terms of community qualities, respondents cited the natural beauty and the quiet and peace of the area as two primary reasons for living in Gilpin County. Least-liked features of the area included the lack of services, problems with road maintenance, and leadership problems. The two features cited as significant tourist attractions were the historic districts and the scenic views. The two features residents wanted to protect from change were the residential areas and local forests. Political participation in the county rose with age and length of residency in the community, and arts patronage increased with higher education. Residents working in the metropolitan area were less likely than those working locally to be involved in local government, lodges, community meetings, or volunteering, and less likely to be informed through community meetings or word of mouth.

Finally, the study found that "most respondents (56 percent) feel that people in Gilpin County don't look ahead to the future and plan for it, but react to events after the fact" (Colorado Center for Community Development 1991: 30). Nearly 90 percent of the respondents wanted better planning for the future. When asked about desired changes for improving county life in the future, "better leadership" was cited in 25 percent of all responses, followed by "improved road conditions" (about 20 percent). One respondent's written comments reflected the sentiments of many who replied in the "Comments" section of the survey: "We love our home, surroundings, our good friends, and climate—but everything connected with the *county* is an endless struggle in all aspects: economic, political, cultural, educational, with no real expectation of change" (Colorado Center for Community Development 1991: Comments 1).

These two studies provide glimpses of a small community characterized, like most other communities, by both positive and negative qualities. In conversations with Gilpin County residents conducted prior to the gambling vote, people tended to highlight the positive qualities of living in the community, ignoring or rejecting suggestions that there might be negative aspects of the local experience. For example, when asked to describe the people who lived there in the late 1980s, a Central City resident commented that it was "a wonderful place filled with interesting people who didn't have much money. . . . [E]specially [in winter] when there were no tourists, we would all hang out, have a beer and enjoy great fun. . . . [T]here are no places like this anymore." A Black Hawk resident said that town "is made up of capable, intelligent individuals. People here don't look sophisticated, but they have wonderful backgrounds. . . . People choose to live here; life isn't easy here." Residents of the two towns and the county would agree with the description of one resident, who said that locals are "solid, independent mountain people."

Nevertheless, the freedoms of life in Gilpin County have created problems for both individuals and institutions, and these problems at times affect the ability of people to function effectively both independently and as a community. Interviews and observations prior to and during the gambling developments suggest that many people live in Gilpin County because they cannot or will not live in other places, or because Gilpin County is an escape from other places. The sense of community does not depend on whether people get along well or work together, but on an orientation *away* from other places and people. The personality of place developed from these conditions favors as little governmental and social control as possible, and accepts nontraditional behaviors as standard. "Locals are people with an attitude," said one resident, and this attitude supports the practice of freedom in personal lifestyle and nonparticipation in community.

Among individuals, the self-production of local characters meant that some people saw themselves as being above the law or immune from social conventions. Behaviors that would elsewhere lead to criminal records were minimized here. A certain amount of friendly protection and tolerance meant that such actions were usually no deterrent to the perpetrator assuming or maintaining a position in local government. Health officials reported that alcohol and substance abuse problems were common in the community, and letters and opinions printed in the local newspaper confirmed the existence of such problems. Indeed, the 1990 Colorado Center for Community Development survey found that respondents thought alcoholism was the major health problem in the county. One respondent wrote, in a lengthy comment to that survey, "I have noticed this county tends to attract people who have a lot of dysfunctions ... [including] family beaters, drunks, a lot of drug addicts & numerous other dysfunctions.... If you look at our school register of names, of parents living with live-ins, divorced single parents, the % is very high" (Colorado Center for Community Development 1991: Comments 4). Though one should not generalize to all community members from these individual problems, it is important to note that many residents perceived and talked about the existence of such problems across the community.

Institutional dysfunctions are of concern because they affect the capabilities of communities to function effectively for the welfare of all citizens. In Gilpin County, institutional problems were evident in the perennial battles between local entities. Central City feuded with Black Hawk, the towns feuded with the county, and some local residents battled with outsiders (including the Opera House Association, the governor, and the Denver media). The root cause of such conflicts seemed to be a passionate, though at times strangling, love for the history and meanings of Gilpin County and its mining towns. The outcomes of such sentiments were manifest in attempts to control or manipulate social and civic community processes by groups or individuals who felt they had special vision or special authority in the community. Residents objected to the "old boy network" of Central City, the persistent anger of a former longtime Central City mayor after he had been voted out of office, and the impression of family dynasty management in Black Hawk, but it seemed that little was ever done to change the situations that produced conflicts.

Governance was one local issue that stimulated much public discussion. Community decision-making processes were traditionally familial, colloquial, and informal. Residential and business longevity often equated with community power. Some residents felt that community decision making was not always public, as issues of concern were sometimes discussed and resolved at private meetings in such places as the Central City Elks Club. The informal, behind-the-scenes operation of local government favored by some with power was seen as restrictive and even dangerous by those outside the elite groups. Moreover, informal government often perpetuated ineptness by protecting friends, and was ineffective in assuring accountability.

The dominant impression of Gilpin County in the time period just prior to the introduction of the gambling proposal was that the community balanced uneasily between rural provincialism and cosmopolitan sophistication. By the late 1980s, Gilpin County appeared to be populated by people who had chosen to accept the problems of rural, mountain living as the price of the opportunities and freedoms of personal lifestyle. Each group of residents had an agenda. Miners wanted freedom to mine without federal and state restrictions; county residents gave up local participation for peace and isolation; businesspeople wanted the benefits of a more favorable economy, as long as the tourists went away after spending their dollars. There seemed to be little agreement about what constituted "community," and even less effort exhibited toward creating a desired community. History remained a strong pull, drawing residents away from the demands of contemporary society. At the same time, urban life was encroaching farther into the mountains, bringing stresses as well as opportunities that could not be addressed with traditional methods. Under such conditions, it was only natural that the gambling proposal would be introduced with the rationale that each community group would receive substantial benefits with little personal or collective cost.

3

THE RHETORIC OF DESPAIR

The primary purpose of the resolution . . . is not to promote gambling. . . .
Keep in mind that we are not talking about casinos. . . . It is hoped that tourists will come to these towns year-round, not only to engage in limited gambling, but to stay in the hotels, eat in the restaurants, and shop in the stores.
— State Senator Sally Hopper (*WRC*, Apr. 13, 1990: 2)

The social movement in support of gambling began in Central City with
private discussions among government leaders and local businessmen. Interviews with the key proponents revealed that a primary stimulus for discussing
development issues was that the Central City water system was in a state of
severe disrepair, yet there were no local or state monies available to fund
improvements. Leaders in that town also felt a need for some type of development that would help extend the tourist season and job possibilities beyond
summer. They claimed that ski area and other mountain resort development
had drawn tourists away from Gilpin County; as a result, sales tax and other
governmental revenues were inadequate to meet community needs. As the
Central City manager remarked, there was "no way to compete with the ski
areas, not with a little town of 250 residents during the summer" (Hidahl
interview1994).[1]

Among the many possible development strategies discussed, gambling
was not a sudden or unexpected idea for the Gilpin County communities. As
noted in chapter 2, gambling had been suggested and even implemented in

the early opera years to enhance local revenues. Circumstances had never been favorable, however, for gaining the necessary state legislative approval. By 1988, though, the tide was turning. Public acceptance for lotteries seemed to be on the increase, and the development of small-stakes casino gambling in Deadwood, South Dakota (another Western boom-and-bust gold town) signalled the rise of more positive public attitudes about casinos. If Deadwood could have gambling, reasoned some local leaders, it might be possible to convince people that Central City should have it, too.

TOURISM DEVELOPMENT AND PUBLIC RHETORIC

The public campaign to bring gambling to Central City originated with presentation of the idea by the mayor in the local Gilpin County newspaper, the *Weekly Register-Call*. The mass media often play a significant role in tourism development campaigns, introducing key spokespersons, serving as a forum for community debate, and sometimes even advocating particular actions relative to the development (Watson 1989; Janowitz 1967). Given the importance of public discussion in most community growth processes, it is surprising that the study of rhetoric surrounding proposed tourism developments is so often neglected by social scientists. Leaders, residents, and outsiders always discuss and debate the tourism growth options in the mass media and other public forums, evaluating suggested development alternatives for feasibility, benefit, and consistency with community ideologies. Verbal and written messages, in the form of information bulletins, public appeals, reports from community meetings, local newspaper columns, editorials and letters, or government pronouncements, assume status as visible artifacts of the development process. By tracing community rhetoric over time, researchers can begin to understand how and under what conditions development proposals arise, why they succeed or fail, and how communities are transformed in the process of negotiating central arguments and images.

Messages related to tourism development are introduced into communities with existing social relationships, cultures, and history. In the course of a development campaign, new messages are given meaning when they are (either purposefully or inadvertently) linked by key spokespersons with taken-for-granted community meanings and practices. New messages represent broad ideological statements, prominently defining the kind of reality promoters or opponents wish to create. Spoken and written messages are not static but are continually "massaged," shaped, and repositioned by a variety of communicators throughout a development campaign—and, if the campaign is successful, throughout the community implementation and adaptation processes as well. The communicators whose messages are most persuasive, or who speak more loudly or more often in the public debate, tend to be seen as powerful actors in the development process, even if they eventually find themselves on the losing side of the campaign.

The difficulty of studying the rhetoric of tourism development is apparent given how quickly messages fade from public view. Spoken messages remain in public consciousness only as long as an issue is publicly debated, or "sound bytes" persist, or images or ideas are called upon in comparison to other events or issues. Mass media provide wide public access to messages; however, these messages are continually replaced with others that appear to have equal, if not greater, importance. Even when an issue remains prominent over many months or years, audiences typically tune in to only some parts of the message, and they may be unlikely to clearly remember much about earlier messages. Moreover, new audience members may not know or understand the contextual factors surrounding earlier messages, or may be unaware of historical relationships among participants involved in the discussions, so their ability to decipher and understand new public messages may be limited.

Because spoken messages are transitory, other channels of communication are needed to reinforce or corroborate past messages and to present new messages. In this respect, local newspapers and other written documents are invaluable sources of information, because they can confirm impressions about issues that might have been only fleetingly evident in spoken communications (Gephart 1993; Preister 1987; Motz 1983; Janes 1958). As Motz (1981: 278) argued, using historical narrative documents such as newspapers and public documents in research about community development impacts provides a longitudinal view of the local social climate, places current changes in context, and describes a community's "typical way of responding to change." Local newspapers give visibility to many types of structured messages, including public information and reports about significant local events; identification of important community leaders and citizens; and "features" (stories, letters, opinions, photographs, announcements) illustrating meaningful social and cultural aspects of community life. Each type of message can be seen as a piece of a puzzle that shows how people think about their towns, their environments, their history, and their associations with one another. Because written media such as newspapers are often archived in public libraries and/or computer databases, they can easily be used as sources for detailed analyses of tourism development issues over time.

Stamm (1985: 36) suggested that local "newspapers help build expectations about the community" among residents and newcomers, and thus stimulate some forms of community association and participation. This is because locally produced newspaper articles and stories represent one approach to organizing relevant community symbols and meanings and disseminating them across community groups. People in communities learn about, and perhaps come to share, ideas about who they are as a community through repetition of meaningful stories and narratives about their participation, and the participation of others, in that place. Johnstone (1990: 5) explains that, "Just as narrative structures our sense of self and our interactions with others, our sense of place and community is rooted in narration. A person is at home in a place when the place evokes stories, and, conversely, stories can serve to create places." This idea is well illustrated in Ryden's (1993) exposition of the folklore of the Coeur d'Alene mining district in Idaho, of which he concludes (p. 241), "Unlike simple geographical locations, which exist objectively, places do not exist until they are verbalized, first in thought and memory and then through the spoken or written word." Such narratives are then called upon in personal and mass-mediated discussions to legitimize some community proposals and development claims and to reject those that do not fit with local images of self and place.

Because newspapers are published, sold, and distributed across a community, the messages contained in their pages achieve a certain independence and credibility, at least among readers who have some emotional or tangible investment in local happenings. This group includes not only local residents, businesspeople, and leaders, but also those who have either moved away or are thinking of moving into the community, as well as those who have developed attachments to the community even without living there. Because any of these people might publicly express their views about community issues in the local newspaper, each potentially contributes to the framing and managing of local issues. Short of being quoted in a news story, the most common outlets for the presentation of personal sentiments that call upon communal meanings are the "Opinion" columns and "Letters to the Editor" appearing in a local newspaper. Supplemented with other methods of data collection and analysis, review of letters to the editor and opinion columns provides a wealth of information about the transformation of community during periods of change.

Although letters and opinions are not unbiased or complete accounts of community sentiments and attitudes, they constitute a series of texts explaining different perspectives on community choices, decisions, and goals. News accounts of local events may be more nearly objective, but opinions and letters contribute the personal viewpoints of motivated citizens who draw upon community ideologies to frame and focus issues for public debate. The agendas of residents are potentially different from those of local publishers and editors. For example, Rystrom (1991) found that opinions and letters written by local citizens often illustrate different biases than editorials provided by the staffs of local newspapers. His research showed that letters to the editor primarily focused on local topics, whereas editorials focused on issues of statewide concern. In addition, both editorials and letters tended to be written in response to governmental issues discussed in previous issues of the paper, but letters were more humanistic than editorials, and were more concerned with the implications of governmental decisions for local lifestyle and environment.

There are a variety of methods for studying narrative discourse, including content analysis, rhetorical criticism, and various forms of humanistic analysis (Smith 1988). These involve quantitative approaches (objective measurements of word or phrase frequencies, themes, images, or other categorical items) as well as qualitative methods (informed judgments and interpretations by a critic about an author's intent). Whichever methods are used, there are always dangers in relying solely on secondary data sources for understanding community changes. These problems include content rigidity, measurement errors, variation in data collection methods, contextual effects, and item selection bias (Webb et al. 1966). In conjunction with other research methods, however, systematic analyses of secondary and historical materials provide researchers with a deeper understanding of the complexities of community responses to change. These materials also constitute an extensive data pool not widely utilized by social researchers, particularly those engaged in tourism impacts research.

THE PRESS IN GILPIN COUNTY

News reports, letters to the editor, and opinion columns published in the *Weekly Register-Call* formed the basis for analysis of the pro-gambling campaign and its effects. Both quantitative content analyses and qualitative thematic analyses were used to evaluate the texts, and several specific questions guided the analysis of newspaper contents. What historic conditions influenced the form and content of the gaming proposal? How did people describe their community and its qualities and needs? What were the relevant issues supporting claims of the pro-gambling proposal? What were the roles of local and external spokespersons in keeping the gambling issue in the public consciousness? What expectations were raised about proposed implementation of gambling in the communities?

As described in chapter 1, the *Weekly Register-Call* is the primary newspaper of Central City, Black Hawk, and the unincorporated areas of Gilpin County, and has maintained a long history and presence in the community. Prior to the development of gambling, the *Weekly Register-Call* had a circulation of about 2,000. The newspaper is published each Friday in the form of a folded broadsheet. Historically, the paper has been limited to four pages, except for issues that included publication of special public notices, disbursements, or tax delinquency. Review of the newspaper for several years prior to and during the gambling campaign shows that variability in presentation was slight, although the size of the paper and type styles changed slightly over time.

The front page of the *Weekly Register-Call* typically presents a major local story in the top right quarter of the sheet, and covers most of the top left quarter with a black-and-white photograph from a current community event. News that always makes the front page includes reports about issues discussed at Central City and Black Hawk council meetings and at meetings of the Gilpin County commissioners, and other accounts of significant local events or activities, such as local festivals, accidents in mines, blizzards, or graduation. Occasionally, the front page will carry a story about events farther from home (such as problems at the new Denver airport, or the fiftieth anniversary celebrations of World War II), but this is rare. The only departure from this pattern is the last December issue each year, in which a month-by-month account of what the editors felt to be significant happenings in Gilpin County is summarized beginning on the front page.

Letters to the editor, and opinion and commentary columns, are consistently located on page two of the paper. These and other items of community interest—births, obituaries, book reviews, calendar of events, advertisements, community bulletin board, and school news—are sometimes continued onto page three. Classified advertisements and public notices are usually placed toward the back of the paper, along with a column entitled "Turning Back the Pages," which excerpts items from the community newspapers of 30, 60, 90, and 120 years ago.

The *Weekly Register-Call* experiences the typical problems and possibilities common to many rural papers. Local reporters sometimes attend only to particular elements of community life, and local issues—discussed and resolved on a different schedule than the publishing schedule—sometimes receive incomplete presentation in the paper. As a longtime resident and former mayor of Central City, the publisher often uses his column as an arena for either social boosterism or social vendetta. Gilpin County residents rely on the *Weekly Register-Call* for local news, but realize that the paper is oftentimes only a supplement to the real happenings of the community. Indeed, its primary fault has been that it may not quite "cover what people were really talking about, like somebody's going to buy the Gilded Garter and change its name or the big fight behind the Toll Gate [Saloon] last weekend—all the stuff people really talk about" (Cady, in Gunn 1989: 28). Despite shortcomings, though, the *Weekly Register-Call* serves the community in two ways: by disseminating local news and announcing local events, and by evaluating, supporting, and contributing to local culture.

THE COMMUNITY PRIOR TO GAMBLING

Because new issues emerge into preexisting fields of community interaction, a review of community issues prior to gambling introduction is helpful as a basis for understanding the extent to which the gambling idea drew upon local images and meanings. A content analysis of news articles, letters, and opinion columns published in the *Weekly Register-Call* between January 1988 and September 1989 (the twenty-one months prior to introduction of the gaming proposal) revealed patterns in community practices and interactions that confirm the research findings from the two studies discussed in chapter 2. Community issues taking center stage during the pre-gambling period included problems with local telephone service, mining property tax assessments, and dogs running loose in the county; opposition to increased local business taxes in Central City; the need for community recreation programs; and a school superintendent recall petition. Many positive letters to the editor also appeared in the paper, usually to thank local volunteers, participants, and sponsors of community events.

Countywide, the significant issue of public debate was a proposed dam in Clear Creek canyon south of Black Hawk and Central City. The project was intended to provide water for metropolitan communities and create reservoir recreation opportunities by submerging Highway 6, the primary canyon traffic route to Gilpin County. Community rhetoric about the project was predominantly negative, with leaders and citizens highlighting the costs of the project to Gilpin County. In the words of those writing letters to the editor about this issue, geographic isolation, economic ruin, and community decline would likely result if the dam were built.

An analysis of key themes discussed in the letters to the editor of the *Weekly Register-Call* was also conducted. Words and phrases that referred to what it was like to live in Gilpin County were extracted from the texts of these letters and grouped according to predominant themes. An iterative process of sorting produced six general categories: Environmental Beauty; Interesting History; Pride in Local Volunteers; Tourism as a Primary Industry; Economic Depression; and Local Conflict. The first three categories refer to very positive aspects of living in Gilpin County. People wrote about their love of the natural beauty, the mountains, wildlife, forests, clean air, landscapes, peace and quiet, and the rural atmosphere of the area. They also appreciated the historic surroundings and took pride in the efforts of local volunteers and groups who contributed to an improved quality of life.

The last three categories paint another picture of life in Gilpin County. Recognizing that tourism was the primary industry of the county, letter writers expressed mixed feelings about whether tourism could sustain them in the future. Authors perceived that the county had been "in a depression for the last five years," that tourism was slowing and property taxes were increasing, and that "we are heading toward a ghost town." Only one letter writer felt that mining and milling industries were still vital to the local economy. The Local Conflict category offered possible explanations for community uncertainties. The conflicts and antagonisms among residents and governments of Gilpin County that had been identified in studies by external researchers are also reflected in the letters to the editor. Indeed, these letters suggested that local feuds were common: the approximately thirty entries in the Local Conflict category accounted for more than twice the number of phrases generated for the combined set of five other thematic categories.

Two different types of local conflicts were discussed by letter writers: personal and institutional. Personal conflicts were suggested by phrases and words that negatively evaluated the behaviors of other community residents. For example, letter writers described some of their neighbors as "apathetic," "uncaring," "isolated in their own homes," or "always bickering among themselves." Several writers called upon their neighbors to unite as a community, to stick to facts rather than letting emotions rule public discussion, and to stop telling lies about other residents. A few writers provided explanations for why residents tolerated these kinds of personal conflicts. "[W]hat's a Gilpinite without a gripe?" asked one. Another suggested that "people live in Central City because they could not or would not live in organized society."

Another set of comments in this category referred to conflict between local institutions, particularly governments. The issues addressed in these letters covered conflicts between Central City and Black Hawk, between the towns and the county, and between each of the local jurisdictions and the Denver media. Writers claimed that there was "blatant, irresponsible politicking" locally, that officials were "stupid and irresponsible," and that local governments typically functioned to provide "band-aid surgery, not long range planning." A tendency toward "the good old boy tradition" of governance was said to be manifest across the community: "City councils serve their own purposes," "citizen input is not taken seriously by elected officials," and "citizens are seen as intruders" by leaders. There were also complaints about the "carnival atmosphere" of Central City's saloons, and the "malicious attacks" of the Denver media against the community in general and Central City in particular.

The overview of themes discussed in letters to the editor of the *Weekly Register-Call* shows that residents had both positive and negative feelings about their community. Though many residents who wrote letters to the newspaper saw positive aspects to life in Gilpin County (natural beauty, mining heritage, some kinds of local involvement), some people were also unhappy over local governance and community direction. Remarks about a continuing economic slowdown, a decline in tourism, the negative types of some tourism experiences offered, and the development plans of outside forces that influenced local conditions (such as the Clear Creek dam proposal) all contributed to the image of a community debating its future. These conditions set the stage for introduction of the gambling proposal.

PROMOTING GAMBLING IN CENTRAL CITY AND BLACK HAWK

The first public mention of gambling appeared in the *Weekly Register-Call* in September 1989, when Central City's mayor, Bruce Schmalz, was quoted as saying, "[I]f kept small . . . legalized gambling . . . could provide jobs, becoming a real boost to a slumping economy" (*WRC,* Sept. 8, 1989: 1). The image of entertainment gambling as a natural feature of a Western gold mining town was invoked, but Schmalz reassured residents that only limited stakes gambling (defined as slot machines, poker, and blackjack, with no bets exceeding $5.00) would be allowed. The link with economic improvement was a useful preliminary rhetorical strategy, responding as it did to perceptions of declining economic conditions across Gilpin County. As a respected business leader and well-liked mayor, Schmalz was also a particularly powerful and credible spokesman for the gambling cause. Shortly after his announcement, Black Hawk joined with Central City in promoting local gambling. A Black Hawk alderman, debating the merits of the proposal, explained that he saw gambling as "a form of entertainment, a pleasant pastime for a day or an evening, rather than a high-stakes competition" (*WRC,* Sept. 15, 1989: 1).

When Mayor Schmalz introduced the gambling idea in the pages of the *Weekly Register-Call,* most citizens did not know that he was speaking both as mayor and as a member of an informal group of Central City business and government leaders who had been meeting for several years to discuss economic development.[2] In fact, when formally organized as the nonprofit "CCPI" (Central City Preservation, Inc.) later that fall, the group claimed to have "been getting together regularly over the past few years, and [to] have been pursuing the possibility of legalized gambling for three years" (*WRC,* Nov. 10, 1989: 1). The "Support Program Package" (CCPI, no date) that introduced CCPI to the public described a local history of gambling, goals of the group, rebuttal to concerns about the development of limited stakes gambling, and expectations for transforming the gambling idea into a state ballot issue. As the document explained, CCPI was created to:

cultivate, promote, foster, sponsor and develop among people the appreciation, understanding, taste and love for historical buildings, structures, architecture, style and design within the area; to promote and to secure ways and means to preserve, protect, enhance, perpetuate and restore those structures and designs; and to otherwise do all lawful things necessary to accomplish those purposes.

Although historic preservation was the stated interest of CCPI members, their primary goal was the legalization of gambling. Much of the Support Program Package document was devoted to a discussion of "Limited Gambling Pros, Cons, and/or Possible Concerns," but that heading was somewhat misleading, as the report actually stressed primarily positive outcomes that could be expected from gambling. The authors wrote, for example, that gambling would "revive the flavor of the true frontier gold mining life" and contribute to "the unique 'Old West' atmosphere of Central City and Black Hawk" (Item 2). Limited gambling was proposed as "a supplement to and not a replacement of existing business in the area" (Item 3), and visitors were predicted to be primarily day-trip tourists, not those seeking "a final vacation destination" (Item 4). The authors provided their own evaluation of the recently initiated gambling operations in Deadwood, South Dakota, claiming that "[Deadwood's] biggest problem is parking . . . and other than being financially better off, there has been little change in local lifestyles and little change in the residential property market" (Item 10). Though others later debated the accuracy of this last statement, there was little basis for argument at the time. Deadwood's gambling halls had just opened in November 1989, in the same month that CCPI publicly announced its formation, and any statement about the effects of gambling in Deadwood was premature.

The use of historic preservation as a stimulus for the pro-gambling campaign was a clever and effective manipulation of meaningful local images and symbols. As a designated National Historic Landmark District, Central City, Black Hawk, and the surrounding mining areas had independent, external confirmation of their historic significance. In addition, the presence of old Victorian buildings, derelict mining structures, and mine tailings dumps scattered on the hillsides also evoked strong personal sentiments from people who lived in the area. "There's something magic about this place," said one resident about Central City. The frontier, mining, and opera history struck a chord with residents and visitors alike, linking together otherwise divergent groups across the community.

As described in the initial news report, CCPI's rationale for promoting gambling was that it could not only provide funds for historic preservation, but also could reduce Central City's mill levy, provide jobs with high salaries, increase property values, and fund improvements to local services (*WRC*, Nov. 10, 1989: 1). Other than two news articles in the *Weekly Register-Call* mentioning CCPI activities, the first correspondence from the group beyond the Support Program Package appeared in the form of a letter to the editor of the newspaper in early December 1989. Noting that the main goal was to allow Colorado voters to decide the issue of gaming development on the November 1990 ballot, the co-chair of the Public Relations Committee outlined the positive merits of the proposal, concluding, "This is a proposition where everyone can win" (*WRC*, Dec. 8, 1989: 2). The practice of highlighting positive gains while ignoring potential negative outcomes is also typical in other types of developments, particularly those in rural western communities. As Cortese and Jones (1977: 80) wrote about the western energy boomtowns they studied, "Perceptions of economic impacts before they occur seem to ignore the negative aspects. Most people said that when they first heard of the project . . . they believed the boom would bring a wave of prosperity in which everyone would benefit."

The idea that gambling was to be "an attraction" grew from initial claims about its "limited" nature (low betting limits and restricted area) and the anticipated beneficial effects of gambling operations. The term *Mom-and-Pop gambling* was often used to describe the type of gambling anticipated by promoters. Slot machines would be placed in existing local businesses, covering only a small portion of available floor space. The overall image was one of harmless entertainment for tourists and substantial benefits for community businesses and residents. In his first communication, Schmalz had suggested that gambling would not change either the look of Central City or the lifestyle of its residents. To reinforce this idea, CCPI organizers explained in a March 1990 letter to the editor that the 40 percent tax rate they proposed for businesses offering gambling would "provide a nice profit for operators while keeping gambling as an attraction rather than allowing it to become an industry in its own right" (*WRC*, Mar. 2, 1990: 1). No objections to this proposed tax rate emerged locally or among metropolitan spokespersons.

Signals that the gambling campaign was being waged for reasons other than simply local economic development emerged over time. Schmalz had alluded in the September 1989 news story to the idea that local gambling would attract Denver conventioneers; this theme was later repeated by Black Hawk council members. Over time, CCPI members began to speak more and more openly about their intent to place the issue on the state ballot so that all Colorado citizens could vote on it, and they were explicit about using gambling revenues for historic preservation both locally and statewide. A letter to the editor from the CCPI vice president, Lary Brown, published in the December

29, 1989, issue of the *Weekly Register-Call*, took the campaign to a new level. Brown insisted that "gambling revenues could also help delay increases in taxes for Colorado residents, which are already among the highest in the nation" (p. 2). The statement was clearly meant to obtain the support of voters across Colorado for gambling development in Central City and Black Hawk. Though the logic of his argument was unclear, it apparently worked. No one publicly challenged the claims, and by the end of January 1990, only four months after the initial announcement by Schmalz, a Gilpin County realty company was reporting huge increases in requests for available property "by speculators who want in on the proposed 'action'" (*WRC*, Jan. 26, 1990: 1).

Though introduced in September, and followed by several news items in the fall of 1989, the gambling proposal stimulated little public discussion among Gilpin County residents until January 1990, when the first citizen's letter to the editor appeared. That letter, evaluating the pros and cons of the gambling idea, initiated the public debate about the proposed development. It also stimulated a generally unsuccessful effort to evaluate the claims of proponents against "facts" from other gaming areas. Page one news articles appearing in the *Weekly Register-Call* in January, February, and March 1990 reported anecdotal evidence about the experiences of citizens in Deadwood, South Dakota, based on the impressions of Gilpin County residents who had independently visited that town to evaluate the outcomes of gambling. The first article was extremely favorable, focusing on positive outcomes of the gambling projects. The second article presented and discussed primarily negative impacts. The third news article provided the response from CCPI members. Despite their earlier claims that gambling development in Deadwood had had few negative impacts, CCPI members assured Gilpin County residents that the Colorado proposal had been written to minimize problems such as those experienced in Deadwood. Indeed, CCPI members said they expected "little negative impact on the local community if gambling is approved" (*WRC*, Mar. 2, 1990: 1).

It was difficult to assess the claims of either proponents or opponents, though, as the commentary on both sides was speculative; objective, independent data seemed to be missing from the public debate. As news articles about the gambling issue continued to increase in the *Weekly Register-Call*, letters to the editor began to appear more frequently, too. Many of these expressed skepticism and uncertainty about the far-reaching claims of campaign organizers, though many authors were also quite open-minded about the possibilities of limited gambling. From September 1989 through April 1990 (thirty-four issues of the weekly newspaper), twenty-two news articles were written about or contained references to the gambling issue, whereas eleven letters to the editor discussed the possibilities and problems of gambling. All of those letters were published between January and April.

By April 1990, enough concern had apparently been expressed by local citizens to prompt the CCPI vice president to pen an angry letter to the local newspaper; the letter was also distributed across the state to other local newspapers. Entitled, "The real facts behind the limited gambling proposal," the letter claimed that "some people have been very effective in distorting the facts or ignoring them altogether" (*WRC*, Apr. 6, 1990: 2). Reiterating the merits of the proposal, Lary Brown (who later also claimed to be the author of the proposed gaming legislation) chastised those who had made "rash statements" about the proposal, ignored the historic preservation aspects of the proposal, and failed to comprehend the "overall tourism benefit to all of Colorado."

This letter marked the end of civility in the campaign for gambling in Colorado and the beginning of direct confrontation between supporters and those who questioned the supporters' assertions. The introduction of the gambling idea in Gilpin County had been characterized by a certain innocence and simplicity: gambling was entertainment, the community benefits were all positive, historic buildings would be saved, and even the state would profit. After April, however, the battle lines formed. The tone of the rhetoric became more strident, positions became polarized, and those opposing the gambling idea, including Governor Roy Romer and some residents of the towns and county, were attacked by local organizers. A "rhetoric of despair," highlighting the alleged decline of the community, was formalized, taking center stage in the escalating confrontation.

THE RISE OF THE RHETORIC OF DESPAIR

Public discussion about gambling in the *Weekly Register-Call* accompanied legislative negotiation of the proposal. Gambling proponents from Central City and Black Hawk had defined the scope and elements of the pro-gambling proposal by November 1989, and had, in February 1990, presented a resolution to the state legislature asking for a constitutional amendment to allow gambling in the towns. That proposal was debated among legislators during the remainder of the winter and early spring. During this time, Cripple Creek, another prominent Colorado gold rush town located in Teller County west of Colorado Springs, became the third town to join the gambling campaign. At the end of April 1990, the initiative to allow gambling in the three former gold mining towns was rejected by the Colorado Senate. In response, CCPI members initiated a statewide petition drive aimed at obtaining enough signatures of registered voters to place a pro-gaming amendment on the state ballot. In August, the Colorado Secretary of State's office verified the petition signatures and approved the measure. Amendment 4 thus became a statewide issue, to be voted on in the November 1990 election.

In April 1990, apparently anticipating the defeat in the state legislature, two local committees—the Preservation Initiative Committee in Central City and Black Hawk, and the Cripple Creek Preservation Initiative Committee— had organized to coordinate financial and promotional efforts supporting Amendment 4. In conjunction with CCPI, the two PIC groups raised a war chest of about $595,500 in contributions. These monies paid for the signature campaign, consulting advice, lobbyist activities, and campaign promotion. Many of the contributions were local in nature: only a small portion was made by out-of-state citizens or businesses, and the contributions reports do not identify any of those as having ties to major casino interests in New Jersey or Nevada. Of the contributors, however, a substantial number of local business-people in Central City and Black Hawk made multiple donations, some apparently totalling between $10,000 and $15,000 per businessperson (Colorado Secretary of State 1990b). The issue of community decline had been invoked to promote the pro-gaming cause, but the relatively large sums donated by small businesses in the Gilpin County towns suggests that at least some local shop owners were not in a situation of imminent demise.

If the introductory period of the gambling proposal (September 1989 to April 1990) was characterized by innocent hopefulness, the signature collection period up to the statewide election (May 1990 to early November) can be identified by increasing local attention and a new confrontational tone. Figure 3.1 illustrates changes in the number of news articles, letters, and opinions

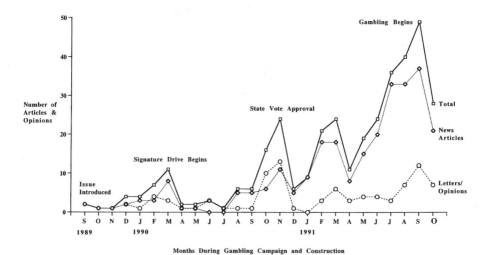

Figure 3.1   News Articles and Opinions in the *Weekly Register-Call*, 1989–1991

published in the *Weekly Register-Call* across the course of the gambling campaign. The number of news articles increased between November 1989 and March 1990, reflecting the efforts of CCPI to push its message to the forefront of public discussion. When the legislature failed to approve the gambling measure, the quiet efforts of the grassroots signature-gathering campaign went almost unnoticed in the local press. After the signature petitions were approved by the Secretary of State's office, though, news articles increased at a dizzying pace. The published letters and opinions generally followed a similar pattern of growth, with peaks forming around significant events in the campaign.

The gambling proposal was not the only issue discussed in the newspaper between September 1989 and the first week of November 1990, just before the statewide vote; it was, however, the issue that got the most newspaper space. In addition to the gambling issue, other issues relevant to community living conditions received attention. Brief excitement was generated over a proposed gold and gravel placer operation near Rollinsville, which the county commissioners eventually denied. The historic Gilpin Hotel in Black Hawk suffered a major fire in December 1989, and other local problems continued: letter writers said that dogs ran loose, telephone service was inadequate, and road maintenance was shoddy; residents were concerned about county environmental issues; local volunteers were praised; and requests to renew newspaper subscriptions were noted. But, as if suddenly realizing that the gambling proponents were serious about the proposal, most letter writers focused on the gambling issue once the signature petition process was initiated.

The signature drive was notable for its revised, unified, single message: gambling would assure local and state historic preservation by increasing tourism in Gilpin County's towns and across the state. Freda Poundstone, the newly hired campaign manager who was also a professional lobbyist from the Denver metropolitan area, promised to work hard to promote the gambling measure: "With the state economy in such dire straits . . . Colorado voters will favor a proposal that should increase tourism across the state" (*WRC*, Sept. 28, 1990: 1). As part of the signature drive, CCPI sold tokens depicting the Coeur d'Alene mine building decaying above Central City. Flowery news commentary by a local reporter demonstrated that the *Weekly Register-Call* was a partisan supporter of CCPI and the pro-gambling effort. "Felled by age, lack of upkeep and strong winds [the building] stands for what CCPI wants for our county—historic preservation" (*WRC*, Aug. 3, 1990: 3).

The Coeur d'Alene structure was one symbol of decline, but others were added later. Throughout the period from May to November 1990, community conditions were continually portrayed as desperate. In meetings and letters to the editor, supportive citizens spoke of the "sagging economy" and "lack of

The decaying Coeur d'Alene Mine structure above Central City symbolized community decline during the pro-gambling campaign.

opportunity," noting that "all we want is a chance." There was a pervasive sense that the community was on the brink of death and could be saved only by gambling development. Comments by state senator Sally Hopper, who helped direct the proposal through the state legislature, confirmed the image. She interpreted the CCPI plan with the comments that appear at the beginning of this chapter, concluding with the idea that, without gambling, the towns would likely "crumble before our eyes or become ghost towns" (*WRC,* Apr. 13, 1990: 2).

Gambling tourism was positioned as the solution to all local problems. Negative aspects of the proposed development continued to be downplayed or ignored. In September 1990, a fourth article about gaming impacts in Deadwood, again primarily negative, was published in the *Weekly Register-Call.* The previous week's paper had included a report about the murder of a Deadwood casino owner. Although there was no response from CCPI, people voicing opposition to the gambling proposal were attacked by another source. "It is amusing to listen to . . . what the 'naysayers' are ranting and raving about in their hysterical attempts to destroy the one chance for survival and restoration of three Colorado mining communities," wrote the newspaper publisher William C. Russell in October (*WRC*, Oct. 19, 1990: 2).

The acknowledgment of the tourism and salvation merits of the gambling proposal structured all subsequent discussions about the issue. The campaign gained a stronger focus: historic preservation and local economic growth through gambling would also boost local and statewide tourism revenues. Failure to support the proposal, according to promoters, meant certain, immediate death for Black Hawk, Central City, Cripple Creek, and their counties. Tourism and historic preservation were presented as inherently positive, acceptable, and even necessary requirements for local life. In contrast, images of decay (the Coeur d'Alene mine), decline (Gilpin County economy), and impoverishment (local people), were called upon to illustrate the consequences of challenging the proposal. Such rhetorical positioning shifted public attention away from the reasonable but unaddressed topic of whether gambling was the only or best solution for local economic woes, and directed the discussion entirely toward the topic of what kind of gambling was appropriate. Given such clear choices, who could argue against developing tourism for historic preservation while saving individuals, communities, and history?

During the period from September 1989 to November 1990, forty gambling-related news articles, and an equal number of letters to the editor and opinion columns, appeared in the *Weekly Register-Call*. About 60 percent of the letters were opposed to some or all aspects of the gambling measure. In announcing a public meeting to discuss the gambling initiative, CCPI proponents were quoted as saying, "There is a lot of misinformation out there" (*WRC*, Oct. 5, 1990: 1). In news reports from three public meetings held in September and October 1990, however, what seemed to be bothering citizens was the lack of *enough* information "out there" that responded to their very real concerns about the community's future. For example, at an October 1990 meeting, so many citizens spoke out against the gambling proposal that the invited legislators expressed surprise: "Senator [Sally] Hopper said she had been under the impression that virtually everyone in the community supported the gambling initiative. . . . Representative [Sam] Williams also thought support for gambling was overwhelming" (*WRC*, Oct. 5, 1990: 1).

Comments such as these worried some residents. Campaign leaders had been successful in convincing many local voters and their two key legislators that gambling was the solution to local problems, and the more than 70,000 valid signatures of registered voters in Colorado (*WRC*, Aug. 24, 1990: 1) seemed to provide further justification of the cause. The fact that local citizens and others in the state who opposed the gambling developments were poorly organized and not very vocal contributed to the perception that everyone was in favor of gambling. Two organized anti-gaming groups collectively raised only about $28,700 to fund the opposition effort. "United Citizens Against Gambling," originating in nearby Idaho Springs in Clear Creek County, but listing a Black Hawk resident as its treasurer, raised only about $6,700 from citizens and a Denver corporation (Colorado Secretary of State 1990b). The bulk of the opposition money, about $22,000, came from dog racing associations and clubs, including the Interstate Racing Association. Five large contributions from such clubs, totalling between $3,500 and $5,000 each, were made to the "Save Gilpin and Teller Counties" group based in Black Hawk. Although Governor Romer spoke out against the gambling initiative, he was not prominent in the opposition. Engaged in a battle for his own reelection, it is likely that actively working against the gambling measure would have alienated a large proportion of his constituency (Lamm interview 1994).

Because all efforts were focused on the gambling proposal, local leaders made no effort to discuss other economic development alternatives. In later interviews with CCPI representatives, it was clear that they felt there had been adequate discussion of alternatives during the years leading up to 1990, and that only gambling could provide the desired community benefits. Politics in Central City and Black Hawk during the confirmation period remained relatively stable, though tensions were high between those favoring (the apparent majority) and those opposing the gambling initiative. In Cripple Creek, however, three members of the city council were voted out of office in August 1990, apparently for their anti-gambling views (*WRC*, Aug. 31, 1990: 1). When Central City alderman and famous artist Angelo DiBenedetto, who was vehemently opposed to the gambling initiative, proposed a series of public debates with CCPI campaign manager-lobbyist Freda Poundstone, he was ignored (*WRC*, Oct. 5, 1990: 2).

CAMPAIGN THEMES IN THE PUBLIC FORUM

The campaign period extended for about a year, from first announcement of the gambling idea, in September 1989, to the statewide vote on Amendment 4 in November 1990. To understand the form and content of campaign arguments, letters to the editor of the *Weekly Register-Call* published during this time period were reviewed. Using the same approach as employed in reviewing letters prior to the gambling campaign, words and phrases that referred to what it was like to live in Gilpin County were extracted from the texts of letters, iteratively sorted, and grouped according to predominant themes. This process produced four general categories reflecting themes during the campaign time period: Environmental Beauty; Social and Cultural Qualities; Economic Fragility; and History and Historic Images. The Economy category contained almost twice as many phrases as the Natural and Social/Cultural environments categories; the History category contained more than double the number of entries in the Economy category.

The two categories representing Natural and Social/Cultural environments included words and phrases illustrating the most positive and appealing aspects of living in Gilpin County. These included the values associated with living in a mountain environment (peace, quiet, being away from the city) and the scenic beauty of the natural surroundings. In contrast to pre-gambling-proposal times, an additional category of Social and Cultural Qualities emerged, including words and phrases about meaningful positive aspects of the social and cultural environment. During the gambling campaign, many people wrote letters specifically discussing Gilpin County's positive social and cultural characteristics. These letters contained phrases such as, "we love our town and would do nothing to hurt it," "wonderful people live here," "residents are independent, strong willed, and radical," and people who once lived here had "colorful, imaginative and romantic personalities." This category, then, represents a more reflective sentiment among letter writers than was evidenced prior to introduction of the gambling proposal.

The category titled Economic Fragility contained words and phrases that were similar to the pre-gambling category with the same heading. For example, people noted that Gilpin was "a depressed county," that "we are on the verge of economic destruction," and that "we are a poor, small county but have high property tax rates." In contrast to the time period prior to introduction of the gambling proposal, however, this category seemed to contain more strongly voiced comments than were evident before September 1989. One letter writer commented that "we are like a third world country," and another dramatically wrote, "[W]e languish in obvious weakness, decay and ruin, financial decline, and impending absorption by Jefferson County" (an adjacent metropolitan county). Several letters called upon readers to "give us a break," and "vote for a new beginning, a new prosperity, a new era of strength and vitality." Taken together, the comments in this category suggest that writers were adopting the claims of the gambling proponents and stretching the rhetoric of despair to more and more extreme positions in an effort to galvanize support for the gaming proposal.

Phrases in the final category, History and Historic Images, tended to describe general qualities related to history of the area, including: "Old West Victorian mining towns," "old western mining images," "antiquated buildings," and the "unique, historic, colorful Opera House." Writers explained that history was "the primary attraction here," and that the "flavor and richness of western Victorian images" was provided by "shabby but grand remnants of our

Proponents promised that gambling would provide revenues for renovation of local historic structures, including the Williams' Stables building in Central City.

historic past in Central City and Black Hawk." Only three letter writers mentioned that the historic resources of the towns were in decline. Most focused, instead, on the grandeur of past days and the legacy that must be preserved for the future.

If the letters to the editor are any indication, economic issues and historic preservation were of primary interest to the citizens of Gilpin County during the campaign for gambling. A total of thirty-three citizens had letters and opinions published in the newspaper between December 1989 and election day in November 1990. No other forms of tourism or other economic development choices were discussed during this period; the comments of letter writers referred only to the merits of the gambling proposal. The efforts of proponents to rationalize gambling legalization for purposes of historic preservation seem to have appealed to local publics, as reflected by an increasing number of references to the historic values of Gilpin County. As the campaign continued toward the statewide vote in November 1990, though, authors of letters expressed more dramatic and despairing views of community economic conditions, even though no authors offered objective data to support their assertions.

EVALUATING CAMPAIGN CLAIMS

The study of community rhetoric illustrates changing community sentiments and images over the course of a tourism development campaign. Analysis of messages throughout the development process illustrates how social actors, both powerful and naive, used persuasive messages to create and manipulate issues that ultimately had consequences for community residents and visitors. In the uncertain climate of community tourism decision making, what passes as effective or successful political rhetoric is not necessarily the equivalent of truthful rhetoric. Suggestive, compelling, persuasive rhetoric stimulates people's imaginations and galvanizes local support by using emotional appeals that draw upon community symbols and myths. In such a political climate, impressions often matter more than evidence.

Had anyone made an effort to evaluate the legitimacy of proponents' claims, they would have found that images of the community's imminent death were vastly overstated. Census data show that Gilpin County was not a wealthy area, but social and economic conditions there paralleled trends across Colorado throughout the 1980s. Table 3.1 displays comparative data for Gilpin County and the state of Colorado for 1980 and 1990. Selected social and economic characteristics for Central City and Black Hawk are also included for comparison with the 1990 county-level data.

In comparing Gilpin County to the state, the data show that between 1980 and 1990, both county and state increased their proportions of persons sixty-five years of age and older, their percent unemployed, and the proportion of persons below poverty level. In each case, the percent increase in Gilpin County was less than the percent increase for the state as a whole. In other categories, Gilpin County residents were better off than the statewide average. The county had proportionally more high school and college graduates; higher median household, family, and per capita incomes; and proportionally fewer persons, families, and households below poverty level in 1990 than the state average. County retail sales also increased between 1980 and 1990, although examination of data reveals variation in year-to-year trends throughout the decade.[3] In addition to the data in this table, it should be noted that county property taxes, a measure used by gambling proponents as an example of community decline, were (on a per capita basis) higher than the statewide average in 1976–1977, about the same as the state average in 1981–1982, and substantially lower than the state average in 1986–1987, according to the *County and City Data Book* (1983, 1988, 1994). Data show that over this time period, about 80 percent to 85 percent of the total tax base in Gilpin County was attributed to property taxes, a proportion about average in comparison to all Colorado counties.

Table 3.1 Selected Social and Economic Characteristics, 1980 and 1990

	Colorado		Gilpin County		Central City	Black Hawk
	1980	1990	1980	1990	1990	1990
Population[a]	2,889,964	3,294,394	2,441	3,070	298	246
Proportion 65 or older	8.6%	10.0%	6.6%	7.2%	12.1%	11.4%
% high school graduate or higher	78.6%	84.4%	87.0%	93.0%	88.4%	80.7%
% college graduate or higher	23.0%	27.0%	25.6%	29.5%	21.9%	7.7%
% Unemployed[b]	5.0%	5.7%	7.9%	8.2%	10.8%	18.2%
Median household income[c]	$18,056	$30,140	$19,436	$31,898	$24,712	$19,722
Median family income[c]	$21,279	$35,930	$21,849	$36,218	$29,375	$28,750
Per capita income[c]	$7,998	$14,821	$7,920	$15,267	$14,331	$9,732
Persons below poverty[d]	10.1%	11.7%	10.1% n = 247	10.6% n = 321	17.9% n = 53	20.7% n = 50
Families below poverty[d]	7.4%	8.6%	7.7%	7.1% n = 62	13.5% n = 10	14.9% n = 11
Female-headed households below poverty[d]	26.0%	29.9%	30.3%	23.5% n = 23	38.5% n = 10	50.0% n = 9
Persons working outside county of residence	29.9%	31.3%	69.9%	71.3%		
Retail sales	$9.8 M, 1977	$21.3 M, 1987	$7.9 M, 1979	$9.2 M, 1989		

Sources: 1980, 1990 U.S. Census of Population; 1983, 1994 County and City Data Book; State of Colorado Department of Revenue.

[a]Population totals are estimates based on samples.

[b]Unemployment rate is percent of total civilian labor force unemployed in 1982 and 1991. The data in the table are from the 1983 and 1994 County and City Data Books. These figures differ substantially from data provided by the Colorado Department of Labor and Employment, which lists the following totals for Gilpin County: 1980: 5.2% (5.9% for Colorado); 1982: 9.9% (7.7% for Colorado); 1984: 5.5% (5.6% for Colorado); 1986: 7.5% (7.4% for Colorado); 1988: 5.6% (6.4% for Colorado); 1989 (when gambling was proposed): 5.3% (5.8% for Colorado); 1990: 3.5%, later revised to 2.6% (4.9% for Colorado).

[c]Median and per capita income data are for 1979 and 1989.

[d]Poverty level data are for 1979 and 1989.

There was just cause for concern in Gilpin County, but it was not because "the County was dying," as gambling proponents claimed. Instead, the county was gaining at the expense of Central City and Black Hawk, a situation that apparently went unnoticed by town and county leaders. Table 3.1 shows that, by 1990, people living in Gilpin County's two historic mining towns were worse off than those living in unincorporated areas of the county. Black Hawk had an 18.2 percent unemployment rate and Central City had a 10.8 percent unemployment rate, both above the 1990 county average of 8.2 percent. People living in the towns were older, poorer, less well educated, and more likely to be living below the poverty level than those living elsewhere in the county. These differences were most dramatic for the 250 or so residents of Black Hawk; Central City was more similar to the county as a whole, but still trailed on many social and economic indicators. These conditions were not of recent origin, though. According to population trends presented in Table 2.1 (chapter 2), Black Hawk's population had been stable since about 1920, whereas Central City's population had remained at about the same level since 1950. The number of residents across all incorporated and unincorporated parts of the county, in contrast, had been expanding since 1960.

The data in Table 3.1 reflect the post–1920 historical decline of the Gilpin County mining towns, and the post–1960 growth of unincorporated parts of the county as exurbanites moved to the area. This trend had been previously noted by the study coordinator of the 1990 Gilpin County Citizen Survey (discussed in chapter 2), who commented, "[P]lace of work [is] a key stratifier ... as Gilpin County is, I believe, simultaneously mountain community and exurban community" (Jones 1991). As he and others had observed, most residents living in unincorporated Gilpin County worked outside the county; many had professional jobs and substantial incomes, were highly educated, and owned large houses in county subdivisions surrounded by national forest lands. Provided one could afford the cost of mountain living (costs that included reduced or nonexistent public services, long travel times to and from work, and lack of private business services locally), Gilpin County provided substantial scenic amenities along with the personal privacy and freedom of lifestyle.

Though many Gilpin County residents were better off in 1990 than in 1980, others—primarily the elderly, those marginally employed, and those living in the towns—were not. The claims that the county was "dying" were untrue, but such claims provided powerful imagery, and were likely a more effective rhetorical strategy than the truth: the towns had been in decline for about half a century, but the county had been growing substantially over the past thirty years.

THE CAMPAIGN AS IDEOLOGY

Campaigns are rhetorical processes in pursuit of power. All spokespersons, both for and against issues, work to persuade those who have not yet declared their positions and to influence those whose decisions are not yet firm. The goal is not only to control the outcomes of decision making, but also to shape images of reality and thus influence the process and content of the debate preceding decision making. As Edelman (1988: 11) noted, the uses of particular words, phrases, and images "are strategies, deliberate or unrecognized, for strengthening or undermining support for specific courses of action and for particular ideologies." Community ideologies, which are selective perspectives about reality presented by members of particular groups of people, precede and structure the collective responses of people to change. Ideological explanations tend to have logical and simplistic arguments, utopian visions, and symbolic forms. They are the interpreted histories of a people, given primacy by spokespersons who wish to advance a cause. As Shibutani (1986: 504) explained, however, "The new histories are not necessarily fabrications; the historians select and emphasize different events of the past and interpret them from another standpoint." Ideologies support and give meaning to specific action choices.

As the gambling campaign showed, rhetorical strategies do not necessarily have to be truthful to be effective. Indeed, strategies based on incorrect data or impressions may also be very useful politically (Freudenburg and Gramling 1994a). The rhetoric of despair illustrates this point. Even prior to the gambling campaign, letters to the editor published in the *Weekly Register-Call* drew upon unsupported negative images to suggest that Gilpin County residents were poor and the economy depressed. The gambling campaign repeated and embellished the same theme, contributing to the persistence of the myths of community decline. Such claims, enlivened to some degree by the traces of decay visible in every gold tailings pile and historic building in the area, gave the appearance of being legitimate, in part because they were familiar, but also because they were presented by credible spokespersons such as local government leaders.

The myths of community decline were also compelling for another reason: they reconstructed, adapted, and repeated the unique local history known by nearly all Gilpin County residents. For example, the image of boom-and-bust mining towns along the Western frontier was historically accurate, but it was also invoked by current residents to give meaning to their own contemporary experiences. People celebrated Gilpin County's past in community events. They created new words, such as "Zeke" and "pointylanders," to separate themselves from outsiders. According to residents, Gilpin County was not only a special place in the past, it was also a special place now, and by implication local people must be considered special, too. Such converted myths reinforced the pervasive culture of individual freedom, fostering a solidarity against others who might question the lifestyles, claims, or expectations of Gilpinites.

Increases in the rhetoric of despair from earlier to later stages of the campaign discouraged objective evaluation of gambling or other possible development alternatives. At the very heart of the gambling campaign was the basic assumption that tourism, in general, was a desirable growth strategy for Gilpin County. Whether tourism was the best or only development alternative, or whether some forms of tourism might be more desirable than others, were issues that were never addressed. In this campaign, tourism depended solely on gambling development. Yet, gambling proponents provided no specific evidence that this development strategy would be superior to other development options, justifiable with regard to costs and benefits, or a suitable complement to community character or goals.

Even though some debated its moral suitability, the idea of gambling was compelling because gambling was consistent with the history and culture of Gilpin County. The Western towns on the American frontier, after all, had supported a variety of gambling activities in earlier mining and opera times. In addition, the gold miner's ever-present hope for a return to the boom days was an expression of a gambling attitude favored in many rural Western places. History, real and imagined, was important in Gilpin County, and because both proponents and opponents claimed ownership of the same historical background and symbols, the key strategic issue of the campaign was how to marshal historical facts to support one's own position, while also neutralizing the arguments of opponents. The problem was solved when gambling proponents cleverly turned the debate into an argument about personal values, ignoring the calls for evidence and discouraging reasoned discussion of the potentials and pitfalls of the gambling proposal.

In the gambling campaign, economic gain was stressed over potential social, cultural, environmental, or political consequences. This is not unusual in tourism development campaigns, as Richter (1989: 21) summarized from her analyses of political aspects of tourism development: "The announced rationale is always economic.... The political objectives and pressures are usually not mentioned. The social costs and economic risks are pooh-poohed as the whines of no-growth nay-sayers." For gambling development, the merits of the proposal were evaluated less on objective analysis of the benefits and costs of gambling and more on the personal characteristics of those challenging the idea. As organizers framed the issue, those who opposed, disfavored, or were uncertain about the gambling proposal deserved to be seen as obviously against the well-being of the communities and their history. For many responsible citizens, this was clearly untrue; they were simply exercising the right to debate the merits of the proposal by participating in the process of community decision making. However, the escalating arguments about values, and the resulting polarization of positions about the gambling development, created increasingly wide emotional rifts within the community.

Freudenburg and Gramling (1994a, 1994b) describe this political strategy as "diversionary reframing." As a campaign proceeds, claimants on one side of the debate divert attention from their critics' concerns by reframing the discussion around other topics. In many cases, the other topics introduced into the debate include the legitimacy of, and values held by, the opponents themselves. In other words, any persons who question the claimants become themselves the object of criticism, and are labelled as irrational, un-American, against progress, or even worse. The result of such a process is that the campaign becomes less about the real issue (the merits or problems of gambling development) and more about the political beliefs of potential opponents ("They just want our community to remain impoverished!"). Under such circumstances, values become central, negativism escalates, and objectivity about real issues related to development disappears.

In the gambling campaign, examples of diversionary reframing were evident in the angry rebuttals made by proponents to questions raised in citizens' letters to the editor. The CCPI vice president, Lary Brown, for example, wrote in an April 1990 letter that "[S]ome people have been very effective in distorting the facts or ignoring them altogether" (*WRC,* Apr. 6, 1990: 2). He continued: "Rash statements that limited gambling will cause alcoholism, child abuse, homelessness and prostitution are designed to incite the misinformed." Angry rhetoric such as this had little to do with objective analyses of data, but much to do with giving opponents a bad name. The implicit challenge to citizens who were following the gambling campaign in the *Weekly Register-Call* was to beware of asking too many questions about the proposal, lest they be labelled as people who distort facts, make rash statements, or incite others who were equally misinformed.

By diverting attention from sensitive issues associated with gambling development (What if the development fails? How can the community control growth? Who would be accountable? Who is really behind the proposal and what do they have to gain from it? Who might lose in this gamble?), and by relying on the rhetoric of despair, proponents successfully created a problem in need of resolution. Then, having contrived the crisis of imminent community demise, proponents set about providing the solution: vote for gambling and the community will be saved. Their skill in manipulating the campaign allowed almost everyone to buy into some part of the proposal. Business owners and managers could expect more dollars in their cash registers; government leaders' power and authority would be enhanced by managing a new kind of community tourism; residents could anticipate more opportunities for local entertainment and reduced taxes. Everyone would join in saving historic buildings. Even some of the most skeptical of county residents were charmed by the apparent simplicity and spirit of the gambling proposal. One resident who voted for gaming, but later spoke out about the spread of the developments, said, "It sounded like harmless fun, a few slot machines in every little business. This was going to be an added attraction."

The single-minded focus on gambling tourism, the use of diversionary reframing as a central rhetorical strategy, and the use of historical symbols and images to confirm the suitability of gambling for the community all contributed to a successful campaign. On November 6, 1990, the legislation allowing limited gaming in three Colorado mountain towns (Central City, Black Hawk, and Cripple Creek) was approved by the voters of Colorado. Gambling was slated to begin October 1, 1991. Among Colorado citizens voting on the amendment, 57.3 percent (574,620) voted in favor of gambling development, while 42.7 percent (428,096) voted against (Colorado Secretary of State 1990a: 208). Of sixty-three Colorado counties, only eight failed to support the pro-gaming amendment. In Gilpin County, the rate of passage of the ballot amendment was even more favorable. A total of 1,506 Gilpin residents voted, a 65.2 percent turnout from 2,309 registered voters in the county. Of these, 66.3 percent (999 people) voted in favor, while 30.6 percent (461 persons) voted against the amendment to allow gaming development. Only 3.1 percent of Gilpin County voters (46 people) failed to vote on this issue (Colorado Secretary of State 1990a: 208). The *Gilpin County Advocate* (Nov. 8, 1990: 1), a small, newer tabloid, titled a front-page story "The boom is back for Gilpin," and printed above its name the word *JACKPOT.*

NOTES

1. It is unclear how Central City's Jack Hidahl, then city manager, came up with a number of 250 in the summer as a population estimate when gambling was introduced in 1988. The 1990 Census of Population had counted 335 people living in Central City and 227 living in Black Hawk. Central City's population had been relatively stable since the 1980 Census of Population.

2. Apparently some of the meetings of CCPI organizers and supporters took place—before, during, and after the gambling campaign—at the

Central City Elks Club. This raised the ire of some local citizens and businesspeople, especially women, who were not allowed in the club at certain times, effectively limiting their participation in some of the relevant "community" meetings. The old-boy network of Central City politics is an issue that emerges in all time periods in the community; it became particularly problematic for citizens, however, during the course of gambling development. The issue of local politics is discussed in greater detail in chapter 7.

3. Chapter 6 provides more detailed data showing unemployment trends from 1984–1994. Except for a two-year period in 1986–1987, Gilpin County had a lower rate of unemployment than the state as a whole. In 1986 and 1987, the state rates were exceeded by only a few tenths of a percentage point.

4

CONSTRUCTING AN INDUSTRY

[T]he whole campaign to promote gambling was to help the merchants in the towns. The merchants were deceived into thinking that they would benefit. Now we're all losing our leases.
— Central City businessman (*WRC*, July 12, 1991: 8).

With "boom buttons" for sale in local shops, passage of Amendment 4 in November 1990 marked the beginning of a new growth period in Gilpin County. A sense of euphoria and accomplishment spread throughout the community. Hopeful letters began to appear in the *Weekly Register-Call* exhorting residents and leaders to work together in creating a successful gambling development. In the weeks after Amendment 4 passed, the dark-suited, briefcase-carrying speculators, increasing in number and peering at buildings as they walked along the main streets of the towns, seemed like characters in a new local comic opera. After all, there had been little interest in buying or selling either commercial or residential property in the previous several decades.[1] In hindsight, though, the arrival of the speculators foreshadowed tragi-comedy; the romantic notions of a new boomtown were soon to be dashed by the realities of the construction period.

One immediate consequence of gambling approval was the appearance of a "new" language spoken by the speculators and developers. As outsiders began to infiltrate the community, residents unexpectedly found that they had been using the wrong words to describe the impending tourism development.

According to the newcomers, the correct term for what was about to happen in the community was *gaming*, not *gambling*. Even news articles and letters in the *Weekly Register-Call* reflect dissemination of the new language from speculators to local proponents, and then across the wider community. In letters to the editor published after the vote, use of the word *gambling* declined and use of the word *gaming* increased significantly.

Simultaneously, the word *casino* appeared more and more frequently in public discourse, marking an obvious departure from Senator Hopper's 1990 claim that "we are not talking about casinos." Residents had thought of noncasino gambling as a few slot machines in every local business, but the term *gaming* implied an industry in which casinos were the featured attraction. It would be easy to blame the new financiers and developers for these linguistic manipulations, but the transformation was subtle, and no CCPI members or other local leaders made any efforts to correct those using the terms *casinos* or *gaming*. Silence allowed the words to become common, and symbolized a reorientation in the structure of the tourism development and a subtle loss of local control, without any evidence of formal community discussion or agreement.

FROM CAMPAIGN TO CONSTRUCTION

The pro-gambling campaign was important not only because it succeeded, but also because it stimulated community discussions about desired and appropriate futures in Gilpin County, the nature of community, and the qualities of place. As illustrated by the analysis in chapter 3, these community conversations had real consequences: specific organizations and individuals were elevated into powerful positions as community spokespersons; levels of community conflict rose and fell as symbols and intentions were questioned; certain aspects of community history were favored and others were downplayed; realtors were contacted by potential investors requesting information about available property; residents voiced opinions in letters to the newspaper; and elected officials, mass media, and other publics outside the community began to attend to Gilpin County happenings.

Such anticipatory impacts associated with proposed community developments, common in tourism and other growth schemes, are not always acknowledged or understood by either participants or observers. The failure of tourism researchers to adequately examine community impacts produced prior to the operation stage of a new development project can often be traced to uncertainties surrounding the actual starting point of project preparations. Comprehensive tourism planning often occurs only after a growth option (such as gambling, a ski resort, a new sports stadium, or other development) has been selected, and is not always a rational or linear process (Getz 1986;

Gunn 1994; Haywood 1988; Wheeller 1991). As Murphy (1983: 180) observed, tourism planning is often ad hoc and remedial, "responding to changing markets and local emergencies, rather than to coordinated strategies pursuing a planned goal." Consequently, researchers focus primarily on the postopening effects of development, which are often easier to delimit than the community processes leading up to decisions about tourism choices.[2]

Although few tourism researchers have written about anticipatory growth effects, researchers studying rural western regions have found that impacts occurring even prior to the opening of major construction projects often have significant consequences for communities (Leistritz and Murdock 1981; Murdock and Leistritz 1979). For example, Brown, Geertsen, and Krannich (1989: 586) documented instances of social disruption occurring during rapid growth in an energy boomtown in Utah, noting that "even greater changes occurred during the period after announcement of the project but before the commencement of rapid growth." Evaluating the social and economic impacts of large-scale technological projects, Freudenburg and Gramling (1992: 937) concluded that "[s]ignificant social changes ... take place both before and after the phases of the most intense physical activities (construction, production, expansion)" of projects. They explained,

> The opportunity-threat phase of development often produces not just expected impacts, but *actual* impacts—significant, empirically verifiable changes that would not take place but for the announcement of a proposed development or activity, the actions taken to encourage, discourage, or otherwise influence the outcomes, and the social definitions of the development that emerge. ... Disruptions can result not just from the threats and opportunities themselves, moreover, *but also from the contentiousness of debates*, including debates over whether the threats and/or opportunities of a proposed development are being "legitimately" perceived [p. 943].

The gambling campaign illustrated rhetorical aspects of anticipatory effects, but the construction period stimulated even more numerous and more tangible community changes. Beginning with the vote to approve gambling in Black Hawk, Central City, and Cripple Creek, the formal construction period stretched from November 1990 to "Opening Day" on October 1, 1991. Construction-related activities also continued beyond the start of gambling operations, but the most intense period of community organizing, planning, and renovating was compressed into the narrow, eleven-month time frame between the vote and the opening of gaming. This period was characterized not only by visible community changes, but also by a prevailing sense of urgency, uncertainty, and emotional loss.

PLANNING FOR COMMUNITY CHANGE

The idea that gambling would present an added attraction to the existing business configuration and Western mining-town image of Central City and Black Hawk had seemed an unshakable premise of the promotional campaign. Supporters had claimed that community revitalization through gambling would provide long-term economic growth, accomplished with sensitivity to local historic, cultural, and natural resources, and producing minimal negative impacts. But the "Eureka!" heard when the gambling amendment passed in November 1990 set in motion a flood of information seeking, investment, and construction across the Gilpin County gaming towns.

Although Central City and Black Hawk were quiet and calm the day after the vote, a large new "For Sale" sign greeted residents and visitors to a Main Street business in Central City that morning. Soon, other "For Sale" and "Going Out of Business" signs blossomed on businesses and homes in the two towns. Before the end of 1990, the first indications of real estate speculation in Gilpin County became apparent. Property in the commercial zones of the towns suddenly, and unexpectedly, achieved value far beyond market prices.

"For Sale" signs sprouted across Gilpin County once gaming was approved. This view of Central City shows the Catholic Church at left, and the Coeur d'Alene Mine on the hill above the town adjacent to a mine tailings pile.

Between November 1990 and September 1991, more than $46 million in property transfers were recorded in Central City and Black Hawk, with commercial property selling at a premium. Indeed, Gilpin County property sales for the calendar year 1991 were nearly $66.3 million above the total of $10.6 million counted in calendar year 1990.[3] One building in Central City, valued at $14,000 before gambling was publicly mentioned, listed for sale during the campaign at $35,000, and sold after approval of Amendment 4 for $235,000. A parking lot at the south end of Central City's Main Street, owned by the publisher of the *Weekly Register-Call,* sold for $5 million. The Belvidere Theatre building in Central City transferred for a whopping $10 million.[4]

The Victorian Nugget gift shop, managed by one of the organizers of the pro-gambling campaign, was one of the many Central City businesses that closed. The building was sold for casino development.

Requests for research on property titles and boundaries so overwhelmed the county recorder's office that clerks were forced to institute limited research hours for potential investors. "We can't get anything done any more with all these people coming in," said one employee.

During the initial round of real estate speculation, and in concert with the linguistic turn from "gambling" to "casino gaming," it became apparent that a focused planning effort would be required to maintain some measure of local control over the proposed developments. Government leaders in Central City and Black Hawk thus placed moratoria on construction projects in each city. The six-month hiatus, from late November 1990 through April 1991, was to be dedicated to planning and community preparations for gambling.

Because gambling development was an uncommon venture and outside the experience of community leaders, the assistance of external planning firms and consultants was sought to direct and coordinate local planning efforts. Though residents called for collaborative planning between the two neighboring towns, Black Hawk and Central City each independently hired different planning firms to address their own critical developmental concerns. A concession to broader planning concerns emerged when the state of Colorado's Department of Local Affairs made available a limited sum of money for a county-wide regional planning council. Coordinated by David Williams, a Denver planning consultant, in concert with governmental representatives from both towns and Gilpin County, the group met regularly during the construction period. According to Williams and others, though, this group was effective only in an advisory capacity, having no implementation power and few financial resources beyond the consultant's salary.

By January 1991, a series of community meetings was initiated in each town to discuss development issues. Community planning meetings served a variety of functions. They were a place for residents to air concerns, for community leaders to outline priorities and strategies, for hopeful developers to obtain information and seek concessions from the local leadership, and for planners to guide local choices. Unfortunately, the process was neither as free from conflict nor as outcome-oriented as anticipated. Agendas were long, meetings were scheduled nearly every night of the week, discussion seemed endless, consensus was often lacking, and decisions were frequently postponed. The local alternative newspaper, observing the commotion, asked, "What's wrong with our town meetings?" and answered: "Here's what: most of the people are now from some other town" (*LKC*, Feb. 1, 1991: 7). The act of meeting, though, gave a sense of accomplishment, and the reports of discussions printed in the local newspaper substantiated the impression that planning for gambling was well under way.

The platform of new issues that suddenly arose with the promise of gambling development was extensive and more complex than previous community experience. Key issues in both Central City and Black Hawk revolved around procedures for upgrading local infrastructure (roads, electricity, sewage capacity), developing transportation and parking systems, arranging bonds for water system improvements, protecting historic amenities, and maintaining a positive quality of life for local citizens. Although the broad issues of concern were obvious, there were substantial conflicts over proposed solutions. Leaders and consultants generally worked on what was practical, tangible, and immediate, such as zoning requirements, transportation issues, and parking problems—issues that could be rendered in architectural drawings. Residents, though, continued to debate broader lifestyle issues, such as how to maintain local gathering places, keep impacts out of the county, and minimize disruptions to local patterns of life.

It became apparent, especially in the organizational meetings held by Central City and Gilpin County, that although citizens and planners used the same terms to describe their concerns, the words had different meanings for each group. For example, when residents talked about quality-of-life issues, they were expressing concerns that local gathering places would be lost, that traffic jams and parking would adversely affect daily life, and that "private" local places might be lost as a result of development. Planners, however, talked about quality of life in terms of how to construct a workable transportation system, how to manage parking, and procedures for improving sewer and water systems. In other words, planners talked about making local systems work better, whereas residents talked about helping local people feel better. When residents proposed radical solutions based on their visions of community (such as eliminating parking lots in Central City, or disallowing parking near county subdivisions), these ideas were met with snickers from planners and government leaders who had already assumed that growth, not restriction, was the desired outcome of gambling development. Claiming that leaders were not listening to their concerns, residents reported heightened tensions and anger as the planning period wore on.

In addition to the ever-increasing items of business on the agendas of local government meetings, gaming development placed demands on local leaders that could not possibly be handled under traditional forms of governance. As one local leader explained, "Right now it's crisis management. Everyone's so overwhelmed ... they can't think down the road." Yet, external investors were concerned about competitive advantage in the race to construct and operate their new casino ventures. They wanted fairness and equity in the conduct of local regulations, timely discussion and decisions by local leaders, and a willingness by the leadership to collaborate in creation of the new gaming industry. Instead, the external entrepreneurs often found a resistance to formal procedures and structure, and flexible interpretations of appropriate governing process. This was especially true in Central City, where the old-boy network of government and business leaders continued to govern in a traditional manner, much to the irritation of new casino developers. The growing frustrations with local leadership were increasingly evident in newspaper reports and letters discussing issues of local conflict.

MINING THE PAST: MORE HOLES IN THE GROUND

When the Black Hawk and Central City building moratoria ended in late spring 1991, the uncertainties of planning were replaced with the vigor of gambling-related construction. Having been encouraged by the excitement of property speculation and hopeful rhetoric about a new boom in the community, residents were emotionally unprepared for the extensive construction apparently required to transform historic structures into functional casinos. According to developers, the buildings were so old that massive renovation and replacement were necessary. However interesting the buildings constructed in the late 1800s were, decades of limited upkeep had taken a toll. Historic buildings were structurally unable to accommodate the anticipated numbers of gaming devices and tourists, meet fire and safety codes, and provide access for handicapped visitors.

Extensive construction also occurred for another reason: casino developers had a more liberal interpretation of *renovation* than did local residents. Gaming industry entrepreneurs claimed that renovation could be accomplished only by gutting interiors, discarding most exterior walls and facades, and extending buildings farther back into mountainsides or higher into the sky. As construction reached a peak during the summer of 1991, all the dust, debris, noise, and construction traffic jams prompted a resident to chastise, "I don't think that this is what the voters voted for" (*WRC,* June 14, 1991: 1).

The gaming amendment had as its central focus local and statewide historic preservation. In an effort to ensure that proposed casino developments would fit with local ambience and be as historically accurate as possible, all renovation plans were required to receive approval from historic review boards in the gaming towns. With veto power over construction plans or designs submitted by casino owners, the Black Hawk Historic Architectural Review

Construction at the corner of Eureka and Main Streets in Central City in September 1991 — just days before casinos opened for business—delayed traffic and raised tempers.

The historic preservation merits of gambling development were questioned when casino construction appeared to require massive destruction. Several shops at the south end of Central City's Main Street were demolished to create space for Bullwhackers Casino. Only the facades facing Main Street remained; these were incorporated into the design of the much larger casino, but are now indistinguishable to casual visitors.

Commission and the Central City Historic Preservation Commission emerged as two of the most powerful agencies in local government. They alone could prevent or limit development based on an assessment of the historic merits of the proposed design. Their efforts were hardly ever without controversy, though. Historic review decisions usually stimulated arguments, either from residents who opposed the option, or from new industry representatives who felt they were wasting time and money changing window casings, doorknobs, signs, and other features of their planned casinos.

The issue of historic accuracy took different forms in the two gaming towns. In Central City, most buildings in the commercial zone were visually intact but had suffered serious effects from aging. The renovation process usually required gutting the interiors of the historic buildings, removing old or rotting wood, and stabilizing the foundations and remaining walls. In some cases, approval was given to enlarge the buildings by chiseling out the back walls into the hillsides. Rooftop additions, however, were discouraged; when crews were seen building what appeared to be a penthouse addition on to the roof of one building, they were fined and the offending structure was removed. The most extreme cases of "historic preservation," and the ones most disturbing to local residents, were those where entire buildings were torn away, leaving only facades to be incorporated into entirely new constructions. Bullwhackers in Central City is an example of this kind of "renovation."

Black Hawk had some of the same problems as Central City, but there were fewer original historic structures in the commercial center of town. There were, however, many frame buildings that had been modified over the years and were in various stages of decay. Because Black Hawk was historically the "city of mills," a decision was made to allow gaming construction "in the style of" the old ore-crushing mills. This opened the door for demolition of several old buildings and the construction of very large, new casinos. For example, only the front twenty feet of the Gilpin Hotel were saved; the fire-damaged remainder was torn down, part of the hillside behind the hotel was removed, the building was extended back into the hillside, and an addition was made to the south side, making the building about four times the size of the previous hotel. Other buildings, even though not fire-damaged, experienced the same fate. On several occasions, usually when approval from the local historic review board was not forthcoming in a timely fashion, buildings tended to fall down unexpectedly. For example, Bullwhackers in Black Hawk is built on the site where some parts of an historic building were to be preserved. The structure mysteriously began to crack and collapse during renovation (*WRC*, Mar. 6, 1992: 1), and it was subsequently demolished as a safety hazard, thereby circumventing the ruling of the historic review board.

Remaking buildings "in the spirit" of the old mining towns introduced new development criteria that had never been discussed in the pre-gaming campaign or planning stages. The result was an outpouring of negative public sentiment. The approval of several large casino projects in each town, some as new buildings and others as consolidations of smaller shops in adjacent buildings, added to fears that the community was being lost to developers. Some gaming proponents rationalized the building projects as a natural outcome of new economic activity and progress. In interviews, they implied that because historic buildings were already in disrepair, and because historic interiors had been revised with the passage of time, the physical changes should not be interpreted as "losing" local history, but as "preserving" all that was left. As one local supporter of gaming development noted in an interview, "What we've lost [through gaming renovation], we were losing anyway." For those residents who had strong attachments to local places and to the very idea of an historic Western mining town, this was not a convincing argument.

Black Hawk's historic Gilpin Hotel on Main Street unfortunately suffered a fire shortly before the top photo was taken. When the property was sold, casino developers tore down all but the front section of the structure and excavated the hillside behind the building to construct a large casino. A side view of the building under construction is shown in the bottom photo. The new Gilpin Hotel and Casino is about four times the size of the historic structure.

The renovation and reconstruction of Main Street historic buildings were seen by residents as an attack on the "real" history of Central City and Black Hawk. This outcome, though, had apparently been expected by some campaign organizers. Lary Brown, CCPI vice president, wrote in a letter to the editor of the newspaper, "When I wrote Amendment 4, I realized that its passage would require massive construction to be done all over town and that it would sometimes be an inconvenience to surrounding businesses" (*WRC*, Aug. 23, 1991: 2). The timing of this revelation—"inconvenience" had never been a consequence mentioned by gambling promoters during the campaign—added to a growing sense of community betrayal. "Outside money drives this County now," reported one resident in an interview.

The destruction and renovation of downtown areas contributed to a widespread sense that local people, culture, and the unique qualities of place were threatened. In a sense, the historic preservation issue became the public expression of private and communal anger and dismay about all aspects of the development that could not be adequately verbalized. These included the meaning of community, the value of the unique landscape, the sense of the past, and the sacredness of community history for both self and community definition. "If the people of Gilpin County could vote on gambling now," said one elected official, "it wouldn't pass."

LIVING THROUGH THE BOOM

The construction period was the time when the community costs of gambling development began to become evident. Mixed emotions of fatigue, excitement, and uncertainty affected the entire community. Some of the people least able to cope with the developments were the most severely affected. Others, even if not directly impacted, saw the community changes and shared in the sense of loss. Only those profiting from the development seemed to remain hopeful.

The initial excitement of property speculation did provide some measure of local entertainment. The competition for business positioning was so fierce that, for several months, the *Weekly Register-Call* ran a new column entitled "Rumor Roundup." Reality and accountability seemed less important than being first with a new idea, and nothing was too outrageous. A gondola was proposed to transport visitors from a parking area several miles away to the gambling halls in Central City; a group of metropolitan area pilots introduced their idea for a helicopter service linking Denver, the ski resorts, and the gambling towns. For a time, when driving along a narrow, unpaved mountain road in an unincorporated area of Gilpin County, one would encounter an elaborately designed sign detailing a developer's plans for a 360-acre "Dory Hills Village: Condos, Helipad, Shopping Mall, Shuttle Buses, Apartments," and more. The sign eventually disappeared, after financing failed and local residents spoke out against the project. Obviously, speculation had its limits: building a helipad on the side of a mountain approached the unimaginable.

The construction period brought an end to many local services in Black Hawk and Central City. One of the first building projects in Black Hawk was conversion of the former auto repair and towing service along Highway 119 into a large, new casino. Later, although the owners had promised to try to remain open, the fortuitous location of a nearby gas station/grocery business proved to be its downfall. The shop closed and the building was enlarged into the three-story Black Hawk Bullwhackers. Residents could no longer buy gas or even get a bottle of milk or a loaf of bread in the towns. In Central City, several gift shops, the old pharmacy museum exhibit, the locally favored Toll Gate and Gold Coin Saloons, and later, the Golden Rose Hotel and the liquor store, all closed, to be converted into casinos. As one observer noted, the towns were beginning to feel more like theme parks and less like centers of community.

The owners who made millions by selling or leasing their properties were not blamed for having good fortune, but the repercussions of their success spread across the community. Building owners could benefit from the sale of

Business revenues suffered throughout the construction summer of 1991, as parking and pedestrian access were affected by casino and infrastructure building projects.

their previously unprofitable structures, but those who rented shops or apartments found that they were unable to renew their leases. In many cases, leases were canceled so owners could sell the buildings or land. As increasing numbers of Main Street businesses were displaced during the year prior to the opening of gambling, the manager of a jewelry shop expressed his anger in the quote that appears at the beginning of this chapter. Gambling development was supposed to help local businesses profit, but "[n]ow we're all losing our leases" (*WRC,* July 12, 1991: 8). As the campaign had been waged primarily with contributions from local businesspeople, their eviction seemed to be the ultimate betrayal.

The construction summer of 1991 produced a sharp downturn in revenues for shops that attempted to remain open, as tourists had difficulty gaining access to sidewalks, stores, and parking. New business and occupational taxes imposed on storefronts in both Black Hawk and Central City at that time, which were intended to raise local revenues in preparation for gambling development, stimulated negative feelings toward local leaders from the businesspeople who experienced the brunt of the construction impacts. Several new businesses did appear during the construction period, though all were related to the casino industry. Early in 1991, casino development consultants and a slot machine company moved into vacant buildings. In general, however, rapid speculation and casino construction reduced activity in other business sectors, and new service businesses beyond casino-related enterprises failed to arise during the construction period.

A variety of public activities and services were also affected. Construction crews now used the medical services of the local clinic, so the small staff was increasingly overworked. The library was beset with requests for local information, and the bookmobile was forced to cancel its stops in Central City and Black Hawk because construction activities prevented parking in the usual places. A residential parking permit system was implemented so that homeowners' cars would not be towed. Parking was now to be restricted to fee-collecting lots, even if the visitors were coming to town for reasons other than gambling. Saloons and cafes where locals had regularly met closed when the buildings were sold to casino developers. Some residents, including those who had sold or leased buildings for windfall profits, and those who had reservations about living in a gambling town, moved away. As daily life was transformed, a sense of loss for community and history, coupled with a feeling of loss of control over local living conditions and choices, prevailed.

Residential areas were also affected by casino construction. Situated on a prime land parcel near the center of town, the Black Hawk trailer court housed about twenty residents, most of them elderly. When the Gilpin Hotel was sold to a Boulder, Colorado, casino development group for more than $1 million, the trailer park land was included in the sale. By April 1991, the residents had received eviction notices. Each household was offered a stipend of $1,200 as compensation for quick relocation of the trailers. Because of regulations prohibiting trailer houses in county subdivisions, though, most of the residents were unable to relocate in Gilpin County.

When the plight of the trailer court residents was made public, a letter to the editor in the *Weekly Register-Call* (*WRC,* Sept. 20, 1991:2) encouraged county commissioners to uphold the restrictions against trailers locating in county subdivisions. The issue was not that county residents were opposed to the elderly residents moving into subdivisions, but rather that they feared an influx of trailers housing casino employees if covenant restrictions were eased. Restrictions remained, and because no local solution could be found to the displacement of the elderly Black Hawk trailer park residents, most were forced to move away from the area.

The injustice of elderly residents being evicted from their homes as a result of gaming development created much public anger. When asked about the situation during an interview, a local government leader and supporter of gaming dismissed the incident, saying, "Those trailer park people don't really add much value to the community anyway." The insensitivity of such a comment—especially in view of the fact that most of the elderly residents had been longtime community members—pointed out the prevalence of commitment to growth and economic gain, no matter what the cost. As another resident explained in an interview, "Well, you have to give a little to get a little." Ignored by many, though, was the issue of who was giving and who was getting. Though it is impossible to measure, a Gilpin county health professional later speculated that the deaths of several local elderly people during and immediately after the construction period were related to the disruption of their lives as a result of the new developments.

Outside the towns, in unincorporated areas of the county, residents also began to feel unanticipated pressures on their daily habits. As gambling construction progressed, traffic volumes increased dramatically on the primary Gilpin County roads, and residents took to driving the unpaved mountain roads to and from work rather than waiting in endless traffic jams in the one-mile-long Gregory Gulch, watching their towns undergo renovation. Though gambling activities were to be allowed only in the towns and not in the county, there were spillover effects in the unincorporated areas. Speculators prowled the area, seeking property on which to site parking lots, shopping strips, and other "improvements," and many of these sites were near previously quiet county subdivisions. Development-related changes were threatening the very peace and scenic beauty residents had moved to Gilpin County to enjoy, and the response was strong and negative. Numerous letters appeared in the newspaper opposing the schemes proposed by external developers and demanding that leaders contain the gaming developments in Central City and Black Hawk. The rise of community activism through the formation of neighborhood interest groups began to emerge during the construction period.

The collective community shock experienced during the construction summer of 1991 is revealed by the sentiments expressed in letters to the editor of the *Weekly Register-Call*. The analysis of themes and issues discussed in these letters reveals categories similar to those identified in pre-gambling and campaign time periods, but the volume of letters and the negative feelings expressed were unusual in comparison to earlier time periods. Beginning with newspaper issues published after the November 1990 vote, and continuing through the end of September 1991, just before gaming opened (a total of 47 issues), an extraordinary 206 news articles and 44 letters and opinions about gambling development were published in the local paper. Many of these appeared in the later months of this time period: there was an especially large volume of community letters just before the commencement of gambling in October 1991.

Figure 3.1 in chapter 3 displayed trends in the publication of news articles, letters, and opinions over the course of the campaign and construction periods of gambling development. The third and fourth peaks charted in that figure reflect the time period from January to April 1991 (third peak), and May through September 1991 (fourth peak), both during the construction phase of gambling development. The escalating volume and negative tone of messages across the campaign and construction periods indicate increasing community concern over the outcomes of the development.

Four themes from the campaign phase were repeated in letters written during the construction phase of gambling development: Environmental Beauty, Social and Cultural Qualities, Economic Fragility, and History and Historic Images. Another theme also reappeared in letters written during the construction period: Community Problems and Conflict. Both the History and Conflict categories contained more than twice the number of entries as any other category, and these two are the most revealing categories for understanding the construction period effects.

Phrases contained in the Community Problems and Conflict category during the construction period were, in comparison to earlier times, more confrontational, specific, and extreme in tone. There were general comments about local problems: "this community is noted for cops and drunks, easy drugs, and being a tourist trap, with junk in the shops," "the Opera House

Association has long been given special treatment by Central City," and "don't allow trailers in our nice subdivisions!" There were also phrases and comments related to the proposed gambling industry: "we don't want the gambling disease to spread into the county," and "gaming people think they can come into our town and run it their way." In all comments, personal and institutional conflicts were again evident. Personal conflicts, evaluating the behavior of other community members, included such phrases as, "nothing will get done if everyone argues," "we all need to take a more active part," and "gaming will not make us whole again; there is too much greed, unbridled ambition and conflict of interest here." The institutional conflicts focused on problems between agencies or collectivities: "Black Hawk won't help Central City; Central City won't help Black Hawk," and "outsiders know little about our situation."

The category of History and Historic Images, drawn from letters to the editor written during the construction period, contained extensive comments relating to the observed effects of the proposed gambling development on the historic qualities of the area. The meaningfulness of the historic and natural landscape had been documented in letters prior to gaming, and was evident in letters published throughout the campaign and construction periods. During the construction period, however, the opinions and letters were primarily negative, and gambling development was blamed for the destruction of local historic resources.

More authors blamed than supported the gambling idea, as evidenced by letters that contained references to the destruction of history and the phoniness of the new construction. For example, people wrote, "there's enough interesting history in the Little Kingdom without faking it," "tall buildings would detract from authenticity," and "the parking lot covers history with asphalt." The people held responsible for these changes were identified not by name but by actions. For example, one person wrote that "the business district is being destroyed by people with dollar signs in their heads"; another commented, "the intentions of Central's Historic Preservation Commission are confusing"; yet another noted that "the real power of influence was becoming the historic preservation offices" in the two cities. Taken together, the overwhelming number of entries in this category suggests that historic images of the community became the symbolic expression of all the hopes and fears associated with gambling development.

LOCAL LEADERSHIP AND COMMUNITY DEVELOPMENT

The construction phase of gambling development placed significant strain on community resources and morale. The agenda for community disruption, though, had been set during the campaign period, when a "sanitized" version of gambling was sold to the public. Limited stakes gambling was supposed to bring only fun and entertainment on a very small scale. Gambling was to have been a unique attraction, so that visitors could enjoy a greater range of community tourist activities. Moreover, because gambling was consistent with mining-town imagery, and mining towns were characterized by boom periods, the new gambling boom would simply be a natural extension of Gilpin County history. Such persuasive arguments left residents unprepared for the vast reconstruction that followed the lifting of town moratoria. As residents commented repeatedly during the construction period, "We trusted our leaders" to provide the type of entertainment gambling described in the campaign; "[i]t wasn't supposed to be like this."

What no one seemed to consider was that the local leadership should never have been entrusted with this responsibility. Leaders were far too intimately involved—tangibly and symbolically—in promoting the development to be able to objectively assess the merits of gambling tourism. The problem was not in personal qualities or a lack of skills; indeed, many of the community leaders were people of high standards, capable and thoughtful individuals.[5] Instead, the problem was structural: in rural communities, local governments tend to be comprised of members of the business elite. Business leaders are uniquely qualified for participation in local government (Logan and Molotch 1987). They are often well educated, have ready financial resources, are visible and known across the community, and are more attentive to local governance issues, as the activities of city and county councils directly affect their business success. In addition, members of the business elite tend to be more growth-oriented than other community members, because growth is taken as a sign of business success, and by extension, community well-being.[6] Holding a position in local government is a way to extend a businessperson's power, influence, and vision across the community.

When the pro-gambling group CCPI formed in 1989, it was made up of local business leaders, many of whom also held positions in local government. Such overlapping roles created a conflict of interest: by promoting gambling development, leaders in local government were also disproportionately favoring their own business interests, as business owners or property landlords would be the ones most likely to profit from gambling development. Owners could sell their businesses or properties for profit, or they could use their financial reserves and organizational structure to extend or replace their existing businesses with gambling operations. Because business and property owners (who were also the government leaders) were the segment of the community most likely to profit directly from the development of gambling, the conflict of interest left government leaders (who were also the business owners) ill-suited to represent the collective well-being of the broader Gilpin County community.

The result could only be described as a "slippage of responsibility" (Freudenburg and Gramling 1994a) in which local leaders, charged with protecting the public good, consistently elevated their private interests. Throughout the construction period, town leaders consistently dismissed suggestions that they had any conflicts of interest, justifying their actions by explaining that they knew what was best for the future of the community. They also repeatedly expressed surprise at the volume of negative comments and publicity generated by the construction period activities, explaining that early negative impacts were simply the price to be paid for long-term benefits. As they reflected, the community was only experiencing "growing pains." Such hopeful attitudes persisted throughout the construction period and into later stages of the gambling development.[7] "This is a very exciting time; we're making history," leaders replied to questions about the development. But, with their sights fixed firmly on Opening Day, community leaders failed to understand that local citizens were beginning to have grave doubts about their leaders.

In addition to the slippage of responsibility by local leaders, another factor influenced the eventual outcome of the development: no organization could be held accountable for the construction outcomes. Local leaders, under the organizing group CCPI, had convinced many Gilpin County and Colorado citizens of the merits of gambling by promoting a simplistic image of entertainment gambling. Once Amendment 4 passed, though, CCPI quietly faded from the public eye, while new casino owners and gaming industry representatives began to play more prominent roles in the community. Central City and Black Hawk business and government leaders continued to speak publicly about the gaming developments, but they now represented only one of the involved interest groups.

The easiest people to blame for the discontinuity between what was promised and what seemed to be developing in the towns were the new casino entrepreneurs. The new external owners, though, had never been actively involved in the gambling campaign, so it was difficult to hold them accountable for creating something that vastly exceeded the proposals. Records from the secretary of state's office (Colorado Secretary of State 1990b) indicate that there were no large campaign contributions from the gambling industry, and industry spokespersons had been remarkably silent about the proposal during the campaign. Casino leaders became visible and vocal only after the vote, when gaming owners' groups formed in the towns. One must assume that this was a conscious rhetorical strategy. Industry representatives and potential investors had little to gain by speaking publicly about their hopes and expectations, especially when these hopes diverged from the ideas of gambling promoters, as the evidence of the construction period indicated. It was more advantageous to let citizens debate the merits of the proposed initiative, knowing that the actual development regulations would be set in the future.

Blaming the gaming industry, even for its silence, was also a sensitive issue. As local leaders and some letter writers to the *Weekly Register-Call* reminded residents, the industry was contributing substantial amounts of money to "save" Gilpin County, and the investors could take their business to another gaming-approved town if the local environment was not welcoming. Because local leaders could not be held responsible for the reinterpretation of the gambling proposal, and because the industry apparently deserved gentle handling, residents sought other scapegoats. In the estimation of community residents, the list of potential culprits was long: planning consultants were seen as serving special interests; Denver media were said to be promoting negative stories about construction gridlock, thus keeping tourists away; and construction crews were adversely affecting normal business operations. According to the local leaders, the most obvious failures were the responsibility of the newly formed State Gaming Commission, which they said had manipulated the legal framework of gaming to favor state and industry interests, ignoring local concerns. The one constant throughout the construction period, though, was that local leaders tended to remain unblemished and resistant to attacks on their own complicity in creating the type of development that was emerging along the main streets of the towns.

As the construction period continued through summer 1990, casino owners and industry representatives emerged as powerful and influential figures in the communities. Although some community members were planning to enter the gaming industry, many of the casino developers were people external to the community, including Denver media and sports personalities and West Coast resort developers, who had substantial financing and organizational capability. It was their speculative activities that controlled the pace and scale of growth locally, and their concerns also shaped the agenda of community discussion issues. Comfortable in their roles as corporate leaders, the new casino owners adopted something of a paternalistic approach to the community. For example, a Central City casino owner explained during an interview that his company was working very closely with the local government officials because "We're Coloradans, that's our history up there; we don't want to ruin those towns." Another new casino owner commented during an interview, "Black Hawk was a sleepy little town which had a love/hate relationship with visitors; now people want to be a destination resort rather than a small town. Locals will be surprised at what their community will be." It was obvious that the people who looked forward to the destination resort were those representing the gaming industry and related interests, not local residents.

By the end of the construction period, it was clear that there would be no turning back. The noncasino gambling of the campaign had been entirely replaced with the casino gaming of the construction period. The future was in creating a gaming industry, and the most successful business owners would be the ones with the largest casinos, the most gaming devices, and the best financing. Indeed, gaming industry representatives were quoted as saying that the small, simple, Mom-and-Pop gambling centers envisioned by local people were unrealistic, given renovation expenses, casino start-up costs, financing efforts, and the cash reserves required for successful operation. As one industry representative asked plaintively during an interview, "Don't the local people know there's no such thing as a little bit of gambling?"

Apparently, Gilpin County residents did not know. It was clear from the public outcry that the amount of construction required to turn historic buildings into appropriate gaming sites far exceeded the expectations of residents. While local leaders savored the energy of the construction period, even previously supportive residents from across all segments of the community became progressively unhappier. "I voted for gambling," said numerous residents during interviews, "but I never expected it would be like this."

What was even more curious, though, was why local proponents apparently did not know "there's no such thing as a little bit of gambling" either. Whether CCPI organizers simply underestimated the requirements of gambling development, or whether they deliberately misled voters regarding expected outcomes, remains unknown. Though several CCPI organizers did express surprise at the pace and scale of community changes, the evidence of the construction period suggests that at least some promoters knew that gambling would be bigger than anticipated and were quite willing to live with the consequences. As some of the primary beneficiaries, they had excellent reasons to be circumspect, and they could blame the industry or the state regulators for letting the development get out of control. If there was a stroke of genius in the gambling development, it was in promoting this development in a community accustomed to nonparticipation and acceptance of local leaders' visions.

ASSESSING CONSTRUCTION PHASE IMPACTS

The gambling developments in Central City and Black Hawk present a classic example of the "growth machine" hypothesis proposed by Molotch (1976). The basic premise of the proposal is that localities are places where influential people with common interests in community growth (where "growth" is expressed as competition over alternative uses of land and property) compete to determine the conditions for and outcomes of local development. The participants in the political negotiation of growth issues are not representative of the entire populace, but are primarily those who have a stake in the outcome of growth decisions. These include some governmental authorities, the local business elite who own and invest in land and property, and other growth supporters, including bankers, lawyers, realtors, and community boosters like the publisher of the local newspaper. In other words, the people most active in local politics will be exactly those who wish to affect the politics of resource distribution (Molotch 1976: 317). These elite operators "use their growth consensus to eliminate any alternative vision of the purpose of local government or the meaning of community" (Logan and Molotch 1987: 51).

Growth-machine activities are evident in nearly every segment of the construction phase of gambling development. Indeed, anticipatory impacts of gambling tourism development may be so striking because they vividly expose the functions of the community growth machine to observers who are usually far less than attentive. Two examples of growth-machine politics in the case of gambling development are the lack of local leadership objection to use of the words *casino* and *gaming,* and the focus on planning to accommodate growth rather than to accommodate the special concerns of local citizens. Other examples are also readily available. The speculation for commercial property, and the outrageous prices of buildings and land, reflected the investment value of casino land and property—not, as locals would have liked to believe, preferences for the value of historic preservation. Negative letters to the editor, and the vocal display of communal unhappiness and despair accompanying construction activities, were evidence of a gap between development preferences of the residential community and those of the pro-growth coalition, which included government, consultant, business, and industry members. Finally, conflicts between casino representatives and government leaders marked the maneuverings of competing growth coalitions over local land use and property arrangements.

Although the logic of growth-machine politics is evident in hindsight, it was camouflaged during gambling development by the rapidity of planning and construction and the shifting bases of leadership in the towns. But growth-machine activities are endemic in many kinds of tourism growth, and should not be a surprise in gaming development, where the expected rewards of obtaining choice land parcels and commercial property are exceedingly high. Though tourism researchers have rarely written about growth-machine politics, there is other evidence to suggest that growth machines are inherent in tourism development. Canan and Hennessy (1989) described a case of land use conflict resulting from resort development in Hawaii, and Madrigal (1995) examined two cases of tourism growth-machine operations in the United States and the United Kingdom. These examples reinforce the idea that community negotiations over future uses of land and property resources are central to the development of tourism. In the case of the Gilpin County towns, moreover, the fact that the land was covered by historic buildings escalated the conflicts beyond tangible ownership issues and into the realm of symbolic meanings related to the historic infrastructure.

Growth-machine politics surrounding gambling development in Central City and Black Hawk produced effects that favored some groups of local and external people more than others. The existence of differential benefits supports Molotch's claim (1976: 320) that, under many circumstances, "local growth is a transfer of quality of life and wealth from the local general public to a certain segment of the local elite. To raise the question of wisdom of growth in regard to any specific locality is hence potentially to threaten such a wealth transfer and the interests of those who profit by it." The increasingly negative and combative tone of public discourse during the campaign and construction periods showed the seriousness of the effort to obtain and develop gambling, and should have alerted citizens to the existence of more powerful, external growth speculators for whom land use in Gilpin County was clearly a political and economic benefit.

That leaders seemed to have been unwilling or unsuccessful in attracting capital for economic development prior to the gambling proposal is not a repudiation of the growth-machine hypothesis. Residential disinterest, or the perception that scenery and other amenity resources were more valuable than industry growth, may have accounted for the lack of local action. Krannich and Humphrey (1983: 74) proposed that "growth promotion would be most evident where substantial numbers of local residents have direct business ties and interest." The lack of business interests in the towns among the greater Gilpin County population, many of whom worked outside the community, may have restrained previous growth plans. It is likely, though, that turning community history into private and public revenue through gambling development was simply a more lucrative proposal for local growth proponents, and a solid investment opportunity for external, growth-oriented gaming entrepreneurs as well. In other words, it was a good bet for growth-machine advocates.

LEGISLATIVE PREPARATIONS

While community residents and leaders planned for gambling, and while construction crews rebuilt the towns, the specific requirements of the gaming bill were debated in the state legislature. One item in the law had direct bearing on the discussion of growth-machine politics: the specification that licensed gaming employees or persons with any formal, tangible interest in a casino could not hold elected office. As noted earlier, local business owners and entrepreneurs tended to participate in local politics, but they were also the ones most likely to enter the casino industry. To prevent conflicts of interest, however, the gaming law required that persons participating in gaming operations could not hold elected office; if they held office at the time they entered the industry, they must resign. In September 1991, just before Opening Day, both towns lost their mayors. Bruce Schmalz, mayor of Central City, and Bill Lorenz, mayor of Black Hawk, were longtime businessmen in their communities, and had each converted a section of their businesses into a casino area. The resignation of the two leaders stirred unrest: with a combined total of only about 600 residents, having enough qualified people to staff local government positions and boards became an issue. A leadership vacuum loomed, as other council and board members of local government were also businesspersons planning to enter the gaming industry.

Seen through the lens of the growth-machine model, the resulting clamor over the state regulation prohibiting persons with a casino interest from holding elected office must be seen as a consequence of the threat to established power networks of the community growth machine. The local leaders who had been most instrumental in obtaining gaming development were now forcibly removed from their elected positions of influence. The response from the pro-growth forces in the community was as expected. "There will be problems with who they get on the local councils," said one gaming industry director in an interview. An elected official in Central City agreed that there was "a danger of getting anti-gaming residents on the council in the future," especially because "the people who are good managers are now in the casino industry, not in local government." The executive director of the newly formed Colorado Gaming Owners Association, Stephen Grogan, protested the state legislation in a letter to the local paper, writing, "These forced resignations will cause a leadership vacuum that might lead to disruptive community in-fights, at the critical time that the focus must be on preparing these [towns] and surrounding communities for the anticipated growth impact" (*WRC*, Sept. 27, 1991: 2). Despite the opposition, the law remained. As expected, that small item would change local power relationships in the months after gaming operations began, much to the delight of some community members, but to the dismay of others. The tales of woe emanating from growth advocates should be seen as a natural outcome of threats to their personal economic and political interests, not necessarily as impassioned concern about the well-being of the community.

THE 1990 GAMBLING LEGISLATION

While construction activities proceeded in the new gambling towns, the legal framework for the gaming industry was discussed in committee by the state legislature. In June 1991, Governor Roy Romer signed the Limited Gaming

Act (Article 18, Section 9, of the Colorado State Constitution), promising diligence in maintaining a crime-free industry.

As approved by the voters and described in the law, gaming is allowed only in the commercial districts of three Colorado towns: Central City and Black Hawk in Gilpin County, and Cripple Creek in Teller County. The intent of the law is to raise monies for historic preservation and to support economic development. Under the law, a five-member Colorado Limited Gaming Control Commission appointed by the governor has final authority to regulate gaming in Colorado. Primary functions of this organization are to establish the annual rate for gaming taxes; approve budgets, allocations, and licenses; and evaluate all Colorado gaming rules and regulations. In addition, the Colorado Division of Gaming, organized within the Colorado Department of Revenue, administers the gaming industry in Colorado. Members of the Division of Gaming process applications for gaming licenses; investigate and monitor license holders; handle citizen complaints; observe casino operations; conduct audits; and provide public information about the Colorado gaming industry (Colorado Division of Gaming 1995).

According to the law, gambling activities are limited to "structures which conform . . . to the architectural styles and designs that were common to the areas prior to World War 1" (Article 18, Section 9: 2(b)). In addition, "no more than thirty-five percent of the square footage of any building and no more than fifty percent of any one floor of such building" (Article 18, Section 9: 3(c)) can contain gambling. As specified, the term *limited stakes gambling* refers to games of chance (including slot machines, video poker and blackjack, keno, and the table games of blackjack and poker) in which the maximum allowable single bet is $5.00. The approved hours of operation are from 8:00 A.M. to 2:00 A.M. Patrons must be at least twenty-one years of age to gamble, and minors are excluded from gaming areas of casinos. People who hold elected governmental positions in the gaming towns or counties, along with town managers and planners, are prohibited from having an interest in gaming operations (Continuing Legal Education in Colorado, Inc. 1993: 78).

The primary beneficiaries of gambling tax revenues in Colorado are the State General Fund and the Colorado State Historical Society. The gaming act formalized the distribution schedule for monies accumulated from taxes, fines, and fees paid into the limited gaming fund. Before distributions are made, the expenses of the Division of Gaming and the Gaming Commission are paid. Almost 50 percent of the tax revenues (49.8 percent) then are deposited in the State General Fund (at least 9 percent of these monies are designated for a Contiguous Counties Impact Fund to reduce some of the regional impacts of gaming development, such as increased traffic and law enforcement needs). Twenty-eight percent of the tax revenues go to the State Historical

Society, caretaker of historic properties in the state. Twelve percent of the available revenues are returned to the governing agencies in Gilpin and Teller Counties, proportional to gaming revenues generated in each county; 10 percent is returned to the governments of Central City, Black Hawk, and Cripple Creek, proportional to the revenues generated by each town; and 0.2 percent is contributed to the Colorado Tourism Promotion Fund. The monies deposited in the State Historical Fund are further divided: 20 percent is dedicated to preservation and restoration projects in the three gaming towns, and 80 percent is to be used for preservation and restoration of historic sites and places throughout the state.

In addition to coordinating the development of casino gaming in three mountain towns, passage of the Limited Gaming Act also opened the door for the development of gaming on Colorado's Indian reservations. According to the 1988 Indian Gaming Regulatory Act, states may enter into compacts with Native American tribes living within their borders to extend gaming opportunities onto reservations. Tribes may develop casinos and offer the same games of chance provided at other locations in the state. In Colorado, two tribal casinos now operate in the southwestern corner of the state. The Ute Mountain Ute Tribe opened the first casino in Towaoc, Montezuma County, in September 1992. A year later, the Southern Ute Tribe opened a casino in Ignacio, La Plata County.

The tribes each have one large casino on their lands. Although the intent has been to hire primarily Native Americans for casino operations and staffing, initial training and management has been provided by nontribal management companies. In Colorado, tribes are not required to report their revenues to the state, and revenue from Indian gaming operations is exempt from state taxation, so no accurate estimates of benefits and costs can be made. None of the statistics presented in this book include information about Colorado tribal gaming operations.

NOTES

1. According to the 1983, 1988, and 1994 *County and City Data Books,* twenty-four new private housing units were authorized by building permits in Gilpin County in 1986, and thirty-four in 1992. The data were suppressed in 1981 because of small numbers, but we can assume that the total was fewer than three permits, as three is the lowest number reported for any Colorado county.

2. See Mathieson and Wall (1982), and Pearce (1989), for overviews of tourism impact analysis.

3. Gilpin County property sales increased dramatically between 1991 and 1993, in the early years of casino operation and stabilization of gaming development in Central City and Black Hawk. For example, total county property sales rose from $10,658,800 in 1990, to $76,956,200 in 1991, and to $98,524,700 in 1993. A more detailed comparative analysis of Gilpin County property sales over time is shown in Table 6.4 in chapter 6.

4. The Belvidere Theatre was first sold in July 1991. As of summer 1995, it had not been renovated as a casino, and still sits empty at the end of Central City's Main Street.

5. Some others were not as respectable, however. Community records reveal police actions and court proceedings against several leaders, though these instances of personal failure were generally kept quietly as community secrets. Despite their transgressions, these persons were not prevented from serving in public office, a situation probably common to many rural communities with small pools of willing candidates for local office.

6. Luloff and Hodges (1992) discuss similar issues in a study of the representativeness of local leaders in a forty-five-town area in New Hampshire. They found that local bureaucrats and citizens often differed in their attitudes toward growth, suggesting that "a great potential exists for lay leaders to make decisions concerning growth and development or other issues which do not reflect the attitudes or desires of the citizens" (p. 393).

7. Chapter 7 shows that this strategy resulted in serious political problems for the towns and the county once gaming had opened. This was especially true in Central City, where governmental leaders became increasingly unresponsive to the community and more closely aligned with planning consultants and some casino interests. The only resolution, from the standpoint of citizens, was a series of recall elections that further polarized the community.

PART TWO
THE CONSEQUENCES OF GAMING DEVELOPMENT

The history of Gilpin County and its former mining boomtowns, and the subsequent campaign and construction periods leading to the opening of gaming on October 1, 1991, constitute the first half of the gambling development story in Black Hawk and Central City. The four chapters of Part II of this book (chapters 5 to 8) consider specific types of community impacts resulting from gaming development between 1991 and early 1996. These chapters are topical rather than chronological because impacts occurred in all contexts of local life simultaneously. In an effort to encourage a more objective, reasoned analysis of gambling impacts, these chapters present both quantitative and qualitative data supporting the conclusions.

Chapter 5 details the growth of the casino industry in Black Hawk and Central City. Though campaign promoters initially promised that gambling would be an attraction rather than an industry, the rapid expansion of casinos even in the first year of gaming operations indicated that little remained of campaign promises. The gambling boom was exciting for local people, but it failed in nearly every way to live up to the claims of the gambling campaign: casinos are out of scale with the local infrastructure, are primarily externally owned, and have not substantially improved local employment levels. They have, however, produced substantial revenues for historic preservation locally and across the state. The implications of casino development for the local economies of Black Hawk, Central City, and Gilpin County are discussed in chapter 6. Although supporters point to the huge revenues associated with gaming development as benefits, they often fail to acknowledge that the costs associated with operating larger and more complex local governments are also substantial. This chapter attempts to provide a balanced picture of revenues and costs.

Chapter 7 evaluates the social and cultural impacts of gaming development. This chapter specifically considers changes in community quality of life after the opening of casinos, discussing daily routines as well as community festivals and special events. Analysis of the gaming developments reveals that new forms of cultural commoditization have emerged, as tangible and intangible reinterpretations of history become visible across the community.

The institutional impacts of gaming development are specifically considered in chapter 8. Governmental agencies and private organizations may be severely affected by new community tourism developments. These entities are often required to provide new services without adequate funding or preparation, and they often unexpectedly find themselves engaged in community power struggles that ensue when new community organizations (in this case, casino businesses and owners' groups) arise. This chapter shows how painful the process of community politics can become during and after gaming development.

5

GROWTH OF THE CASINO INDUSTRY

Limited stakes gaming in Colorado appears to be the vehicle that will transport these ... communities from destitution to thriving destination resort economies.

—Walden (1991: 2)

As Opening Day approached, the rhetoric of the campaign had been fully replaced with the new imagery and construction of casino gaming. The transformation of the gambling concept was so complete, and the construction of the new gaming industry so extensive, that the towns looked almost new. Announcing the first pull of the slot machine handles, the irrepressible alternative newspaper, *The Little Kingdom Come* (Oct. 18, 1991: 1), offered a mixed review and contributed a new concept to the local vernacular, proclaiming, "It's good! It's bad! It's big! It's here! WALLET MINING!"

OPENING DAY: OCTOBER 1, 1991

October 1, 1991, dawned bright and cheerful, with Central City and Black Hawk framed by a brilliant blue sky and golden aspen color. Large crowds gathered in the streets before the 8:00 A.M. opening time, applauding as local and state dignitaries ceremoniously opened the casinos, then scrambling for the casino tokens dropped from rooftops by casino employees. Visitors swarmed the seven casinos in Central City and the four casinos in Black Hawk, standing three and four deep around the gaming tables and in front of slot machines. The first jackpot of $1,000 was, oddly enough, won by Central City planning consultant, David Stahl, at the Gilded Garter Casino. Though other local and state officials attended the opening ceremonies, Governor Roy Romer, who had opposed the gambling initiative, was conspicuous by his absence.

While gambling fever drew patrons into casinos, another kind of lucrative industry was in evidence on local streets: auto towing. The lack of parking near casino entrances forced visitors to leave their vehicles on the shoulders of State Highway 119 and along both sides of the narrow incline of Gregory Gulch. Visitors walking to casinos, and drivers in cars seeking parking spots, then competed for the remaining space in the middle of the narrow roads. Despite the towns' advance planning efforts, parking was clearly a problem, and it would continue to be one of the most vexing, long-lasting concerns associated with the gaming developments.

By midday on October 1, 1991, much of the traffic crush was centered around the intersection of Highways 119 and 279 in Black Hawk. A state patrol officer on duty at that site explained that the Black Hawk traffic jam was the result of incomplete visitor information and lack of signs. People generally

After casinos, the most lucrative local businesses were parking lot management and auto towing services for illegally parked vehicles.

knew that the casinos were located in Central City and Black Hawk, he said, but many were confused about the spatial relationship between the towns. When they arrived at the intersection and saw the Black Hawk casinos, tourists often thought they were in Central City. Many visitors were unaware that they had to drive another mile west up Gregory Gulch to reach Central City. Others were under the impression that all the available parking was in Black Hawk; they expected shuttle buses to drive them to Central City casinos.

The officer noted that five new state police officers had been hired to patrol the Gilpin County highways, and another five had been hired to patrol in Teller County near Cripple Creek's gaming developments. He confirmed that there was no coordination of law enforcement and police work among the towns, the county, or the state. In his opinion, the most significant problem evident on Opening Day was the need for signs directing people to parking areas and shuttle bus stops. In addition to confusing Central City with Black Hawk, people had no idea where to park, where to catch a shuttle bus, or how often the shuttle buses ran. A shuttle bus driver later commented, though, that scheduling was impossible when the traffic was so thick.

Up Gregory Gulch in Central City, cars and people swarmed across the landscape, though traffic jams were less severe. Security people from private firms, hired by the casinos and the town, kept traffic flowing. A doorman at the Teller House said he was glad to be stationed by the door, because the crush of people, the noise of the slot machines, the smell of cigarette smoke, and the exuberant commotion inside the casino gave him a headache. In fact, he wished that "someone would open a non-smoking casino!" As the largest casino in Central City on Opening Day, the Teller House presented visitors with 168 slot machines, 80 poker machines, and 8 blackjack tables. More than 200 people had waited outside the Teller House doors in advance of the 8:00 A.M. opening, and the casino had been congested with gamblers all day.

If Opening Day was any indication, the casino industry in Colorado was headed for overwhelming success. Indeed, the first year of gaming produced wagers, revenues, and tax returns in amounts more than double the expectations of experts. Revenues continued to rise even after the novelty of the first year of gaming ended, though the industry experienced fluctuations during the early stages of operations. Although the first year of gaming was characterized by rapid expansion of casinos, by 1994 and 1995, a more stable, leaner industry had emerged in the Colorado gaming towns.

TAX RATES ON GAMING REVENUES

One of the primary, albeit controversial, functions of the Colorado Limited Gaming Control Commission is to set the gaming tax rate each year. Unlike other states that have established fixed tax rates on casino revenues, Colorado retains an option to adjust the tax rate on an annual basis. In accordance with the claims of early promoters of Amendment 4, the gaming legislation allows the tax to be set "up to a maximum of forty percent of the adjusted gross proceeds" (Article 18, Section 9: 5(a)). The term *adjusted gross proceeds* (AGP) refers to the amount of money wagered by casino patrons minus the amount paid out by casinos in individual winnings.

The suggested 40 percent tax rate had been used by the early CCPI promoters of the gambling initiative to reassure voters that the casino developments would be truly limited. How promoters arrived at a figure of 40 percent is unknown; no other state has ever had a tax on gaming revenues higher than 20 percent. Even in the comparable small-stakes gaming industry of Deadwood, South Dakota, gaming revenues are taxed at only 8 percent (*Rocky Mountain News*, Sept. 30, 1992: 49). Nevertheless, the proposed 40 percent figure was never questioned until summer 1991, when gaming commission members began publicly debating the tax levels. Casino owners and managers, previously silent on the tax issue, suddenly began to protest loudly against the 40 percent tax rate. Claiming that the gaming industry would fail if the tax were set at such a high level, industry representatives threatened to take their development plans elsewhere.

Those confrontations resulted in the establishment of a graduated tax rate for the first year of gaming, with yearly negotiations producing revisions to that initial schedule. Comparisons among the tax rate levels for four years of Colorado gaming are presented in Table 5.1.

Table 5.1   Tax Rates on Adjusted Gross Proceeds, 1991–1995 (M = millions)

Oct. 1, 1991–Sept. 30, 1992		Oct. 1, 1992–Sept. 30, 1993		Oct. 1, 1993–Sept. 30, 1994		Oct. 1, 1994–Sept. 30, 1995[a]	
AGP	Tax Rate	AGP	Tax Rate	AGP	Tax Rate	AGP	Tax Rate
< $440,000	4%	< $1.0 M	2%	< $1.0 M	2%	< $2.0 M	2%
$440,000–$1.2 M	8%	> $1.0 M	20%	$1.0 M–$2.0 M	8%	$2.0 M–$4.0 M	8%
> $1.2 M	5%			$2.0 M–$3.0 M	15%	$4.0 M–$5.0 M	15%
				> $3.0 M	18%	> $5.0 M	18%

Source: Colorado Division of Gaming, *Gaming in Colorado: Fact Book and Abstract* (1993, 1994, 1995).
[a]This rate is also in effect for the gaming year that begins October 1, 1995, and ends September 30, 1996.

For the first year of gaming operations, the tax was scaled at 4, 8, and 15 percent, based on the level of adjusted gross proceeds earned by each casino. Adjustments in subsequent years reflect efforts by the gaming commission to provide tax relief for smaller, Mom-and-Pop casinos (the lowest tax rate, for example, was reduced a further 2 percent for the second year of gaming), and later to relieve the tax burden on larger casinos (reducing the rate from 20 to 18, 15, or 8 percent in the third year of gaming). These levels, obviously, are well within the 40 percent maximum promoted by the early organizers of the gambling initiative. Table 5.1 is also instructive for showing the growth in the size of Colorado casinos, as the base AGP levels have risen in each gaming year as larger casinos have been built and smaller ones have gone out of business. In the 1994–1995 gaming year, "small casinos" are those that earn up to $2 million in AGP. These would have been considered the largest casinos in the first gaming year.

Three general lessons are evident in the annual manipulations of the Colorado gaming tax rate. The first is that the ability to manipulate tax rates is quite desirable from the perspective of the state, especially one that has vested interests in maintaining or improving the amount of tax revenues deposited in the State General Fund. At the same time, such actions are quite undesirable from the perspective of casino owners and investors. As a case in point, the elevation of the second-year tax rate on "large" casinos (defined that year as those for which adjusted gross proceeds exceeded $1 million) generated a large amount of new monies for the state. It raised the tax rates 5 percent for all casinos that had previously been paying 15 percent, and it also raised the tax rates 12 percent for some of the middle-sized casinos that had paid only 8 percent in the first gaming year. The angry response stemming from this adjustment (a *Rocky Mountain News* article dated September 30, 1992: 10, quoted a casino general manager as saying, "They just killed us") indicates that the first-year tax rates were extremely generous for casino owners. The second-year adjustments meant that owners would now be forced to operate without the latitude of the large financial reserves they had enjoyed in the first gaming year.

The second lesson, related to the first, is that interactions exist among many variables associated with casino development, and tax rates cannot be considered in isolation from other factors. Investors claim that adjustable tax rates create uncertainties in the market, reducing potential investment in a given area. Under this logic, developers are said to prefer more stable regulatory environments, and so are more likely to invest in areas where the tax rates are both stable and low. This is only partially true, though: casino development emerges where substantial populations, both residential and tourist, can be captured easily by the industry. Riverboats move to areas that are both more populous and also have more desirable tax rates; casinos are built near large markets as long as the tax rate is within reason and the profit potential is agreeable. The effects of tax rate increases are never isolated.

The third lesson learned from the gaming tax adjustments draws from the second: effects of local actions extend beyond the immediate borders of the local community. The adjustment of second-year gaming tax rates, in concert with other community conditions and industry expansion at the end of the first gaming year, may have redirected a small portion of Colorado casino investment to other places in the United States. Owners and managers said in interviews that they would rather invest in more stable and inviting markets, such as those offered by states promoting riverboat gaming, than extend operations in Colorado. There were also unconfirmed reports that other states used the Colorado situation in a marketing ploy to entice investors away from Colorado. With the increasing development of gaming across the United States, such competitive actions are likely to become more common in the future.

Had the first-year tax rates been slightly higher, the rapid introduction and expansion of large casinos would likely have been slowed, thus allowing smaller establishments to gain a stronger foothold. It is clear in hindsight that the gaming commission did not "kill" the industry with the second-year tax assessments, even though the rates were increased for casinos earning more than $1 million in adjusted gross proceeds. The manipulation of the tax rates, however, did widen the gap between large and small casinos in the second year. Subsequent adjustment in the third gaming year indicates that not only did most of the existing Colorado casinos earn more than $1 million in AGP (and a substantial number earned more than $2 million and $3 million), but also that the commission probably erred in setting rates far too low for the first year, and far too widely apart for the second gaming year. The outcry over the 20 percent tax rate, and the perception that the gaming commission was taking advantage of medium-sized casinos, makes it unlikely that gaming tax rates in Colorado will ever reach the 20 percent rate again. They almost certainly will never approach the 40 percent rate suggested by early promoters of the gambling initiative.[1]

CASINOS AND DEVICES

On October 1, 1991, a total of seven casinos were open for business in Central City and Black Hawk; four others greeted Opening Day in Cripple Creek, Colorado's third gaming town. By the end of that month, twenty-one casinos had opened across the three Colorado gaming towns; eleven of these were located in the two Gilpin County towns. Casinos continued to open throughout the remainder of the first year of gambling and also throughout subsequent years. The largest increase in numbers of operating casinos occurred in summer 1992, during the first gaming year. By June of that year, Colorado boasted fifty-six casinos across its three mountain gaming towns, and thirty-three of these casinos were in Central City and Black Hawk. At the end of the first summer of limited stakes gambling, more than seventy casinos (including more than forty in the two Gilpin County towns) were open in Colorado. Table 5.2 illustrates the growth patterns of the Colorado, Black Hawk, and Central City casinos over the first four years of gaming operations.

As increasing numbers of casinos opened, the total number of gaming devices (slot machines, video poker games, and blackjack and poker table games) also rose dramatically, climbing from about 2,000 across three gaming towns in the opening month to a second-year average near 11,000 for the state (Table 5.2). This occurred even though casinos are required to pay an annual device fee to the state Division of Gaming for each slot machine or table game in their businesses. The fees were initially set at $100 per device, but were reduced to $75 per device in 1994 (Colorado Division of Gaming 1993, 1994, and 1995). These fees are in addition to other fees assessed at the local level.

Central City and Black Hawk consistently accounted for about two-thirds of all casinos and all gaming devices in Colorado, although the data show a shift in positioning between the two towns over time. Initially, Central City led Colorado's gaming towns in numbers of casinos and devices. Black Hawk and Central City contended for the top position until winter 1992, when Central City enacted a moratorium on new development in order to address problems associated with the rapid growth. Black Hawk subsequently pulled ahead of Central City and Cripple Creek, increasing its lead substantially by early 1994.

These data illustrate the growth of the Colorado gaming industry, but neglect to show casino failures. The Colorado Division of Gaming's 1993 and 1994 *Fact Books* show that a total of 105 casinos opened in Colorado between 1991 and 1994. A total of 26 casinos began operations in 1991, 58 opened in 1992, 13 opened in 1993, and 8 opened between January 1 and December 15, 1994. During the same time period, 46 casinos closed (21 casinos in 1992, 17 in 1993, and 8 in 1994). Across three gaming years, a total of 29 openings and subsequent closures occurred in the towns of Central City and Black Hawk, with the remaining 17 in Cripple Creek. Because some of the closed casinos were later reorganized and reopened under new management, the same building in a town might contain several different casinos operating under different licenses at different times.

Table 5.2   Numbers of Casinos and Devices: State of Colorado and Gilpin County Towns, 1991–1995

	October 1991–September 1992						October 1992–September 1993					
	Colorado		Black Hawk		Central City		Colorado		Black Hawk		Central City	
	Casinos/ Devices		Casinos/ Devices		Casinos/ Devices		Casinos/ Devices		Casinos/ Devices		Casinos/ Devices	
Oct	21	1,920	4	448	7	696	75	11,578	19	3,282	23	4,029
Nov	25	2,237	4	455	10	912	76	11,587	20	3,247	23	4,167
Dec	27	2,497	4	455	10	937	70	11,030	21	3,276	21	3,976
Jan	32	2,868	7	733	12	1,045	63	10,027	19	3,183	18	3,526
Feb	34	3,467	8	811	13	1,559	64	9,774	20	3,276	18	3,394
Mar	35	3,578	9	906	13	1,563	64	9,812	20	3,301	18	3,407
Apr	38	3,809	9	912	14	1,612	66	10,246	22	3,600	18	3,429
May	43	4,759	11	1,106	15	2,105	69	11,316	22	3,563	19	4,010
Jun	56	7,202	15	1,701	18	2,883	67	10,952	20	3,347	18	3,732
Jul	68	10,525	17	2,556	22	4,093	65	11,070	21	3,838	16	3,404
Aug	72	11,447	16	2,676	25	4,363	64	10,819	21	3,792	15	3,165
Sep	76	12,001	18	3,004	25	4,347	63	10,684	21	3,751	15	3,180
Avg[a]	44	5,526	10	1,314	15	2,176	67	10,741	21	3,455	19	3,618

For the state as a whole, more than 40 percent (43.8 percent) of casinos closed at some point after their opening. In the individual gaming towns, Black Hawk had the best ratio of openings to closings: only 36.7 percent of all Black Hawk casinos closed within three years of opening. Cripple Creek had a 42.5 percent closure rate, whereas Central City saw more than half of its casinos (51.4 percent) close during the first three years of operations. Across the state, the highest closure rate was in 1992.

Small casinos, especially those that opened in the earliest months of the industry, were more likely to close than others. For example, by December 1992, fifteen casinos had closed. Many of these were in Central City: the Miner's Pick employed only 32 people and had 55 slot machines and 4 card tables; the Red Horse casino had 135 devices, but closed only 16 days after it opened; Molly's Casino had only 40 slot machines. The largest closure was the poorly located Silver Hawk in Black Hawk, with 243 slot machines; it closed in November 1992. Several other casinos closed in January 1993 to avoid paying taxes and device fees during the slower winter tourist season. Smaller casinos were especially vulnerable to tax increases, but they also had fewer financial reserves and less organizational capacity to compete against the larger casinos that opened after 1992.

Business failures were blamed on a host of problems. Investors were said to have had false expectations stemming from the euphoria of overwhelming returns in the first months of gambling activity, when demand was high but

Table 5.2 (*Continued*) Numbers of Casinos and Devices: State of Colorado and Gilpin County Towns, 1991–1995

	October 1993–September 1994						October 1994–September 1995					
	Colorado		Black Hawk		Central City		Colorado		Black Hawk		Central City	
	Casinos/ Devices		Casinos/ Devices		Casinos/ Devices		Casinos/ Devices		Casinos/ Devices		Casinos/ Devices	
Oct	62	10,336	21	3,693	14	3,127	58	11,498	20	4,561	16	3,458
Nov	63	10,326	21	3,681	15	3,154	58	11,318	19	4,363	16	3,381
Dec	65	11,445	23	4,779	16	3,181	59	12,359	19	4,334	17	4,403
Jan	60	11,020	22	4,624	15	3,109	57	12,152	19	4,395	15	4,229
Feb	59	11,067	21	4,631	15	3,134	58	12,555	19	4,566	15	4,235
Mar	58	11,009	20	4,459	15	3,185	56	12,243	19	4,567	13	3,923
Apr	59	11,067	20	4,508	15	3,086	57	12,406	19	4,660	13	3,930
May	60	11,349	20	4,625	16	3,184	59	13,126	20	5,040	14	4,112
Jun	61	11,460	21	4,738	16	3,178	59	13,003	20	5,049	14	3,982
Jul	62	11,623	20	4,621	16	3,253	60	13,169	20	5,066	14	4,003
Aug	61	11,634	20	4,647	15	3,205	59	13,049	19	4,959	14	3,949
Sep	60	11,510	20	4,613	15	3,218	59	13,055	19	4,992	14	3,936
Avg[a]	61	11,154	21	4,468	15	3,167	58	12,494	19	4,713	15	3,962

Source: Colorado Division of Gaming
[a]Average number of casinos and devices per gaming year.

the supply of casinos low. The Colorado gaming industry had overbuilt in the first year, when casinos and devices reached their highest numbers, and the earnings per device declined precipitously. According to industry analysts, the first lucrative year of gaming had seen casinos receiving about double the industry average for returns on gaming devices.

Experiencing the effects of increased competition, many of the smaller casinos attempted temporary downsizing by reducing the number of gaming devices (thus reducing rental and tax payments on the machines), limiting hours of operation, and laying off employees for the slower winter season. In most cases, these strategies failed. Other casino owners blamed their more unfortunate colleagues for poor management, though inadequate capitalization of smaller casino companies combined with increased competition from larger casinos was a more objective assessment. Those whose businesses failed blamed traffic delays on local highways, a shortage of parking space in Central City, competition, excessive tax rates levied by the gaming commission, high rents in the casino districts, and construction cost overruns for their bad luck.

The casinos that remained in operation following the 1992 industry belt-tightening were generally larger than those visible in the first year of operation, and new casinos planned beyond 1993 were more on the order of casino/hotel resorts than Mom-and-Pop establishments. For example, the Central City and Black Hawk Bullwhackers casinos together had more than 1,200 devices in 1992; the opening of Harvey's in Central City in 1994 added about 1,000 gaming devices along with 118 hotel rooms and 180 underground parking spaces. In addition to the large selection of gambling devices, the mega-casinos provided restaurants, shows, and entertainments, gifts and bonus coupons for patrons, and an array of publicity that drew visitors to their doors and kept them inside the premises. Large casinos also had the financial ability to take out full-page advertisements in metropolitan area newspapers, produce television and radio commercials, buy billboard space in Denver and along Interstate 70, and distribute casino newsletters and magazines featuring stories about jackpot winners and company expansion plans. Even more effective were the casino shuttle buses that drove gamblers from metropolitan area locations directly to the front door of the casino, while the buses served as movable advertisements for the casinos.

As the first four years of the Colorado gaming industry came to a close, the local industry trend was away from many small casinos and toward mega-casinos that combined hotel, parking, entertainment, and gambling opportunities. Black Hawk had emerged as the leader in numbers of casinos and devices, and industry spokespersons saw a bright future for converting that town's Main Street into "a world famous strip . . . the central point for gaming in Colorado" (*Rocky Mountain News*, Sept. 24, 1992: 52). By June 1994, the Boulder, Colorado, firm that owned the Gilpin Hotel Casino in Black Hawk proposed to build a "New Gilpin Hotel Casino and Mining Exposition" resort across the street from the original casino (*Boulder Daily Camera*, June 3, 1994: 12A). That project, which would include 70,000 square feet of gaming space, 125 hotel rooms, restaurants, parking, and a conference center, would be the largest casino resort in Colorado if approved by regulatory agencies. The proposed site was the pre-gaming location of the Black Hawk trailer court; the elderly residents who had lived there had all moved away.

Table 5.3   Adjusted Gross Proceeds by Quarter: Colorado and Gilpin County Gaming Towns, 1991–1995 ($)

	October 1991–September 1992			October 1992–September 1993		
	Colorado	Black Hawk	Central City	Colorado	Black Hawk	Central City
Oct–Dec	23,128,786	6,650,614	10,547,705	47,571,740	18,430,449	16,176,015
Jan–Mar	31,595,201	10,230,005	12,917,378	54,522,562	23,325,105	17,789,842
Apr–Jun	41,594,671	11,084,267	18,236,824	65,117,600	26,407,200	21,400,020
Jul–Sep	59,317,021	16,455,906	24,033,923	76,967,397	31,828,788	22,539,388
Total	155,635,679	44,330,792	65,735,830	244,179,299	99,991,542	77,905,265

GAMING REVENUES AND TAXES

If one could survive the pitfalls, there were substantial profits to be made in the Colorado casino business. Indeed, early economic returns exceeded all predictions. Table 5.3 shows that adjusted gross proceeds (AGP) for the state of Colorado as a whole increased dramatically in each year of operation, from more than $155 million in the first gaming year to more than $371 million after the 1994–1995 gaming year. The casino industry exhibited steady gains for each quarter of the year, though adjusted gross proceeds tend to peak in the summer months and decline in the fall and winter months of each year. Across the state, however, each subsequent season produced even higher revenues than the previous year's comparable season. In Black Hawk, with the exception of fall 1994 and winter 1995, a pattern of generally increasing revenues from each quarter to the next, and tremendous gains between October 1991 and September 1995, has been the norm. Central City initially saw very large increases in adjusted gross proceeds in the first year of gaming operations, but the promise of early growth was not maintained, and returns fell to a much lower rate in subsequent years. By 1995, though, revenues exhibited large gains once more, though Central City's contributions to statewide AGP has fallen to about half that of neighboring Black Hawk.

Statewide increases in adjusted gross proceeds have provided substantial gaming taxes accruing to the state for distribution according to the Limited Gaming Act formula. Table 5.4 shows that as adjusted gross proceeds rose, gaming taxes paid to the state increased from $17.7 million in the first operating year to about $45 million by the end of the fourth gaming year. The casinos in Central City and Black Hawk, located closest to the Denver metropolitan area, account for about 75 to 80 percent of all revenues and taxes; Cripple Creek casinos provide the remainder. Because tax rate changes become effective each October, collected taxes sometimes show wide variation for that quarter.

With gaming tax monies far greater than expected, distributions from the Limited Gaming Fund have been extremely generous (Table 5.5).

Table 5.3 *(Continuied)*Adjusted Gross Proceeds by Quarter: Colorado and Gilpin County Gaming Towns, 1991–1995 ($)

	October 1993–September 1994			October 1994–September 1995		
	Colorado	Black Hawk	Central City	Colorado	Black Hawk	Central City
Oct–Dec	63,233,125	30,579,329	17,284,557	81,334,321	43,313,132	18,436,820
Jan–Mar	72,033,024	38,756,466	16,544,072	87,110,765	43,652,608	23,668,546
Apr–Jun	77,688,899	41,915,040	16,003,302	95,787,853	48,814,778	23,670,219
Jul–Sep	94,628,405	49,718,629	18,717,514	107,211,996	53,106,339	25,887,268
Total	307,583,453	160,969,464	68,549,445	371,444,935	188,886,827	91,662,852

Source: Colorado Division of Gaming, *Gaming in Colorado: Fact Book ad Abstract* (1993, 1994, 1995).

Table 5.4   Gaming Taxes Paid by Quarter: Colorado and Gilpin County Gaming Towns, 1991–1995 ($)

| | October 1991–September 1992 | | | October 1992–September 1993 | | |
	Colorado	Black Hawk	Central City	Colorado	Black Hawk	Central City
Oct–Dec	1,972,945	679,927	935,400	3,763,092	1,808,151	1,492,354
Jan–Mar	3,600,221	1,236,962	1,520,999	8,319,910	3,785,549	2,809,066
Apr–Jun	5,219,237	1,433,819	2,397,866	11,109,532	4,657,054	3,703,674
Jul–Sep	6,934,185	1,905,815	3,075,865	13,863,227	5,619,320	4,328,437
Total	17,726,588	5,256,523	7,930,130	37,055,761	15,870,074	12,333,531

Across four years of Colorado gaming, the total revenues, fees, and fines deposited in the Limited Gaming Fund have exceeded $147.7 million. Subtracting operating expenses and escrow required to administer the gaming program, the fund has distributed, over four years, a total of $119 million to various accounts. The amount distributed has grown rapidly: more than $9.1 million was distributed after the first year of gaming, nearly $30.5 million was distributed in 1993, more than $37.7 million was distributed in 1994, and about $41.7 million was distributed in 1995. Historic preservation in particular has profited significantly from the gaming revenues, as more than $33.3 million has been granted to the State Historical Society for improving historic properties and funding projects related to historic preservation. Several hundred projects have already been funded across the state, with projects chosen in competitive proposal review processes. Projects have included preservation planning, repair and restoration work, and survey and evaluations for identified historic properties.

Each gaming town government, and each participating county, has also received substantial amounts of money from its proportional share of the Limited Gaming Fund. Black Hawk has gained $5,380,030 in new revenues, followed by Central City's $3,387,123, and Cripple Creek's $3,093,356. Gilpin and Teller County have also profited, with Gilpin County receiving in excess of $10.5 million and Teller County receiving more than $3.7 million. These new revenues are in addition to revenues from other taxes levied by the gaming towns on casinos, including device fees and parking and impact assessments. Because the Limited Gaming Fund monies are distributed only after a gaming year concludes, distributions to Gilpin and Teller Counties are made only after some gambling-related impacts are felt. Unlike the gaming towns, the counties do not receive any locally generated income from device, parking, or other impact assessments placed on casinos.[2]

Table 5.4 (*Continued*) Gaming Taxes Paid by Quarter: Colorado and Gilpin County Gaming Towns, 1991–1995 ($)

	October 1993–September 1994			October 1994–September 1995		
	Colorado	Black Hawk	Central City	Colorado	Black Hawk	Central City
Oct–Dec	4,227,805	2,639,815	1,058,996	4,683,998	3,604,202	571,385
Jan–Mar	9,614,979	5,633,453	2,281,468	10,523,886	6,281,394	2,828,425
Apr–Jun	12,147,806	7,014,088	2,514,786	13,568,149	7,620,881	3,428,541
Jul–Sep	15,208,199	8,587,402	2,974,393	16,382,207	8,637,141	4,118,624
Total	41,198,789	23,874,758	8,829,643	45,158,240	26,143,618	10,946,977

Source: Colorado Division of Gaming, *Gaming in Colorado: Fact Book ad Abstract* (1993, 1994, 1995).

The revenue and tax data illustrate the benefits of advantageous location and a relatively permissive development agenda. Black Hawk's position as the gateway to Gregory Gulch, the one-mile-long road that leads to Central City, has rewarded that town with a superior location for attracting passing gamblers. The extensive development of extremely large casinos along Black Hawk's previously undeveloped and unpaved Main Street, along with the visible parking lots near casino entrances, provides visitors with visual information that casinos and parking are readily accessible. In addition, the relaxed and generous approach to town redevelopment—Black Hawk had few commercial historic structures to preserve, and the preservation guidelines were not rigorously enforced—led to a very desirable climate for gaming industry investment and expansion. As a result, the Black Hawk casinos have produced the highest revenues and taxes among the three Colorado gaming communities.

When Black Hawk surged ahead of Central City during the winter of 1992, some Central City entrepreneurs blamed the Denver media for spreading rumors that there was little parking in Central City. News articles and letters to the editor in the *Weekly Register-Call*, however, consistently reported that even local residents felt that parking was one of the most serious issues related to gambling development in Central City. In response to their loss of relative advantage, Central City casino owners developed a broad marketing campaign designed to inform visitors that Central City is a different town from Black Hawk, that casino parking is convenient, and that an exciting tourist experience can be had by visiting Central City casinos. The messages are not always accurate ("Keep going two miles past Black Hawk up the canyon," announced one radio message in 1993, although the distance is barely a mile), but the efforts are certainly more focused.

Table 5.5   Distribution of Limited Gaming Fund Monies, 1992–1994 ($)

	Fiscal Year 1992[a]	Fiscal Year 1993	Fiscal Year 1994	Fiscal Year 1995
Expenses, Escrow, Carryover	4,343,877	5,066,927	6,078,451	9,711,699
General Fund	4,114,136	13,424,676	16,558,799	17,013,267
Contiguous Counties	425,000	1,754,059	1,895,234	2,325,995
Tourism Promotion Fund	18,229	60,959	37,738[b]	83,345
State Historical Fund	2,552,124	8,534,228	10,566,724	11,688,347
County Governments	Total: 1,093,768	Total: 3,657,526	Total: 4,528,596	Total: 5,000,721
	Gilpin: 790,095	Gilpin: 2,648,049	Gilpin: 3,365,200	Gilpin: 3,765,606
	Teller: 303,673	Teller: 1,009,447	Teller: 1,163,396	Teller: 1,235,115
Gaming Town Governments	Total: 911,473	Total: 3,047,939	Total: 3,773,830	Total: 4,167,267
	Black Hawk: 263,783	Black Hawk: 1,138,405	Black Hawk: 1,862,385	Black Hawk: 2,115,457
	Central City: 394,629	Central City: 1,067,998	Central City: 941,948	Central City: 982,548
	Cripple Creek: 253,061	Cripple Creek: 842,536	Cripple Creek: 969,497	Cripple Creek: 1,029,262
Municipal Impact Fund[c]			377,423	416,727
CO. Dept of Transportation[d]				997,000
Total Funds Distributed	13,458,607	35,546,314	43,816,751	49,054,641

Source: Colorado Division of Gaming, Gaming in *Colorado: Fact Book and Abstract* (1993, 1994, and 1995).

[a]Gaming funds accounting occurs on a fiscal year basis (July 1 to June 30), not on a gaming year basis (October 1 to September 30), so totals do not match gaming tax totals in Table 5.4. Moreover, Limited Gaming Fund monies include not only tax revenues, but also application and licensing fees and fines.

[b]The proportion of monies deposited in the Tourism Promotion Fund was affected by a technical error. See the 1994 Fact Book.

[c]A portion of the revenue in the Contiguous County Impact Fund was dedicated for a "Municipal Impact Fund" for Woodland Park and Victor, CO, in 1994; the 1994 Fact Book shows discrepancies for this total. The figure closest to the reported Total Limited Gaming Fund revenues was used above.

[d]A portion of the revenue in the Contiguous County Impact Fund was designated for the Colorado Department of Transportation in the 1995 gaming year.

GAMING TOURISTS: TRAFFIC INCREASES

For local residents, a direct consequence of casino development was a rapid increase in the number of vehicles and tourists visiting the communities. A month-by-month comparison of traffic counts over the first four years of gaming is given in Table 5.6.

The volume of vehicles passing over two traffic counter points in Gilpin County is recorded by the State Transportation Department. The first counter, located south of Black Hawk along Highway 119 just north of Highway 6 (Clear Creek Canyon), records daily traffic volume entering Gilpin County from Interstate 70 and Clear Creek Canyon roads. The second counter is situated north of the gaming towns, and counts traffic volume from canyons leading to Boulder and Jefferson Counties, and from Nederland, Boulder, and Estes Park along the portion of Highway 119 known as the Peak-to-Peak Scenic Highway.

Prior to gaming development, little traffic passed the counter at Highways 119 and 6. The annual average for daily traffic in 1986 and 1988 was estimated by the Colorado Department of Transportation at only 2,900 cars. The average rose slightly over the next several years, but had increased to only 3,050 cars by 1990. At the start of gaming, the department began to release data for monthly averages of daily traffic at the two counter locations. These numbers show a rapid and continuing increase in traffic volume throughout the first few years of gaming development.

Several trends can be noted from the traffic data. Most visitors approach the Gilpin County gaming towns from the primary southern access routes of Interstate 70 and Colorado Highway 6, which lead into the Denver and Golden metropolitan areas. Traffic volume has continually increased since the start of gaming operations, even during the winter months that had much lighter volumes at the beginning of gaming development. Further, traffic is not just increasing overall: it is rapidly increasing in the summer months, and also spreading out into the "shoulder seasons" of spring and fall. Reading across the rows or down the columns in Table 5.6, it is clear that traffic totals in each month of each year are being overtaken by even larger numbers in subsequent years.

Increases in traffic volume result from heavier use of the roads by gamblers travelling in private automobiles, but other factors also affect traffic volumes. Bus tours to the gaming towns are popular for both metropolitan-area and out-of-state residents, and some companies make regular runs on a weekly or daily basis. Additionally, because there is limited housing available in Gilpin County, many casino employees commute to work by car or bus from counties closer to the metropolitan area, thus increasing the traffic load on the roads

Table 5.6   Gilpin County Traffic Volume: Number of Vehicles at Two Counter Points[a]

| | Highway 119 North of Highway 6 | | | |
	1991–1992	1992–1993	1993–1994	1994–1995
Oct	8,712	11,862	12,049	13,989
Nov	6,283	9,010	9,935	12,911
Dec	6,912	8,428	11,070	13,241
Jan	7,294	9,675	12,113	13,523
Feb	9,056	9,762	12,375	13,069
Mar	8,808	10,842	12,544	13,507
Apr	9,385	10,964	12,600	13,401
May	10,597	12,342	13,826	14,286
Jun	12,510	13,025	14,422	15,198
Jul	14,654	15,311	16,755	17,667
Aug	14,450	14,484	(15,558)[b]	16,471
Sep	13,074	13,367	(15,506)[b]	14,755
Avg[c]	10,145	11,589	13,231	14,335

| | Highway 119 South of Highway 72 | | | |
	1991–1992	1992–1993	1993–1994	1994–1995
Oct	2,233	2,316	2,423	2,494
Nov	1,493	1,638	1,761	1,992
Dec	1,598	1,575	1,798	2,050
Jan	1,613	1,677	1,833	2,055
Feb	1,790	1,674	1,928	2,068
Mar	1,641	1,771	1,960	2,118
Apr	1,857	1,800	1,917	1,994
May	2,262	2,213	2,595	2,356
Jun	2,776	2,738	2,964	3,083
Jul	3,355	3,388	3,723	3,930
Aug	3,302	3,238	3,369	3,634
Sep	3,180	3,300	3,506	3,158
Avg[c]	2,258	2,277	2,481	2,578

Source: Colorado Department of Transportation.

[a]These data are monthly averages of average daily traffic. Prior to the development of gaming, the Department of Transportation reported annual averages for daily traffic. For 1986, 1988, and 1990, these were, respectively, 2,900, 2,900, and 3,050 vehicles.

[b]The traffic counter at this location failed in August and was repaired in mid-September 1994. The totals for those two months are estimates.

[c]Average number of vehicles crossing counter location per gaming year.

leading to Gilpin County. Added pressures on the main roads and other secondary canyon roads have affected the habits of local residents, who complain that traffic has reached unreasonable proportions at all hours of the day and night. Lending support to their claims is the increase in accidents and road emergency situations since the beginning of gaming. Nearby cities, especially Golden and Boulder, have borne much of the expense of police patrol, accident and emergency response, and rescue operations in the canyons leading to the gaming towns (*Denver Post,* June 15, 1992).

The number of gamblers visiting Black Hawk and Central City is not known, according to the Gilpin County Chamber of Commerce, nor are data available regarding the proportions of gambling visitors from outside the state. As Eadington (1976: 53) noted, though, "for casino gambling to be economically successful, it needs to draw tourists as its main customers." Tourists provide "new" monies to the local and state economy, whereas the quarters and dollars spent by residents recirculate monies that might otherwise be spent on other types of entertainments. A 1995 study suggested that the mountain town casinos were enticing at least a portion of Colorado tourists, because casinos were identified as the third most popular Colorado attraction for out-of-state tourists and conventioneers in 1993 (Center for Business and Economic Forecasting, Inc. 1995). Central City and Black Hawk were traditionally tourist places, so it is probable that they hold equal fascination among some groups now that gaming has emerged. The difficulties of access to the towns, though, including increased traffic volume and the lack of free parking, have been well documented in the media since gaming began, and at least some former visitors refuse to return to the towns, either because of perceived difficulty in getting there or because they disapprove of gambling. There remains a need for more detailed research about who gambles in Colorado.

CASINO MANAGEMENT AND OWNERSHIP

In the initial years of gaming operations, about three-fourths of all casino owners in Central City and Black Hawk were from outside Gilpin County. About half of those external owners were entrepreneurs from the Denver metropolitan area, and the other half were owners and investors residing out-of-state. Metropolitan-area owners and financiers included those with interests in automobile dealerships, real estate, sports, hotels and restaurants, radio and television stations, and other businesses. The earliest out-of-state investors were primarily real estate, resort, or hotel developers from California and Nevada. The first foreign corporation to become involved in the Colorado casino industry was Tivolino, a Swiss company that leased the Teller House from the Central City Opera House Association. Other foreign firms subsequently expressed interest, and by 1995 large gaming companies, such as Harrah's and Caesar's Palace, were staking a presence in the local area.

By the end of four years of Colorado gaming, it is evident that few small casino operators can compete with the large gaming corporations now present in the local area. The smaller casinos that remain viable in the Gilpin County gaming towns are those in which the entrepreneurs have substantial personal financial reserves, other sources of income, ownership of their buildings, and lean gaming operations. The success of larger companies and the decline of smaller gaming halls has reduced diversity and contributed to a more sophisticated, standardized, local gambling experience.

There is increasing evidence of strong ties linking Colorado gaming entrepreneurs with other national gaming ventures. Some of the external owners entered the Colorado market with existing interests in other gaming locales, such as Mississippi riverboats, Nevada casinos, and South Dakota gaming ventures. For example, Virginia Lewis, owner of the Gold Mine casino in Black Hawk, previously operated a casino on a South Dakota Indian reservation. Others have used their Colorado gaming experience as a springboard for involvement in gaming projects in other parts of the country. Bullwhackers Central City and Bullwhackers Black Hawk are managed by Hemmeter Partnerships, a hotel and resort conglomerate known for its resort properties in Hawaii. After the opening of the two Bullwhackers casinos, the company transferred the corporate headquarters from Los Angeles to Golden, Colorado, to oversee the local casino businesses and to facilitate expansion to other gaming sites across the United States. This company has recently been active in Mississippi riverboat gambling and in the conglomerate associated with the forthcoming New Orleans mega-casino. Harrah's, which owns casinos in Atlantic City, New Jersey, and Nevada, and operates riverboat casinos along the Mississippi River, bought an interest in Central City's Glory Hole casino in December 1993, and opened a large casino in Black Hawk that same month (*Denver Post*, Dec. 22, 1993). Another company, owned by Merv Griffin, the television entertainer and New Jersey hotel/casino operator, took on a managing role in Lilly Belle's casino in Black Hawk. After operating only a few weeks, that casino was closed by the State Gaming Commission because the owner had apparently failed to disclose critical information during the licensing process (*Denver Post*, Feb. 18, 1994).

Although casino industry representatives were invisible during the gambling campaign, they developed a strong and powerful presence in the gaming towns after the passage of Amendment 4. By early winter 1992, independent casino owners' associations had formed in each of the three Colorado gaming towns to coordinate local marketing and promotional efforts and present a united front in state lobbying. A single Colorado gaming owners' association was attempted but was short-lived; resistance to collaboration was strong, as each gaming town considered the others to be competitors for gamblers' dollars.

A survey of Gilpin County organizations (Stokowski 1993a) revealed that, by spring 1993, the casino owners' associations were seen by other local organizations in Black Hawk, Central City, and Gilpin County as influential participants in community discussions. Respondents felt that local governments, the school district, and the casino associations had substantial power in influencing community direction. When asked to identify the Gilpin County organizations with which their organizations were most closely linked, the three most-cited groups were the Gilpin County government and the Black Hawk and Central City casino owners' associations.

As casino owners became more powerful through organization, individual gaming owners worked to strengthen ties with local governmental leaders. Interviews with community leaders in 1992 revealed that linkages between Black Hawk government leaders and Black Hawk casino owners, and between Central City government leaders and Central City casino owners, were described as much stronger than existing linkages between Central City and Black Hawk government leaders. The new relationships with casino owners were partly the result of increased interaction between local government leaders and casino developers, as local regulations were created and enforced. At least in Central City, though, the close connections between casino owners and local government officials raised concern among residents, who worried about a "slippage" of community responsibility (Freudenburg and Gramling 1994a; 1994c) among government leaders.

In addition to their other roles, the local casino owners' associations were the primary mechanism by which the gaming industry lobbied against the expansion of Colorado gambling in 1992 and later. Casino owners in Black Hawk, Central City, and Cripple Creek contributed substantial campaign sums to the anti-gambling movement in an effort to preserve their monopoly. The coordinator of the industry group explained the position of the industry, stating at the end of the first gaming year, "this [is] a perilous time for the casinos in the three towns" (*Rocky Mountain News,* Sept. 27, 1992: 120). In the same article, a Central City casino executive was quoted as saying, "The revenue possibilities of limited gambling are limited." Reports from the Division of Gaming, noting huge gains in wagers, revenues, and gaming taxes, when juxtaposed against the doomsday rhetoric of gaming owners, served as a counterpoint to the industry perspective and alerted Colorado citizens that the casino owners' claims were somewhat less than true. The strategy was clear, though:

casino owners, particularly those with the largest casinos, could not afford to let the gaming commission know how well they were doing, or taxes might be raised. Likewise, they could not afford to let the public or competitors know if business declined, because gamblers might go to other establishments and competitors might take advantage during unstable times.

CASINO EMPLOYMENT

Employees who work in the Colorado gaming industry must be licensed by the Division of Gaming. A variety of licenses are offered based on type of participation in the industry (device manufacturer or distributor, casino owner or manager, key and support employees), and each requires different application processes and investigations. The required application and licensing fees for casinos jobs range from $100 for a support license (nonmanagerial positions in casinos) to $150 for licenses for "key" personnel (managers and owners), who also must pay a one-time $1,000 background check fee.

In June of each year, the Division of Gaming conducts a survey of casino employees working in the Colorado gaming industry. This survey is used to help determine distribution schedules for a portion of the Contiguous County Impact Fund monies, which are drawn from casino tax revenues. Table 5.7 compares the residence reports of casino employees over the first four years of Colorado's gaming industry. As these data show, Central City and Black Hawk casino employment has remained relatively stable across the period, with about two-thirds (66.9 to 68.6 percent) of all Colorado casino employees working in the two Gilpin County towns. Although the real number of Gilpin County residents employed in casinos has increased from 312 to 522 over the same period, the relative proportion of Gilpin County residents to all state casino employees has increased only slightly. In fact, Gilpin County residents accounted for only about 10 percent to 12 percent of all persons employed in Gilpin County casinos between October 1, 1991, and 1995. Most Gilpin County casino workers live in adjacent Denver, Jefferson, Boulder, Clear Creek, and Grand counties. According to the 1994 report, only two persons from Teller County, fourteen from Park County, two from El Paso County, and twelve from Douglas County reported working in the Central City or Black Hawk casinos. No Gilpin County residents were reported that year to be working in Cripple Creek casinos.

Table 5.7 Casino Employee Residence Reports

	July 1, 1992	July 1, 1993	July 1, 1994	July 1, 1995
Total Colorado Casino Employees	4,760	5,101	5,343	6,450
Working in Gilpin County casinos	3,184	3,499	3,654	4,337
	66.9%	68.6%	68.4%	67.2%
Working in Teller County casinos	1,576	1,602	1,689	2,113
	33.1%	31.4%	31.6%	32.8%
Casino Employees Living in Gilpin and Contiguous Counties				
Gilpin County	312	398	448	522
Clear Creek County	243	231	247	273
Boulder County	153	141	144	176
Grand County	1	0	2	2
Jefferson County	1,205	1,476	1,736	2,049
Other counties, including Denver	1,219	1,258	1,079	1,329
Total	3,133	3,504	3,656	4,351
% Gilpin County casino employees who reside in Gilpin County	9.8%	11.4%	12.3%	12.0%
Casino Employees Living in Teller and Contiguous Counties				
Teller County	948	984	1,185	1,444
Douglas County	48	13	16	18
El Paso County	566	520	391	473
Fremont County	48	21	34	69
Park County	17	59	61	95
Total	1,627	1,597	1,687	2,099
% Teller County casino employees who reside in Teller County	60.2%	61.4%	70.2%	68.3%

Source: State of Colorado, Division of Gaming, "Contiguous County Employee Survey."

Because such a small proportion of Black Hawk and Central City casino employees live in Gilpin County, many ride shuttle buses to work or drive in private vehicles. Employee transport is subsidized by the casinos, but other benefits, such as health insurance or sick leave, are often provided only for employees who have passed a half-year probationary period. For many casino service positions, wages are higher than minimum but not extravagant; the average is about $6.00 to $7.00 an hour, with tips providing extra income. Although the casino developments did little to reduce the large numbers of Gilpin County residents who commute to professional jobs in Denver, Boulder, and other metropolitan cities, some marginally employed local residents took part- or full-time casino jobs because their former service or laborer positions were "boring." As one said in an interview, "It's exciting to work in the casinos." In addition to the entertainment value of these jobs, wages are better than alternative work as janitors, bus drivers, or waiters outside the casino industry, and the work is not seasonal.

INDUSTRY ISSUES

Although revenues, taxes, tourists, and employment far exceeded all growth expectations, the development of gaming also stimulated community outrage over the lack of correspondence between the original intentions of the gaming initiative and the actual outcomes of development. According to gaming proponents, the blame for the discontinuity could be traced directly to the gaming commission's interpretation of the 35/50 percent rule. As written in the legislation, "no more than thirty-five percent of the square footage of any building and no more than fifty percent of any one floor of such building" can be used for gaming (Article 18, Section 9: 3(c)). The inclusion of this rule was in response to the Deadwood, South Dakota, law that limited casinos to thirty gaming devices per building—an effort that produced many creative attempts at redefining the concept of a *building*. Could the second story of a structure be considered a separate building if there was an outside staircase leading to it? Could an internal partition be used to divide a single structure into two smaller ones, thus creating two buildings? Colorado campaign organizers believed that their legislative refinements would avoid these problems, place a reasonable limit on gaming devices, and also encourage casino owners to maintain retail business space in buildings.

When casinos with hundreds of gaming devices began to appear, though, local CCPI organizers (many of whom, by then, had opened or invested in small casinos) charged that the State Gaming Commission had reinterpreted the 35/50 percent rule. As a local person who also owned a small casino explained in a 1992 letter to the commission, "The apparent enforcement policy of the [Gaming Commission] provides that only the device and place where one sits or stands to play that device is considered gaming area.... [T]he aisles between and passing through the gaming devices are not considered to be gaming" (Grimes 1992). In other words, aisles, walls, change booths, attics, kitchens, and casino merchandise counters, all without devices, could be defined as nongambling spaces. With this interpretation, proportionally more space of each floor and building could be given to gambling devices, which earn more money for the owner than postcards, trinkets, and souvenirs. Such selective measurement gave the appearance that entire floors of buildings were devoted to gaming devices, akin to Las Vegas or Atlantic City casinos.

The practical implications were evident: if a commercial building was to be assessed at the highest and best use—gambling—then it must also be able to devote substantial space to that activity in order to recover as much income from the business as possible.

Complaints about misapplication of the 35/50 percent rule were voiced primarily by the smaller casino owners who were, by the second gaming year, quickly going out of business in the gaming towns. Images of Mom-and-Pop gambling, where a few slot machines in every business would bring economic vitality to the community, were replaced with new images of a serious gaming industry. Local proponents blamed the Gaming Commission for not uphold-ing "their" gambling proposal, but the issue was more complex than that. Had local residents read industry newsletters, though, they would have been fore-warned that members of the Colorado Gaming Owners Association were publicly discussing future industry plans as early as July 1991, three months prior to Opening Day. One newsletter (Colorado Gaming Owners Associa-tion 1991: 2; capitalization and punctuation consistent with original) article read, for example:

> If the Gaming Tax is anywhere above 9%—you will know for certain that those in control do not want to see this industry flourish as a business—but as window dressing to quaint little mountain shops—and they will be out to punish you for coming up with a great idea on how to improve local economies. . . . At this point . . . there are no supporters of the new Gaming Industry in the Governor's office. . . . If you plan on being in the limited gambling business in Colorado you are in the Wilderness. Only with an active and financially strong Association will you have friends to help fight the battles.

In 1993, just two years after limited stakes gambling was initiated in Col-orado, and despite the layoffs and closures by the Colorado casino owners, gaming industry spokespersons proposed that the $5.00 betting limit be raised to allow greater competition and casino development. Higher limits would draw more tourists, allow owners to reinvest and expand their businesses, and create more employment, claimed industry speakers (*Boulder Daily Camera*, Oct. 20, 1993: 6B). Just a year earlier, while blaming the state for allowing casino development to expand beyond what residents had anticipated, former Black Hawk mayor Bill Lorenz had expressed an interest in enlarging his casino, Otto's, to take advantage of the excellent business opportunities asso-ciated with gaming in that town (*Rocky Mountain News*, Aug. 1, 1992: 55).

NOTES

1. This, of course, is not unthinkable: a financial disaster or recession, in which general funds of the state treasury come to depend primarily on gaming tax revenues to make up shortfalls in other revenues, may change the conditions that affect tax rate adjustments. If that situation were to arise, the largest casinos would no doubt attempt to exert political influence by threatening to move their operations to more generous states.

2. This situation is the reverse of that for other kinds of boomtown communities, such as those developing large-scale energy projects. In those communities, the project is situated in the county, so impact mitigation monies are paid to counties, while affected towns suffer problems created by the influx of new residents without having adequate financial resources to cope with new needs. See the discussion about front-end problems in chapter 6.

6

ECONOMIC IMPACTS OF
GAMING DEVELOPMENT

Two bedroom house, drapes and rugs throughout, clean. $300, in Black Hawk.
—*Weekly Register-Call* (Nov. 3, 1989: 7)

IN TOWN: Black Hawk, just off Gregory Street. Immaculate, two bedroom, one bath home. All appliances and fireplace. GARAGE, WASHER, DRYER, CENTRAL! $795.
—*Weekly Register-Call* (Mar. 13, 1992: 5)

The development of the gaming industry in Black Hawk and Central City produced substantial economic, social, and institutional effects. During the first several years after Opening Day, gawkers and gamblers populated the community, while construction crews conjured up new casinos from historic structures or empty space. Charter buses and shuttle vans zipped across the hilly landscape and along mountain roads. "No Parking" signs blossomed along residential and commercial streets, and "pocket parking lots" were tucked into every wide spot along Gregory Gulch and Highway 119. The metallic clinking of coins and the electronic bells and whistles of slot machines echoed across the historic centers of the towns, competing with the continuing noises of construction and traffic.

In 1991, parking fees ranged from $3.00 an hour, for spaces a few steps from casino doors, to $5.00 a day for more distant parking served by shuttle bus. In summer 1992, when demand seemed endless, some parking operators began charging up to $8.00 a day for parking, and several larger casinos instituted valet parking to guarantee that their best patrons would spend more time in the gambling halls and less time on the roads searching for parking spaces. But parking fees varied with the economic fortunes of the community. A downturn in Central City's gaming revenues during the second and third gaming years encouraged casino owners in that town to underwrite parking for visitors. Visitors paid $5.00 to park in a municipal lot, but then received a portion of that amount back in gaming tokens or quarters from participating casinos. This sleight of hand allowed visitors to feel they were getting something free in the process.

A month after Opening Day, a new boardwalk stretched in front of a construction site that would become the Black Hawk Bullwhackers casino. The gas pumps and market previously in that space had been removed, forcing residents and visitors alike to drive eight miles in one direction, or fifteen in the other, to obtain gas. Groceries could be obtained only in adjacent counties. A large brick addition to the Black Forest Inn restaurant had opened as Otto's Casino, and along Gregory Gulch, several old shops were replaced with bulldozed clearings in anticipation of casino construction. Above Central City, the three-level triangle parking lot (a tailings pile dumped on top of Central City's old railroad station when the Glory Hole was mined), which had sold for $5 million in the pre-gambling speculation period, was newly paved and opened for parking.

With so many cars in the parking lots and on the roadways, one also expected to see crowds of people. Instead, the streets were nearly empty. Central City's Main Street had been closed to all private vehicles and redefined as a mall; only pedestrian, shuttle bus, and emergency vehicle traffic were allowed. As there were few benches or seats to encourage leisurely sitting, people clustered on the sidewalks, waiting for the shuttle buses. Large buses and small vans, painted with the logos of casinos or bus companies, then swooped into the designated stops, disgorged gamblers who immediately disappeared into the caverns of the casinos, and whisked others away to their cars. Open doorways gave glimpses of people pulling the "one-armed bandits" lined up in long straight rows inside the casinos, but the views from outside were restricted. Most casinos in Central City had hung voluminous, frilled curtains in their windows, and some gaming halls in Black Hawk had only tiny windows or none at all on the first floor. The Gold Mine casino, for example, has only a few darkened windows that prevent patrons from looking out and passers-by from looking in, a technique often adopted in casino construction.

Proponents claimed that benefits from limited stakes gambling would be significant and widespread, improving the economy and quality of life in the gaming communities and increasing tourism across the state. Economic data from the first several years of gaming operations show that the state of Colorado has received impressive tax benefits; that Black Hawk, Central City, and Gilpin County have obtained considerable revenues; and that economic profits extend to adjacent counties. Other economic gains include increased year-round local employment, reductions in residential property taxes in the gaming towns, and the construction of needed community infrastructure. There have also been economic costs, but because these are more difficult to quantify, they have generally been ignored by evaluators. Considering all economic benefits and costs, however, the 1994 opening of Harvey's, the first large hotel/casino in the area, demonstrated that little remained of the "few slot machines in every small business" image that had been presented by CCPI organizers in the 1990 pro-gambling campaign.

LOCAL BUDGETS: REVENUES AND EXPENDITURES

Gaming development had an immediate impact on the local budgets of Central City and Black Hawk. Town and county governments typically have several fund types from which to draw in managing revenues and expenditures. In Central City, Black Hawk, and Gilpin County, there are two established fund types: Governmental Funds (the largest category of these is usually general funds, but special revenue funds, debt service funds, and, in some cases, capital projects funds are also included under this heading), and Fiduciary Funds (trust accounts that contain expendable interest and nonexpendable principal monies). In addition to Governmental and Fiduciary Funds, the towns and county also have other sources of money, including carryover funds from previous years and transfer funds.

Beginning in 1990, Central City and Black Hawk received substantial new revenue, primarily in the form of local fees assessed on casinos for gaming devices, parking, and other gaming impacts. After the conclusion of each gaming year, the towns also received tax monies from the Limited Gaming Fund proportional to their contributions to that account. As revenues increased, expenditures rose, too. Gaming development meant that the towns needed new water and sewer infrastructure, more skilled administrative employees, and additional governmental services, such as planning. Gilpin County, which cannot tax casinos directly, did not receive immediate gains from gaming development, but eventually received substantial amounts of new revenue through property taxation, sales of county-owned property, and tax distributions from the Limited Gaming Fund. In all three jurisdictions, gaming taxes and other new revenues are deposited in various accounts of the Governmental Funds, depending on the needs of the governing entity, and monies from various funds are used to pay expenses.

Table 6.1 displays longitudinal trends in revenues and expenditures for all fund accounts for each of the governmental entities in Gilpin County. It is evident from this table that the towns and county operated on exceedingly small budgets prior to gaming, and were heavily affected by gaming development. Although total funds show exorbitant increases in revenues and expenditures after gaming was instituted (the gains are on the magnitude of hundreds and thousands of percentage point increases in the two gaming towns), the table also shows that these gains were staggered for towns and county. Black Hawk and Central City experienced initial growth spurts during the 1991 year, when new casinos first provided tax monies and impact fees for local coffers. The towns enjoyed even larger growth rates after 1991, when the industry expanded, larger casinos began to predominate, and early industry stabilization was achieved. Gilpin County, in contrast, saw little financial impact until 1992, when revenues from the sale of county assets and disbursements from the Limited Gaming Fund became available.

Table 6.1   Financial Statements: Black Hawk, Central City, and Gilpin County, Colorado ($)

Black Hawk: All Fund Types		
	Revenues	Expenditures	Fund Balance
1989	138,671	77,162	299,576
1990	127,290	163,708	263,158
1991	773,402	533,470	810,140
1992	5,262,517	5,161,719	500,793
1993	8,221,519	5,588,020	2,268,275
1994	9,970,280	8,184,333	4,152,953

Central City: All Fund Types		
	Revenues	Expenditures	Fund Balance
1989	428,995	323,456	184,292
1990	347,686	331,708	142,570
1991	1,043,189	1,769,885	2,119,787
1992	6,220,389	5,759,504	10,504,676
1993	7,633,279	6,837,280	10,150,674
1994	6,383,481	4,764,301	4,440,061

Gilpin County: All Fund Types		
	Revenues	Expenditures	Fund Balance
1989	1,934,479	1,751,766	813,683
1990	1,971,219	1,962,707	939,796
1991	2,273,370	2,409,113	933,981
1992	3,641,655	3,695,594	1,138,381
1993	10,934,599	4,299,792	7,887,283
1994	6,817,303	13,359,801	6,289,785

Source: Audited financial statements of Black Hawk, Central City, and Gilpin County, Colorado.

The audited financial statements and town budgets provide glimpses of the relationships between the towns and their respective gaming industries. For example, the message from the city manager accompanying Central City's 1994 budget proposal indicated that town administrators were eager to adopt measures supporting gaming industry growth in that town. This brief document read, in part, "In another move aimed at supporting the gaming industry's tenuous economy, the Council has agreed to not increase overall device fee rates" (City of Central 1994: 1), and "[T]he budget is . . . responsive to the needs of our primary industry, gaming. Cuts have been made in several areas to take on a more active role in causing industry growth and ultimate stabilization of City services and resources" (p. 4). In contrast, Black Hawk's 1994 budget message from that town's manager appeared more impartial, considering interests of both gaming businesses and local residents beyond the gaming industry: "With the near completion of gaming development, the advent of second tier development (hotel, retail and housing development) will be pressing. . . . We know we will be able to work with existing residents and businesses as well as with future residents and businesses to successfully keep the historic integrity of the area intact, yet allow for the needs and opportunities of the 21st century to flourish" (City of Black Hawk 1993: 8). Such different positions are a reflection of the divergent fortunes of each town with respect to its individual gaming industry.

BLACK HAWK FINANCES

In preparation for gaming development, the Black Hawk government assessed on each casino operating in that town fees of $800 per gaming device and $2,000 for each allocated parking space.[1] These fees were in addition to state device fees and casino and employee licensing requirements. The impact fees provided the town with revenues to be used for developing local infrastructure and for mitigating problems that gaming might produce. Parking fees, for example, were used to construct a town-owned parking facility that was intended to relieve casinos of the burden of providing their own parking lots. The Miner's Mesa parking area, a four-minute drive up a steep mountain road, and served by shuttle buses to the Black Hawk casinos, opened behind schedule in 1992. The lot, claimed to be the largest private parking facility in Colorado, can currently accommodate 3,000 vehicles, but expansion plans would provide future parking for a total of about 10,000 vehicles. The project has never been a complete success, as casino patrons prefer to park their cars near the gaming halls, and casino managers benefit by marketing their establishments as having close, convenient parking. Moreover, Black Hawk has not restricted the development of other competitive parking lots in the commercial zone of the town, so Miner's Mesa has not received the business it should. Nevertheless, future goals for the site include development of "terraced picnic areas, recreational areas and an entertainment amphitheater to establish the mesa as a concert facility, ideal for headliners" (*Gilpin Gazette*, Apr. 1993: 2).

The Miner's Mesa parking facility above Black Hawk, with spaces for 3,000 vehicles, is said to be the largest parking facility in Colorado.

Table 6.1 shows changes in revenues, expenditures, and fund balances for all fund types used in Black Hawk's governmental accounting between 1989 and 1994. Most gaming revenues were initially deposited in the general fund of governmental revenues, but as gaming revenues increased astronomically, monies were placed in special revenue and debt service funds. The first substantial revenue effects of gaming development in Black Hawk were experienced in 1991, when the town collected more than $546,600 in local device and impact fees from casinos. Licenses, permits, and taxes also showed large gains in 1991, and the town also received $300,000 in revenue by issuing excise tax revenue bonds "to purchase professional and engineering services during preparation of studies and analysis of infrastructure, capital improvements and planning requirements" related to development of limited gaming (City of Black Hawk 1991: 26).

Further increases in Black Hawk revenues were visible in town budgets after 1991 as well, corresponding to the rapid expansion of gaming development. The largest gains were seen in increased tax revenues (which grew from about $96,000 in 1989, to about $140,600 in 1991, to more than $3.5 million by 1993), licenses and permits, and charges for governmental services.

Intergovernmental transfer revenues, only $23,000 in 1991, grew to include distributions from the state Limited Gaming Fund, fines and forfeits, and gaming and impact fees, contributing $1.9 million to the general fund and $2.3 million to special revenue funds by 1994.

Huge increases in expenditures are also evident beginning in 1991, particularly in the areas of governmental operations, public safety, and public inspections. Spending on public safety, for example, grew from $4,689 in 1989 to more than $1.8 million in 1994, as the result of creation of a two-dozen-officer, independent Black Hawk police department (prior to gaming, Black Hawk had contracted policing activities with the county). Expenditures for public works also grew substantially between 1989 ($21,692) and 1994 (about $1.5 million). The influx of new revenues associated with gaming development allowed the Black Hawk government to provide new services beyond the traditional options. Planners were hired, and a new category of parks, recreation, and culture appeared in the budget for the first time in 1992, along with new entries for capital outlay (with more than $9.6 million in expenditures in 1992–1994) and debt service.

In the accounting system used by Black Hawk government, monies from gaming are combined with other tax monies and intergovernmental revenues and deposited in both general and special revenue funds. According to the 1994 Black Hawk budget, gaming-related revenues accounted for about 85 percent of the total revenues in the general and special funds. Longitudinal comparisons of revenues and expenditures in all fund types (Table 6.1) reveal that revenues have grown between 1989 and 1994 from about $138,000 to more than $9.9 million, whereas expenditures increased during that same period from about $77,000 to just less than $8.2 million. During this time, the town has been able to save substantial sums of money and has been able to invest in both necessary and discretionary community improvements. These benefits have not been without penalty. As Linda Martin, the city manager, wrote in the preface to the 1994 Black Hawk budget, "The infrastructure needs, increase in organizational capacity of the city government and community impacts to existing residents have been far beyond anyone's imagination" (City of Black Hawk 1993: 2).

CENTRAL CITY FINANCES

Table 6.1 shows trends over time for revenues and expenditures in all fund types managed by Central City government. In preparation for gaming, Central City government taxed casinos for gaming devices at the rate of $1,000 per slot machine or gaming table per year, and imposed fees-in-lieu-of-parking for which casinos paid $200 per space per year. These fees were in addition to the required state device and licensing fees. With enthusiastic early growth in the Central City casino industry, the town was able to collect more than $375,000 in device fees in 1991 alone. Device taxes and disbursements from the Limited Gaming Fund were the primary sources of new monies added to the town budget after 1990, as revenues in all fund types grew from about $348,000 in 1990 to more than $7.6 million in 1993. Hefty increases were also evident in other revenue categories, including new funds from licenses and permits, charges for services, and intergovernmental transfers.

Expenditures from all fund types also rose dramatically, increasing from a sum of about $332,000 in 1990 to more than $6.8 million in 1993. General government services, public works, and public safety were the primary budgeted expenditures between 1988 and 1990, with total costs for these activities ranging between $273,000 to $308,000. By 1991, though, expenditures in these categories had more than doubled, and by 1993 Central City was spending in excess of $2.8 million to provide these public services. Some of the public safety costs were due to expansion of the local police force: the Central City Marshall's office grew from a few officers, before gambling, to fourteen officers and five information and administrative personnel by 1993.

In addition to these expenditures, Central City spent money for other services once gambling had been approved. Capital outlay and debt service became two of the largest budget items beginning in 1992, and the town has spent about $200,000 a year on traffic control since then as well. Striking increases are also apparent in the public relations category, which, according to financial audits, averaged expenditures of just under $50,000 a year in 1989 and 1990. The 1993 audit, though, shows that Central City's expenditures on public relations had grown to more than $402,000, with most of that amount dedicated to promotions and advertising. The 1994 budget requested more than $578,000 for a four-person public relations staff and continued marketing efforts. The rationale for the increase was described in the 1994 Central City budget document by Jack Hidahl, the city manager, who wrote, "Probably the most dramatic change in 1994s budget is the doubling of the public relations budget. Council has responded strongly to the gaming industry's request for healthy investment in this area" (City of Central 1994: 1). By late 1995, though, when Central City was expecting a revenue shortfall in the 1996 budget, the marketing board appropriation was cancelled (*WRC*, Dec. 15, 1995: 1).

One unique feature of Central City's budget is the large proportion of long-term debt accumulated by the town since gaming was instituted. Prior to gaming, the town had an outstanding balance of $534,000 on 1981-issue general obligation water bonds to fund water system improvements. Once gaming had been approved, the town issued other bonds to help prepare for gaming, raising its long-term debt to more than $23 million. The bonds included more than $3 million to improve the water system (1991 bonds), more than $3 million to fund infrastructure projects (1991), about $7.7 million to finance a new water system (1992), more than $6.8 million for transportation system development (1992), and $850,000 for street and sewer improvements (1992). All bonds are payable between the years 2,002 to 2,012. The total of all 1992 and 1993 fund balances, shown in Table 6.1 as more than $10 million, is due primarily to proceeds derived from the bond sales.

Comparisons of revenues and expenditures show that gaming development produced strong economic gains for Central City. The bonded indebtedness of the town, however, requires that administrators devote considerable monies to annual debt service payments, a circumstance that limits other expenditure options. As a result, local government leaders must actively foster casino industry growth as the primary policy option for the next fifteen or twenty years. Such a strategy (which lends credence to the growth-machine hypothesis introduced in chapter 4) leaves Central City vulnerable to shifts in national economic well-being and gaming industry trends.

Moreover, other policy actions on the local level, such as Central City's enforcement of a second building moratorium between April 1992 and January 1993 (discussed more fully in chapter 7), may in the long term produce consequences that potentially affect the town's ability to meet its financial commitments. Such political decisions also have broader regional implications. The second moratorium had the effect of reducing investment in Central City and transferring it to Black Hawk, as investors whose projects were stalled by the decision became wary of the political climate in Central City and the intentions of its leaders. Black Hawk proved to have a less restrictive growth environment and a more favorable location. Additionally, the Central City moratorium decision affected the ability of the Gilpin County government to complete a $10 million property sale that would have provided it with monetary resources to reduce county impacts much earlier in the development. It appears that Central City's initial boom in investment and construction misled town administrators into an attitude of invincibility, and then, by necessity, into a position of close association and collaboration with the growth-minded gaming industry.

One of the ways in which Central City administrators are attempting to reclaim some of the gaming market share lost to Black Hawk in 1992 and 1993 is a concerted effort to subsidize parking and allow new casinos to develop parking structures that look historic. In the preface to the 1993 town budget, Central City administrators even described a promotional program

Central City's casino industry declined considerably between October 1992 *(top)* and January 1993 *(bottom)*, as a result of casino closures and Central City's second building moratorium.

intended to "attract visitors throughout the year and to promote the City of Central as a fun and friendly place to visit with the proper resources for all visitors (parking, etc.)" (City of Central 1993: 1). Casino owners are highly supportive of this effort. In fact, plans for a $7.5 million parking garage to house 520 vehicles were announced in late 1995 by Harvey's Wagon Wheel casino in Central City, the largest gambling hall in Gilpin County (*Denver Post,* Oct. 18, 1995: 4B, 5B).

GILPIN COUNTY FINANCES

Because the gaming developments are located only in Central City and Black Hawk and not throughout Gilpin County, only the towns receive direct economic benefits from the industry. The county has no direct taxing authority beyond property and sales taxes (it cannot apply device fees or parking impact fees, for example), and it becomes a participant in regional planning only at the invitation of the towns and the industry. Nevertheless, Gilpin County does experience impacts from gaming development, and the legislation allows the county to receive a portion of the Limited Gaming Fund tax revenues to mitigate any problems that arise.

Limited Gaming Fund revenues, however, are available only after the gaming year in which they were produced, so the affected county suffers what rural sociologists and economists have called a "front end problem" (Cummings, Schulze, and Mehr 1978). That is, in places undergoing rapid growth, demands for new services and impacts on existing services and infrastructure precede the potential economic gains that may accompany the development. Communities in transition have substantial needs for new infrastructure, public services, housing, and governmental capability, but often have few financial resources available prior to the planned development to address these needs. Also, "if the anticipated growth does not occur, the community will be overprepared and stuck with half-finished or unneeded facilities and buildings as well as large bills" (Lillydahl and Moen 1983: 215). This situation was evident in Gilpin County; only in fall 1992, a year after gaming had begun, did the county receive about $600,000 in gaming tax revenues from the first year of gambling. This sum was useful, but was a relatively small amount with which to address road improvements, judicial needs, police services, and social services concerns that had earlier accompanied the preparations for gaming.

The lag in county revenues compared with town revenues becomes apparent upon review of the audited financial statements (Table 6.1), which show that revenues for all fund types increased only in 1993, whereas expenses rose visibly beginning in 1991. Gilpin County received small grants from the state for impact assistance prior to gaming in 1991, and received about $60,000 more in revenues from property recording fees, building fees, and property taxes that year—yet the revenues from all governmental funds increased by only 15 percent between 1990 and 1991. Between 1992 and 1993, however, revenues in those funds jumped more than 60 percent, and continued to rise dramatically through 1994. In 1993, sales of assets and more than $1 million in gaming tax revenues together produced more than $7 million in new governmental revenues. Property taxes similarly lagged. Accounting for only about $1 million in revenue in 1989, property taxes were by 1994 producing nearly $5 million in governmental fund revenues, primarily as the result of taxes on commercial properties (which were largely casinos).

The overall balance for all governmental fund types remained low until 1993, as county expenditures roughly matched revenues in the early years of gaming development. The costs of providing general government services, and judicial and public safety services, increased dramatically beginning in 1991. According to Gilpin County audits, the total county payroll in 1989 had been $666,071; in 1991, it was about $800,000, but by 1994 it had increased to $1.48 million. Other substantial increases in expenditures were seen between 1992 and 1994: general government expenditures exceeded $1 million, and judicial and public safety services, along with capital outlay and debt service on a new jail and courthouse facility, together exceeded the $10 million mark by 1994.

COUNTY LABOR FORCE

Beyond governmental finances, economic benefits from gaming development have appeared in the form of increased employment opportunities and improved personal incomes for local and area residents. Though nearly 90 percent of the Gilpin County casino employees live in surrounding urban counties, local residents who wish to work in the casino industry can usually find a job. In contrast to the seasonal work available in pre-gaming days, most jobs are now year-round, the wages are somewhat higher, and health care benefits are often part of an employee's job contract. A study from Regis University's Center for Business and Economic Forecasting, Inc. (1995: 7), estimated that in 1993, the average annual payroll per gaming employee was about $25,781, including taxes and benefits. This figure is still less than the 1990 median household and median family incomes in Gilpin County, though it is higher than the median household and per capita incomes in Black Hawk and Central City (see Table 3.1 in chapter 3; U.S. Department of Commerce 1994).

The competitive market for casino jobs in Central City and Black Hawk initially drew workers away from positions with local governments, the school system, and public services. Gilpin RE–1 school, for example, lost bus drivers and janitors to casino jobs, and some town and county employees left their positions to open new businesses or work in gaming. As local governmental revenues increased, though, salaries for noncasino employment also rose. Wages for town administrators and police officers, in particular, improved, and are now competitive with salaries in surrounding urban areas. These increases, in the context of the small community population, and the need for expanded staffs to meet the demands of the new development, have allowed "outsiders" to move into positions of local importance. The police services are no longer comprised only of "local boys," and the administrative staffs of local government are increasingly likely to be comprised of people who live outside Gilpin County or who have just recently moved there.

Table 6.2 profiles changes in unemployment rates in the Gilpin County and Colorado labor force over the eleven-year period from 1984 through 1994. Comparative data are also provided for the Denver metropolitan area and adjacent counties that contribute employees to the Gilpin County casino industry. These data show that, except for 1986 and 1987, Gilpin County had lower unemployment rates than the state as a whole, a circumstance that contrasts with the claims of gambling proponents that the county was in desperate shape. Moreover, the increase in unemployment rates between 1984 and 1987 was not particular to Gilpin County, but reflected a statewide pattern of economic recession. These data suggest that Gilpin County more closely reflects urban rather than rural counties in unemployment patterns over time. In contrast to these patterns, Clear Creek County, adjacent to Gilpin County's southern border, and sharing its mineral-dependent history, exhibits more extreme high and low variations in unemployment patterns.

Gilpin County appears to have profited with increased employment during both the construction (1990–1991) and operation (1991 and later) phases of gaming development. The construction period may also have had a spillover effect in Clear Creek County, as that county exhibited a remarkable decline in unemployment after 1989. The current unemployment rate for Clear Creek County remains lower than annual rates in the decade of the 1980s, though all counties experienced increased unemployment after the very low rates of 1990 and 1991.

The effects of gaming development on unemployment rates in counties contiguous to Gilpin County are not clear. The recovery period in Grand County began before gaming construction in Gilpin County, and it is unclear whether the construction period in the gaming towns benefited Grand County; few casino employees currently live there, however. The urban counties of Jefferson, Boulder, and Denver each exhibit a similar pattern of declining unemployment between 1989 and 1993, with the exception of an

Table 6.2 Colorado Labor Force: Annual Averages of Percent Unemployed For the State, Gilpin County, and Contiguous Counties (%)

	1984	1985	1986	1987	1988	1989	1990[a]	1991[a]	1992[b]	1993[b]	1994[b]
Colorado	5.6	5.9	7.4	7.7	6.4	5.8	4.9	5.0	5.9	5.2	4.2
Gilpin County	5.5	5.8	7.5	8.0	5.6	5.3	2.6	3.3	5.3	4.3	3.0
Denver MSA	4.8	4.9	6.6	7.2	6.0	5.4	4.3	4.4	5.3	4.7	3.9
Jefferson County[c]	4.4	4.5	5.7	6.4	5.3	4.8	4.0	4.1	4.6	4.1	3.3
Clear Creek County	8.6	7.8	9.9	11.3	9.3	7.1	4.1	4.2	5.5	6.6	4.7
Grand County	4.6	4.5	5.1	6.1	4.5	3.8	3.9	4.3	6.1	5.7	3.8
Boulder County[d]	4.2	5.1	6.0	5.7	4.8	4.5	4.5	4.4	5.0	4.5	3.7

Source: Colorado Department of Labor and Employment, Labor Market Information: Colorado Labor Force Review, Data Supplement 1992; Colorado Labor Force Review, Data Supplement 1994; Colorado Labor Force Review, Data Supplement 1995.

[a] 1990–1991 statistics are from Colorado Labor Force Review: Data Supplement 1994 (adjusted to reflect 1990 census data and 1993 Current Population Survey results).

[b] 1992–1994 statistics are from Colorado Labor Force Review: Data Supplement 1995 (adjusted to reflect 1990 census data and 1994 Current Population Survey results).

[c] Jefferson County is also included within Denver Metropolitan Statistical Area (MSA) totals, but is separated out here to compare with other contiguous counties.

[d] Boulder County is referred to as "Boulder-Longmont MSA" in source material.

unexplained increase in 1992. Denver and Jefferson Counties contribute the largest proportions of casino employees to the Gilpin County gaming industry, though the total numbers of casino employees would constitute only a very minor proportion of total metropolitan employment.

Although proponents of gambling claimed that many Gilpin County residents would be able to obtain local jobs in the casino industry and give up their long commutes into the metropolitan area, this was primarily a public relations ploy. The small proportion of Gilpin County residents among all employees in the Gilpin County casino industry is an indication that other factors are more important in affecting employment choices. For example, many local residents do not have, or cannot obtain, the licensing and training required to hold service positions in casinos. Other people live in Gilpin County because it offers an individualistic lifestyle, and personal freedom is of greater importance than a steady job. In addition, well-educated county residents who are fully employed in well-paying, professional jobs in the metropolitan area are similarly unlikely to choose new employment in the casino industry. The mixed feelings about new opportunities for local employment were illustrated in an interview with one local resident, who said, "People here complained about having no work; now they complain about having to work!"

RELATIONSHIPS BETWEEN CASINO AND NONCASINO BUSINESSES

Though the development of casino gaming was intended to stimulate local businesses by creating a year-round economy in Gilpin County, nearly all the shops in Central City and Black Hawk closed during the construction period. When Central City experienced a downturn in casino revenues during the second year of operation, and several smaller casinos closed, entrepreneurs attempted to open businesses in some of the newly vacant storefronts. Of the five businesses that were open in Central City in January 1993, four were owned by persons who either had a casino interest or had made substantial sums of money selling local properties. In January 1994, two small groceries opened in Central City; one was still operating in summer 1995.

Enterprising individuals found new ways of making money in conjunction with the gaming developments. Early on, local entrepreneurs sold or leased property, or opened casinos or parking lots. More innovative approaches emerged over time. Some residents created new cottage industries related to gaming. One couple opened an after-hours casino cleaning service, and another formed a casino token-sorting service. In addition, at least ten new Black Hawk and Central City bed-and-breakfast accommodations displayed brochures at the Gilpin County Chamber of Commerce in summer 1995.

"Accidental" ventures also produced lucrative returns. One couple, for example, made $750,000 in profit simply by attempting to sell their property, when potential buyers reneged on the purchase contract and forfeited the nonrefundable earnest money deposits (*Denver Post,* Nov. 4, 1992: C1, C5).

Casino development did stimulate variety in the restaurant services sector of the retail economy. Varied, inexpensive restaurants, including fast-food places, are now available in the commercial areas of the towns, benefiting local residents as well as tourists. Few restaurants exist, however, outside the casinos, as almost all existing cafes, restaurants, and saloons closed when buildings were converted to casinos.[2] Indeed, new businesses providing necessary community services have been slow to emerge, and there seem to be significant lag effects in the development of new services beyond casino-related enterprises. Because property in the commercial zone of each gaming town is assessed at the commercial (casino) rate, it is economically inefficient for non-casino businesses to open in the casino district, and local governments have not provided enticements for other businesses to emerge.

The effects of gaming development on the local economy are traced in Table 6.3, which displays county retail sales over time. Table 6.3 shows that total county retail sales more than doubled between 1991 and 1992, growing from about $15.6 million to more than $35.2 million, and remaining above $28 million even after 1992. This rapid growth trend subsequent to the opening of gaming contrasts with the more typical pattern of incremental gains and losses evident in the decade of the 1980s. For example, county retail sales grew overall between 1980 and 1988, improving from $7.9 million in 1980 to $10.2 million by 1988, but the growth was not linear: some years showed large gains and others experienced slight declines from the previous year.[3] Although the overall trend was positive, promoters of the gambling campaign apparently focused on the minor fluctuations from year to year, claiming that such variability foreshadowed the demise of the community.

Table 6.3 also illustrates how the relative distribution of retail sales across towns and unincorporated areas of the county changed once gaming was established. Prior to gaming development, businesses in Central City accounted for about 50 to 56 percent of all retail sales receipts; Black Hawk contributed 26 to 31 percent, and the remainder could be attributed to county businesses. In 1990 (the primary construction period), and 1992 (the first full year of gaming), though, retail sales in Central City accounted for about 75 percent of all county retail sales receipts. The construction period was the time when most Central City businesses closed and were converted to casinos; the redistribution of retail sales in 1990 may have occurred as merchants sold off their inventories. The increase associated with 1992, the first full year of

Table 6.3   Gilpin County Retail Sales, 1988–1994

	Total Retail Sales ($)	Central City (% of county total)	Black Hawk (% of county total)	Remainder (% of county total)
1988	10,202,715	5,165,983	3,153,672	1,883,060
		50.6%	30.9%	18.5%
1989	9,253,315	5,130,654	2,640,727	1,481,934
		55.5%	28.5%	16%
1990	16,251,810	12,483,195	2,289,174	1,479,441
		76.8%	14.1%	9.1%
1991	15,624,738	9,350,867	2,880,939	3,392,932
		59.9%	18.4%	21.7%
1992	35,215,390	25,090,066	6,260,143	3,865,181
		71.3%	17.8%	10.9%
1993	29,005,682	12,057,725	11,542,499	5,405,458
		41.6%	39.8%	18.6%
1994	28,856,270	12,054,582	12,695,148	4,106,540
		41.8%	43.9%	14.2%

Source: State of Colorado, Department of Revenue.

casino operations, likely reflects the continued construction activities and the rapid growth in the casino industry that year. County retail sales since 1992 exhibit a more stable pattern characterized by a more even distribution between Central City and Black Hawk, with each now contributing about 40 percent to the total county retail sales.

The effect of gaming development on traditional county business activities is reflected over time in the variability in numbers of establishments by Standard Industrial Classification category. Between 1980 and 1994, the proportion of establishments in mining, manufacturing, government services, and retail trade (eating and drinking establishments) all declined, whereas the proportion of businesses in construction and services (especially amusement, recreation, and lodging services) rose. Thirty-one establishments were involved in retail trade in 1980, a total that remained relatively stable until 1992, when it declined to fourteen, falling to eleven by 1994. Retail trade establishments had accounted for about 44 percent of all businesses in Gilpin County in 1980, but comprised only about 9 percent in 1994. At the same time, services grew from nineteen in 1990 (about 27 percent of the total), to sixty-seven in 1994 (about 55 percent of all Gilpin County establishments). About two-thirds of the total number of services after 1990 were in the amusement/recreation category that includes casinos. These trends indicate that Gilpin County had enjoyed a more diverse mix of businesses before gaming was instituted.

Beyond retail sales receipts and the SIC business classifications, trends in Gilpin County business structure can be traced in data about numbers of employees and average wages. Data from the Colorado Department of Labor and Employment reveal that between 1980 and 1991, the average annual number of Gilpin County businesses varied between 68 and 87 establishments. The average annual number of employees hired by those businesses increased from 341, in 1980, to 393 in 1990. The average annual wage also improved on a yearly basis, rising from $7,581 in 1980, to $11,291 in 1985 and $13,679 in 1990. Gaming development, though, had a noticeable effect on each of these indicators. The average number of businesses grew to 125 in 1993, while the average number of people employed per year jumped to 701 in 1991, and to more than 3,900 in 1993. Annual average wages increased to more than $15,800 in 1991, and to about $17,790 in 1992.

The development of gaming also affected the functions of the Gilpin County Chamber of Commerce. Prior to gaming, the Chamber had been a small, volunteer organization with little revenue and a primary mission of providing information to summer tourists. The development of gaming was accompanied by the establishment of the first paid director's position for the Chamber, but the emergence of casino owners' associations in Central City and Black Hawk, along with in-house casino marketing, cast doubt on the central position of the Chamber as representative of businesses in the community. Moreover, because so few noncasino businesses remained after gaming was established, the role of the Chamber was further thrown into question. For a time after the opening of gaming, the Chamber was even forced to relocate outside the towns, when the land on which it had been housed was sold. After several moves, the administrators leased space in a Black Hawk building along Gregory Gulch, but hours of operation were sometimes erratic and access unpredictable.

In 1995, a more active, locally representative, reorganized Chamber began to emerge. Although six of the twelve officers of the board of directors were casino representatives, and conflicts between the town governments still influenced their support for and participation in Chamber activities, the organization seemed more focused. The current Gilpin County Chamber of Commerce serves the community by positively representing noncasino local businesses (primarily small lodging businesses) and by strengthening regional linkages that had previously been dormant. Financing for the Chamber of Commerce, though, given the competing marketing efforts of the two local casino owners' associations and the independent marketing efforts of local governments, remains a serious problem (*WRC*, Nov. 25, 1994a: 1).

PROPERTY ISSUES

The approval of the gambling amendment had an immediate impact on the local real estate market. Speculators convinced of the viability of gaming in Colorado eagerly purchased, sold, and resold buildings and land in Central City and Black Hawk. The strongest sales were initially seen in Central City, where a $53 million increase in sales occurred between 1990 and 1991 (Table 6.4).

Table 6.4   Gilpin County Property Sales, 1989–1995

	Gilpin County	Black Hawk	Central City
1989	8,879,500	147,100	1,629,800
1990	10,658,800	667,400	1,867,000
1991	76,956,200	9,887,800	54,948,200
1992	74,100,600	18,830,800	31,708,900
1993	98,524,700	32,132,700	46,426,300
1994	48,097,100	11,347,600	9,141,500
1995	45,475,600	13,404,200	6,344,300

Source: Property sale records, Gilpin County Clerk and Recorder.

Although the land rush continued over the next several years in that town, total yearly property sales declined in comparison with property transfers in Black Hawk. Counting only $147,100 in property sales in 1989, Black Hawk's land became more valuable as that town moved into prominence in the gaming industry. Property sales in Black Hawk showed startling gains between 1990 and 1993, reaching more than $32 million by 1993. Though 1993 was the peak year for property transfers, total county sales remained strong even in 1994 and 1995, especially for Black Hawk.

Property sales indicate the value investors are willing to place on development opportunities. In the Gilpin County gaming developments, the economic gain represented primarily extralocal inputs into the local economy. In addition to property sales, the economic effects of gaming development appeared in the pattern of assessed valuations and property taxes for Gilpin County. Table 6.5 shows changes over time in assessed valuations for the five property categories recorded by the county assessor. Between 1988 and 1991, the actual number of schedules and the assessed value of residential, commercial, agricultural, and metalliferous properties in Gilpin County remained relatively stable. Industrial property values increased substantially in 1991 and again in 1994. These increases were the result of structural improvements and

Table 6.5 Gilpin County Assessed Valuation, 1988–1994 ($)

	1988	1989	1990	1991
Total Residential	28,394,320	27,012,410	27,153,670	26,056,690
Total Commercial	3,839,700	3,953,360	3,636,560	3,639,080
Total Industrial	15,400	13,860	13,760	41,060
Total Agricultural	212,650	245,860	195,440	190,100
Total Metalliferous	3,299,600	3,251,880	3,173,060	3,199,170
Total Assessed Valuation	37,596,870	36,381,570	35,906,390	34,795,600

	1992	1993	1994
Total Residential	41,233,490	32,267,500	32,190,120
Total Commercial	70,681,910	89,133,340	109,586,780
Total Industrial	41,210	48,410	81,340
Total Agricultural	135,960	145,830	124,420
Total Metalliferous	3,221,600	6,531,570	5,498,720
Total Assessed Valuation	117,054,970	130,183,350	150,047,280

Source: Abstract of Assessment, Gilpin County Assessor's Office.

renovations to the few existing industrial businesses, and were unrelated to the gaming developments.

After 1991, the assessed valuation for the entire county increased by more than 300 percent, with most of the addition attributable to commercial property assessments, primarily from gaming-related improvements. After the opening of gaming in 1991, the pattern in assessed valuations for all except commercial properties became more variable. For example, valuations were higher in 1992 for residential properties, but declined after that; assessed valuations for agricultural land fell considerably after 1990; and though valuations for mining properties doubled in 1993, they declined slightly in 1994. Changes in the metalliferous category are particularly interesting because they illustrate subtle and almost invisible pressures brought upon the community as a result of gaming development. Some of the increase in assessed valuation in this category is due to reclassification of patented mining claims according to new identification procedures, but much of the increase can be traced to the buying and selling of unworked mining claims in the southern portion of Gilpin County. The stimulus for this type of speculation is apparently the proposal to construct a southern access route to Central City that would bypass both Black Hawk and much of the narrow, winding Highway 119 roadway.

The effect of gaming on local mill levies and taxes in Black Hawk and Central City is presented in Table 6.6. These data show that, as the assessed value of all local properties increased, the mill levy percentage decreased dramatically. The largest proportion of the tax burden is carried by the casinos,

Table 6.6   Central City and Black Hawk: Taxes to Be Collected, 1988–1994

	Central City			Black Hawk		
	Assessed Value ($)	Mill Levy (%)	Tax ($)	Assessed Value ($)	Mill Levy (%)	Tax ($)
1988	4,705,440	10.601	49,882	2,262,330	9.720	21,990
1989	4,403,870	11.332	49,904	2,111,050	10.460	22,082
1990	4,348,070	11.475	49,894	2,095,610	10.460	21,920
1991	4,078,150	11.025	44,962	1,829,310	2.500	4,573
1992	76,322,010	0.631	48,159	11,596,220	0.414	4,801
1993	64,552,830	0.631	40,733	31,782,370	0.158	5,022
1994	70,919,990	0.631	44,751	44,419,780	0.118	5,242

Source: Abstract of Assessment, Gilpin County Assessor's Office.

and residents pay proportionally so little in property taxes now that Central City's 1994 budget included the statement, "the operation of the City is almost free to the residential taxpayer" (City of Central 1994: 3). Residential tax collections in Black Hawk show extreme declines in 1991 and after, as leaders in that town collected smaller amounts of taxes from local residents and larger amounts of taxes from casino property owners. The mill levy was thus reduced to almost zero, and residential property taxes were allowed to decline considerably. Central City experienced a more variable gaming industry, and the second moratorium affected the flow of local device and gaming tax revenues. As a result, property tax collections remained generally stable, even as the mill levy was reduced, because the mill levy remained proportional to assessed valuations.

Although Black Hawk and Central City leaders have attempted to place more of the tax burden on casinos and less on residents, individual properties in the towns are differentially affected based on their location relative to the casinos. Properties in or near the commercial zones of the towns, including buildings, vacant land, and residential dwellings, were most likely to see increased property valuations based on their privileged locations. A property is taxed at the rate for the highest and best use of that location, not on the actual use. Even if property in the casino zone is unimproved, the fact that it could potentially be developed into a casino-related project means that it will be valued for and taxed at the casino commercial rate. Increased property valuation creates an excellent climate for selling property or for retaining property for later sale, but it is undesirable for those renting (who might be evicted by a landlord wanting to sell) or for those unwilling to sell (who must now pay exorbitant property taxes). New renters also pay higher costs for leasing apartments and houses near the casino area, as the combined effects of property taxation, location, and limited availability in the local housing market produce higher rents.

Residents in unincorporated areas of Gilpin County have been affected in different ways by the casino developments in the towns. After gaming was established, property taxes dropped for most residents across the county. One homeowner, for example, saw his tax bill decline from $1,200 to about $400. The trend is beginning to reverse, however, partly in response to changing market values for property across the county. The county assessor reports that more people are moving into Gilpin County (many from out of state), and they are willing to spend more money for vacant land and housing. As the sales prices increase, assessed valuations for all properties also increase, and all county property becomes more valuable. This favors sellers but is not entirely desirable from the standpoint of residents who wish to retain lower rates for property taxes. As one resident observed, though, it was difficult to feel sorry for people who owned property they could sell, if they wished, for substantial and in some cases extravagant gains. For at least some residents of unincorporated Gilpin County, though, the issue is perhaps more about preservation of a particular lifestyle than about whether a house or acreage can be sold for several thousand dollars more than could have been obtained in the past.

REGIONAL AND SECONDARY IMPACTS OF GAMING DEVELOPMENT

Although casinos are contained in the central commercial zones of Black Hawk and Central City, both positive and negative impacts associated with the gaming developments extend beyond the borders of those towns, affecting other areas in Gilpin County and other counties in the region. Some of the adjacent and nearby counties receive benefits in the form of more diverse employment opportunities, more tourist visits, improved retail sales and property taxes, increased housing rentals, and a more active business climate. At the same time, gaming development has produced negative effects, such as increased traffic congestion on state and county roads leading to the gaming towns, higher demands on existing services in nearby counties, and requests for new or expanded services for existing and incoming residents as well as tourists. The town of Golden, in particular, has experienced considerable problems related to police and emergency services provision for Clear Creek Canyon, Colorado Highway 6, which has seen exorbitant increases in traffic from gaming employees and casino patrons.

A study prepared for the Colorado Division of Gaming by the Lincoln Company (1992) attempted to assess the early effects of gaming development on counties contiguous to Gilpin County. Adjacent counties are eligible to receive funds from the Contiguous County Limited Gaming Impact Fund, a source of revenue established under the Limited Gaming Act that comprises monies drawn from the gaming taxes deposited into the General Fund. By law, at least 9 percent of the General Fund gaming tax revenues are reserved for mitigating impacts in the eight counties adjacent to the gaming counties of Gilpin and Teller.

Counties adjacent to Gilpin include Boulder, Clear Creek, Grand, and Jefferson. The Lincoln Company consultants concluded that Grand County, northwest of Gilpin County, and having no direct highway access into Gilpin County, was and would likely remain primarily unaffected by the gaming developments in Central City and Black Hawk. In contrast, Clear Creek County, immediately south of Gilpin County via Highway 119, was, even as early as 1992, experiencing substantial and mostly negative effects from the gaming developments. Boulder and Jefferson Counties—urban communities with larger populations and resources—were expected to "absorb economic impacts and have greater potential to benefit from dollars spent by gamblers and employees away from the gaming area" (Lincoln Company 1992: 5). In relation to Gilpin County, the most affected cities were, in order, Idaho Springs (Clear Creek County), Golden (Jefferson County), and Nederland (Boulder County). The smallest of these, Nederland, cited traffic and traffic offenses as the largest concerns related to the development of gaming in Central City and Black Hawk.

The study team found that in 1992, retail sales revenues were up in every county adjacent to the gaming counties of Gilpin and Teller. There were also increased pressures on local services in each adjacent county stemming from gaming development. Contiguous counties reported higher agency workloads at all governmental levels, needed more law enforcement officers, and required additional personnel and maintenance equipment for roads. Clear Creek County, in particular, had several unique problems related to the nearby gaming developments. That county provides solid waste management services for Gilpin County, and after gaming initiation trash volume increased considerably. In addition, higher wages for jobs in Gilpin County had an adverse effect on employment in Clear Creek County. Employees were lost to Gilpin County jobs, and those "who remain and the replacements must be paid at a higher rate than formerly if they are to stay" (Lincoln Company 1992: 9).

The Lincoln Company study was conducted during an early stage of gaming development. A 1995 study prepared by researchers at the Center for Business and Economic Forecasting, Inc., at Regis University in Denver, Colorado, considered broader issues related to the economic impacts of the Colorado gaming industry. This study team concluded that the gaming industry in

Colorado was a $300 million industry with substantial direct and indirect economic benefits. In addition to revenues received in the form of state tax revenues and local fees paid to gaming towns, casino gaming activity also produced "about $13 million in revenue from sales of food and beverages and other operating and non-operating sources during the first nine months of business . . . [and] about $30 million in revenue from sources other than gaming" during 1993 (Center for Business and Economic Forecasting, Inc. 1995: 6). Study authors also estimated multiplier effects of the gaming industry at $661 million in spending and $259 in earnings (p. 11) for the Colorado economy. Even though many of these effects were felt in communities outside Central City and Black Hawk, the authors believed, based on numbers of jobs available and growth in wages, that "the economic health of these former mining towns, which had little or no economic activity, has improved immeasurably" (p. 12).

Both the Lincoln Company study and the Regis University report provide details about direct and indirect economic impacts associated with gaming development. However, neither one evaluated the leakage of economic resources away from Gilpin County, and the analyses tend to be vague about the precise locale where economic benefits are likely to accrue. This is a critical issue for Gilpin County residents in particular. Because so few services supporting either the operation of the casino industry or the local residential population are available within Gilpin County, and because only a small proportion of casino employees are drawn from the pool of county residents, there are substantial leakage effects as monies drain out of the community toward external suppliers. Moreover, the lack of gas, grocery, and other basic retail services in Gilpin County indicates that little spending (from casino businesses, employees, tourists, or residents) will recirculate in the county. As Crompton (1995: 18) noted, "Only those dollars remaining within the host community after leakage has taken place constitute the net economic gain to that city." Because direct, indirect, and induced economic impacts are minimal to nonexistent in Gilpin County, it is curious that consultants can claim such large economic gains for that county. Almost all of the economic gains (with the exception of additions to local government revenues through taxes) accrue to metropolitan area communities and the external gaming corporations, which are national, not regional, in origin.

Because so many gaming employees and owners live outside Gilpin County, the solutions for reducing leakage effects are immigration, increased housing availability, greater economic diversification, and expanded training of local people (Mathieson and Wall 1982). Many of these solutions are undesirable, however, in the view of some Gilpin County residents who believe that gaming development and its impacts should be contained in the towns and not allowed to spread across the county. Some community groups, in fact, continue to fight against expansion of new housing, parking areas, and relocation of government services into mid-county areas, explaining that their goal is to retain the natural beauty and rural quality of Gilpin County. Nevertheless, several new housing developments are currently in the planning stages for undeveloped areas west and south of Central City.

There are other evident problems with the economic analyses of gaming in Gilpin County. Consulting teams have tended to ignore opportunity costs (the value of alternative choices and growth strategies) and measure only growth benefits, omitting the short- and long-term local and regional costs of development. Communities considering gaming development as an economic development strategy usually "are interested in knowing how much extra income the host community will receive from the injection of funds from visitors" (Crompton 1995: 21), but such estimates require more sophisticated cost-benefit analyses. Given the problems identified previously, along with the dearth of information about gaming tourist characteristics and visitation patterns to the gaming towns, available economic analyses must be considered oversimplifications at this time.

CASINO CONTRIBUTIONS TO COMMUNITY

Since the inception of gaming in Black Hawk and Central City, the gaming owners' associations, and several specific casino owners, have supported community efforts and programs. A few casino owners have donated computers and money to the schools, provided financial support for community social events and festivals, contributed to the library building fund, held community nights at casinos, given resident discounts on meals and purchases, and made financial contributions to scholarships and other worthwhile causes. One of the largest donations was made by the Glory Hole Saloon and Gaming Hall, which contributed $25,000 in 1992 to the Gilpin County Historical Society for preservation of "Old 71," the historic steam engine that now rests in front of the Coeur d'Alene mine on a hillside above Central City. Other casino owners, notably Virginia Lewis, owner of the Gold Mine Casino in Black Hawk, have been especially generous in making contributions to local projects related to youth recreation, child care, and the needs of the schools. Despite individual generosity, though, it cannot be said that there is a substantial philanthropic sentiment among owners and operators in the local casino industry. Most of the gaming businesspeople have invested in the community on the basis of favorable economic conditions—not to save a community, but to secure a profit.

Some local residents still have mixed feelings about "casino folks," whom locals view as people who came in and took over the town. A Black Hawk government official said in an interview that he approved of the casino leadership because "they know how to get things done, how to get from A to B," and were not participants in the "old boys club" or "family management" that had prevailed in the past. Other residents are more reserved in their judgments, describing casino owners as paternalistic, maintaining a type of "we know what's best for the locals" attitude. These residents note that relationships between local residents and casino people are based on economic exchange, not on emotional commitment to the lifestyle and place. As a demonstration of the gulf in understanding, Lew Cady, editor of *The Little Kingdom Come*, gave a sample of casino workers an informal quiz about significant historic events and people in Gilpin County. He reported that few knew anything about the mining history, significant people, or important events of Gilpin County.

ECONOMIC COSTS

The initial economic impacts of gaming development were uneven. Some local property owners became instant millionaires, whereas others, such as shop lessees and renters, were forced to vacate their properties when the buildings were sold for casino development. As the towns reoriented their business structures toward the gaming industry, economic benefits began to emerge. Town and county revenues increased dramatically, employment opportunities became available for those wanting to work, and secondary benefits accrued as a result of casino contributions to local community institutions. Though the economic benefits of gaming appear to be substantial, contributing monies to the local and regional economies and to the state as a whole, economic costs are also visible in the gaming community.

An analysis of direct economic impacts from gaming shows that, rather than creating a diversified economic base, Central City and Black Hawk are now heavily dependent on gaming revenues for meeting their enlarged schedules of expenditures. Maintaining a stable or growing casino industry has become a political and economic necessity. Dependence on a single industry makes the towns extremely vulnerable to fluctuations in demand for gaming and sensitive to trends in the national organization of the casino industry. The corporations involved in the Gilpin County gaming industry have investments in other United States gaming markets that provide flexibility in responding to external threats. The gaming towns of Gilpin County, though, have become economic monoliths dependent on the choices of the small set of gaming businesses operating in their towns.

The single-industry growth model, of course, replicates the traditional pattern of Gilpin County mining resource dependency, and invites comparison to what Freudenburg (1992) terms "addictive economies."[4] Such communities are often highly unstable, because if their source of revenue slows or dries up, they have few other revenue streams with which to pay for their extensive expenditure commitments. The dangers of dependence solely on gambling tourism, and on the companies and conglomerates currently forming the business mix in Gilpin County, raise concerns about future economic and community directions, particularly in Central City, where the level of bonded indebtedness is worrisome.

The development of gambling tourism, seen by some local leaders as an approach to community salvation, must also be evaluated for what it has constrained. Any development produces opportunity costs, or choices that are forgone by decisions to accept one development agenda instead of another. Central City's choice to become known as a gaming town, for example, has already produced consequences. Some opera patrons will not return to the opera; attendance has declined at local historic sites; and community festivals have either disappeared or become entertainments funded and produced by the casino industry for tourists, rather than inexpensive celebrations of community. In addition, all future decisions for community growth will now be evaluated in terms of congruence with the gaming industry, as gaming industry leaders will have increasingly broader input into decisions about community futures.

The adoption of gaming as a development strategy produced direct economic costs for residents forced to relocate their homes or shops when properties were sold for gaming, and contributed to increased inflation in the housing market that forced some low-income persons out of the community. The economic costs of gaming development also include the replacement of existing community services with gaming halls, the lack of private investment outside the casino sector, and the lag effects (Stokowski 1993b) visible in the local economy. Rubenstein (1984: 64) reported a similar trend in the Atlantic City, New Jersey, casino developments, in which there was a "lack of control by government and community groups within Atlantic City. . . . [It] appears that rapid development in the casino sector . . . directed the pace of noncasino redevelopment." Arguments that economic diversity will occur in the future, or that growth in other sectors was unlikely to occur without gaming development, are simply hopeful assumptions about the power of gaming development to stimulate other growth. Indeed, the potential for vertical integration of the casino industry with other hotel, airline, transportation, and tour operations raises fears that the host communities of Central City and Black Hawk will have their historic, cultural, and natural heritage and amenities become merely the support staff for casino industry expansion.

NOTES

1. Knowing that parking and traffic congestion would be significant issues in the success of gaming, Black Hawk and Central City each determined that casinos should pay parking impact fees that would be used by the towns to construct parking facilities. Fees-in-lieu-of-parking were assessed on each casino based on a complex formula considering casino size, number of gaming devices, and current parking capabilities.

2. The Black Forest Inn, a restaurant owned and operated by former Black Hawk mayor Bill Lorenz, is the only restaurant remaining from the pre-gambling days in either Central City and Black Hawk, and is the only restaurant not located inside a casino. It is, however, linked with Lorenz's casino operation, Otto's Casino, by a passageway.

3. The county retail sales figures for 1980 to 1987 are (in millions):

1980	$7,947	1984	$8,705
1981	$8,525	1985	$8,948
1982	$8,321	1986	$8,654
1983	$8,172	1987	$9,124

4. Freudenburg (1992) uses the term "addictive economies" to describe rural communities and regions with historic dependence on natural resource extraction activities such as mining, logging, and fishing. The argument here is that the historical patterns of social interaction in such communities structure future decisions, even after the resource has played out or the community has progressed to another stage of development. The prevailing approach is one in which short-term solutions are favored over longer-term goals, and critical, skeptical analyses of the merits of growth often do not exist. In other words, rather than evaluating alternative futures, local leaders often respond with increasing desperation and claims of hopelessness about their situation, chasing any solution that might provide temporary relief. Such approaches are inherently dangerous, because, as Freudenburg (p. 328) explained, "the forces that buffet rural communities are far broader than those that originate within or can be controlled by the communities themselves."

7

SOCIAL AND CULTURAL IMPACTS OF GAMING DEVELOPMENT

People live here because they don't want to live other places. Or can't. Because they are fiercely independent and individualistic. . . . The community was founded by some of the most independent types on the American frontier, prospectors and miners. And the attitude still prevails. As does a saloon-oriented culture.

— *The Little Kingdom Come* (Feb. 16, 1990: 2)

In addition to impacting economic arenas of local life, tourism development can also affect social and cultural aspects of community. Rapid community development affects the quality and fabric of community life by revising interaction possibilities, interfering with the ability to conduct community activities, and transforming elements of community and landscape that contribute to personal and collective identity. Impacts are visible in the activities of voluntary and private organizations, in new physical arrangements of local spaces, in patterns of informal socializing, in the routines of daily life and regular events, and in challenges to shared meanings of communal experiences. The informal, social interactions and occurrences that arise in community living are important because they provide structure, a sense of permanence, and a reality to daily life. As Bellah et al. (1985: 154) explained, "People growing up in communities of memory not only hear the stories that tell how the community came to be, what its hopes and fears are, and how its ideals are exemplified in outstanding men and women; they also participate in the practices—ritual, aesthetic, ethical—that define the community as a way of life."

Especially in small, rural communities, people feel they can count on the regularities of community life to give meaning to personal and collective experience. Because many of the interaction patterns and rituals are largely taken for granted, though, communities often make little preparation for their preservation, and the subsequent alteration of such valued qualities is usually accompanied by shock and anger. Residents in developing communities often speak of a profound sense of loss and sadness because "what they had" before the development, even if it could not be precisely articulated, is now gone. Although it is difficult to quantify some of the effects, the cumulative social and cultural impacts of rapid tourism development are very real in the experiences of local people and should not be ignored in tourism development planning.

REGULAR ROUTINES

Prior to the development of gambling, the local environment in Gilpin County was usually uncluttered with visitors, and spatial constraints were few. Residents had a number of special local places, including saloons, cafes, and fraternal clubs, where community gatherings took place. In fact, the entire streetscape was often a place for meeting and socializing. Except in the summer tourist season, cars were few and far between, and benches, stone walls, curbs, and even the middle of streets were treated as gathering spots. Beginning with the construction period in Central City and Black Hawk, however, residents' daily life patterns were disrupted considerably. The renovation or replacement of buildings obliterated many of the local gathering places where residents socialized. A new physical landscape—one that was pristine, controlled, repainted, larger in scale, and dedicated primarily to the business interests of casino owners—emerged over the first several years of gaming development. In addition, as shops and businesses closed, some longtime residents were displaced and others moved away; old-timers and neighbors became less visible among the panorama of visitors, construction crews, and casino employees flooding the towns.

There were many subtle cues that the after-gaming community life would be different from life before gaming. The Christmas tree that formerly tilted with homemade ornaments each year in the middle of the main intersection of Central City's crossroads, Eureka and Main Streets, has been moved out of the way of shuttle buses and vans, and is now more formally decorated and anchored on a sidewalk at the southern end of Main Street, near the larger casinos. Planters and hanging baskets beautify Central City in the summer, lending a resort atmosphere, and the hills around Black Hawk frame new, sturdy, brick casino buildings marching down Main Street with formal precision. Night skies are no longer completely dark, as huge light fixtures glow over the new hilltop parking lots, diffusing light pollution into the windows of homes overlooking the towns. Banners and signs now stretch across Black Hawk streets and along buildings. (Banners apparently are an effective casino marketing tool, and the penalties for violating local sign codes are relatively minor.) The *Weekly Register-Call* gained pages after gaming began. Post-gaming issues typically have six or eight pages, and occasionally reach twelve pages of content. The format of the paper has remained about the same as before gaming, but police and ambulance reports, casino advertisements, and want ads are given more space.

Even local churches were affected by the development of gaming. Traffic and parking problems reduced attendance at services, and some congregations were offended by the new emphasis on gambling. Special arrangements were made with parking lot owners to provide reserved spaces and shuttle services for Sunday worshipers, but scheduling weddings and funerals in the midst of peak gaming traffic was a challenge. Most of the churches just worked quietly around the new gaming industry, but one church organization mounted a creative publicity campaign aimed at reaching a wider set of faithful. Between December 1994 and March 1995, St. Paul's Episcopal Church of Central City ran an advertisement in the *Weekly Register-Call* attempting to get a share of the gambling tourist market. The ad invited gamblers and casino employees to "Come Meet Jesus!" at the church, conveniently located "Behind Central Palace Casino."

The initiation of gaming had consequences for the local pub culture. Saloons and cafes where some residents gathered for socializing closed as buildings were converted to casinos. Residents commented that even *The Little Kingdom Come* seemed to have lost a bit of its edge and outrageousness in the first few years after gaming was established. The editor explained that writers had to exercise some discretion now that casino people were reading the paper. Tall tales, rumors, and jokes that appeared harmless sometimes had repercussions for local people working for casinos. Colloquial and external cultures clashed as new casino industry owners and managers targeted by the *LKC* press found innuendo less comical than did the local pranksters. In December 1995, in fact, *The Little Kingdom Come* published a letter from an attorney, claiming his client, the general manager of the Lady Luck Casino in Central City, had suffered damage to his reputation as a result of a satirical report in the *LKC* discussing management practices at that casino (*LKC*, Dec. 12, 1995). The attorney and client agreed not to pursue legal action if the

LKC printed an apology and a retraction. The local sense of humor was apparently no longer fashionable in Central City.

New kinds of tourists and new kinds of construction also framed the growth experience after gaming was approved. A visible symbol of change was the first-ever traffic light raised in Black Hawk just before gaming began, in September 1991. Located at the busy intersection of Highways 119 and 279, it was later joined by a second stop light less than half a mile away, at the south entrance to Black Hawk. Coupled with traffic directors standing in the middle of intersections, hawkers calling to drivers to park in their lots and patronize their casinos, new "No Parking" signs across the community, and "Parking: $5.00" signs at every wide spot in the road, the landscape around Central City and Black Hawk began to take on the characteristics of an adult theme park. Lending a surreal feeling to the drive through the towns was the absence of people on the streets. Almost everyone was indoors in the casinos, and the landscape had been given over to car parking.

Parking issues and traffic volumes were two of the most serious concerns expressed by residents at all stages of gaming development. Prior to gaming, many kinds of private and official local business were typically conducted in person. Tax bills were paid at the county offices in Central City, the county seat, rather than mailed; people received their mail at post office boxes in Central City or Black Hawk, rather than at home; and churches, restaurants, and shops were all located in the towns, not in unincorporated areas of the county. A trip to town represented a social event as well as a means of conducting business. With the advent of gaming, though, traffic jams and in-town parking restrictions became deterrents to normal community activities.

In preparation for gaming, the Central City and Black Hawk governments instituted a residential parking permit system. Residents were required to display parking stickers on their cars and the cars of their guests to ensure that vehicles would not be towed. Any cars parked in residential areas without permits were subject to removal. The basic idea of providing guaranteed residential parking was sound, but the need for any type of parking permit in a community inspired by rugged individualism produced feelings that the towns were under siege. As one community planner noted during an interview, "Parking had more to do with the loss of a sense of community and place than anything else."

Parking permits were an effort to control residential impacts, but business and governmental parking had been inadequately addressed in the preparations for gaming. When Main Street in Central City was closed off to personal vehicles, and when both gaming towns adopted a pay-for-parking system, nongambling as well as gambling visitors were affected. Only a few "official business" spots were available at the county courthouse, at the post offices, and at local government offices. People coming into the towns to eat at a restaurant, pay bills at the courthouse, attend the opera, serve jury duty, or visit the museum also paid the parking costs associated with gaming development. Moreover, although local residents felt that they should receive the same privileges of "tolerant" law enforcement enjoyed prior to gaming, the enlarged police staffs (who were unable to differentiate nonlocals from locals) seemed to exhibit excessive vigilance about parking violations.

The visual and symbolic reminders of community change fostered a collective sense of panic that set in during the construction period and extended into the first several years after gaming operations began. In interviews, residents used the words "culture shock" to describe their experiences during this time period. "In spring 1991," observed one resident, "a panic set in among people as their town was being torn apart. No one was prepared to see building interiors gutted." The unexpectedness of extensive construction, the sense of loss of local history, and the commotion of tourists and gaming traffic in the casino towns led people to believe that the community was out of control. In conversations, residents reported higher levels of stress and feelings of isolation. One complained, "We don't know where people are, we don't know the names of the people we're seeing around town." Another put the feeling in very personal terms: "We just don't have a feeling of small town closeness anymore. . . . Now I don't know if someone dies unless I see it in the paper."

The displacement of neighbors and renovation of historic buildings into casinos contributed to feelings of powerlessness among residents. Unlike in other boomtowns and some destination resort towns, population increases were not from residential in-migrants, but from the daily flood of tourists in the gaming towns, and from the heavy traffic on formerly quiet highways and local streets. After gambling began, casual sightseers, strolling visitors, and socializing residents all but disappeared from local sidewalks, replaced by employees hurrying to work or lunch, traffic control guards motioning cars and people to keep moving, and gamblers walking purposefully from one casino to another. Residents in the towns complained about casino shuttle buses going past their homes to parking lots at all hours of the day and night, and also about casino patrons trespassing on their properties. The pace of local life had quickened.

An exact record of residential population increase due to gaming development has been unavailable in the towns and county. Colloquial accounts confirm that Black Hawk and Central City both lost population as gaming was established, but now casino employees are beginning to share vacant rental housing, and populations in the towns are creeping upward. There has been

Prior to gambling development, nearly two dozen elderly residents lived in a small trailer park along Black Hawk's unpaved Main Street *(top)*. Sale of the land to casino developers displaced the residents and their trailers; for a time, the lot was used for gambler and construction worker parking *(opposite page, top)*. By summer 1995, the trailer park lot was a paved parking area for gamblers, Main Street had been paved, and casinos lined the west side of the street *(opposite page, bottom)*. Note the enlarged Gilpin Hotel and Casino in the center.

little new home construction in the county, though officials report that housing vacancies have been reduced. Between 1990 and 1995, Gilpin County voter registrations increased by only 2.5 percent, from 2,309 to 2,369. In November 1995, though, county administrators were unable to provide an estimate of county population. "We can tell you that the Census said there were 3,070 people living here in 1990, but we have no idea how many live here now," said one person, who added, "The 'guess-timate' around here is about 3,900 people living in Gilpin County now." When pressed to say whether newcomers were gaming employees, and whether they resided in Central City, Black Hawk, or other areas of the county, the official repeated, "No one really knows."

Though in-migration of casino employees to residential subdivisions of Gilpin County has as yet been limited, there are continued pressures to develop parcels of county land into single homes, apartments, and condominiums for casino employees. Many county residents fear that the housing impacts of gaming development may eventually spread beyond the gaming

towns, turning Gilpin County into suburbia. As one resident explained in an interview, "Now our County has some money and everyone wants things— road equipment, services; are these really necessary? We wanted a mountain lifestyle. Now they're bringing in everything we moved up here to get away from. . . . [W]e don't want to live in the suburbs." Housing pressures, particularly for service employees, have negatively affected other Colorado resort communities, and the continued rhetoric of the gaming industry and some local leaders supporting "gaming destination resorts" worries residents who fear losing their quiet mountain environment to the spread of rental or multiple-unit housing.

After the second building moratorium, Central City's proposed water storage project raised particular concerns because it implied county-wide growth that had never been mentioned during development preparations. In 1992, as a solution to raw water storage and availability needs, Central City officials proposed construction of a seventy-foot-high dam and reservoir in upper Chase Gulch. The reservoir would initially store about 600 acre-feet of water, but could be expanded to hold 1,175 acre-feet of water eventually. Town leaders justified this size by projecting a tenfold increase in town and area population growth. By the year 2,000, according to town leaders and planners, the number of Central City residents would likely increase from 350 to 3,500 residents, and the overall county population would increase from about 3,000 to more than 30,000 residents. Prior to gaming, one community

Central City's new reservoir, under construction in Chase Gulch in July 1995, began to store water in winter 1996.

leader interviewed had commented, "People live here because they don't want lots of folks around." Gaming-related developments were clearly failing to protect that aspect of community life.

Although Central City's population exceeded 3,500 people at the height of the gold rush, nothing in the history of Gilpin County indicates that regional growth of this magnitude is reasonable. The experiences of ski area development and ski resort communities in the Colorado Rockies and else-where, though, indicates that anything is possible if water is available. Gilpin County citizens, working individually and as members of interest groups, were unable to slow or decrease the size of the proposed Central City water project, despite the fact that there are households downstream of the dam. By early winter 1996, the reservoir had begun to be used for water storage.

Other proposals to expand access, particularly to Central City, continued to be discussed in late 1995. A southern access route through the Lake Gulch and Russell Gulch areas, proposed in 1992, and estimated at $33 million for construction, received support from casino owners who wished to draw some of the gambling market away from Black Hawk. Others proposed developing new housing in Russell Gulch to accommodate casino employees and gaming visitors. In one of the most extraordinary proposals yet described, a group of entrepreneurs suggested that Central City's parking problems could be solved by asking gamblers to park in Idaho Springs, located along Interstate 70 in Clear Creek County, and ride a conveyance through an existing mining tunnel to Central City. The Argo Tunnel, constructed between 1893 and 1910, and 4.16 miles in length (Cox 1989: 109), links mines in Idaho Springs with those above Central City. It has been closed since 1943 because of a mining-related flood. Given that "the Argo Tunnel discharges more than 740 pounds of alu-minum, iron, manganese, and zinc into Clear Creek each day" (Colorado Department of Public Health and Environment 1995: 1), the cost and effort of cleanup to accommodate such a plan would be exorbitant. Yet, proponents claim that this scheme would add a unique mining-town flavor to the experi-ence of gambling in Central City. More to the point, it would keep potential gamblers away from Highway 119 and the Black Hawk casinos. The enter-tainment value of this expensive proposal, linked as it is to the contrived and often vacuous rhetoric of "authentic mining town experiences," almost guar-antees that someone will take it seriously.

OPERA UNDER THE INFLUENCE OF GAMING

Prior to gaming development, life in Gilpin County had a distinct seasonal rhythm. Summers were alive with opera productions and community festivals, and homes on the hillsides and Central City streets were populated with musicians, performers, seasonal residents, and tourists. Singers, musicians, and other affiliates became a community within a community, with some returning year after year to perform or work in Central City. Autumn sometimes brought day-trip sightseers on aspen color tours. Winter and spring were off-seasons, and few tourists wandered through the towns and their shops or restaurants.

Gaming development changed these patterns by producing a year-round economy in Central City and Black Hawk. Although the number of gaming visitors did fluctuate by season, few days or months of the year could now be considered off-season. The gaming activities were mapped over existing community events, images, and meanings, producing substantial impacts for arts and historical organizations and their activities. The opera was one of the foremost organizations affected by gaming development.

The Central City Opera House Association spoke out publicly against the development of gambling when the CCPI proposal became public. Yet, in a turnabout that still irritates some local residents, the Association was one of the first to profit from the approval of gaming. Shortly after the gaming amendment was passed, the Association announced that it had signed a thirty-year rental agreement with Tivolino, Inc., a Swiss company, to develop gaming in the Teller House. In exchange for monthly rent and several million dollars worth of renovations and improvements to the 1872 structure, the Opera Association allowed the tenant to offer gambling in the lower floors of the Teller House building. Representatives from the Association explained their actions by noting that gaming would exert a heavy burden on taxable properties owned by the Central City Opera House Association, and would adversely affect summer opera performances by increasing traffic and limiting parking in Central City (Johnson 1992). To survive in Central City, they explained, gaming revenues were needed to meet the anticipated additional operating costs.

The growing pains associated with gaming development, including traffic and parking problems, business closures, and ongoing casino construction, did indeed affect attendance at opera performances. Beginning with summer 1992, the "general manager . . . admitted there was a fifteen percent drop in ticket sales [and the Association had been] approached by other non-gaming, mountain towns to move the opera there" (Young 1993: 111). Not only were season ticket holders not renewing their seats, but walk-up ticket sales also declined, apparently because gamblers were not likely to be opera patrons. Former opera supporters expressed concerns that parking would be difficult, travel along mountain roads with gamblers who had been drinking would make for an unsafe and stressful trip, and the loss of historical qualities to a contrived gambling hall imagery in Central City would be depressing.

In response to these concerns, the Opera House Association instituted a system of guaranteed parking for opera patrons, a shuttle bus service from the Central City parking lots to the front door of the Opera House, and a bus service for opera subscribers from the Denver metropolitan area to Central City. The cost of such services, recovered in part from parking fees, has been substantial for the Association, but these actions have probably retained some patrons and enticed others to return. A patron survey insert in the 1993 season preview, along with a concerted public information and reassurance effort, also contributed to positive public opinion. Reports from the 1995 summer season, in fact, suggest that opera attendance has improved, and now approaches pre-gaming numbers.

The arrangement with Tivolino, an established entertainment company, has proven lucrative for the Association. Gaming profits have been used to make needed renovations to the Teller House and to other local Association properties. A $2 million low-interest loan from the Teller House to the Association, in return for reduced rent, allowed the Opera House Association to construct a new rehearsal hall in the old McFarlane iron foundry, just west of the Opera House. Opened in June 1994, and dubbed "Holler Hall" by local wits, this project seems to indicate a long-term commitment to opera in the community.

There are both tangible and intangible benefits in continuing opera/community relationships. The opera stimulates a particular kind of local tourism, bringing an artistic vitality to the summer season and accommodating visitors with historical tours of the Teller House and Opera House. Local residents are sometimes used as supernumeraries for nonsinging parts in opera performances. The pageantry of opera openings provides the community with a festive occasion attended by society and political leaders, and the event is well covered by the local and metropolitan press. Local residents benefit from the residency of singers and musicians in the community. Impromptu performances are ongoing throughout the summer, and the artists sing for church services and other local events. The positive image of the Central City opera extends across regional, national, and international boundaries, and supporters express strong sentiments about continuing the operatic tradition in the community.

One value of the opera is that it diversifies community tourism beyond retail offerings and gaming opportunities (Ditmer 1992). Like gambling, opera plays upon the fantasies of patrons, but addiction to opera is more socially acceptable than addiction to gambling. Opera celebrates the past history of theatrical performances in Central City and Gilpin County on a scale that is appropriate to that place, unlike the new casinos, many of which have produced a contrived generic image of Western frontier gambling on a scale and form out of character with the local place. Four years after the introduction of gaming, though, it appears that opera and gambling may find coexistence uncomfortable in Central City, as promoters of each diverge in their visions for the future, in the community images they elevate, and in their strategies for reaching desired goals.

IMPACTS ON COMMUNITY FESTIVALS AND EVENTS

Other voluntary and private associations were also affected by the development of gaming. The Gilpin County Historical Society, a nonprofit organization that preserves the history of the area, owns and manages a variety of properties in Gilpin County and the gaming towns. Premier among these is the Gilpin County Historical Museum in the old Central City schoolhouse on High Street. The museum had served about 5,000 visitors a year prior to gaming development, but visitation fell to about half that number in the first few years after gaming was established. Some of the decline was due to fewer school tours coming to the new gaming area. Other problems included inadequate publicity, problems with access and parking at the museum, inconvenient hours of operation for casual visitors, and potential incompatibility with gambling. By the summer of 1995, volunteers at the museum reported that visitation is improving, as some gamblers (and other nongambling visitors to the towns) who desire a more diverse recreation experience in the community are spending a portion of their time at the museum.

Members of the Historical Society were divided about the adoption of gaming as a development strategy. A representative noted, "People love the towns passionately, but there didn't seem to be any other way [to save them] than gaming." Although Historical Society members expressed mixed feelings about the extent of renovation needed to turn local buildings into casinos, they are delighted with the benefits brought by the taxes collected from gaming operations. Under the gaming legislation, the Gilpin County Historical Society became the administrator of gaming tax monies that are returned to the county for distribution for worthy historic preservation projects (the towns of Black Hawk and Central City also receive monies from the Limited Gaming Fund for historic preservation). Throughout the county, these monies have been used for preservation and restoration projects that have local historic merit, including repairs to the Coeur d'Alene mine above Central City, the Opera House and other historic structures, rock wall repairs, cemetery maintenance, oral history projects, and improvements to historic residences.

The Gilpin County Arts Association, a group that celebrated its forty-fifth anniversary in 1992, organizes an arts show and sale each summer in Washington Hall, one of the two frame structures to survive the 1874 fire in

Central City. This group reported that, after gaming was introduced, show visitation declined by about 50 percent from years prior to gaming, and art sales were also drastically reduced. Only with some financial assistance from Central City was the summer arts show able to continue past 1993. Visits to the Lost Gold Mine, a private venture in Central City that offered a short gold mine tour and gift shop, also declined by about half when gaming was introduced. Previous visitors had been families on outings, but families tended to stop visiting Central City once casinos began operating. There was little for children to do in the town, and no one under twenty-one years of age is allowed in the casinos.

A series of community festivals traditionally marked the social calendar of Gilpin County and its historic towns. Each June, "Lou Bunch Day" celebrated the last madam to operate a house of ill repute in Central City. The entertainments included bed races down Main Street in Central City, chorus lines performing song-and-dance routines, and the election of Madam of the Year, Sporting House Girl, and "Dandy Dan" at an evening banquet. A "Jazz Fest," begun in 1977, drew crowds over a long autumn weekend each year, with bands performing in local saloons in Central City. A "Cemetery Crawl" was organized by the Historical Society each October to tour historic cemeteries in the Gilpin County mining area. "Ghosts" of past residents would talk to visitors about their lives, and an annual dinner with a guest speaker was held in the evening. An arts-and-crafts "Wintershire" festival was held each December in Central City in an effort to draw tourists to the community for a bit of Christmas shopping.

The development of gaming had noticeable and primarily negative effects on local community festivals and celebrations in the years immediately following the start of gaming. Attendance declined at all events, and several were cancelled or reconfigured. Wintershire was scaled back in 1994 after a disappointing season in 1993. The Jazz Fest was an early casualty. That festival had attracted about 3,000 visitors each year between 1977 and 1990. After gaming was established, though, attendance plummeted, and by 1992, only 700 visitors attended the weekend performances (Granruth interview 1994). The event had traditionally been held in local saloons, but these were now casinos, so few suitable spaces were available. When several casinos agreed to serve as locations for the musical performances, a new problem arose: it was extremely difficult for organizers to control access to the paid events when casinos worked on the opposite principle of trying to entice as many people as possible into their gaming halls. The lack of hotel rooms was also a deterrent, as was the lack of commitment from Central City. After sixteen years, the traditional event faded from the local scene, apparently incompatible with gambling and local visions for the future. In 1995, the jazz festival was reconfigured, though, as a primarily casino-produced street festival.

Lou Bunch Day events were also nearly thwarted in 1992 when Central City government leaders, under pressure from casino owners, refused to close Main Street to casino shuttle traffic for more than an hour and a half. That year, many of the Lou Bunch Day events celebrating Central City's history were held in Black Hawk. Local public outcry was substantial, and casino owners, apparently realizing the economic potential of the event, began to actively recreate the festival as a casino-sponsored Central City celebration. In 1995, extensive publicity efforts were undertaken in support of the festival (*WRC*, June 16, 1995: 4). The Master of Ceremonies and event director were nonlocal casino representatives; the expanded entertainments included street bands, mock gunfights, food booths, dances, and the more typical bed races and banquet.

The professionalization of community festivals and events by casino interests has resulted in increased attendance for the events that have survived. Marketing efforts are more focused and effective, and publicity about events appears more regularly in the metropolitan papers. Some might consider the Cemetery Crawl, in particular, a success story, as it saw increases in participation in 1994 and 1995. The casinos have also been underwriting and adding new festivals to the agenda of community events, though these tend to be highly commercialized and largely stereotypical of resort community programming. Fourth of July fireworks, New Year's Eve fireworks, food festivals ("A Taste of Central City"), and musical events are becoming standard fare. Such efforts expand the entertainment offerings of major casinos beyond their in-house theaters, and entire streets become performance stages. The apparent collaboration of local governments with casinos in this effort reveals how profit motives and competition are insidious in the development of a gaming industry. Local people do not provide community festivals and events for their own enjoyment any longer; casinos produce the shows, but for very different reasons.

One event that appears to have remained primarily local in nature is the Gilpin County Fair, held outside the gaming towns in mid-county each August. One county resident explained that only at the Gilpin County Fair in 1993 was her sense of community restored. The fair brought out local people who had disappeared amid the crowds of tourists in the gaming towns, and reestablished a feeling of neighborliness and local involvement that had been missing since the beginning of gaming development. She commented, "People whom I hadn't seen in a long time were there, and I began to feel a sense of kinship with 'the survivors' of the development process."

REINTERPRETING HISTORY

By 1994, the furious pace of the early gaming development efforts had abated. The community still experienced conflicts, particularly over local governance and leadership issues, and several major construction projects continued, but a general battle fatigue and resignation replaced the shock and sadness that had been so prevalent among residents earlier in the development. A new phase of analysis and reflection emerged, and residents began to take stock of the community changes. The towns were different, but historic building facades were visibly improved; there were more restaurants, and the competition between casinos had produced cheaper meal prices; some of the casino owners were charitable to community causes; old-timers were finding new places to congregate in some of the smaller locally owned casinos; and even *The Little Kingdom Come* had rediscovered its sharp wit. One resident expressed the view of others, that it was now a "different, more interesting experience to go into town, as there are more things to show people when they visit, and more interesting places to eat."

Observations like these stimulated more generous interpretations of the community and gaming development process. One resident rationalized, "Central City and Black Hawk have been boom and bust towns for their whole existence; this is just another phase." Even negative issues were turned into positive outcomes: "The traffic doesn't bother us; it looks alive here now, it feels alive here," said one couple. When asked whether gambling had changed the character of the community, one resident said, "It wasn't a nice place to live before: there were no services, the cost was very high for things like water and electricity, and high school kids couldn't get jobs." Highlighting the improved business qualities of the new gaming area, a former local government leader said, "It was an extremely quiet sleepy mountain town with very relaxed rules and a lot of boredom for seven months of the year. Now there are more rules than we ever imagined, lots more stress, and great opportunities." Another resident made the point more succinctly: "It's not a better place to live now; it's a better place to do business now."

The reinterpretation of the community as a place to conduct business, replacing a view of the community as a place for quality living, was a subtle indicator of broad shifts in community representation. Gaming development covertly, but continually, called into question many of the images and meanings of Gilpin County history, reconstructing the "real" history of the mining towns and presenting a more sophisticated, sanitized version of the past to residents and visitors alike. In response to the casinos' reinterpretations of local history, the gaming towns also reconsidered their heritage, and began to produce newly contrived representations of their own past history. The result was a continually shifting panorama of authentic and imagined symbolic representations of frontier mining-town gambling.

The two local agencies that had the most power over specific development projects were the Black Hawk Historic Architectural Review Commission (HARC) and the Central City Historic Preservation Commission (HPC). Because they had veto power over construction plans and designs submitted by casino owners, they could prevent or limit development, and did so on the basis of their interpretations about the accuracy of each proposed design and how it fit the historic character of the towns. Initially local people lauded their efforts, but the extensive visible renovation ("destruction," as some termed it) eventually turned public sentiment against the historic protectors. Numerous articles in local and metropolitan papers called into question the procedures of the historic boards. Casino representatives voiced anger about what they saw as unreasonable restrictions on their business plans and investments. The stresses of the role finally overcame the Central City HPC administrator, Alan Granruth. He resigned, explaining that he had worked very hard for historic preservation in the town, but felt his efforts were being minimized by others with a political agenda and by the bitter fighting among local people (Granruth interview 1994).

Historic building renovations and new building construction had initially been justified by the need to renovate historic buildings for use as more solid contemporary casino structures. As established gaming companies entered the Colorado market, though, a second goal emerged: more competitive casinos would have to be larger casinos. Local government leaders, understanding that larger casinos would also produce more tax revenues for the town, approved proposed development plans. Massive construction suddenly became justifiable. The proliferation of huge building cranes sprouting across the landscape inspired one local person to quip in 1993, "We had enough holes in the ground before gambling; now we've got even more, and they're all high tech!"

The local historic preservation boards, charged with approving developers' construction plans, became the direct guardians of community heritage. The two towns had different philosophies about historic preservation, but standards were relatively consistent within each town. Central City had a substantial number of historic buildings, and was generally strict about requiring downtown facades to be kept relatively intact. Black Hawk, with less historic infrastructure, allowed more new construction, but required that new casinos be built "in the style of" gold mills, typical residential housing, or commercial district shops. The flexibility of Black Hawk was appreciated by casino developers. One said during an interview, "Casino making in this town is easier

Black Hawk's Kwik-Mart grocery and gas station operated at the corner of Highways 119 and 279 prior to gaming development. When the first photo was taken in December 1991 *(top)*, the owners had opened a small casino in the building and had removed the gas pumps to expand parking. The loss of the grocery and gas station left the towns without either service just as gaming began. By August 1992 *(bottom)*, the lot and historic building had been sold to Bullwhackers for casino development. When the building began to crack during reconstruction, the original structure was demolished and a new, oversized casino was built on the lot.

than in Central City. There's no strength to the Historic Preservation committee, and people can build their own building to suit what they want." The adaptability of Black Hawk government leaders, though, was attacked by numerous residents on the grounds that community history was being lost. When, in August 1995, an 1863 building in Black Hawk was demolished to make way for expanded casino parking, community outrage was immediate. An editorial in the local newspaper cautioned residents that there seemed to be a conflict of interest on the part of the Black Hawk aldermen who had approved the demolition permit: they had recently been guests at a Las Vegas hotel whose marketing director was a stockholder in the casino next to the historic Black Hawk building (*WRC,* July 21, 1995: 2). Summarizing the community sentiment, Dan Monroe, a Gilpin County historian, wrote sarcastically in *The Little Kingdom Come* (Aug. 4, 1995: 1), "When does something priceless become valueless? When it stands in the way of additional parking."

Although preventing historic buildings from being torn down or falling down unexpectedly was a considerable challenge for the towns, local preservation oversight committees were reasonably successful in controlling neon signs, unusual paint colors or effects, sign lettering, and structures entirely out of character with the surroundings. The repainted and repaired buildings certainly made the towns look cleaner and more orderly, even though real gold mining towns could hardly have been described as tidy. It was the interiors of buildings, though, that most directly challenged the preservation agenda.

Interior renovations were beyond the scope of the historic preservation committees, but some casinos attempted to work appropriate interior design into their renovation plans. The Teller House, Glory Hole/Harrah's, and the Gold Coin casinos in Central City, and the Gilpin Hotel in Black Hawk, attempted to provide consistent interpretations of local history, succeeding to various degrees. Other casinos, however, were less attentive to historic detail. Papone's Palace casino in Central City featured a glittering array of glass ceilings and walls, and a multitude of chandeliers, even though historic pictures show that authentic historic interiors usually had tin ceilings, patterned wallpaper, and more subtle lighting. An escalator in one casino, glass-enclosed elevators in others, and even a fake "exploding" gold mine in Harvey's casino in Central City were industry innovations designed primarily to accommodate, entertain, and entice visitors. In response to negative comments by local residents, one town government official commented about the alterations, "You can't expect us to put these old buildings under glass and never make any changes."

The conversion of Main Street buildings in Central City and Black Hawk did produce a new visual experience for residents and visitors alike. Under increased pressure from larger casinos and more powerful casino owners' associations, historic preservation guidelines began to be interpreted more flexibly. A new level was added to the top of the Glory Hole casino in Central City, blocking the full view of the Catholic Church that stood on the hillside above Main Street. Black Hawk's Main Street became a continuous row of new casinos, dwarfing traditional buildings such as the historic Lace House. By winter 1995, Fitzgerald's Casino in Black Hawk completed a large parking structure with fake rock walls that were built into the hillside near the intersection of Main Street and Highway 279. At the same time, Harrah's in Black Hawk began excavating the hillside behind its casino further south on Main Street to construct its own parking garage.

In the process of construction, small, historic houses and the "real" rock walls formed by hand by laboring Cornish miners were removed for safekeeping. Many eventually were incorporated, in "improved" condition, into casino projects, albeit on a substantially transformed scale. Dramatic examples of this type of "historic preservation" can be seen in Central City Bullwhackers, which is a new structure built around an old, Main Street shop facade, and the historic mine shaft house that was incorporated into a section of Harvey's Casino in Central City. If one did not remember the shaft house structure from pre-gaming days, it would be impossible to recognize it once Harvey's had taken shape around it. Supporters of the gaming developments pointed out, though, that without gambling, these historic buildings would have decayed in place.

By and large, casino organizational philosophies dictated the type of attractions that emerged in the towns, and these were generally not meant to remind local people of their special history. A case in point was the fate of the Gold Coin saloon in Central City. The Coin was nearly 100 years old when gaming was established in 1991, and was much loved by local residents. The original bar fixture was intact, and historic decorations and artifacts on the walls and ceiling created a special ambience. As Charlotte Taylor, editor of the *Weekly Register-Call*, wrote in that paper, "There is a need for an eye of familiarity in the midst of a hurricane of change. . . . To many of us, the living history represented by the mementos at the Coin are . . . physical reminders of some very good memories, a community scrapbook, if you will" (*WRC,* June 25, 1993: 3).

The Gold Coin was purchased during the gaming construction period, and for a year after June 1991, the bar was closed while the building was reinforced and a casino built in another part of the structure. The Coin reopened with a large, exuberant party for local residents in July 1992. Several different owners later, the Lady Luck Casino of Las Vegas took over operation of the casino/saloon. After more renovation closures, local people were shocked to find their beloved hangout converted into a soda fountain/ice cream parlor, with many of the historic artifacts apparently lost, stolen, or otherwise missing. The owners eventually removed the door handles from the outside of the bar doors, so patrons could exit, but not enter, the venerable space from the sidewalk. As a columnist for *The Little Kingdom Come* (June 16, 1993: 1) wrote, "The Gold Coin ... died recently on a Central City street. ... [Some] believe the Coin was a victim of Casino's Disease, the virulent and extremely contagious ailment that had laid waste to Central's core area. Early symptoms are excessive redecoration and feverish activity, followed by spasmodic grand openings ... [and finally] delusions of grandeur, lethargy ... and death." Though the Coin saloon was later returned to being a saloon, not a soda fountain, and another local reunion party was held in November 1995, the entire process had demonstrated how the fate of significant local places was entirely dependent on the fortunes of the casino industry.

Historic interpretation also followed casino organizational philosophies. In both gaming towns, casino employees wear stylized Western clothing and fanciful costuming.[1] Doormen dress as Western outlaws, and female greeters in skimpy feathered dresses and high heels suggestively hint at a "wild West" imagery of gunfighters, train robbers, and "ladies of the evening." Historical writings show, though, that the Gilpin County towns were not typical of the rough mining camps portrayed in movie Westerns. Outlaws did not gallop through the towns, the murder and crime rates were low, and vices (fights, gambling, prostitution) were limited and generally kept under control. These towns had the usual array of mining camp enticements, to be sure, but they are memorable not for a rowdy past, but for their contributions to Colorado history, evident in the multiethnic populace of the communities, the important political and business leaders who lived and mined in Gilpin County, and the artistic and theatrical legacy of the towns. The intentional creation of a movie-set history implies that, at least in the eyes of some casino owners, the real history is not "real" enough to attract patrons into the new gambling parlors. More authentic images must be devised.

The presentation of casino historical illusions was reinforced by the efforts of local governments to mimic the gaming developments with new cultural presentations of their own. As Hall (1994: 187) explained, "nostalgia and heritage have become components of the tourist experience with local government playing a major role in reconstructing and representing whole places as heritage objects for the tourist gaze." Miner's Mesa parking lot above Black Hawk, for example, has a huge entrance gate designed to look like a composite, generic mining structure; a weathered old mine shaft house (the real thing) resting on adjacent property is dwarfed by the parking structure.

The inauthentic, mining-inspired structure at the entrance to Miner's Mesa parking facility contributes to the creation of historical illusions.

In Central City, a publicity brochure produced by the town marketing group after gaming began contains the following extravagant, contested, claims:

> Not everyone who came West struck it rich, but those who settled in Central City were never hard up for wild times.... Dance halls and bars were brimming.... [N]o mining town was complete without a Red Light District and Central City's was notorious.... Today, folks are still striking it rich with the largest and most authentically restored casinos in Colorado.

In Central City, too, local government leaders announced that a troupe of "Shady Ladies of the Motherlode" (apparently modelled after the casino greeters who represented ladies of the evening) would be, from August 1994 forward, the "city ambassadors." Rather than representing some of the many other women who lived in that town—immigrant miners' wives, Victorian society ladies, or Western pioneer women—as community ambassadors, the provocative Shady Ladies symbolically elevate a contrived version of community history and culture. Though described as a troupe that celebrates the "role of the successful business woman in the old West" (*WRC*, Nov. 25, 1994b: 1), this group implicitly demeans the past and contemporary status of local women. Historic records show that Central City, unlike other, wilder Western mining towns, had only a limited "red-light" district, and history apparently recalls the name of only one local prostitute, Lou Bunch. The presentation of Shady Ladies as community representatives implies that real history is irrelevant in the context of advancing politically defined community economic goals.

The Shady Ladies, exploding gold mines, fake mining structures, and imitation buildings are attempts to tantalize visitors with a notion of gambling as a slightly immoral activity carried out in a "wild West" setting. Unlike other forms of popular or cultured theatre in Central City and Black Hawk, the gaming developments impose their imagery over the entire landscape, suppressing innovation, imagination, and the truly authentic cultures of the historic community and place. Although heritage is fast becoming a desired component of many kinds of tourism development, Hall (1994: 180) cautioned that "[t]he representation of heritage will have substantial implications for both collective and individual identity and hence for the creation of social realities." In this instance, reshaping a community into a tourist attraction by controlling all possible elements of the recreation experience creates yearnings for a past that never existed in this place. As Urry (1990: 109) explained, "nostalgic memory is quite different from total recall; it is a socially organized construction. The question is not whether we should or should not preserve the past, but what kind of past we have chosen to preserve."

The new images associated with gaming tourism development are deeply entrenched products of organizational cultures. For example, Bullwhackers casinos have implemented a performance ideology: "Employees are called cast members and they dress in costumes rather than uniforms. Collectively, cast members are called Troupe Bullwhacker. Gamblers are guests who are to be cushioned in ornate Victorian elegance" (*Rocky Mountain News,* May 10, 1992: 7C). This type of impression management is not intended to facilitate local historical understanding, but to replace the reality inside and outside casino doors with a more provocative appeal designed to attract gamblers and their bets. Indeed, one could speculate that the more an industry talks about creating a "fantasy" for visitors, the more likely it is that visitors will surreptitiously be convinced to play a scripted role in the alleged drama, and the less likely it is that the development will be consistent with local culture or history.

The academic literature of heritage tourism development describes the process of exploiting culture and heritage for commercial purposes as "cultural commoditization" (Smith 1989; Turner and Ash 1975). As van den Berghe (1993: 180) explained, "The commoditization process does not stop with land, labor, and capital but ultimately includes the history, ethnic identity, and culture" of communities of people. Gaming tourism not only packages the culture and history of a community to make it more saleable, but the industry also contrives and imposes new cultural realities that are "hyper-real" in form.[2] Eco (1986: 6) characterized this approach as an effort to achieve "immortality [through] duplication." It is distinguished by blurred passages between the real and the contrived, so, "as Baudrillard famously argues, what we increasingly consume are signs or representations. . . . This world of sign and spectacle is one in which there is no real originality. . . . Everything is a copy, or a text upon a text, where what is fake seems more real than the real" (Urry 1990: 85). The contrivance of new practices, cultures, and history is so subtle and pervasive that it appears both reasonable and necessary in the context of the gaming development.

The only suitable metaphor for such intentional management of the tourism and recreation experience is that of a theme park dedicated to satisfying the short-term pleasures of passing tourists. Greenwood (1989: 179) argued that "[t]reating culture as a natural resource or a commodity over which tourists have rights is not simply perverse, it is a violation of the peoples' cultural rights"—but there is little enough understanding of how the process occurs and even less of how it might be reversed. The theme park nature of Gilpin County's gaming towns, though, is readily apparent to visitors and observers, and is not denied by industry spokespersons. Newspaper columnist Jack Kisling (1992) wrote, soon after the opening of gaming, "Spurred by the discovery of underground gold in the 1950s, Central City's founders built the town in a godawful hurry. Then it decayed at leisure, gradually reaching the advanced state of dilapidation it was in when gambling was discovered last year. Since then its rebuilders have worked at the furious pace of the founders, and now, less than a year later, the Disneyfication is all but complete." Early in the operation phase of the development, an industry analyst proudly rationalized the development in a gaming bulletin, writing, "If the whole world is a stage, and it surely is in Black Hawk, Central City and Cripple Creek, the play has begun before the set has been completed" (Walden 1992: 2).

Oddly enough, the real history of Gilpin County and its eminent mining towns goes almost unnoticed. When the 135-year anniversary of the discovery of gold, and the 120-year anniversary of Central City's Great Fire both occurred in May 1994, they were acknowledged only in the *Weekly Register-Call*. Both of these events were defining moments in the history of Gilpin County and Colorado, yet neither was commemorated publicly in the gaming towns in 1994.

A SENSE OF COMMUNITY, A SENSE OF PLACE

The notable characteristics of Black Hawk and Central City as two of the earliest Colorado mining communities, and their memorable history and landscape features, were qualities of place that were poorly articulated in the planning process for gaming. Prior to gaming development, the central images of mining boom and bust, and opera restoration, bounded community life. Surrounded by symbols of the past in decaying buildings, mine tailings on the hillsides, and historic cemeteries, and sheltered within the mountain ethos that celebrated a frontier spirit, rugged individualism, and personal freedom, most Gilpin County residents revelled in the belief that they were unique and extraordinary. The sense of geographic remoteness to the county, and the celebration of formal and informal theater in opera productions and daily life, combined to produce a sometimes surreal engagement with the outside world.

The sensitivity expressed by Gilpin County residents toward the natural and historic environments of the local area parallels what Willits, Bealer, and Timbers describe as a type of "rural mystique." People often "view the various aspects of rurality in positive terms and . . . reject negative images of rural life. . . . [This imagery] involves an aura of treasured and almost sacred elements" (1990: 575). Moreover, these treasured elements of rural life, which give meaning to communal and personal life, are often the very features used symbolically to appeal to and attract tourists in plans for economic development. Sustainable tourism development "relies on . . . the utilization of natural, historical, cultural, and human resources in the local environment as tourist attractions" (Burr 1995: 1). Tourism developers thus expropriate community symbols for industry profit.

The language and objects associated with the mountain environment, mining history, and frontier attitudes of Gilpin County life were the symbols by which residents formed and demonstrated a sense of place, community, and self-identity. As Cohen (1985: 21) observed, "Symbols are effective because they are imprecise. . . . They are, therefore, ideal media through which people can speak a 'common' language, behave in apparently similar ways, participate in the 'same' rituals. . . . Individuality and commonality are thus reconcilable." Symbols are ambiguous and pliable, and different interpretations are used to justify and provide meaning for contemporary actions. This is why people with different characteristics and goals can collectively define themselves as a community, distinct from others, and exceptional in their shared history. People "construct community symbolically, making it a resource and repository of meaning, and a referent of their identity" (Cohen 1985: 118).

Prior to gaming development, Gilpin County residents could not be said to constitute a fully cohesive, participatory community, but they were united in their passion for creating private retreats and supporting personal freedom and individualism. As one resident explained, "There were always controversies here, but we were more cohesive. We could all go to the same meetings and know each other." Although residents differed in their interpretations of a quality living environment, with some favoring the beauty of the mountains, nature, and rurality, others appreciating the historic qualities of the area, and others partial to the obvious individual freedoms, many people lived in Gilpin County because it brought advantages not present in other places. They invested in that place as a way to retain the ideals of a desired past. As one resident explained, the value of living in Gilpin County was that everyone had freedom to do as they wished, and people "didn't get in each other's way." Unusual and extraordinary people congregated there because quirky behaviors were tolerated and there were few social or institutional constraints.

These conclusions parallel those of a pre-gaming survey of Gilpin County residents conducted at the University of Colorado at Denver (Colorado Center for Community Development 1991). Researchers found that respondents felt strongly about community historic areas and scenic mountain views, and that residential areas, forests, and the historic district were places that residents wanted to protect from tourists (p. 20). When asked to write in their own words about what they liked most about living in Gilpin County, the natural beauty of the mountain and forest environment, and the peace and quiet, were the two most frequently cited items; lack of services, road maintenance, and leadership problems were the top-ranking worst features of local life (p. 26). A sense of community was measured by evaluating residents' levels of participation in local organizations and by their efforts to keep informed about community affairs. These results consistently indicated a disparity between metropolitan-area workers (primarily those living in unincorporated Gilpin County) and those working in the local area. Metro-area workers were less informed and less involved, and volunteered less.

Although the ideals of Gilpin County living can be celebrated, one should not romanticize the pre-gaming community conditions. Kinship and shared involvement in local organizations linked residents only to a degree. One longtime resident said, "People in the towns stick together, but people in the County go their separate ways." Elderly people, low-income or indigent people, and those living a marginal existence on the fringes of society were often ill-served by the community, which extolled individuality rather than civic virtue. Colloquial accounts reveal numerous instances of individual and collective dysfunctional behavior, tolerance for antisocial and even dangerous activities, and entrenched conflict. One medical professional who had observed the community over many years stated, "People here seem to have a lot of unfocused anger. Resentments simmer just below the surface." Fractured along lines of residence, residents could be more generally characterized by an orientation away from other places and people, not toward a cohesive community.

Gaming development challenged the symbols and conceptions of everyday life. Power and control over community decisions shifted from residents to their elected leaders and hired planners, and then to casino interests. Ideals of personal freedom, the "live and let live" attitude, and reluctance to change disappeared under the onslaught of rapid growth. One resident expressed what many felt, namely, "We lost our community for the price of prosperity. It's good if you can take part in the benefits, but a majority of people don't. Many are unhappy with this progress, others are envious." Community members, particularly those living in unincorporated areas of the county, agreed that the scale and pace of construction were overwhelming and unexpected, that community desires had not been met, and that the entire county had been irrevocably changed by gaming development. Leaders resolutely reminded residents, though, that even though gaming development was different from what even the leaders had expected, it would benefit the community in the long run.

When impacts occur in tourism or other forms of rapid community development, and especially under conditions where the changes conflict so strongly with a community's view of itself and its natural and historic surroundings, qualities of self are also at issue. This point was illustrated in the comments of one local resident, who remarked, "The gaming people aren't members of the community; they don't care about the place or hang around up here. The new folks don't even know who the old ones are!" In other words, residents felt lost in the new social and physical arrangements of the community. They were also offended at not being recognized as the unique characters they thought they were.

NEW COMMUNITY SERVICES

The anticipated riches of gaming development gave residents incentive to undertake projects that had seemed unimaginable before 1991. One of these was construction of a new Gilpin County Public Library structure. Prior to gaming development, the library was situated in the first floor of a house in mid-county; the upstairs of the house was a rental unit not associated with the library. Located about eight miles north of Black Hawk along Highway 119, the library was a central place for local socializing. A person could learn more about the workings of the community by visiting the local library for an afternoon than by interviewing some community leaders. Residents would stop to get books or videos, and would stay longer than they had intended, to gossip and discuss local issues with the librarian and other patrons.

In 1992, because of the favorable climate of property speculation associated with gaming development, the owner of the house placed it on the market. The listed selling price of $285,000 far exceeded a before-gaming listing price of $92,500. Despite being overpriced for the mid-county market, the willingness of the owner to sell stimulated county leaders and the library board to think about their future needs.[3] Gaming-related construction in Black Hawk and Central City had already affected the library bookmobile. In September 1991, the library had been forced to cancel its regularly scheduled weekly bookmobile stops in the towns, resuming operations only in 1993 when special arrangements were made for the bookmobile to use private parking areas.

In 1992, efforts were initiated to raise funds to construct a new Gilpin County Library. An active Friends of the Library group conducted numerous fund-raising activities, including book sales, a locally performed play, and blackjack and poker tournaments held in Central City's Glory Hole casino. Initial funding was raised through individual, governmental, and corporate donations, including $41,000 in contributions from both town governments and Gilpin County, grants in the amount of $114,000, and a total of $8,000 from two casinos. Funds totalling $625,000 for completion of the project were obtained from county residents with passage of a general obligation bond issued in November 1993. The lack of support from casinos was perceived by the Friends group to indicate an unwillingness by casinos to support local community projects. According to one library supporter, philanthropic rhetoric by casinos should be considered mostly as hollow promises.

In historic mining-town fashion, a celebratory dynamite blast in September 1993 marked the groundbreaking for construction of the new library. The first half of the structure was operational in January 1994 and the second half was completed in March 1995. The uses to which the new library building will be put are diverse. One wing is reserved for traditional library functions; the other provides space for community meetings. Interest groups across the community, including political parties, health clinic and library board members, and groups associated with community projects, began to use the new community gathering place immediately. Now that the structure has been built, though, money for operating it is scarce. The challenge for the future will be to raise new funds to pay utilities and maintain the building, and to purchase books and equipment.

Residents are extremely positive about their investment in the new library, and the facility serves as a model of what interested, active citizens can accomplish when they work together. The library, however, is less a consequence of gaming development than an expression of dedicated effort by groups of residents with a clear community goal. Gaming development was important for the process primarily as a stimulus for encouraging people to think more hopefully about their future together.

A similar process was observed in the efforts of residents to formalize community child care and community recreation programming after gaming was established. Recreational opportunities were a community priority, given the increasing concern about meeting the needs of children and teens in a place given over to adult entertainments. Several casino owners, primarily people who had been local residents before gaming, did provide video arcades and other attractions for children, and there were many ideas to develop family activities such as movie theaters, day care, a waterpark, and a golf course, but these were speculative at best. In the interim, the Gilpin County Recreation Commission and the Gilpin County Child Care Association were formed to provide day care for children and recreation services for children, youth, and adults in the Gilpin County community.

The recreation commission is staffed by three board members, one from each local governmental entity, providing a solid example of collaborative efforts by Gilpin County, Central City, and Black Hawk. Though the group had proposed forming a parks and recreation district based on new tax monies, the effort was not supported by the casino owners, who objected to several aspects of the plan. A news report in the local paper reported that a spokesperson for the casino associations "said casinos could not be expected to be the 'cash cow' for all the community's needs. [Barnes] cited financial statistics indicating that few casinos are thriving financially" (*WRC,* Aug. 5, 1994: 1). Funds for the Gilpin County Recreation Commission are obtained from grants from the towns and county. In summer 1995, the organization was able to provide services such as youth and adult exercise programs, children's camp and day care programs, and classes and lectures. The Gilpin Commission on Child Care, another cooperative venture between the towns, the county, some casino owners, and state agencies, has coordinated the construction of the first child care center in the county.

A COMMUNITY FOR THE FUTURE?

Community leaders said during the campaign and construction periods of gaming development that because growth was being confined to the commercial areas of the towns, local residents would experience few negative impacts. Time has proven this assessment incorrect. Obvious social and cultural impacts, including extreme increases in traffic and visitor volumes, reinterpretations of local heritage, and visual transformation of the natural and historic landscape, have been accompanied by widespread emotional distress. The geographic conditions of the gaming towns will probably continue to affect traffic flow and congestion problems, but the persistence of sentiments such as anger, depression, or bitterness over the changes may be more significant for community vitality. New socializing and gathering places will always be found by entrepreneurial people; community trust and hopefulness require collective encouragement, support, and participation.

The gaming developments in Central City and Black Hawk confirm the findings of Rubenstein (1984), who concluded in his study of casino development processes in Atlantic City, New Jersey, that social costs are associated with the economic benefits of casino development. Interviews with community residents reveal that many feel that economic gains for Central City and Black Hawk have come at the expense of quality of life throughout the county.[4] Many community members also believe that gambling development would not be approved if residents could vote on the proposal again today.

Promises of social and economic benefits accompany all forms of tourism development, but what is unclear is when material benefits can or should be expected by the local populace. Anticipated benefits can only be judged from a basis of realistic time projections, an analysis that requires longitudinal research and reliable initial data. As Lillydahl and Moen (1983: 216) pointed out, "key data for forecasting population growth and other impacts in ... areas undergoing economic development are the employment plans of industry," but these plans are not always known, or may be misrepresented or withheld. Further, if campaign claims are used as a basis, analysts may not know if spokespersons are reliable or credible sources, or whether they have a personal stake in the outcomes.

The next decade of gaming operations in Black Hawk and Central City may produce benefits for the community, but there will surely be associated costs in the increasing urbanization of the county and towns in the service of the gaming industry. Efforts are under way, for example, to develop employee housing near the towns and to create new attractions for residents and visitors. A Denver developer has proposed a golf and convention resort in tandem with single- and multiple-unit housing complexes near Central City (*Boulder Daily Camera*, Mar. 8, 1993: 1A, 2A), and other projects are also being discussed. The golf/resort scheme would require Central City to annex approximately 350 acres (about half the size of the current town) and provide water, sewer, police protection, and other utilities and services.

The community of the future will likely comprise people quite different from the current set of residents, and the positive expression of values cherished in the past—individualism, innovativeness, humor, theatricality, ruggedness—may be diluted under the influence of newcomers. By introducing new residents into the area, however, gaming development may also lead to fewer negative expressions of community ethos, including fatalism, personal or collective disability, self-centeredness, passivity, and escapism—an outcome that may benefit the community. Old and new residents may also become more attached to the community of the future, finding that participation in a shared economy stimulates a greater sense of community (Goudy 1990; Fischer 1982; Wellman 1979). In addition, the industry-contrived Western interpretations of the new gaming towns may stimulate a new historical consciousness simply because they are presented in such compelling and appealing fashion. Indeed, van den Berghe (1993: 626) suggested that "sometimes such creations or recreations become the basis of a cultural revival, acquire over time a secondary authority of their own, and are reappropriated by their creators."

What seems clear from analyses of the social and cultural impacts of gaming development is the need for both old-timers and newcomers to work together toward a more *civic* community. Putnam (1993) described a *civic community* as one that has the following characteristics: residents are active in public affairs, are linked in horizontal relationships of reciprocity and cooperation, are respectful and trustful toward one another, and are involved in local associations that reinforce norms of public-spiritedness. As he explained, "social capital" in the form of institutionalized positive behaviors can help resolve problems of collective action introduced by historical circumstance. "Social trust, norms of reciprocity, networks of civic engagement, and successful cooperation are mutually reinforcing" (Putnam 1993: 180). The kind of Gilpin County community that will matter for the future is not merely one where residents have visions for the future, or feel an attachment to place, or have a viable industry, but one where residents are willing to participate and collaborate in pursuit of civic humanism. As Wilkinson (1992: 109–110) explained, we must hope "that the development machine will be collared, that there will be a majority of civic leaders imbued with the public interest and determined to achieve a sane, stable growth that will build lasting, close-knit, self-reliant communities" in the future.

NOTES

1. Fortunately, the aqua-suited, Mob-inspired gangsters serving as doormen for one Central City casino enjoyed only a brief tenure at their posts.

2. See Eco (1986) for a discussion of hyperreality. Daniel Boorstin's (1961) analysis of the gullibility of Americans seeking and creating "pseudo-events," along with Dean MacCannell's (1976) analysis of tourism as a personal quest for "authenticity," are reminders that the creation of a

tourism experience is often a strategic cultural and political decision stimulated by economic reasons for public consumption. Urry (1990) elaborates this point in detail.

3.   The house still had not sold by early 1995.

4.   Comparable processes of community transformation through tourism were described by Powers (1986) in his discussion of how Hannibal, Missouri, recreated itself as a tourism venue by reinterpreting the legacy of Mark Twain to advance a goal of economic growth. See also Greenberg's (1986) entertaining story about the transformation of a poor farm into a cultural tourist attraction. That fictional example contains a most memorable line about the manipulation of reality: "Why don't you realize that *authentic* doesn't mean *real*?" (p. 171).

8

INSTITUTIONAL IMPACTS OF GAMING DEVELOPMENT

You got your gambling, Black Hawk and Central City. Well, *you* keep it! It's your mess, your lie. . . . We don't want the disease to spread into the County. NO PARKING LOTS, no gambling-related businesses. This greed frenzy must stay confined.

—Gilpin County resident (*WRC,* July 19, 1991: 2)

The *institutional impacts* of tourism development are those related to changes in organizational business practices, the availability and use of public and private resources, and the structure and form of political relationships. Institutions are people organizing to govern, to socialize, to educate, to provide for individual and communal well-being, and to solve community problems. Specific institutional impacts may include, among others, changes in the organizing capabilities of local governments; changes in patterns of crime or criminal behavior that affect police and emergency systems staffing; new demands on local health care providers, social services, and schools; and transformations of the natural environment affecting resource management practices. As a result of tourism development, for example, more police officers may be needed to patrol the streets, community meetings may last five hours instead of two, and town and county offices may have to hire new employees.

The severity and persistence of institutional impacts depends on the preparations made by a community to plan for and control the ensuing development.

As Richter (1989: 19) pointed out, "scholars, policy makers, the travel industry, and community leaders need to understand that there is often a political agenda—wise or foolish, benign or selfish, compatible or incompatible— underlying the explicit tourism program. It ... should be factored into planning, implementation, and the monitoring and evaluation of tourism development projects." Whereas chapter 7 considered impacts related to public and private community social institutions and informal arenas of local social life, this chapter focuses on the impacts of gambling development that relate specifically to governmental entities in Gilpin County.

INSTITUTIONS OF SOCIAL CONTROL: PUBLIC SAFETY

The ability of the community to protect its citizens and visiting tourists is an important function of community institutions. Although many growth strategies raise concerns about police protection and crime deterrence, gaming development seems particularly problematic in this regard. Gaming tends to raise fears about organized and incidental crime, carrying as it does overtones of illicit activity, shady accounting, and even violence. Whether community members or tourists personally experience crime, or whether they observe or hear about crime and perceive it to be a problem, leaders must work to reduce crime opportunities and also to manage public perceptions. Four years after the start of gaming in Colorado, most community members believe that State Gaming Commission regulations have been generally effective in maintaining a "clean" industry, even though local criminal activity is up markedly since gaming began in 1991.

Early impacts from gaming development were felt in the Gilpin County sheriff's dispatch center, which was deluged by calls from visitors requesting information. Throughout the first year of gaming, a significant proportion of police time was spent in writing citations for drunk driving (primarily to non-local offenders) and parking violations, and in serving court papers. Many of the court proceedings were related to property disputes, a problem that arose when old mining deeds and boundary records proved to be incomplete. Officers in each town also assisted in police, ambulance, and fire calls for the other entities. During spring 1992, there were also more cases of domestic abuse requiring police involvement. Law officers were uncertain of the reason for the increase in abuse cases, but speculated that the instances were related either to people stressed by the uncertainties associated with community transformation, or to more police training and more aggressive protection services.

Alcohol appears to be involved in many of the types of crimes emerging in the gaming towns. Police reports show that alcohol-related injuries (drunken people falling down and injuring themselves) and vehicular accidents in which alcohol is involved are increasing at alarming rates. In the six months after gaming began, six fatalities occurred on the canyon roads leading to the gambling towns, five more than were recorded during the same time period the previous year. During the same period, fifteen alcohol-related accidents occurred, though there had been only three in the previous year. Criminal escapades, such as people stealing shuttle buses or other vehicles, and scams by employees to rob casinos, are also becoming more common.

Since gaming began, a significant proportion of police time has also been spent in ticketing parking violators. Parking was such a vexing problem in the small towns and narrow inclines of Gregory Gulch that both residents and visitors were adversely affected. The amount of effort devoted to controlling parking is evident in the number of citations written by Black Hawk and Central City police. From distributing almost no tickets before gaming began, Central City police issued 5,412 parking tickets in 1992, and about 1,000 in each of the next two years. Black Hawk police cited increasing numbers of parking violators, with tickets rising from almost none prior to gaming, to 2,331 in 1992, and to 2,842 by 1994.[1]

The increased demands on local police forces could be addressed only by expanding the size of the police forces. The Gilpin County sheriff's office employed five officers before gaming began, but the staff had grown to nine by 1992, and included fourteen deputies, dispatchers, and sergeants by the end of 1993. The Central City police force expanded from two-and-a-half officers to eighteen by 1994. In the process, the marshall, Elmo Gatlin, was suspended, then resigned in early 1993, on charges of improper administration of the community Christmas drive; some questionable hiring decisions also plagued that force.[2] Black Hawk, which had had no police force and contracted police protection from Gilpin County prior to gaming, created a new force that grew from eleven to twenty-seven personnel (officers and administrative staff) between 1992 and 1994.

With the improved town budgets, salaries for officers and detectives in the Black Hawk and Central City police departments increased by $15,000 to $20,000, a necessary condition for attracting experienced candidates from outside the community. Salaries for Chief Bruce Hartman and officers in the Gilpin County police force lagged behind those of the other two entities, but improved after 1993 with increased county budgets. New police chiefs in both Black Hawk and Central City have given those departments a more identifiable character and shape, though not without friction. The efforts of the Black Hawk chief of police, Jerry Yocum, to build that force into a professional organization have raised concerns about a lack of local cooperation with other local organizations. Yocum created a new dispatching center that operates independently from Gilpin County's dispatch process, duplicating local services and potentially causing confusion about officer activities. Residents see this as a continuation of turf battles in the local area.

An influx of money from gaming impact fees and tax revenues accruing to Black Hawk and Central City governments paid for personnel additions and new equipment and supplies, including vehicles, radios, computers, office space and renovations, and office furniture. Unlike the towns, the county had no direct source of gaming revenue, and had to fund initial purchases with external grants; it eventually received disbursements from state gaming tax revenues to support the expansion of county services. As police services became more bureaucratized, each jurisdiction formalized training and response procedures to replace the informal methods remaining from pre-gambling times. Larger staffs and the scrutiny of the state over the gaming towns also resulted in more rigorous and exact crime reporting.[3] Because many of the new officers were drawn from outside the community, rather than from the local residential population, and some had been trained in larger metropolitan areas, they presented themselves as more professional and objective than earlier members of the local police forces. Nevertheless, an exposé on police incompetence, poor training, and personnel problems in the gaming towns appeared in a Denver investigative tabloid even as recently as 1994 (Bowers 1994). Longtime Gilpin County residents also charge that the new police officers have little respect for old-timers, and fail to maintain the helpful and flexible attitudes and standards enjoyed in pre-gaming times.

The primary duty of the new police staffs is to control crime, but despite the expansion of the police forces, increases in serious crimes were apparent after gambling was initiated.[4] The relationship between community crime and gaming is a relatively understudied topic in the social sciences, and published studies tend to focus primarily on individual factors, such as why some people commit gambling crimes (Lesieur 1977), or gambling as a form of deviant behavior (Frey 1984; Findlay 1986). Among researchers who have studied community effects, Friedman, Hakim, and Weinblatt (1989: 622) found, in a study of Atlantic City gaming, that "[v]iolent crimes [were] on the average 78 percent higher, burglaries 41 percent, vehicle thefts 30 percent, and larcenies 3 percent" after casinos opened. These crimes also "spilled over" in the region, affecting communities that received few economic benefits from gaming. Hakim and Buck (1989: 414) added that, even controlling for "the effects of increased community wealth, policing, unemployment, travel time, and population . . . there was less crime before the introduction of casinos" in Atlantic City.

Albanese (1985) also found a strong correlation between the number of casinos and total crimes in Atlantic City in seven crime categories (murder, forcible rape, robbery, aggravated assault, burglary, larceny, and motor vehicle theft), but suggested that these increases were offset by huge increases in average daily populations visiting the casino city. In other words, even though raw totals of crimes had increased, people were somewhat less likely to be victimized because the numbers of tourists visiting the city had also increased. Hakim and Buck (1989: 415) noted, however, that even if tourists were less likely to be involved in a crime, the local community still carried the cost for services that accompanied increases in crime, such as the added costs of police protection, the potential costs of increased court activity, imprisonments, and associated government administration.

In documenting changes in crime related to gaming developments in the Colorado gaming towns, county-level crime statistics from time periods prior to, during, and after the onset of gaming in October 1991 were reviewed. Data about criminal offenses and arrests published in the annual reports of the Colorado Bureau of Investigation were analyzed. Colorado reports seven common "Index Offenses," subdivided as either "violent crimes" (murder, forcible rape, robbery, and aggravated assault) or "property crimes" (burglary, larceny-theft, and motor vehicle theft). "Arrests" data contain statistics on a wide array of offenses, only some of which are reported here. There is no correlation between total number of offenses and total number of arrests, as one person may be arrested for several offenses, or one arrest may "clear" (solve) several different crimes.

Data in the crime reports are summarized for state, county, and jurisdiction (city or town police force), and reflect *reported* crimes, not *all* crimes. Because some criminals are never caught, and some crimes are never solved, the success of public protection measures can only be incompletely estimated. It is important to understand, however, that crime data represent a census, not a sample, of reported crime. The ability to assess changes in crime patterns in a county varies with the constraints of local conditions, and there are some peculiarities associated with crime reports that are not immediately visible to persons outside the local communities. Prime among these are the characteristics of individuals charged with making the reports. For example, some years ago, the medical practitioner/coroner in Gilpin County had a habit of designating persons deceased from gunshot wounds as "died of natural causes"! Murder and manslaughter statistics for those years, then, are probably inaccurate portrayals of actual circumstances.

Table 8.1 shows that before gaming (1989–1990), most categories of offenses increased only marginally or remained stable in Gilpin County, while

Table 8.1   Total Index Offenses: Gilpin County, Colorado, 1989–1994

	Total Index Offenses	Murder and Manslaughter	Death by Negligence	Rape	Robbery	Aggravated Assault	Burglary	Larceny and Theft	Motor Vehicle Theft
1989	133	—	—	—	—	4	47	73	9
1990	127	—	—	1	—	11	39	73	3
1991	151	1	—	—	1	22	38	85	4
1992	359	—	—	—	6	29	46	259	19
1993[a]	323	—	—	1	—	37	50	222	13
1994[b]	(230)	—	—	—	(2)	(19)	(58)	(144)	(7)
% Increase: 1991–1993	113.9 %	—	—	—	—	68.2 %	31.6 %	161.2 %	225 %

Source: Colorado Bureau of Investigation, Department of Public Safety.

[a]The 1993 report includes only ten months of data from Central City.

[b]The 1994 crime data underestimate the volume of crime for many places in Colorado because the state adopted a new reporting process in mid-year. As a result, many Colorado places, including the gaming towns, failed to report crime totals for the entire year. The Gilpin County sheriff reported crime for only six months, the Central City marshall reported only seven months of data, and the Black Hawk Police Department reported only nine months of statistics.

a few even decreased. After gaming was initiated in 1991, though, large increases were seen across several offense categories. In real numbers, it is clear that there was less crime before than after gaming development. The largest proportion of crimes, both before and after gaming, were property crimes (burglary, larceny-theft, motor vehicle theft), though one category of violent crime (aggravated assault) increased after gaming development as well. Of the offense categories shown, larceny and theft offenses and motor vehicle theft increased most dramatically between 1990 and 1993.

In addition to data about index offenses, arrest data provide information about specific categories of crime for which people were arrested in given jurisdictions. Only twelve of twenty-seven arrest categories reported in Colorado are shown in Table 8.2; categories that show no or few arrests either before or after gaming (for example, loitering, embezzlement, and arson) are excluded. In Gilpin County, most categories of arrests were relatively stable from 1989 to 1991; after the opening of gaming, though, total arrests increased by about 306 percent (1991 to 1993). By far the largest increases in raw numbers occurred in the DUI category (driving under the influence of alcohol), which accounted for an increasing proportion of all Gilpin County arrests between 1990 and 1993. The percentage of arrests for narcotics and drug offenses, assaults, disorderly conduct, forgery and fraud, and other crimes, increased as well. Prostitution, often thought to accompany gambling development, shows little change in total numbers, though more arrests are reported in the most recent years than in the years prior to the adoption of gambling. Local police attribute the low numbers in this category to the fact that no hotels were available in Gilpin County's gaming towns until the end of 1994; most gamblers and tourists were, and remain, day-trip visitors. Officers comment that they have concerns about prostitution moving into the area with the opening of planned casino hotels.

There are many reasons why offenses and arrests may rise when gaming is adopted as a growth strategy, including larger and more vigilant police staffs, more tourists visiting the community, an increased number of at-risk properties (such as hotel rooms), the flow of larger amounts of money, and expanded personal opportunity for involvement in unlawful activities (see Roehl (1994) and Albanese (1985) for a discussion of some of these risk factors). Another explanation may be that the state as a whole is experiencing increased crime. To check this possibility, Gilpin County crime trends were compared against state patterns. Both before and after gaming was established, the total number of offenses and arrests in Gilpin County accounted for only a minuscule proportion (less than 1 percent) of all state offenses and arrests. More striking, though, is the fact that after-gaming trends in the

Table 8.2   Gilpin County Arrests, 1989–1994

	Total Arrests[a]	Felony Assault	Simple Assault	Narc and Drug	DUI	Liquor	Disord conduct	Forg and Fraud	Vandal	Weapn	Prost and Sex	Family Offenses	Gambling
1989	232	4	11	9	136	1	7	1	1	3	3	5	—
1990	200	9	15	3	81	5	6	2	11	1	—	2	—
1991	185	13	11	5	84	7	9	1	8	1	—	—	2
1992	698	28	52	22	262	28	54	5	15	6	4	3	8
1993	751	30	28	55	410	20	25	21	7	6	4	3	5
1994[b]	(814)	(13)	(20)	(15)	(269)	(6)	(21)	(23)	(1)	(4)	—	(9)	(9)
% Increase: 1991–1993	305.9%	130.7%	154.5%	1,000%	388%	185.7%	177.7%	2,000%	−12.5%	500%	—	—	286.3%

Source: Colorado Bureau of Investigation, Department of Public Safety.

Categories: Felony assault; Simple assault; Narcotic and drug violations; Driving under the influence of alcohol; Liquor law violations; Disorderly conduct; Forgery, fraud, and counterfeit; Vandalism; Weapons violations; Prostitution and other sex offenses; Offenses against families and children; Gambling.

[a]The data presented do not sum to the total arrests because data for only twelve of twenty-seven arrest categories are reported here.

[b]The 1994 crime data underestimate the volume of crime for many places in Colorado because the state adopted a new reporting process in mid-year. As a result, many Colorado places, including the gaming towns, failed to report crime totals for the entire year. The Gilpin County Sheriff reported crime for only six months, the Central City marshall reported only seven months of data, and the Black Hawk Police Department reported only nine months of statistics.

gaming county are opposite to trends at the state level. Total state offenses and arrests have declined since 1991, whereas total offenses and arrests in Gilpin County have increased since then.

Between 1989 and 1994, the estimated population of Gilpin County grew only slightly, and it is unlikely that huge increases in offenses and arrests can be attributed solely to local people, who showed little proclivity for excessive crime prior to gaming. There have, however, been large increases in numbers of vehicles passing highway counters since gaming began in 1991, as reported in chapter 5. Traffic volume at the Highway 6 and 119 intersection in Gilpin County increased by about 216 percent between 1991 and 1993. A conservative estimate of visitors to the gaming towns would multiply the total number of vehicles by at least three or four people per car to account for multiple riders and for vehicles arriving on routes different from those that pass this spot.

Because both crime and visitor numbers are increasing, it is reasonable to ask whether both are increasing at the same rate; that is, are people facing the same risk of being victimized by crime as they were before gaming? Calculating an index of offenses per capita (offenses divided by resident population), and an index of offenses per vehicle (as the actual number of tourists is unknown, but the number of vehicles is documented, this is a conservative proxy measure of tourist visits) shows that if only Gilpin County residents are considered, the per capita crime rate has increased somewhat in the years after gaming was established. Although only about 4 residents out of every 100 in the county might have experienced an index crime in 1990, nearly 11 out of every 100 in 1992, and about 10 out of every 100 in 1993, were likely to be victimized. If, however, gaming "vehicles" (tourists proxy) are considered as the baseline for analysis, the crime rate falls during time periods both before and after gaming. That is, between 4 and 5 "vehicles" (visitor groups) out of every 100 vehicles (visitor groups) would be the victim of crime in 1989, compared with only about 3 in 1993. In other words, tourist visits have increased faster than crime, slightly reducing the chance that people will be victims of crime. As it is likely that there are more visitors per vehicle with gaming, the number of potential crime victims would actually be even less than projected.

The conclusion is that although actual numbers of index offenses and arrests increased with gaming, the current likelihood of any individual being a crime victim in Gilpin County has decreased, because the tourist population has risen faster than the number of crimes. Although gaming development is related to an increase in crime, crime has not grown proportionally to the increased numbers of gamblers visiting the county. This finding is opposite to the conclusions of Freudenburg and Jones (1991) who, in their analysis of crime in rapid-growth energy boomtowns, found "significantly greater increases in criminal activities than in populations" (p. 638). The differences may be due to the fact that, to this point, gamblers have constituted a primarily transient population in Gilpin County, whereas construction workers and project employees in energy boomtowns often move to the affected town and become residents. Once hotels are built in the gaming towns, and more casino employees move to the area, the crime figures will probably show a different pattern.

The data are not as negative as gaming opponents suggest, but they do indicate some serious effects of gaming development in rural communities. There are clearly new community costs associated with crime in the gaming boomtowns, and these costs have not, to this point, been eradicated by economic gains from gaming. An increase in real numbers of crimes places new demands on local government payrolls (for police and emergency personnel salaries) and infrastructure (for jail and court facilities). In addition, local perceptions of criminal behavior may produce community fear or conflict, or stimulate other criminal behavior.[5] Tourists may also be averse to visiting an attraction where reports or perceptions of crime are elevated.

It is not yet clear whether gaming behavior produces increases in crime, or whether crime increases are simply the result of huge increases in tourist visits to the towns. A very preliminary comparison of crime trends in Colorado gaming counties compared with crime trends in three nongaming resort counties in Colorado (San Miguel, Pitkin, and Summit) suggests that gaming *per se* may produce different forms of criminal behavior than do other resort communities, regardless of the visitor increases common to both types of counties. The three nongaming resort counties exhibited a slower rate of population growth, a more erratic pattern of changes in index offenses and arrests, more juvenile arrests, and a higher proportion of crimes against persons (rather than against property) than did the gaming counties. It may be that gaming communities of any size are likely to see sectoral increases in crime, such as increased property offenses rather than violent personal crimes, or increases in specific types of arrests (related to banned substances, aggressive behaviors, and money-related violations) and not others. Given the very early stages of gambling tourism development in Colorado, however, these differences may be due more to structural conditions associated with varying levels of resort development than to differences in the types of tourism entertainments.

With criminal arrests up markedly since gaming was instituted, the county jail has been one of the most affected community institutions. In 1990, the jail averaged about six or seven prisoners a day, but by 1993, twenty-five to thirty offenders were being jailed per day. Because the Gilpin County facility, located in the basement of the county courthouse, could hold only ten inmates, the others were transported to Clear Creek, Jefferson, and Eagle counties for incarceration. Not only did this involve transport time and pay for officers involved in the exchange, but the costs to house and feed inmates in Gilpin County and other jurisdictions was also borne by the county; this expense reached several hundred thousand dollars after gaming. This situation highlighted the differential costs and benefits of gaming development: the towns received gaming revenues directly, but the county had no direct taxing authority over casinos and was forced to wait for either disbursements from the Limited Gaming Fund or property tax collections. The delay in benefit accrual proved a substantial problem, particularly for addressing criminal and court impacts of gaming development (*WRC,* Dec. 25, 1995:1).

Once revenues became available in 1992, the Gilpin County commissioners initiated efforts to construct a new justice center in mid-county. The choice of site produced an immediate, negative outcry from residents living in a nearby subdivision, who protested having jail facilities in their neighborhood and who opposed the urbanization of the mid-county area. Residents also felt that the decision as to the site had been made without adequate public input, and that the project should not be allowed to go forward without guaranteed water and sewer infrastructure.

Despite continuing bitter public meetings and contentious letters to the editor of the newspaper, the need for a new jail was evident and pressing and construction moved ahead. A recall election of county commissioners responsible for approving the facility failed, and the justice center opened in August 1995.

The new Gilpin County Justice Center was built in mid-county near an established housing subdivision, against the wishes of many residents. This photo was taken in July 1995, shortly before the facility opened.

The building holds the new jail, district and county court facilities, the sheriff's department, county nursing and social services offices, an office for the state patrol, two community rooms, and offices for elected county officials. In addition to space for 54 inmates, the facility can be expanded to accommodate more than 100 prisoners if necessary. According to the county nurse, who also serves as jail nurse, the crimes for which people are now incarcerated in Gilpin County have become increasingly complex, and the criminals have become more dangerous, in comparison to pre-gaming times. It is unlikely that Gilpin County will ever again see local petty offenders sitting on the front lawn of the county courthouse, having lunch, reading the newspaper, and enjoying the sunshine—a relatively common sight in the years before gambling was introduced.

One of the consequences of more active policing is that the court system has become overloaded with cases that cannot be heard in a timely manner with limited staff. Tables 8.3 and 8.4 show longitudinal patterns in district and court case filings for relevant cases. These data correspond to the time periods before gaming, during the establishment of the new industry, and during the first several years after gaming became operational. Unfortunately, the fiscal year is opposite to gaming years, so the data are not directly comparable; the trends, however, are the crucial issue in these tables. The data shown are for Gilpin County cases only. Cases attributable to Jefferson County are not included in these tables because, despite their rising numbers, Gilpin County cases constitute a relatively small proportion of the total First Judicial District caseload.[6]

Table 8.3 shows that between 1988–1989 and 1993–1994, the total number of cases filed in district court increased by 50 percent, with civil cases (growing by 56 percent) and criminal cases (increasing by 65 percent) exceeding that rate. Indeed, only probate and mental health cases showed no clear patterns of rising incidence. The largest proportions of filings both before and after gaming were for civil and criminal cases. Civil case filings were typically disputes over real personal property, failure to complete property sales transactions, money demands, or personal injury suits. Criminal offense filings primarily included offenses against property, drug and narcotics offenses, offenses against persons, or fraud.

Cases filed in county court (Table 8.4) show similar increasing patterns between 1988–1989 and 1993–1994, rising 68 percent over that time period. Traffic cases accounted for about 63 percent of all county court filings before gaming, and remained at about that level even after gaming was established; nevertheless, the increase in raw numbers (from 507 to 1,529 cases) after gaming began is staggering. Small claims cases and misdemeanors showed the

Table 8.3   District Court Filings: Gilpin County Cases, 1988–1994[a]

Fiscal Year[b]	Domestic Relations	Civil	Probate	Juvenile	Mental Health	Criminal	Total
1988–89	23	41	12	10	3	25	114
1989–90	25	36	8	25	0	27	121
1990–91	23	42	12	13	2	21	113
1991–92	21	63	14	23	1	21	143
1992–93	27	122	6	31	1	71	258
1993–94	34	94	11	17	2	72	230
% Increase: 1988–89 to 1993–94	32%	56%	—	41%	—	65%	50%

Source: Colorado Judicial Branch annual reports.
[a]Gilpin County and Jefferson County constitute the First Judicial District of the Colorado court system. The numbers reported here are for Gilpin County-related filings in district courts only.
[b]The fiscal year runs from July 1 of one year through June 30 of the next.

most dramatic gains (up 82 and 80 percent, respectively), but all other categories were also rising.

These dramatic numbers also indicate other associated problems. Prior to the introduction of gambling, the Gilpin County Courthouse in Central City housed the small jail, county offices, and courtrooms. A very small parking area accommodated county sheriff's vehicles, a few key county employees, and visitors. Parking for other employees, citizens serving jury duty, and other visitors

Table 8.4   County Court Filings: Gilpin County, 1988–1994 (a)

Fiscal Year[b]	Civil	Small Claims	Traffic	Infractions	Misde- meanors	Felony Complaints	Total
1988–89	33	9	507	127	97	31	804
1989–90	33	13	470	60	118	24	718
1990–91	29	16	246	32	113	25	461
1991–92	30	24	686	74	234	31	1,079
1992–93	58	56	1,622	297	391	80	2,504
1993–94	74	50	1,529	290	480	96	2,519
% Increase: 1988–89 to 1993–94	55 %	82 %	67 %	56 %	80 %	68 %	68 %

Source: Colorado Judicial Branch annual reports
[a]Gilpin County and Jefferson County constitute the First Judicial District of the Colorado court system. The numbers reported here are for filings in Gilpin County courts only.
[b]The fiscal year runs from July 1 of one year through June 30 of the next.

was available along streets and in the immediate vicinity of the courthouse. With the initiation of gaming and the disappearance of free neighborhood parking, courthouse activities were severely restricted. Citizens on jury duty, residents or visitors paying fines or bills, researchers, and others using the courthouse were forced to pay (at gamblers' rates) for parking. As early as mid-December 1991, only two months after gaming began, county judge Fred Rogers also described the local court system as extremely overcrowded (*WRC,* Dec. 13, 1991: 3).

COMMUNITY MEDICAL AND HEALTH SERVICES

The impacts of tourism development on the provision of medical, health, and social services are often difficult to measure, but are important for assessing community impacts of tourism development. It is particularly difficult to obtain baseline secondary data for these services in rural communities, due to patient confidentiality requirements, personnel changes, funding level variations, or simply the fact that longitudinal data are often unavailable. Serendipity, though, sometimes provides comparison data. For example, one effort that attempted to assess community health care in Gilpin County was the "Community Health Promotion Evaluation Program," a research project of the University of Washington's School of Public Health and Community Medicine. Between 1988 and 1992, study organizers evaluated health promotion and prevention activities in 26 communities in the western United States; Gilpin County happened to be one of the study communities.

Surveys were conducted at three time periods that happened to coincide with notable moments in the gaming development. The first survey was conducted prior to the gambling campaign, the second was conducted during the construction phase (overlapping several months after October 1, 1991), and the third survey was conducted after gaming was operational. Researchers asked public leaders from all segments of community life to evaluate seven factors (leadership, political support, planning, coordination, funding, availability, and utilization) related to community efforts to reduce six specific health problems. The identified health problems included: health promotion for adults; health promotion for adolescents; prevention of tobacco abuse; prevention of substance abuse; prevention of adolescent pregnancies; and prevention of cardiovascular disease and cancer (Community Health Promotion Evaluation Program 1989, 1991, 1993).

Results of the University of Washington studies show that mean scores for Gilpin County respondents were uniformly low across all variables.[7] Funding for health promotion and utilization of services were seen as the two most evident problems in health promotion in Gilpin County. Respondents believed, however, that funding had increased with the advent of gaming development for at least three health areas: health promotion for adults, health promotion for adolescents, and prevention of substance abuse. Between the first and third study periods (i.e., during the time in which gaming development was established in the community), respondents saw political support, planning, leadership, and coordination decreasing for most of the health promotion items.

It is not clear from these data whether community interest and mobilization around specific health issues was a response to a particular health or social problem existing in the community, or the result of efforts by individual community leaders to provide prevention services before problems arose. Community leaders confirmed in later interviews that support for local health care has been uneven. A few dedicated professionals had provided leadership in the community, but resources and institutional support were often inadequate. Nevertheless, community consciousness may be raised when a single practitioner begins to conduct seminars and training programs for community members, and political will to support programs may emerge. This was the case with the county nurse, who developed community programs in the early 1990s to reduce tobacco abuse, substance abuse, and heart disease.

To assess the effects of gaming development on community medical and health services provision, a series of interviews with community health professionals was conducted beginning in 1992. These conversations indicated that gaming development had had significant impacts on several aspects of community medical provision. One of the most obvious impacts was in the relocation of the Gilpin County nurse, county social services, and mental health coordinator from their offices in Central City to a set of trailers in midcounty. The move was required when the Clark Annex building was put up for sale by the county. The sale fell through when Central City declared its second moratorium, but the offices were moved anyway. Other changes were seen in the types of problems that accompanied gaming development, and in the groups served before and after gaming. New demands on community social and medical services are not unusual under conditions of rapid growth. Indeed, Cortese and Jones (1977) identified similar trends in western energy development boomtowns.

The workload for the county nurse, for example, increased as a result of gaming development. Initially, the nurse was asked by the county to provide increased adult immunization services and to develop server-intervention programs for casino workers who provided alcoholic beverages to patrons. The number of adult immunizations increased from 56 in 1990 to 220 in 1991, with casino employees accounting for the large increase. In 1992, when the staff at Columbine Medical Center in Black Hawk took on the role of providing services for casino employees, the county nurse's role was reduced. After a new county nurse was hired in 1994, a new policy of attending primarily to residents was established. The nurse is a central contact person who provides rides, telephone and in-person check-ups, screening, information, and referrals for county residents. According to the county nurse, these functions have helped restore some sense of community among local people, particularly elderly citizens, who had felt overlooked in the early years of gaming development.

Prior to gaming development, the Black Hawk branch of Columbine Family Heath Center, a federally financed rural health clinic, was located in the upstairs offices of a building in Black Hawk's commercial zone. Before gaming, clinic visits totalled slightly more than 3,200 patient contacts a year, but nearly 2,000 more patients visited the clinic in 1993 compared with 1989. According to the center's administrator, Diane Rittenhouse, the substantial increase in patient encounters was due primarily to the role of the clinic as a provider for employee health insurance and worker compensation programs for construction crews and casino employees. A new billing and records clerk was eventually hired.

After gaming began, the continued expansion of casinos around the clinic facility eventually made parking unmanageable for staff and patients alike: only two short-term spaces were available near the clinic entrance. In 1993, when the owner of a nearby parking lot proved unwilling to continue to provide parking spaces for clinic patients and staff, the clinic was forced to relocate into prefabricated buildings erected in the casino zone near the south end of Black Hawk's Main Street. The buildings were provided by Provenant Health Partners through St. Anthony's Hospital in Denver. The lot, provided by Gilpin County, had available parking, and the clinic operated there from early 1993 until July 1994, when that location also was reclaimed for gaming development. During that time, the administrators entered into a joint operating agreement with Provenant Health Partners to provide primary and urgent medical care.

When the Main Street location later became unavailable, the entire building was moved to another spot midway between Central City and Black Hawk along Gregory Gulch. The use of this desirable spot, with its spacious parking area, was donated by E. Norman and Mildred Blake, lifelong residents of Black Hawk and parents of the clinic director. As long as the casino developments remain primarily in or adjacent to the main business zones of the towns and do not disperse along Gregory Gulch, the clinic is likely to remain in this location.

Traditionally, the clinic specialized in serving low-income patients, elderly residents, school children (for sports and school physical examinations), and indigent patients from the Gilpin County and Clear Creek County area. During the construction period before gaming, and during the casino operations period after October 1, 1991, the profile of patient visits changed. Although the low-income residential population served by the clinic did not change dramatically before and after gaming, clinic doctors and administrators were overwhelmed with the volume of new construction workers and casino employees using the center, and with the billing and records paperwork required to coordinate insurance payments. In the baseline years of 1989 and 1990, the largest proportion of patients were 11–20 years old (21 percent of all patient visits in 1989 and 24 percent in 1990). The next largest group of patients were those aged 31–40 (14 percent of the total in 1989 and 16 percent in 1990). In 1991, however, corresponding to the most intense period of construction and to casino Opening Day, the largest age groups visiting the clinic were, in order, patients aged 31–40 years (20 percent of the total visits) and adults aged 41–50 (18 percent of total).

Clinic visits by adults remained high through 1994, while the relative proportion of children, teenagers, and elderly declined. In fact, the number of elderly patients decreased from 11 percent of the total in 1989 to only 3.6 percent in 1992, probably reflecting the difficulties of clinic access and patient departures from the area. Although patient contact sheets are not always complete with respect to diagnoses, notations indicating anxiety, depression, or hypertension increased substantially after 1990, peaking in 1991 and 1992. This period corresponded to the time of most rapid construction and gambling tourist increase in the community.

Along with increased demands for medical services, there have also been significant increases in demand for the ambulance service of Gilpin County since gaming began in Central City and Black Hawk. From January through August 1992, 387 patients were transported by ambulance, compared with only 181 patients transported during the entire previous year (1991) and 131 transported during all of 1990. The largest increases during 1991 were seen between October and December, the months during which gambling began locally. Ambulance personnel report that the increase in numbers of patrons was due to greater numbers of visitors, particularly elderly visitors unused to the high altitude, not to new kinds of ailments. The majority of incidents that require ambulance services are altitude-related problems such as fainting, blood pressure problems, and diabetic problems, exacerbated by drinking alcohol and the excitement of gambling. Before October 1, 1991, the ambulance service was staffed by ten to fifteen volunteers; after October 1, 1991, they organized a volunteer staff of about thirty-five people.

By 1995, demands on the ambulance service were stabilizing. The ambulance service tended to get medical calls, especially for elderly patients or those unused to the altitude, whereas trauma and accident calls were limited. The number of patients served had reached a plateau of about 100–120 calls per month, with half of these for transport and the other half for medical check-and-release on site. This monthly total sums to between 1,200 to 1,440 patient contacts per year, compared with a patient load of 194 persons in 1990 and 299 in 1991, so the impact on ambulance service has been substantial. The volunteer staff, as well, has been replaced by two permanent ambulances staffed with paramedics and EMT personnel, twenty-four hours a day. When necessary, a third ambulance staffed by volunteers is called from the community. Gilpin County Search and Rescue continues to operate the ambulance service, with financial support from Black Hawk, Central City, and Gilpin County.

The health and medical impacts were not unanticipated, but only limited county funds have been available for improving service provision in these areas. It is startling to realize how short-staffed these agencies are in comparison to how many community members and tourists they serve. It appears that government officials in the towns are willing to ignore the substantial difficulties experienced by the county in funding these services, and to rely on the willingness of volunteers and donations to keep necessary services afloat.

The need for well-funded emergency service organizations was demonstrated at several points after gaming began when local personnel participated in injury accident response teams. The most dramatic of these occasions was a crash on Highway 119 in August 1995, in which a drunken motorist hit a bus carrying gaming tourists, killing two and injuring forty-two (*Denver Post*, Aug. 28, 1995: 1A, 8A). This tragic accident raised new concerns about the safety of the two-lane mountain roads leading to the gaming towns, and about the role of alcohol in contributing to accidents. The state Department of Transportation had made numerous improvements to the roads, including repairing pavement, adding pullout lanes for slower drivers, installing guard rails, adding lights in tunnels, and improving signage. Nevertheless, the narrow canyon roads, coupled with drivers who may be alcohol-impaired, are a potentially lethal combination. Though the driver of the auto in the car/bus crash in August had not been gambling and drinking in the casinos, he had been drinking while camping in the county. Moreover, many other accidents have occurred when casino patrons attempted to drive home after gambling and drinking. An unpublished study of alcohol-related traffic accidents in the gaming county was reported to have found that, "in the first year of gambling, 57 percent of alcohol-related accidents involved people driving away from the gambling towns, but about 43 percent [of alcohol-related accidents could be attributed to people] driving *toward* the gambling towns" (*Denver Post*, Aug. 30, 1995: 1A, 24A).

COMMUNITY SOCIAL SERVICES

In addition to community health services, some of the most difficult impacts to measure are those related to the provision of social services. The county provides a number of programs for low-income and needy people in the community, including financial aid services, child protection services, Aid for Families with Dependent Children (AFDC), administration of child support payments, programs for elderly, and community mental health services.

Impacts in several of the programs administered under social services can be traced directly to the development of casino gaming. With the advent of gaming, for example, demand for financial aid services decreased by about two-thirds, as people who were once income-eligible for the program took jobs in the gaming industry and earned salaries higher than the qualification level. Food stamps and low-income energy assistance payments decreased by about half, when some low-income residents took casino jobs paying minimal, but year-round, salaries. The number of individuals eligible for medical disability services declined, as residents unable to afford the higher, gambling-induced rents across the county moved away. Several child protection cases were also directly related to gaming. In 1992, about five or six cases of child neglect (less than 10 percent of all child protection services cases) were related to gambling activities; these were primarily cases in which children were left alone in parked vehicles while parents gambled. Although only a small proportion of the total community mental health caseload is related to gaming, about five cases in 1992 concerned residents suffering stress and anxiety about community changes, work arrangements, and living situations.

Other changes in social services provision appear to be independent of gaming development. The demand for child protective services in Gilpin County, for example, has increased since 1991, rising from about seventeen open cases a month to about thirty-four, but the increase is related to organizational restructuring rather than gaming. A new County Social Services director, and new caseworkers hired from outside the community prior to the start of gaming, have a more aggressive, preventative philosophy than earlier staff, accounting for much of the increase in caseload numbers. In addition, some 1995 programs have a wider scope of services available than in pre-gaming times, so increases in program enrollment simply reflect institutional priorities.

Employment in the casino industry appears to have an indirect effect on some types of social services. In 1992, about twenty child protection services cases (35 percent of the total) were "related" to gaming in the sense that at least one parent was employed in the casino industry. These cases include children who were left alone, or with an elderly grandparent, while a single parent was at work. The data, however, are insufficient to determine a causal relationship between gaming employment and child neglect or abuse.[8]

Another type of social service program may be an indicator of broader trends in gaming development employment. The caseload for child support payments increased from sixty-three cases in September 1991 (pre-gaming) to about eighty-three cases in September 1992 (the end of the first gaming year). In each of the twenty new cases, the absent parent either lived in Gilpin County or worked in the Central City or Black Hawk gaming industry. As most of the divorce or support orders originated in either Nevada or South Dakota, a pattern of "casino employment migration" may be emerging through child support payment cases. That is, there may be a pattern of employment-trained people following gambling jobs from state to state, forming a new kind of migrant worker. Some of the effort to collect child support payments then falls upon the community where the liable parent is employed.

If employment migration proves to be a pattern common to all kinds of urban or rural areas where gaming is developed, community institutional effects may potentially be seen in either child support cases (when the liable parent takes a casino job locally), or in local educational systems (when a single parent with children obtains a job in the local casino industry). In Gilpin County, the effects of gaming development on schooling and educational provision are mixed.

The Gilpin County RE–1 school educates students from pre-kindergarten through grade 12, the last year of high school. Gilpin RE–1 is the only public school in the county, though some students living in the northernmost areas of the county attend Boulder County schools, and a few others attend private schools outside Gilpin County. Anecdotal evidence from interviews with community leaders confirms that with the development of gaming in Central City and Black Hawk, the Gilpin County school lost some low-wage employees (custodians, secretaries, bus drivers) to casino jobs that paid higher salaries. Casino owners, however, have supported student projects and fundraisers and have contributed scholarships and equipment to the school.

Colorado Department of Education data representing before, during, and after periods of gaming development reveal little variation in student enrollment, teacher retention, or student-to-teacher ratios. From 1987 to 1994, student enrollment was relatively stable at between 337 and 351 students in all grades. Similarly, the number of teachers remained relatively constant throughout the period, as did student-to-teacher ratios. It appears that any outflow of students from the community as a result of gaming has generally been balanced by an inflow of new students. A school spokesperson, though, noted that some of the new students seem "different" from local students. As children of casino employees, they are more likely to be from single-parent families, have a more transient and worldly lifestyle, and pose more disciplinary problems.

Finally, although Gilpin County has no Gamblers Anonymous groups, there are unconfirmed reports of rising attendance at Gamblers Anonymous meetings in Denver and other metropolitan areas since gaming was established in the Gilpin County towns.

ENVIRONMENTAL QUALITY

Tangible impacts of gaming development may be observed in changes to community natural resources, but in many cases these changes have been only poorly monitored and quantified over the course of casino development. The substantial proportion of public lands (about 52 percent is in public trust) in Gilpin County means that a variety of state and federal resource agencies potentially have a stake in the process and outcomes of gaming development. Air and water quality, forest management, mining land use, wildlife migration, recreational use of public lands, and noise and light pollution were some of the issues that came to the forefront with gaming development. In addition to concerns about public lands management, private mining properties were subject to development restrictions based on their level of toxic mineral contamination, and responsibility for cleanup was a point of negotiation between land owners and potential casino developers. A 1992 telephone survey of natural resource managers revealed that natural resource agencies experienced both direct and indirect impacts on lands under their jurisdiction in conjunction with the start of gaming.

Golden Gate Canyon State Park, administered by the Colorado Division of Parks and Outdoor Recreation, recorded an increased number of visitors around the start of gaming, and projected a need for more camping sites. That agency expected "shoulder season" usage in the off-peak times of spring and fall to increase, as gambling tourists sought camping sites near the gaming towns. By 1995, though, a spokesperson for that park explained that the impact had not been as great as expected, as gamblers were apparently unlikely to be campers. The largest impact, in fact, was increased traffic on the canyon roads to the park when the primary routes to the gaming towns experienced accident delays. Increased traffic on roads around the park also meant more use of park restrooms along the route, though restroom users rarely purchased a park permit to allow access into the area. Using a state park restroom is apparently not "using the park" in the minds of automobile tourists.

Similarly, the U.S. Department of Agriculture's Forest Service anticipated in 1991 that an outcome of gambling development would be an increase in the number of illegal residences springing up on forest land, and an increase in special use requests. The Forest Service manages extensive tracts of national forest land in Gilpin County, including portions of the Roosevelt National Forest and the Arapahoe National Forest, and is a partner in managing the Peak-to-Peak Scenic Highway (Highway 119) extending north from Black Hawk to Estes Park. The forest lands offer campgrounds, timber harvest opportunities, cattle grazing permits, wilderness access, mining permits, and scenic amenities. In 1995, a Forest Service employee reflected that the agency had anticipated much more impact than had actually occurred after gaming was established. Squatters had not been as large a problem as expected, and though the agency received many requests and inquiries about purchasing or developing lands adjacent to or on the forests, very few developers followed through with specific applications.

The U.S. Department of Interior's Bureau of Land Management is responsible for scattered small plots of land in Gilpin County that are used primarily for dispersed recreation, grazing, and mining. That agency, along with the state's Mined Land Reclamation Board, was concerned that former mining areas would prove to be an attraction for tourists who might be unaware of the large numbers of open mine shafts remaining in the area, or who might remove historic artifacts from county ghost town areas. A program to cap open mine shafts across the county was given added incentive by the introduction of gambling in the Gilpin County towns. The potential dangers to tourists were obvious after reports like the one that appeared in 1992, describing the experience of an intoxicated man who fell into a mine shaft as he and a companion searched for a shortcut from Central City to Black Hawk. Gilpin County Mine Rescue was called out in the middle of the night to pluck the man from the hole in the ground; he was not severely injured (*WRC,* Sept. 11, 1992: 1).

One prominent force in Gilpin County resource management is the Environmental Protection Agency (EPA), which, along with the Colorado Department of Health, monitors the review and cleanup of the county's "Superfund" sites. The mining districts around Idaho Springs and Central City were added in 1983 to the list of national Superfund sites under the name "Clear Creek/Central City Superfund Site" (Colorado Department of Public Health and Environment 1995). In Gilpin County, Superfund locations include mine tunnels, waste dumps, and soil and water resources contaminated with heavy metals from mining operations. These areas often have dangerously high concentrations of cyanide and arsenic (used to leach gold from rock), as well as other heavy metals such as lead, zinc, and manganese. Because these sites are considered dangerous to humans, animals, and wildlife, cleanup processes are strictly regulated. The process of tracing past site owners and working with new owners, reviewing site conditions, and enforcing and monitoring restoration processes is complex and time-consuming, and even before gaming was approved, the EPA was considered an unwanted meddler by independent-minded Gilpin County miners and others. In 1991, EPA officials said they anticipated even more complicated relationships with local governments, landowners, and casino industry representatives as gaming became operational.

The involvement of the EPA and the Colorado Department of Health with town and county officials and gaming interests, however, produced tangible improvements in the cleanup of some mining hazards and wastes, and in the improvement of local stream flow and water resources. Oversight by these agencies resulted in numerous local environmental improvements. The towns stopped dumping partially treated sewage into North Clear Creek in 1992; the towns and casino developers were prevented from dumping debris into and alongside the creek in 1994; some roads were paved to reduce dust and particulates; acid mine drainage from the National Tunnel was contained; and the Gregory Incline mining waste site was cleaned up by Bullwhackers casino in Black Hawk in 1994 for new use as a paved parking area (Colorado Department of Public Health and Environment 1995). When Central City initiated procedures to build the Chase Gulch water reservoir, the EPA and other agencies were also a factor in the permitting process, assuring that this project would meet environmental standards.

The National Park Service had designated some portions of Central City, Black Hawk, and the Gilpin County mining area as a National Historic Landmark District in 1961 and later. Although the appointment primarily provided for publicity and tax credits on historic properties within the landmark district, the Park Service was not authorized to enforce any restrictions on changes made to the historic area or properties. With initiation of the construction period in the gaming towns in 1991, the Park Service expressed concern about the extensive renovation activities, including the gutting of buildings, the demolition of historic structures, and the erection of incompatible new structures. On several occasions, the agency publicly stated that the historic designation would be under threat if the pace and scale of casino developments continued. As a result of gaming development, the National Park Service placed all three of Colorado's gaming towns on a "most endangered historic landmarks" list in 1992. The towns remain on the endangered list as of 1995.

A large portion of the hillside at the south end of Black Hawk was logged to construct the road and switchbacks leading to the Miner's Mesa parking area above town. The narrow, two-lane Highway 119 is shown at bottom; a row of vehicles can be seen on the incline of the Miner's Mesa road in the center of the photo.

Although federal and state natural resource agencies primarily worked on critical problems, more incremental negative impacts emerged with the construction and operation of gaming. Residents remarked about increased air pollution in the towns from the huge volume of automobile exhaust, extensive noise pollution from bus traffic and tourist and construction vehicles, and increased littering in the commercial zones of Black Hawk and Central City. In addition, the construction of the Miner's Mesa parking lot above Black Hawk created a visual eyesore and extensive deforestation on a prominent hillside. Because the area is well lighted, and the road scar is unimproved, the accommodation of gamblers produced unwanted light pollution and reduced visual quality for residents who valued local scenery and environmental amenities.

Interviews with the state and federal agencies responsible for managing natural resources in Gilpin County were instructive for more than the range of impacts expected from gaming development. Collectively, these agencies demonstrated a reactive rather than proactive approach to dealing with change in towns adjacent to resource lands. With the exception of the Environmental Protection Agency, few of the agencies were involved in continuing dialogues with town or county government officials. Moreover, few mechanisms were in place for facilitating interactions, a unusual situation given the positive values Gilpin County residents continue to express regarding their natural surroundings and the contribution of local public lands to local quality of life.

THE FAILURE OF COMMUNITY VISIONS?

The tangible institutional impacts associated with gaming development were both costly and disruptive to Black Hawk, Central City, and Gilpin County. As residents and leaders sought to explain the mixed and sometimes unsettling effects, they looked first to community visions, then to government structures and planning processes. The process of self-evaluation was not easy, and community conflicts persisted throughout the first few years after the opening of gambling.

Community visions can be defined as those collective ideals and values desired by residents of a locale. These include implicit understandings, for example, about how to keep community spirit alive, or about "how we collectively see the future." Community planners and analysts often believe that articulation of strong, long-term visions is necessary for successful tourism development (Hester 1990; Richardson 1991; Minnesota Tourism Center 1991). Likewise, researchers writing about tourism partnerships have proposed that community visions should be shared by all interest groups with a stake in the development (Bruns and Stokowski 1996, forthcoming). Though highly idealistic, the basic assumption of these writings is that communities able to identify focused, valued futures through participatory action are better able to control development choices and outcomes.

Although citizens may not consciously label their shared goals as visions, hopes for the future appear frequently and visibly in the rhetoric of local public life. As the discussion of community rhetoric in chapter 3 demonstrated, a variety of shared visions were expressed by Gilpin County residents prior to and during the gambling campaign. These included desires to protect the small-town lifestyle, preserve the amenities of the natural and historic landscape, and retain personal independence and lifestyle while revitalizing the local economy. In addition, a vision was clearly specified by pro-gambling CCPI promoters, who claimed that gambling would be developed as an attraction rather than an industry, limited in location and restricted in form, compatible with other local businesses, and nonintrusive on social life. Indeed, the success of the gambling campaign was directly related to the skill of the promoters in expressing their vision of noncasino, limited stakes gambling based on a few slot machines in every little business.

When gaming development subsequently brought extensive physical changes, and the discrepancy between what had been promised in the gambling campaign and the realities of the construction period became apparent, community-wide discussions about visions of the future also multiplied. For example, an alternative, more limited growth model was presented during a community planning meeting when one resident suggested that townsfolk really wanted "no cars in Central City." His proposal was met with laughter and suggestions that he was being unreasonable. For gaming to succeed, explained planners and local government leaders, auto traffic and parking must be managed, not banned. Such commentary made it clear that community leaders were more willing to let the growth machine take its course than to derail or slow it to accommodate alternative growth suggestions.

By supporting the casino development growth policy and ignoring other alternatives, local leaders failed to represent all community interests adequately. Residents had not voted to approve gaming on the scale and magnitude they experienced; they had voted for a small-scale, year-round attraction that would stabilize local businesses. Citizens in Central City, Black Hawk, and Gilpin County were generally much more conservative in their attitudes about community development, and while many were not anti-gaming or anti-growth, they were much less pro-growth than the elected officials. In personal interviews, elected officials acknowledged this point, but commented that "gaming development was good for local people," who, they said, were stuck in the past.

Once the gaming amendment had been approved, and organizers and developers focused on restructuring the community to accommodate the gaming industry, it was almost too late to consider other visions. The dominant ideology of community survival through casino development became the precise vision, thus limiting discussion of what amount of growth was desirable, how growth should be managed, and how gaming fit with other long-term community futures. The presentation of Black Hawk and Central City as "new Western boomtowns" by casino entrepreneurs reinforced that ideology. One casino manager explained the industry vision in an interview several months after the start of gaming, saying, "Gaming is the road to riches for us and the towns." An owner of another casino explained, "We want to preserve and recreate the integrity of this place . . . and attract many different demographics." Linking local history with a contemporary profit motive allowed casino entrepreneurs to create new community meanings through revised rhetoric that focused attention on the benefits of gaming, and allowed industry newcomers to claim a connection to the area's history, thus rationalizing growth.

In considering Colorado gaming development, Long (1995: 192) asserted that the communities "did not start out with a well-conceived vision of how they wanted gaming to look—nor did they have in place the right set of policy enablers and controls to achieve their vision." Although the issue of policy controls is a separate matter, the examples cited earlier contradict the view that coherent visions were missing from the development process. Gaming development, in increasing scope and scale, may not have been the choice of certain residents or groups, but it was certainly a vision of future conditions supported by promoters, developers, and casino entrepreneurs. Similarly, a Gilpin County leader described the consequences of gaming establishment by suggesting that "No one had the ability to create a vision; they only created an industry, and their primary concern was with maintaining a clean, crime-free industry." This charge is also unsupported by evidence: the creation of a gaming industry (in whatever form) *became* the central community vision once gambling had emerged as a potential future course of action in 1989.

This suggests, then, that communities are rarely visionless but are continually considering the merits of potential alternative futures. As the gaming developments in Black Hawk and Central City illustrate, diverse visions were presented and discussed by spokespersons, interest groups, and analysts during the campaign stage of tourism proposals and afterwards. These divergent and often competing visions represented the growth preferences of different coalitions of community interests ranging from growth-machine advocates to growth critics. The conclusion that "there was no vision" cannot be supported with available data; indeed, it oversimplifies more complex issues of decision making, responsibility, and accountability associated with gaming development.

There are several alternative hypotheses, however, that might explain the more complex dynamics of community tourism development. First, certain types of visions may be more likely than others to prevail in the contest over community futures. As suggested by the discussion of growth-machine politics in chapter 4, in the Colorado gaming developments and probably in other tourism growth situations, the visions that tended to predominate were those presented by powerful, wealthy, central participants (internal to the community as well as external) associated with community growth machines. So, though many visions are discussed, only some are supported by powerful leaders, and chosen visions tend to disproportionately reflect growth-machine interests. The selective choice hypothesis might also account for the poor reception given by persons in positions of power to competing visions proposed by nonaligned residents, as seen in the suggestion to ban cars from Central City.

Growth-machine politics may play a substantial role in the choice of which visions ultimately are adopted, but other community conditions may already have set the stage for powerful interests to usurp the development process. Another hypothesis to consider in evaluating the institutional impacts of gaming development is that community leaders typically have vested interests in maintaining the status quo, and so present only very general visions, and procedures for achieving those visions, for local consumption. By keeping visions nonspecific, leaders appear to be attentive to community needs while taking on little responsibility to actually accomplish anything. This was evident in interviews with key leaders in Black Hawk and Central City, who described their pre-gambling community visions in extremely broad terms. A government leader in Central City explained, "We want survival of the community"; in Black Hawk, a town leader said, "We want to go where the citizens want us to go." Surely all residents would have agreed that a position against community decline and for citizens' concerns was desirable; unfortunately, both positions were so hopelessly vague as to be almost meaningless.

There are strategic reasons for leaders to be obscure about community visions. If only generalities are promised, any advances are rewarded; if nothing is accomplished, leaders cannot be held accountable for failure. Moreover, it is easier to blame lack of vision as the cause of failure (the blame is generalized, and no one is directly held responsible) than to blame specific individuals, such as community leaders, for allowing questionable visions to succeed (defensiveness and conflict result). In interviews conducted shortly after the opening of gaming, residents from all community groups expressed confusion about how the gambling developments had become so much more extensive and more overwhelming than anyone had anticipated. "We trusted our leaders to protect us," residents kept repeating; "how could this happen?" The eventual explosion of community anger and despair showed the downside of a strategy of vague visioning. Citizens turned against local leaders and initiated formal procedures to oust incumbents in an effort to reclaim control of town government.

Growth-machine selectivity and existing community conditions are thus likely to influence the outcomes of development, but one could also hypothesize that the implementation process contributed to failures in accomplishing desired development goals. Community visions are framed rhetorically, but implementation requires real and symbolic action, not merely words. If all affected groups and citizens are not equal partners in designing and enacting an implementation strategy, some partners (such as those who are wealthier) may unduly influence the process. Some groups or actors may attempt to stymie the process in an effort to preserve their own position or undercut the role of others. If the circumstances for shared decision making are not already established in communities, though, it is unlikely that either leaders or residents will take the opportunity to create the organizational structures facilitating proactive, shared involvement under conditions of rapid growth, when rhetoric is accompanied by powerful incentives, or when authority is threatened.

Observations from the development and operation stages of gaming suggest three conclusions. First, industry goals were expressed as consonant with growth-machine visions presented by CCPI members, local government leaders, community planners, and casino developers. Second, alternative, competing, or partial visions specified by residents who were outside the promotional groups often were not taken seriously by local leaders, primarily because those in a position to do something about alternative visions had already committed to the tourism growth option. Third, identified visions were almost never accompanied by specific action plans detailing the procedures for accomplishing the desired future outcome. As a result, community visions were reframed as secondary to the economic goals of gaming development; only later, when antagonism against local government leaders for their role in the gaming development grew dramatically, did community members begin to reestablish their voice in community visioning.

GOVERNANCE AFTER GAMING

Policy issues that arise during periods of rapid growth are especially interesting to social scientists because they tend to call into question past community ideologies and force leaders to accommodate new voices in development preparations. The preeminent policy issue in the preparations for gaming was the meaning of *development*. As understood by government leaders and CCPI promoters (and later, casino owners) in Black Hawk and Central City, development meant growth, and growth was to be measured in quantitative terms as year-round economic activity, more jobs, more tourists, and improved individual incomes. More qualitative measures of development, such as greater diversity in the economic base, more flexibility of choice in community growth decisions, greater resiliency in periods of real economic decline, and wider participation in community visioning, were rarely mentioned either during the preparations for gaming or later, after casinos opened. The failure of residents to understand their leaders' growth orientation, coupled with the failure of leaders to temper quantitative growth with quality-of-life benefits, was a volatile combination in the gaming towns.

Development impacts can affect community governance in at least three ways: by placing added stress on existing service provision; by disrupting political and administrative processes or typical ways of doing business in local government; and by stimulating organizational restructuring to accommodate new demands on policy makers and staff. In Gilpin County and the gaming towns, stresses on existing services were visible in police, health, social services, and other public agencies providing for the public welfare. Changes in process were evident in planning, government administration, and policy actions such as hiring decisions, contract services, and public review provisions. These product and process outcomes were, in many cases, accompanied by organizational restructuring in local governments.

The instability of tenure for local government officials after gaming was adopted became a central issue in policy formation and enactment. The gaming law specified that citizens could not simultaneously hold a gaming license and an elected government position, a measure aimed at eliminating potential conflicts of interest between casinos and town governments. For small, rural towns like Black Hawk and Central City, this rule had dramatic consequences. Populations in such towns are often so limited that few candidates are available for local office. Moreover, in rural communities, members of the business elite are likely to serve in local government, but they are also well positioned with financial and property resources to become involved in the new industry. As the growth-machine model predicts, their power and influence could be strengthened considerably if allowed a dual role in government and industry. Naturally, casino supporters protested loudly against this regulation, as their development agenda depended on supportive local government leadership (*WRC*, Sept. 27, 1991:2).

The consequence of this legislation became apparent in the month before Opening Day in 1991, when both Central City and Black Hawk mayors resigned their positions to go into the casino business. Mayor Bruce Schmalz, owner of the Rock Shop and T-shirt Shop in Central City, and Mayor Bill Lorenz, owner of the Black Forest Inn restaurant in Black Hawk, each converted a portion of their buildings into casino areas. Central City's new mayor, Rand Anderson, held office from October 1991 through mid-March 1992 before he, too, entered the casino industry. The next Central City mayor, Dick Allen, lasted less than two years before being ousted in a community recall election in December 1993. Black Hawk politics were considerably more stable.

Mayors were not the only ones affected by the gaming legislation: other members of local government, including council members and staff, also left government positions to take jobs in casinos, open small businesses such as bed-and-breakfast lodgings, or move away. The parade of mayors and other officials away from public service and toward casino jobs raised fears that the gaming towns would experience government failure. With such small town populations, qualified applicants for elected positions were scarce. In addition, the long work hours, evident stress, and relatively low salaries deterred potential candidates. Rapid community growth demanded more specialized jobs and expertise, but these skills were sometimes unavailable locally or were non-importable because of low pay scales and high community uncertainty. Positions such as mayor and council member also required residency in the gaming towns, and although salaries for elected officials and government staff began to improve as town revenues grew, people were more likely to be moving out of the gaming towns than into them, as housing rents were also on the rise.

A creative solution to the problem of leadership continuity was implemented in Central City. There, former mayors and council members were appointed to a newly contrived "Board of Adjustments" that was meant to advise town officials on contemporary issues related to community development. It was reasonable to ask for input from former town leaders, as they could provide historical context and memory of past governance issues, but there were also problems with this approach. Members of the Board of Adjustments included organizers of the pro-gambling campaign, and they were generally positive about the changes to the community. "It's not completely what we expected," said one former, long-term Central City official, "but we just weren't prepared for the huge success of gambling here." According to these leaders, the reasonable course of action now that gaming had arrived was to compete for a good share of the market. In other words, these leaders accepted the sacrifice of community disruption for the bonuses expected from whatever casino entrepreneurs were willing to provide in the town. The prominence of the growth-machine agenda among local government leaders and within Central City's Board of Adjustments worried many citizens, raised concerns about collusion, and fueled suspicions that important decisions were being made behind the scenes rather than publicly.

The shifting power structures of local governance were also apparent in the use of advisors and consultants on town development issues. Soon after the gaming amendment was passed by Colorado voters, consultants were hired in Black Hawk and Central City to direct and advise the planning process. They responded to tangible development needs with plans for physical changes in the towns, providing services that were not within the scope of government capabilities in those small towns. Their role was not to challenge assumptions about growth, but to enact plans for accomplishing tangible development goals. Their visibility and influence in the planning process differed by town. In Black Hawk, for example, the Denver-based firm of Cole and Associates conducted community meetings, advised local government on code compliance, and prepared scale drawings for casino "development zones" along Black Hawk's main streets. In Central City, consultants performed similar functions, but maintained an active community role even past the start of gaming.

More troubling than the extensive use of consultants during early stages of gaming preparations, and into postestablishment organization, was the continued presence of consultants on the town payrolls even several years past Opening Day. Particularly in Central City, consultants seemed to be unusually likely to be promoted into powerful positions in local government. The most obvious example of this phenomenon was David Stahl, project coordinator with Associated Land Consultants, Inc., of Boulder, Colorado, who had been hired to direct the planning efforts in Central City soon after gaming was approved in 1990. Stahl stayed on the town payroll after the opening of gaming, earning substantial fees for consulting on parking, traffic flow, transportation systems, community development, public works, water storage, and other issues. In September 1993, the Central City council proposed hiring Stahl as a local government staff member to oversee seven departments, including planning, building inspection, public works, and historic preservation. The rationale for this proposal was that the town would save consultant fees by placing Stahl on staff (though why Stahl would consider taking a government job with less pay than his consulting income was never revealed).

Local opposition to the proposal to hire Stahl was strong and animated, as shown by several pointed letters to the editor appearing in the *Weekly Register-Call*. Residents objected to the lack of competitive application and hiring practices; a perceived lack of tangible products from Stahl's tenure as a local consultant; the appearance of favoritism, given that Stahl had recruited some town employees and consultants; ethical issues in Stahl's previous employment; and the creation of more complex layers of local government (*WRC*, Sept. 3, 1993: 1; Sept. 10, 1993: 2; Sept. 17, 1993: 23). Nevertheless, Stahl was appointed to be Central City's Director of Community Development and Operations in November 1993. He resigned in March 1994, again becoming a consultant to Central City. Then, in November 1994, after city manager Jack Hidahl resigned under pressure from the casino association,[9] Stahl was appointed to be the acting city manager. Later promoted to interim city manager, he held this post throughout 1995. Apparently satisfied with his performance, the Central City aldermen debated in summer 1995 the merits of requiring that the city manager live in Central City. Though the council tended to favor lifting the residency requirement, local citizens were less favorable. Stahl was not a resident of Central City, a point that added fuel to the hotly debated issue. In the November election, citizens voted to require residency for the person holding the position of city manager.

The case of David Stahl recalled the "good old boy" traditions of governance in pre-gaming Central City, and raised special concerns among citizens who wondered why and how outsiders had become apparently powerful insiders in local governance. The question of who was in charge in the gambling towns became more than rhetorical. The formalization of governance procedures using contrived boards and planning consultants meant that accountability was in short supply. Moreover, it became difficult to even locate community leaders and have a conversation with one, as new gatekeepers appeared at all political levels. Staff were directed to deal with routine procedures and public concerns, leaving leaders free to focus on the critical issues facing the community. In theory, these changes made good sense. For a community that previously had been organized along principles of familiarity and informality, though, increasing bureaucratization was disconcerting. Residents began to feel that access to their leaders was being restricted by overzealous staff members who should not have had that kind of power. Residents also expressed concern when specific gatekeepers exceeded their job duties and began to speak as if they were in leadership roles. As a case in point, residents were shocked when Donna Martin, the secretarial assistant to the county commissioners, suddenly adopted the role of policy spokesperson for the commissioners. Residents, angered at the lack of responsiveness to citizens, questioned the attentiveness and judgment of the county commissioners. Though Martin was later promoted to the position of county manager, the complaints continued.

The situation confirmed what Hall (1994: 150) observed in other tourism development sites, namely, that "local élites and external interests may have a greater influence in directing tourism development processes than many of the people who will be most affected by such development." Some residents of Black Hawk, Central City, and Gilpin County perceived that leaders had incrementally sold off the community to the highest casino bidders. Residents wanted a voice in community direction and assurances that the "unofficial governments" of advisory boards and consultants could be controlled. Residents reported feeling unable to influence the planning and implementation process, believing that many decisions were handled through private agreements made outside the public forum. Indeed, an opinion column published in the *Weekly Register-Call* in 1992 was typically blunt about what residents saw as the root of local problems: "Central City observers have long been aware of an apparent council of marionettes, manipulated by 'staff' and consultants. This impression is magnified by their shunning of public input. . . . It's all a matter of accountability" (July 31, 1992: 2). These sorts of accusations would be repeated, publicly and privately, by numerous residents in conversations over the next three years.

Central City's second building moratorium, imposed during a council meeting in April 1992, added fuel to this fire. After a two-hour executive session, with no public discussion allowed, the aldermen unanimously passed a moratorium on new casino construction in Central City. Projects already approved by HARC could proceed, but no new applications would be accepted until after the moratorium was lifted. Council members explained after the meeting that growth was out of control and special action was needed. The town could not cope with transportation, parking, water, and sewer problems. These issues had all been evident to residents, but local leaders had previously downplayed their significance, explaining that the hired consultants were working on resolving the problems. The moratorium was tentatively set to extend until January 1993.

What appeared at first blush to be a reasonable, if extreme, response to dealing with the problems of rapid growth eventually revealed several strange coincidences. About eighteen projects, including the proposed sale of Gilpin County and school district properties totalling about $15 million, and a number of projects proposed for Gregory Gulch (most involving construction of entirely new buildings), fell through as a result of the moratorium. In contrast, the personal projects of several Central City council members were approved just prior to imposition of the moratorium. Although the moratorium came as a surprise to casino developers and residents, there were reports that some associates of council members had been forewarned. One alderman was alleged to have completed a several-million-dollar property sale using advance knowledge of the moratorium (*Denver Post*, Aug. 28, 1992: 1A, 23A).

As if the moratorium had not stimulated enough conflict, the actions of Central City leaders at other times fueled the fire. The "pizza caper" at one Central City council meeting, for example, appeared to be a symbolic demonstration of power by council members, as well as a rude insult to both potential casino developers and residents (*Denver Post*, June 25, 1992: 1B, 5B). A review of Central City's moratorium was placed last on the agenda, and the hall was filled by potential casino developers awaiting the discussion. Several hours later, when the other agenda items had been resolved, the council called a recess and began eating pizzas at the council table, while audience members looked on in amazement. Only when they had finished eating in front of the crowd did the council discuss the moratorium, agreeing that it should not be lifted until water supply issues were resolved. The "staging" of the pizza caper suggests that the real meaning of the spectacle was to reinforce the attitude of invincibility assumed by Central City council members. New casino owners were unconvinced, and became increasingly irritated by their dealings with the Central City leaders. "Central City is a small town experiencing a boom that is being run by small-town people who want the same power they had when it was small," said the general manager of a small casino that closed after only a few months in business (*Rocky Mountain News,* Sept. 2, 1992: 37).

Other aspects of Central City politics came under greater scrutiny when the moratorium was imposed, and investigative reporters uncovered inconsistencies in the approval process for numerous casino projects even prior to the moratorium.[10] Casino projects that had been approved for development, for example, were sometimes ratified by committees comprised of members who were involved in the property sale for that particular project. It was, therefore, not unexpected that the moratorium stimulated accusations that town leaders were favoring existing casino owners, who wanted to keep development out of the Gulch and centralized along Main and Eureka Streets, thus protecting their own interests against increased competition. Several lawsuits and recall efforts were initiated against Mayor Dick Allen and Alderman Scott Webb, who were charged with attempting to manipulate the development for their own personal gain. The lawsuits and recall efforts were unsuccessful, but the moratorium was lifted in February 1993.

COMMUNITY CONFLICTS

Institutions are shaped by history (Putnam 1993), and community conflicts were not a unique product of the gaming developments. Battles, real and imagined, between Central City and Black Hawk and between the towns and the county, were established practices in Gilpin County, though many individuals took great pains to camouflage their sentiments. "I don't talk to Black Hawk," said one prominent Central City leader during an interview. He explained that his views were typical, even though the official policy was to claim that everyone was so busy working on internal town issues that it was really difficult to find time to drive a mile and meet with representatives from the other town. Interviews with other community officials revealed that, while publicly promoting a need for cooperation, leaders continued the lack of cooperation by blaming the other town for failures in communication. "They want to always do things their own way," rationalized representatives from both Central City and Black Hawk about the others.

Corroborating evidence of local feuding appeared in a series of interviews with community leaders from the towns, county, and new gaming industry in 1992. Nearly all the interviewees reported that cooperation between the two town governments was far below average, and about two-thirds of the leaders thought that cooperation between residents of Central City and Black Hawk was also below average. The only relationships described as "above average" in degree of cooperation were linkages between town governments and Colorado

Division of Gaming officials, and between town governments and casino own-ers' associations.[11] These attitudes were also evident to outside analysts and to new casino owners and managers. "There are so many local factions working against each other and the new casino industry," lamented one casino manager.

Gaming development renewed competitive urges and exaggerated exist-ing levels of community conflict. Though elected officials worked long hours, their efforts were not always appreciated by either local constituents or casino representatives. Charges of favoritism, nonaccountability, and hidden agendas accompanied the planning and development process (*Denver Post*, June 22, 1992: 1B, 2B). Residents who said they had "trusted their leaders" to accom-plish the kind of development promoted in the gambling campaign were bit-ter, and charged that local leaders seemed to be "in the pockets" of the casino industry. Local government leaders retorted that the blame should rest with the State Gaming Commission, which had failed to enforce the spatial regula-tions and the proposed tax rate as intended by campaign organizers. Industry leaders claimed a right to lobby for agreeable business conditions, and blamed local proponents for their naive notion that gaming could be conducted on a Mom-and-Pop scale.

The perception that elected officials failed to listen to, understand, or respond to community concerns dramatized the problem of incommensurate goals. Community leaders had goals opposite to those of many residents, and casino developers had industry plans that were unavailable for public scrutiny. Although strong negative opinions about the pace and scale of community changes had been expressed at all stages of the gambling campaign and throughout the construction period, the operational phase of gaming saw an outpouring of community anger, despair, and unparalleled conflict. Accusa-tions about who was to blame for casinos' taking over the towns became ram-pant. As impacts began to be felt across all institutions and social areas of the community, anger reached a fever pitch, and recall elections became the means by which community dissatisfaction was channeled into action.

The threat of recall elections had been used in previous community con-flicts, but the disappointments and inequalities resulting from gaming devel-opment left residents with few other means of response. The first recall election occurred in Black Hawk in January 1992, when residents attempted to unseat three town council members for allegedly having conflicts of inter-est, violating the open meetings law, and failing to have a legal residence in the town. One of the three recalled council members was replaced after sev-enty-nine citizens (47 percent of Black Hawk voters) cast their ballots.

Recall efforts against Central City Mayor Dick Allen and Alderman Scott Webb, in autumn 1992, stimulated by that town's second moratorium, both failed with about 60 percent of the 150 votes cast in favor of retaining each of the men. That recall had been initiated by two local women, Cindy Gribble and Cynthia Combs, who complained about the obstructiveness, nonaccountability, discourtesy, and secretiveness of Central City leaders. For their efforts, they were portrayed by local government officials as "dangerous" to the town (*Denver Post,* Nov. 30, 1992; Dec. 2, 1992). A second recall effort was initiated against Dick Allen in December 1993. The petition supporting that recall alleged that Allen had failed to maintain his primary residence in Central City, had failed to act personally and professionally in the best interests of that town, and had failed to investigate improprieties in the conduct of town employees. In the weeks leading up to the second recall election, the mayor also was evicted from his home and shop for not paying rent in July 1993, and stood accused of stealing artifacts and vandalizing the premises. This recall succeeded by a margin of 83 to 72 (about 54 percent of 155 votes), the first time Central City residents had ousted a seated elected official.[12]

As the level of community dissatisfaction rose, other kinds of concerted civic participation increased across Gilpin County. Several of these efforts were centered in the county, where residents formed citizen action groups to protest the spread of gambling-related developments into mid-county areas. A precedent for these types of activities had been set with the formation of "Little Kingdom Forest" in 1988 to stop forest clear-cutting in Gilpin County. The unique qualities of the mountain environment were always important to county residents, many of whom had moved to Gilpin County as a retreat from metropolitan-area problems and were adamantly opposed to urbanization of the local landscape. With the advent of gaming, though, as real estate prices in the towns skyrocketed, pressures increased to locate governmental services and business developments in mid-county.

The level of anger prompting these meetings was often intense. "This is not the laid-back mountain community it used to be. . . . Outside influences drive the community now. Money talks," observed one resident. Another commented, "Those of us who voted for gambling were naive. We trusted our Commissioners and local towns to keep control. We were ignorant of the problems—and we were betrayed by the people who pushed gambling."

Two primary citizen activist groups both emerged in 1992. The Gilpin Residents Protective Association (GRPA) began to meet in living rooms in mid-county neighborhoods to consider strategies for protecting unincorporated areas of the county. They were initially formed to protest a proposed parking lot planned for mid-county, and continued to actively lobby against encroachment of any developments felt to be detrimental to county quality of life. Many members of this group were especially opposed to the siting of the new jail facility in mid-county. Another group known as PAVE (Protect Apex Valley Environment) formed to oppose the proposed diversion and damming of North Clear Creek to meet the water needs of Black Hawk, Central City, and the casino industry. About forty members of this environmentally conscious group staged a protest march in the towns in 1992 to oppose water diversion projects under discussion at that time.

As the county groups began to speak more forcefully in public meetings about their visions for the future of the county, their opponents in the gaming towns became angrier. In another example of diversionary reframing, those supporting gaming developments, including town leaders and some county residents, berated the "rabble rousers in the County" for not supporting "the" growth process. Though new levels of partici-

Gilpin County residents placed this sign along North Clear Creek near Apex. Citizen activism emerged in mid-Gilpin County, as residents protested water diversion schemes proposed by the gaming towns.

pation, and a more cohesive sense of community among county residents, emerged as positive products of these meetings, increased anger and resentment among county residents also accompanied the process. Even into 1995, a county resident noted, "Gambling has destroyed this community and many people are still utterly bitter."

One unsuccessful anti-growth effort concerned the siting of the new jail and justice center in mid-Gilpin County near the oldest community cemetery and a quiet subdivision. County commissioners had attempted to work with citizen groups that expressed concern over the location, but the situation was colored by past grievances mapped onto contemporary community needs. As one county resident noted in June 1994, the decision to build the justice center in mid-county was based on planning decisions made many years before gaming. In his words, "The Commissioners aren't rocket scientists, but they're basically good people. They have worked with community groups, kept us informed, and made the best decision they could, constrained by land use decisions made a decade or two ago before there was any thought of gaming development."

Not all residents were this generous, and a new round of recall elections was initiated in the county. An effort to recall all three county commissioners, based primarily on their involvement in choosing a site for the new county jail facility, produced extensive community conflict. The recall petition alleged that the three commissioners had proceeded with development of the justice center without adequate study of alternative sites, without securing water and sewer infrastructure, and in disregard of community wishes. The implications of this recall election were potentially very serious. All three county commissioners would have been ousted from office and replaced with persons who had not held such positions in the past and who had little experience working in county government in the rapidly changing community. The bitter temperament in the community prompted one of the commissioners eventually to choose not to run for reelection, although the recall of the other two commissioners failed soundly.

Many of the community power struggles that ensued during the construction and operation phases of gaming development can be seen as challenges to the dominant male "voice" of community governance in an effort to achieve equal access, information, or equal or greater political position. Traditionally, men dominated the political scene in Gilpin County while women played supporting roles. Men have held the primary positions in local government and have been the primary business owners. Photographs in the weekly paper are more likely to picture men than women in official or informal occasions. Indeed, one of the strongest community complaints about the pro-gambling campaign was that so-called public discussions were being conducted in male-only meetings at the Central City Elks Club. There were also numerous complaints of documents and information being unavailable to citizens, often female, who had different opinions than local leaders.

The debilitating effects of community conflict may be partially mitigated over time, particularly as local residents continued to participate fully in their communities. Letters in the *Weekly Register-Call* expressed, in typical Gilpin County fashion, the willingness of people to contribute to solving community problems, even if community leaders did not seem to take advantage of these offers. As one resident wrote (*WRC,* July 10, 1992: 2), "EARTH TO CITY!! We're out here. We're trying to COMMUNICATE. We have ideas. We can help. Why won't you hear us? If you would accept input from us rather than hide all your heads in the false notion that you have all the answers then maybe we could work things out." By the end of 1994, some negative sentiments had abated, as people who remained in the community came to realize that tolerance coupled with vigilance was the key to the future. The election of several new local leaders also did much to provide a more representative government.

In addition to these changes, a new column in the *Weekly Register-Call* proved to be a catalyst for public discussion among Gilpin County residents. Written by Lary Brown, the former CCPI leader who was later adversely affected by Central City's second moratorium and could not sell his building, the column was introduced in autumn 1993 under the title "Setting it Straighter" (a reference to Central City's news bulletin, "Setting it Straight"). Originally a commentary on the moratorium consequences and the state of Central City's finances, the column became, by February 1994, a regular opinion/analysis report under the title of the "Central City Shaft." Replete with innuendo, the often-vitriolic tone of the commentary suggested that Brown's motives were perhaps not altogether noble or objective. Nevertheless, his column attempted to provide oversight on local government decisions that often seemed to have been made under secretive circumstances or for obscure reasons. Brown attacked the Central City government for paying exorbitant fees to consultants and attorneys, for irregular elections and assessment procedures, poor decisions about expenditures, and other issues of local concern. The value of Brown's column was in stimulating public discussion about issues that were sensitive or not fully addressed by local leaders. Brown's essays were an outlet for community anger, and they allowed the community to vicariously exercise oversight on the leadership and the new gaming industry.

GAMING AND COMMUNITY INSTITUTIONS

Tourism development should be concerned with producing and creating sustainable community futures, not only in economic terms, but also in terms that are human, and on both personal and collective scales. This becomes almost impossible when community institutions are affected by rapid growth processes. The gaming developments in Central City and Black Hawk are not unique in their outcomes. Cortese and Jones (1977: 84) observed that in most of the western energy boomtowns they studied, "there was a high and sometimes complete turnover in leadership positions. . . . In all of these cases we were told that there had been a need for more professional, more competent, more aggressive, or more energetic people." The cases these authors cite include voluntary resignations and appointed replacements. In most cases, the outcome was a turn toward professionalization and formality in governance and agency administration, creating bureaucratic layers where none had previously existed. Such outcomes seem never to be anticipated by communities considering growth issues, yet they are absolutely central to the outcomes of the development.

The institutional effects of tourism development can be seen in the provision of community services and in the negotiation of power, but as Hall (1994: 2) pointed out, tourism researchers have typically "either ignored or neglected the political dimension of the allocation of tourism resources, the generation of tourism policy, and the politics of tourism development." As the gaming developments in Central City and Black Hawk show, though, such issues are relevant to the success of the tourism growth option, as well as to the viability of the community itself.

The community planning processes that preceded casino development and continued into the operational phase of gaming illustrate some of the complexities of governance and citizen participation in rapid-growth tourism communities. The extended planning process demonstrated that small, incremental policy decisions may have substantial cumulative consequences. This was especially true for local transportation planning and the hiring of consultants, most obviously in Central City. The planning process also elaborated a model in which "talk was action," but action was not coincident with decision-making power. For example, public meetings and community forums facilitated citizen participation, but more often than not, residents felt the exercise to be in vain. As a result, the discontinuity across the project agendas and timetables of government leaders, citizens, and industry developers was striking, highlighting a need for more integrative approaches to tourism planning. It was impossible to be integrative, though, when growth interests promoted one set of visions, citizens searched for a collective vision, and industry leaders—appearing on the local scene only after gaming had been approved—presented yet another set of values and goals.

The impacts of gaming development on community institutions confirms that both tangible and intangible changes occur in communities undergoing rapid development. Gaming development may solve some of the economic needs of communities, but there may also be consequent, unanticipated institutional effects. The capability of local leaders and residents to effectively manage the process of planning for, and the outcomes of, large-scale tourism development must be considered in advance. In Gilpin County and its gaming towns, the skills needed to effectively manage tourism development, including political negotiation, entrepreneurship, coalition building, promotion of community involvement, and countless others, were rarely apparent. In addition, more traditional political skills evident in the community, such as working within a small, reliable group of friends and family, holding informal local meetings, and casual adherence to rules, were inappropriate under the onset of the rapid, well-financed process of casino development. In addition, the loss of personal attention and the increasing levels of bureaucratic layering led to a sense of unease among the citizenry, and contributed to the feeling that no one was in control.

The unhappiness that characterized the community between the summer construction period in 1991 and the stabilization of casinos in 1995 is documented in letters to the editor published in the *Weekly Register-Call*. Nearly all the letter writers mentioned politics (particularly Central City politics) as a primary reason for citizen displeasure. Moreover, the letters were penned by a wide variety of citizens, including some who had written letters before, but many who had not. "There is a *big* lack of communication here," wrote one Central City resident, "and most of it is because council and staff seem to hear only those who agree with them" (*WRC*, Dec. 9, 1994: 2). Another resident wrote, "What happened to the people we had in all the offices that truly cared about our little town pre-gaming? We . . . have so many split groups and mudslinging that it keeps me sick and angry" (*WRC*, Feb. 4, 1994: 2). By January 1995, a county resident proposed in an editorial that the north end of Gilpin County should secede from the southern end where the gaming towns were located, writing: "We do not want the northern neighborhoods to become support areas for the gambling industry" (*WRC*, Jan. 25, 1995: 2). He continued, "I find this hatred and animosity among supposed neighbors to be the greatest threat to our lifestyles because it causes people to act in ways that are in the short term only beneficial to their subgroup."

Nearly four years after the start of gaming, residents who remain in the area are beginning to adapt to some of the changes, and some have become less visibly anguished about gaming development and its consequences. This is not to suggest that residents have accepted the industry, the local politics that brought it about, or the consequences of the development. In many cases, they have simply given up those battles, and now fight primarily to contain the effects within the gaming towns. Since recall elections removed some elected officials from office and replaced them with individuals who appear to have broader community goals, it appears that citizens are now attending to the skills and leadership abilities of candidates and their responsiveness to community concerns. Some casino owners express concern that town councils may eventually be fully staffed by residents opposed to gambling, but this seems highly unlikely. The economic viability of the community is now almost entirely dependent on gaming advancement.

NOTES

1. Beginning in 1992, each gaming town contracted with a Denver company to handle parking ticket recordkeeping. A representative from that company explained that seasonal trends, the opening of new parking facilities, and the institution of shuttle bus systems were contributing causes of wide variation in the number of monthly tickets distributed in the gaming towns. In addition, the early aggressive policies, particularly of the Central City police force, regarding ticketing of parking violators accounted for the 5,412 tickets given in 1992. (About 4,600 offenders were ticketed between January and August 1992, and more than 850 visitors were ticketed in one month alone that year.) Such aggressive ticketing had repercussions among visitors, as letters to the editor complaining about the treatment of visitors began appearing in the *Weekly Register-Call*. The problem lay not only in the ticketing process, but also in the removal of automobiles when they were misparked. The towing service's impound lot, located eight miles north of the gaming towns, reportedly charged $85 or more for retrieving a car; this was on top of the cost of a taxi between the gaming towns and the impound lot. Bad publicity eventually forced Central City to offer free parking for a time in the local parking lots.

2. David Hayhurst, a former Denver police officer who had staged his own disappearance during working hours in 1989 (an event that set off a massive missing persons search), was hired by the Central City Police Department in July 1992. Chief Gatlin defended the hiring by saying, "He is a very qualified police officer with good references" (*Denver Post*, July 18, 1992: 1B). By January 1993, Hayhurst was experiencing job difficulties after allegedly choking a drunken driver he had arrested. He was fired at the end of that month for failing to pass his probationary period.

3. This was not true in 1994, unfortunately. The 1994 crime data underestimate the volume of crime for many places in Colorado because the state adopted a new reporting process in midyear. As a result, many Colorado places, including the gaming towns, failed to report crime totals for the entire year. The Gilpin County sheriff reported crime for only six months, the Central City marshall reported only seven months of crime data, and the Black Hawk Police Department reported only nine months of statistics.

4. Stokowski (1996) provides a more detailed overview of crime issues associated with gaming development in all three Colorado gaming towns. See

also Freudenburg and Jones (1991) for an overview of crime issues in rapid-growth energy communities.

5. How do residents in gaming communities subjectively make sense of their post-gaming-development lives? Krannich, Greider, and Little (1985: 193) found, in the energy boomtowns they studied, that although there were no differences in crime experiences between residents of rapid-growth energy communities and those in "non-boom" communities, residents of the boomtowns "exhibited a significantly higher fear of crime" than the others. The authors suggest that boomtown growth stimulates "a powerful social reality, which leads to the conclusion that boom town life is stressful, dangerous, and disorganized" (Krannich, Greider, and Little 1985: 206). These perceptions are encouraged and confirmed by media and interest-group reports of crime, and by the personal interactions of citizens.

6. For example, total filings for the First Judicial District for the 1988–1989 fiscal year were 14,085 (Gilpin County accounted for 114 of these), and for fiscal year 1993–1994, the total was 14,338 (Gilpin County accounted for 230). Although Gilpin County's contribution to these totals has generally been a linear increase, the total number of filings has increased in a nonlinear pattern.

7. Mean scores were computed for all seven factors across all six community health issues. The ratings were based on a scale where 1.0 meant "very weak" and 5.0 meant "very strong" on the factor studied. Results showed that the mean scores from all respondents across all variables concerning health promotion in Gilpin County were grouped more toward the lower than the upper ranges of the scale. Mean scores extended from 1.0 ("very weak") to 4.0 ("strong"), but most were in the "weak" to "medium" range (2.0 to 3.5). Gilpin County scores were generally lower than the mean scores reported for other study communities, though it is impossible to evaluate this in more detail without further information about characteristics of the other communities.

8. Unlike the more conservative accounts of the Gilpin County Social Services director and staff, personnel at the Clear Creek County Social Services reportedly consider any case in which at least one parent is employed in the gaming industry to be gambling-related. Under these assumptions, social services impacts in Clear Creek County, south of and adjacent to Gilpin County, are reported to be even larger than those in Gilpin County.

9. It is unclear whether Hidahl was fired or resigned (*Denver Post,* Nov. 27, 1994: 1C), but there certainly was pressure from both the casino industry and local residents to remove him from office.

10. A series of articles written by reporter Steve Garnaas for the *Denver Post* is particularly revealing. See "Developers: Bias Plagues Central City," and "Builders in Gulch Feel Cheated" (June 22, 1992: B1, B2); "Casino Moratorium to Continue" (June 25, 1992: 1B, 5B); "Central City Alderman Center of 'Tip Off' Probe" (Aug. 28, 1992: 1A, 23A).

11. A series of interviews in 1992, with thirty community leaders from Black Hawk, Central City, and the local gaming industry, confirmed the split between Central City and Black Hawk. About 90 percent of the interviewees reported that cooperation between the governments of the two towns was far below average. On a scale of one to seven, where one was "no cooperation" and seven was "high cooperation," the mean response was about two (1.9). Leaders perceived that residents of the two towns were also not eager to work together on projects. About 72 percent ranked cooperation between residents of Central City and Black Hawk as "below average" (a mean score of 2.4). When asked about the cooperativeness of residents in each town with one another, the mean scores reported for both Black Hawk and Central City residents were about 4.0, or "average" on the scale. The only categories receiving mean scores higher than 4.0 were those involving the towns and their respective casino associations, and the towns and Colorado Division of Gaming officials. About 75 percent of those interviewed felt that cooperation between town governments and Division of Gaming officials was above average (mean score of 5.4), whereas just over half of the leaders interviewed felt that cooperation between local governments and casino owners' associations in that town were slightly above average (4.4 mean score).

    Even into 1993, polarized positions were still visible across the community. In another survey of interaction and cooperation between Gilpin County organizations conducted two years after the start of gaming (Stokowski 1993a), respondents were asked to describe the extent to which organizations in Gilpin County were interdependent. About 47 percent of responding organization representatives agreed with the statement, "Gilpin County organizations generally work independently, but when there are community problems, coalitions of organizations will form to cooperatively address these issues." Another 38 percent, however, believed that "[t]here are many conflicts between organizations throughout Gilpin County, and organizations do not work together to address community problems." Only 4 percent of respondents thought that "[o]rganizations throughout Gilpin County are interdependent, and they often work together to solve community problems."

12. Oddly enough, former mayor Dick Allen was, just a month later, appointed by new mayor Don Mattivi to a position on the Central City Marketing Commission.

PART THREE
THE FUTURE OF GAMING

The Introduction to this book, along with chapters 9 and 10, serve as "book-ends" that frame the before-and-after gambling stories in Gilpin County. The introduction provided an overview of important contextual issues that later influenced the structure and substance of the gaming developments in Central City and Black Hawk. Chapters 9 and 10 consider the implications of gaming development for the local community, and more broadly, for other communities seeking to employ gambling tourism as an economic development strategy.

Chapter 9 traces parallels and paradoxes in the images and economies produced by mining, opera, and gambling. The analysis demonstrates that community issues repeat across all time periods and that a boomtown mythology pervades local life and influences community choices. Though Black Hawk and Central City may be unique locales, the consequences of their gaming developments are remarkably similar to those experienced by other gaming communities. Chapter 10 evaluates the social movement responsible for the dispersion of gambling across the United States, raising questions about the reasons behind the proliferation of gaming, and considering strategies for maintaining community control over gambling tourism growth.

9

THE PARALLELS AND PARADOXES OF GAMING IN GILPIN COUNTY

> Put yourself in our melancholy position. . . . We, and this entire little township with us, have hung on all these endless years because of a single hope: the hope that Guellen would rise again, in all its ancient grandeur. . . . [W]e are merely forgotten. We need credit, confidence, contracts, then our economy and culture will boom.
>
> — Friedrich Dürrenmatt (1962: 65)

Friedrich Dürrenmatt's 1956 play, "The Visit," is a parable about the effects of promised wealth on a depressed community's way of life. Guellen, a fictional small town in Central Europe, accepts a gift of riches from an elderly millionairess and becomes a boomtown. The gift has a condition, though: townsfolk must kill one of their own who wronged the woman when they were both children. As described by the author in a postscript, this is a town where people "aren't wicked . . . only weak, like everyone. It's a community slowly yielding to temptation" (Dürrenmatt 1962: 108). In this play, no one wants to kill the chosen man, but no one acts to stop the murder, believing that somehow, everything will be resolved without the man's death. Of course, it is not.

The story of Guellen illustrates the dilemmas of gaming development in Central City and Black Hawk, where residents waited for outsiders to define and provide a future, trusted that leaders would find a way to retain local control, and discovered that they had traded history and a sense of place for unexpected urbanization. In the process of accepting the "gift" of development riches, the loss of truly unique and important elements of Gilpin County life also brought regrets.

PARALLELS: MINING, OPERA, AND GAMBLING

While Black Hawk and Central City serve as general exemplars of former rural or resource-dependent towns in transition, they also exhibit particular characteristics that influenced the entire gaming development process. Notable among these is the romanticism associated with the assumed uniqueness of life in Gilpin County. Visitors and residents alike valued the qualities of place and community that yielded an impression of stepping back in time and out of the commotion of more urbanized society. Most rural communities have some sense that they are unique. As Fitchen (1991: 252) observed, "Rural communities are presumed by their members to have individual identities, each different from the next. Uniqueness is an article of faith, an untested assumption. . . . The ingredients of uniqueness are not always clear, yet people just 'know' that their community is unique." Not all rural communities, though, hold to that sentiment with the same degree of passionate observance and ownership expressed by people associated with Gilpin County. Such passionate romanticism has rewarding as well as damaging outcomes. Few rural communities, for example, go to the lengths of publishing such a self-reflective, self-congratulatory, entertaining tabloid as *The Little Kingdom Come*. In contrast, evidence of grudges and mean-spiritedness carried across generations reflects an unworthy community spirit.

The natural and historic settings are central to the experience of uniqueness in Gilpin County and the gaming towns. The mountain landscape, along with the cultural landscape of historic properties and evidence of the mining past, provided the basic raw material for tangible and symbolic interpretations of place and people. Landscapes such as these are not merely scenery, but "a constant space in which people operate, a backdrop against which the activities of daily living are carried out, a space that is both setting and symbol of rural life" (Fitchen 1991: 251). The landscapes of Gilpin County are rhetorically organized in public life under the theme of a "frontier" place. Frontiers are characterized by the unknown quality of what lies beyond; in mining, opera, and gambling pursuits, the feeling of being on the brink of the unfamiliar quickens an instinct for chance. Miners tempted fate and luck searching for riches in the unsettled wilderness of the Kansas Territory. Later, a forgotten mining town represented the frontier of possibility for those who organized the renovation of the Central City Opera House and orchestrated the creation of an artistic and preservation-minded community out of the ruins of buildings and memories. More recently, promoters of the gambling initiative overcame a symbolic frontier in convincing others that gambling, long an example of public immorality, was an acceptable, appropriate, and, indeed, desirable community economic development option.

The uniqueness of place is also confirmed in the three predominant industries that have structured these communities. Mining, opera, and gambling are ventures that allow chance and illusion to be transformed into reality. King (1977: 175) observed that mining entrepreneurs understood that the "industry was primarily a high-stakes gamble in which one mine paid to a score that did not, though investors continued to spend in hopes of hitting a jackpot bonanza." Opera restoration was also a gamble for its time in history, given that reconstruction was accomplished prior to the development of paved roads leading to Gilpin County. Long before mountain tourism was common in Colorado, promoters believed that a summer opera festival could revitalize the remote community of Central City, reclaiming art and history from time. The development of the gaming industry was similarly imaginative. Organizers and industry representatives replayed the theme of a new boom in the Rocky Mountains, shaping an industry from images of the past. Promoters refused to be limited by conventional expectations, convincing others that gambling development was their only hope for keeping the community alive. In all three cases, entrepreneurs pushed the limits of possibility,

The juxtaposition of the Gregory Monument in the former town of Mountain City (commemorating the site where John Gregory found rich gold veins in 1859) with a "For Sale: Gaming" sign on the property immediately behind the monument illustrates the unresolved dilemma between preserving historical meanings and selling history for private gain.

refusing to accept unfavorable odds and maintaining a stubborn resolve to ignore or challenge disbelievers.

Pioneers, be they gold seekers, opera patrons, or gamblers, are favored with and motivated by a good measure of imagination and fantasy. All are risk takers challenging and reshaping an uncertain environment, and each draws hope from a "boom" psychology based on the illusion that riches are just one hillside, aria, or slot machine away. Opera lovers and casino gamblers share several traits, not the least of which is that opera and gambling "are both fantasy operations, based on the customer's access to loose change and his willing suspension of disbelief. . . . The main difference between opera and gambling is that gambling always makes money for the management and opera always loses it" (*LKC,* Oct. 18, 1991: 1). Similarly, miners and opera participants continually practice dramatic public performances with the goal of eventually achieving fame and fortune; mining and gambling overlap in the everpresent and addictive hopefulness of hitting the big strike with one swing of the miner's pick or one pull of the slot machine handle. Successful participants in each of these ventures are independent souls, engaged by an optimistic, if not feverish, belief in the reasonableness of their actions.

However celebrated in history, though, the independent and speculative efforts of visionary pioneers are not the only requirements for success. Reliance on external sources of financing, knowledge, and contacts is traditional in the mining, opera, and gambling histories of Gilpin County. Miners depended on investors, the milling industry, transport companies, and other suppliers for grubstakes, contacts, and ore processing. As King (1977: 170) explained, "Eastern money committed to developing the high-risk gold and silver mines of the West liberated local people from total dependence on an erratic industry and at the same time enabled them to build enterprises with a more stable and permanent future." As a result, shipping, farming, transport, railroads, ranching, and real estate businesses grew up in the mining area, helping to stabilize communities. Similarly, opera was reestablished with "society money" from Denver. Prominent families supported the renovation efforts, and the trusteeship of the University of Denver reduced individual liability and helped protect a larger number of historic properties. The theater world also provided performers willing to imagine the possibilities of apprenticeship in a professional mountain theater. Gambling has also quickly succumbed to the control of external capitalization, managers, and employees, simultaneously producing a different kind of development than anticipated by local people.

Mining, opera, and gambling illustrate the consolidation of power for strategic and practical reasons of profit, business autonomy, and image control. The quick establishment of mining laws in the gold camps favored the earliest miners and limited access to resources by latecomers to the camps. Opera organizers bought local homes and business properties that were eventually transferred into tax-free status. Although the Opera Association had a more difficult time convincing community residents and businesses to adopt the proposed scheme of turning Central City into a "Williamsburg of the West," the summer opera festival was the event around which the entire community revolved after mining declined. The gaming development of the 1990s began as a model of community participation and benefit, but the tangible economic and political goals of the industry, particularly as more external casino companies become involved, are far removed from the stated goals of early organizers. Casino companies, in addition, wield considerable power on the local level, now that town governments are financed primarily through casino taxes and revenues.

In all three pursuits—mining, opera, and gambling—community issues repeat across time, and economic growth choices continually conflict with ideas about the appropriate protection of valued community symbols. The conflicts between these images are at the margins, where different interpretations intersect and where social and institutional behaviors and expectations collide. The passions that provoke romanticism about Central City, Black Hawk, and Gilpin County may be the very same passions that stimulate sentiments of exclusion. Having found the qualities of place congruent with goals of personal freedom and choice, insiders see outsiders as threatening private claims of autonomy. Only overwhelming promises of a new boom time, and assurances that the past will remain the same while the future becomes extraordinarily better, seem to temporarily overcome the problem of ownership.

The establishment of a truly comprehensive community growth strategy, absent during the mining and opera periods, and not yet visible in the return to gambling, requires a spirit of collaboration to flourish. Civic-mindedness of this sort, however, is not a practiced skill in many resource-dependent towns. Patterns of noncooperation and favoring personal gain were established early on in the mining period, as King (1977: 177) noted: "The boom psychology that infected people whenever they considered the mineral resources of the West defined success in mining as recovering the largest possible fortune in the shortest possible time." As gaming development shows, the freedom and individualism that so pervade local myths interfere with a communal spirit. Gilpin County remains primarily a setting dedicated to accomplishing special interests, rather than a place to pursue humanistic, collective goals. The lack of collaboration has already proven dangerous in gaming development. Accustomed to boomtown mythology, residents cheered the million-dollar sales of local buildings, failing to realize the implications for loss of meaningful community gathering spots and the social cohesion stimulated in these places. In addition, despite being economically and socially interdependent, traditions of noncooperation between town and county governments have prevented discussions and actions to resolve shared problems and possibilities. Yet, working together could have mitigated some of the negative effects of gaming development across the community.

Just as in earlier boom periods, the long-term future of gaming development is not assured. Mining declined not for lack of effort, but initially because technology was inadequate, and later because metal production was affected by world markets, wars, and environmental consciousness. Opera production was also susceptible to external influences, and when revenues and investments were limited, the festival reduced the number of performances or sometimes closed. Dependent now on the business interests of primarily external gaming corporations, Gilpin County towns are at the mercy of corporations with complex national and international financial affairs and only selective commitment to local issues. As in the mining boom, industry developers, owners, financiers, local and state governments, and others now form an intersecting set of interests in the Colorado gaming industry. The new industry may eventually replicate the mining boom-and-bust cycle, or it may more closely parallel the controlled growth of the artistic community encouraged by opera revival. In either case, the trend will be toward a single-industry town made vulnerable by a lack of internal diversity and external threats to sovereignty.

An important remaining question is whether the gaming developments of Black Hawk and Central City will complement or supplant future choices for economic growth. Previous community activities surrounding mining and opera were complementary because they existed in different areas of the physical landscape, and attracted people who intersected only irregularly. But casinos, located in the central business districts, interfere directly with social and governmental functions of the community, as well as with opera production. In addition, the need for extensive landscape reorganization (including parking lot construction, road repavement, and water diversion projects) to accommodate casinos and visitors potentially limits future mining activities and other opportunities. Draping a new development over another of a different type, particularly when the scale of each is so different, thus has implications for the conduct of established industries. Moreover, as gaming development so aptly illustrates, not only the tangible activities of these industries, but also the images promoted by each, may conflict.

COMMUNITY AND DEVELOPMENT PARADOXES

Although this is a book about two Gilpin County towns, it is also a book that tells two stories. The first is the story of the pre-gaming community, focusing on how historical, social, and economic conditions set the stage for the introduction of gambling by a group of political and business leaders in Central City. The second story is the account of community transformation after gaming was adopted, a narrative that exposes the potential inadequacies of both history and the future. Running between the two stories are themes of contrast and explanation. For example, the first story had as its theme noncasino gambling, whereas the second story centered on free-market casino development. The key actors in the first story were small business owners and community residents, whereas the primary actors in the second story were state regulators, tourists, and casino corporations. The conclusion of the first story was supposed to be historic preservation; the conclusion of the second story was preservation of historic illusions. The moral of the first story was that casinos were undesirable, but the moral of the second story was that casinos were indispensable.

The dynamics that led from the first story to the second story were detailed in previous chapters, but the transformation from before gaming to after gaming uncovered older conflicts and paradoxes in community life that could be understood only in historical comparison. These patterns are comparable to the contrasts Erikson (1976) described as "axes of variation," or essential cultural tendencies and differences inherent in community life. In his classic study of an Appalachian flood disaster, Erikson (1976: 249) proposed that cultures could "be visualized as a kind of gravitational field in which people are sometimes made more alike by the values they share in common but are sometimes set apart, differentiated, by contrary pulls built into the texture of that field." The axes of variation are the array of cultural agreements and contrasts around which people orient their communal lives. They are "not only sources of tension but [also] gradients along which responses to social change are likely to take place" (Erikson 1976: 83).

Erikson identified five different axes of variation in his Appalachian mountain communities, including tensions between tradition and personal liberty, the contrast between assertiveness and resignation, the pull between self-centeredness and group-centeredness, the conflict between ability and disability, and the struggle between the desire for independence and the need for dependence. Similar contrasts can be identified in the Gilpin County character. Residents glorified community history, but their practice of local history was primarily through individual acts of imagination and performance or through interest-group affiliation. Residents celebrated a sense of community as long as community demanded little of them. They sought personal freedoms, but they also condemned individuals whose freedoms were in conflict with their own. They claimed to have competence, knowledge, and skills, but failed to plan or act until absolutely necessary. Finally, they fell into fatalism and indecision when confronted with options for the future. To these dualities, moreover, three other communal tensions could be added: the tension between fantasy and reality, expressed in the formal and informal theater cultures and the sense of escapism inherent in Gilpin County life; the tension between passivity and activism, expressed in terms of variable levels of community participation; and the continual pull between rural and urban society, expressed as growth conflicts.

The gaming developments in Central City and Black Hawk upset the equilibrium of community axes of variation and recast typical patterns of local interaction and meaning in new directions. Construction-induced changes across the natural and historic landscapes of Central City, Black Hawk, and Gilpin County triggered sudden fear about the potential loss of individual and shared values. In addition, the contrived images of Western history presented by the new casinos called into question meaningful elements of the community past. The assault on historical and natural elements of place also symbolized an attack on local residents, who found "their identities as individuals through their occupancy of the community's social space: if outsiders trespass in that space, then its occupants' own sense of self is felt to be debased. . . . A frequent and glib description of what is feared may be lost is 'way of life'; part of what is meant is the sense of self" (Cohen 1985: 109).

Although the slide along some of Gilpin County's axes of variation was an inevitable consequence of gaming development, the outcomes of gaming also reinforced at least one central paradox of that mountain environment. The pervasiveness of a boom psychology permeated every aspect of local life, despite the fact that, as in much of the intermountain West, Gilpin County's mining booms were always followed by periods of bust. Nevertheless, a pervasive communal intoxication and excitement was associated with the very idea of boomtown living. A similar spirit is present in many boomtown communities, according to Gulliford (1989: 6), who wrote about the 1970s energy boom in Colorado: "[S]mall towns were changed overnight by rapid growth. The feeling of excitement, of being part of a larger whole, was an urban attitude new to longtime rural residents. From the family practice physician to the grade school janitor, in a boomtown situation, everyone works hard just to keep up. . . . Residents enjoyed the commotion, and everyone with a job felt needed—though often overworked and overwhelmed."

Communities faced with boom situations often draw upon myths assert-
ing the rights of individuals to profit, appearing to claim that individual profit
is the basis for community benefit. As a result, reliance on the mythology of
boom times reflects commitment to an imagined and romantic personal ideal,
not necessarily a corresponding responsibility for the communal outcomes.
Boom situations do not lend themselves to slow, steady, careful planning, but
to the demands of immediacy and, at times, frenetic decision making. The
boom psychology emphasizes an everpresent and exciting belief that the past
can be repeated with no loss of contemporary qualities or benefits.

The preponderance of this mythology prohibited questions about potential alternative forms of development. Once gaming had been proposed, and
the excitement began to spread across the community, other development
alternatives never appeared on the public agenda. One might wonder, for
example, why the alleged community interest in historic preservation had
never fostered a concerted local development effort prior to gaming adoption.
The support for such attention is apparent, for, as Gunn (1994: 359)
observed, "There is little question about the greatly increased demand worldwide for traveler visits to cultural sites. Critical then is the increased application of creativity, skill, and cultural sensitivity by designers and developers of
these sites in order to enhance visitor satisfactions and perpetuate cultural
qualities that are being threatened." In this country, though, historic preservation has traditionally been left to independent interest groups, and the returns
from renovation are usually incremental. In essence, the boomtown imagery
on which Gilpin County residents depended was incompatible with the participatory, added-value, planned-growth model of most historic preservation
efforts. State leaders were also blamed by residents for not doing enough to
save the historic properties of Gilpin County, despite the available governmental mechanisms for historic designation and tax reductions. The boom
psychology reflects the choice of accepting immediate gain for an uncertain
future, and of rationalizing all consequences as uncontrollable.

In the Black Hawk and Central City developments, the initial excitement about the gambling proposal was out of proportion to all expectations
of what the small development might accomplish in the towns, but the fever
was fueled by promoters' images that these dying communities were barely
able to gasp a last breath of hope. Gaming development was consistent with
boomtown mythology because it replicated the essential elements of the
boom imagery on personal and collective fronts. Gambling was speculative,
risky, and challenging, justified by the possibility of exorbitant rewards;
moreover, the institutionalization of gaming was unique in the political climate of 1990. Additionally, for a community unused to shared attitudes or

activity, the selection of gambling as the primary development option represented a communal focus and commitment toward a shared goal. Residents consistently explained that gambling recalled the former spirit of the towns and fit with community history. No one ever mentioned, though, that bust periods were also part of community history, or that booms had potentially disturbing personal and community consequences.

Hogan asserted that it was not the early mining booms that sustained the community, but rather the bust period that helped it survive into the twentieth century. Focusing primarily on Central City's frontier heritage, he wrote (1990: 78), "Central City was established and sustained not on the tide of economic development but in the wake of economic decline. [Local] entrepreneurial labor and capital were able to control the commercial economy because [external] labor and capital largely abandoned the Central City region in the 1860s." The initial success of mine laborers, and later of shopkeepers and entrepreneurs who provided capital, preserved community autonomy by supporting local interests against the forces of state or national capital and politics.

Hogan's perspective, then, predicts that the corporate, external gaming industry that has emerged in the Gilpin County towns marks the end of domination of community capital and politics by local laborers and local entrepreneurs. The intrusion of "monopoly capital . . . large-scale corporate enterprise and the concentration of assets in a few firms that claimed the bulk of regional and national trade [forecloses] the opportunities for the small-scale entrepreneurs who had traditionally controlled frontier enterprise" (Hogan 1990: 15). The paradox—that the individualistic spirit of boomtown mythology has produced not local control but the absolute antithesis of that, in the form of corporate domination—teaches a lesson that has gone unnoticed by other communities seeking gambling by invoking boomtown rhetoric. As Hogan observed in his study of Colorado frontier communities, "the success of political and economic development efforts undermined the alliance of commerce and industry. . . . [T]he intrusion of eastern capital inspired labor-capital conflict, and the likely resolution was to repress, coopt, and preempt labor" (Hogan 1990: 14). This point was reinforced more generally by Flora (1990: 173), who wrote, "We have become adept at implementing policies worldwide that favor capital. . . . What we have not been able to guarantee is jobs or distribution of income. We need now to turn our attention to policies that favor people over capital, particularly rural peoples in an increasingly global economy."

Will history repeat itself in the Gilpin County gaming towns? The consequences of gaming development in the Gilpin County towns show that fanciful images of past history can neither sustain a contemporary community nor guarantee its resurrection. Images of poor, declining mining towns were effective in obtaining public sympathy and support for gaming development, but they also reinforced a passive attitude inconsistent with adequate community preparation and planning. The image of contemporary decline stood in opposition to earlier boomtown glory days, which, from a distance of several generations, looked especially inviting. Fitchen (1991: 259) explained that "[t]he image of the past as stable, unchanging, and pristine makes the present seem unsettled, dramatically changing, and polluted beyond all hope.... [T]he images of the past ... may make it harder for communities to come to terms with the present and the future." Indeed, one of the remarkable consequences of gaming development was the overwhelming shock and amazement expressed by residents about the reconstructed business districts of the towns. Insulated in their mountain haven, residents had not only placed their trust in local leaders, but had also trusted in the power of community boomtown mythology. As the development process went on, though, it became clear that neither the leadership nor the myths could withstand the pressures of gaming industry development.

RECALLING MINING TOWN GOVERNANCE

One of the consequences of pervasive boomtown mythology was the paradox of boundary relationships. Residents always appeared willing to look to outsiders for assistance while at the same time they blamed outsiders for problems. The sense of dependency on outsiders (and sometimes paranoia about the hidden agendas of outsiders relative to the county) reflects a pattern common across all time periods in Gilpin County history. Ambivalence about outsiders, common to many western places, is justified by popular claims that outsiders cannot understand the special circumstances of living in a rural place, or the special qualities of the people who live in those places. Local failures are thus seen as the failure of outsiders to provide aid in a timely manner. Gambling development was a perfect example of the passivity that allowed such a spirit to flourish.

Prior to the approval of gambling, Governor Roy Romer, in particular, was the target of negative sentiment from local interests, who charged that Romer had no ideas for how to help the community prosper. Whether it was Romer's responsibility to provide growth ideas, when the local community had apparently been rejecting alternatives for many years, was beside the point. It was Romer's opposition to the very idea of gambling development that was seen as an indication of his unwillingness to help Gilpin County at all. Some people believe that the governor actually helped catalyze local support for gambling by virtue of his strong opposition to the proposal: residents vowed to accomplish their objective in spite of the governor's feelings. The negative sentiments against Governor Romer abated only in 1993 when, nearly two full years after the start of gaming, Romer personally visited the towns and toured some of the casinos.

Once the gaming amendment had passed, local complaints were directed toward the Colorado Gaming Commission for ostensibly not regulating the industry in the spirit intended by local promoters. Two issues that caused much local debate were the 35/50 percent rule for casino space usage, and reduction of the proposed 40 percent tax level. Local leaders commented in interviews that "the State bureaucrats didn't know what we had in mind with the rule about space," but one might reasonably ask why CCPI and other local gambling promoters were apparently unable to clarify their ideas before the gaming commission, given their use during the gambling campaign and establishment period of the services of Freda Poundstone, a lobbyist known to be very powerful in Colorado.[1] Some of the explanation seems to be in the positioning of even more powerful casino entrepreneurs, who had formed a lobbying group before the tax and spacing rules were established. Public complaints about the regulations appeared to be simply part of the political process setting the stage for development of a gaming industry in Colorado.

Although local leaders attempted to blame the gaming commission for outcomes of the casino developments, these arguments cannot be supported. In addition, errors and the casual informality of town governments prior to gaming could be partially blamed for problems. In the spring of 1993, for example, members of the Black Hawk town council reported finding a long-lost, unopened letter from the State Gaming Commission, postmarked spring 1992, inviting them to participate in discussions about setting the gaming tax for the 1993–1994 gaming year. The tax had subsequently been adopted without any input from Black Hawk (*Rocky Mountain News*, Apr. 27, 1993: 51A).

The one group blamed most often for local problems was the metropolitan-area mass media. Though the major news media initially adopted a generally balanced and cautious approach toward gambling development, discussing potential positive and negative impacts equally, local growth supporters reacted swiftly against any perceived slight from the media. In one case, news coverage of potential parking problems in Central City—an issue that had been openly discussed in local meetings, written about in the local newspaper, and obvious to anyone familiar with the area—drew the wrath of government leaders and gambling supporters. Media, particularly external sources, always are suspect in the eyes of local growth proponents. As Conover (1991: 112), writing about Aspen, Colorado, explained, "On the one hand, [resort communities] need the press in order to survive. . . . And yet when the press has anything critical to say, they feel victimized."

The basic, though often hidden, issue in these antagonisms is that external media challenge in a very public manner the goals and methods of local growth proponents who are used to maintaining their positions through force of personality, not by resiliency of their long-term goals for the community. The fear is that publics both outside and inside the community will come to ridicule the leadership for ill-conceived ideas. Yet, for towns dependent on tourism, "You need the people from outside, and yet you fear the people from outside. You want them because they provide jobs and affirm that you live in a special place; and yet you spurn them because of their bad manners and the fact that you must serve them" (Conover 1991: 112).

One of the likely institutional changes associated with rapid tourism growth in rural communities is the potential for interorganizational conflicts, especially between traditional community organizations and new organizations. Despite being growth-oriented, local business and governmental leaders in the gaming towns were initially less supportive of extensive growth than were incoming casino owners. Nevertheless, community leaders were eventually drawn into the issue agendas defined by casino owners, and thus lost the power to advance their own agendas and interests. This was illustrated in the local debate over valet parking on Central City's Pine Street. Mark Van Loucks of the Glory Hole/Harrah's Casino in that town proposed converting about fifteen parking spaces of the narrow residential street to casino valet parking. The issue was described in a front-page news article of the *Weekly Register-Call* (Mar. 10, 1995: 1) as follows: "Van Loucks hopes the residents are sensitive to the desperation of the situation of casino businesses. Since the Tollgate [casino] closed, it is necessary 'to rescue' the industry which is in 'very serious shape.' We are all in this together, he said. If the industry goes bust, we're all going down together."

Denver media were blamed for business closures in early 1992. This poster was hung in a closed Central City shop. The owner, disagreeing with the newspaper article, had penned across the text, "How bad was the trip up? Call Denver media!!!"

Though the rhetoric of despair had been used repeatedly throughout the gaming development process to portend the tragic fate of the casino industry and the former mining towns, the Central City council apparently had not come to understand the strategy. Van Loucks's argument was apparently persuasive, because the project was approved by the council on a trial basis (which in Central City usually means that the action will never be reversed). The entire process reflected Gale's (1986: 49) observation that rural leaders often experience a "loss of autonomy that accompanies . . . external involvement [in their community]. This loss includes the reduced ability of rural growth machines to control or manipulate system boundaries." One might also add that rural leaders also lose the ability to control the definition of the situation; by failing to challenge the assertions Van Loucks presented, they essentially showed that the local perspective was equivalent to the casino perspective.

The boundary question also highlighted the coherence, but inherent inadequacy, of local governing structures. In Gilpin County, Black Hawk, and Central City, the community drew its strength and consistency from rituals associated with local history, not from active, participatory engagement with others across the community. People moved to Gilpin County to escape from other places and to live out their images of life in a rural mountain frontier. Collectively, they loved the history, landscape, and culture, but they valued these as symbolic of individual freedoms and choices, not as communal responsibilities to past and future.

Boomtown imagery fostered a spirit of individualism that legitimized the passivity of many residents. A passive spirit, in this case, did not mean an absence of opinion but a willingness to leave the actual decisions of governance to others. As Cohen (1975: 126) wrote about a similar town, "this antipathy to organisation . . . is also a potent resource exploited by politicians who recognise in it a means of maintaining the impotence of the local people and, therefore, of nurturing their own indispensability." The longevity of local leaders promoted a sense of security among residents, who reported in interviews that they trusted their leaders to do what was right for the community. Moreover, local government was best described as entertainment, not active participation to bring about a desired, common future. Because almost nothing ever happened in the towns and county, local governance was simply a way to fill the time while attempting to maintain the local economy with little disruption.

This orientation can be understood only in historical terms, because local politics and governance developed as a reenactment of mining camp organization and structure. Hogan (1990: 3) called the process "Carnival" government because, "[w]hen the laboring classes were economically independent and politically organized, as were the gold miners . . . local government was dedicated to the defense of personal liberty as well as public order." Under Carnival government, miners and other laborers controlled the processes of production and economic exchange, whereas town boosters (who were primarily local merchants and elected officials) attempted to promote the sovereignty of the laboring classes through democratic mechanisms. The Carnival governments of the frontier, then, "were, above all, public spectacles, with frequent elections, parades, and public meetings" (Hogan 1990: 9).

In historic terms, the efforts of the earliest Gilpin County argonauts to quickly establish mining districts and codify regulations about mining activities, procedures of governance, and acceptable public behaviors demonstrated recognition of their authority on the Western frontier. The eventual decline of mining, accompanied by the rise of a merchant town and a service economy, did not reduce the resistance to external control of community assets. Threats against local autonomy were publicly and visibly challenged, as local leaders and townspeople joined forces to preserve the status quo. Vivid examples of their efforts are contained in the historic record. Mrs. Alice Ramstetter's 1949 incarceration in the local jail and the community torchlight parade that protested her jailing, and the outpouring of public sentiment against the proposed 1988 damming of Clear Creek for water supply and recreational purposes, were just two examples. Less dramatic, though equally effective, public spectacles can be found in the processes of gambling development. The pizza caper of Central City governance, recall elections across the community, and the extensive number of public meetings at which the primary goal seemed to be helping people feel better through talking rather than through decision making each illustrated this point.

Carnival governance was an effective means of rural community organization as long as the community was not seen as a potential commodity by external industry financiers. Hogan (1990: 3) suggested that "the development of a national monopoly capitalist class and a centrally administered federal government undermined local control of the economy and government and inspired local resistance to the intrusion of national actors," but this outcome may be more typical in periods of mineral resource extraction than in contemporary times. Certainly there were pockets of local resistance to the influence of external gaming companies, but these were not supported by the local leadership. Offers of millions of dollars to purchase old buildings seemed to confirm the boomtown rhetoric, and minimized attention to the actual and potential problems of boomtown life.

The increasing corporatization and transformation of community festivals and events by the casino industry in the several years after the establishment of gaming extended the power of the external actors and covertly drew local

In hopes of stimulating visitation, casino owners now underwrite community festivals, such as this 1994 Fourth of July Festival on Central City's Main Street. New awnings, signs, and hanging flower baskets now decorate the streets, though few benches remain from pre-gaming times. Once gaming began, Main Street was closed to all private vehicles; only commercial and casino shuttle buses are allowed.

governments into partnership with casinos. The transformation of community rituals was so subtle that only the most detailed observation revealed it. As Cohen (1985: 91) explained, "Frequently, the *appearance* of continuity is so compelling that it obscures people's recognition that the form itself has changed." The promotion of Western-like imagery by casinos provided a common focus and form by which local residents could still identify coherent community symbolism and feel that there was some stability to the present. The images were more polished and slicker, and the structure was more restrained, but the symbolism "manages the change so that it limits the disruption of people's orientations to their community, and enables them to make sense of novel circumstances through the use of familiar idioms" (Cohen 1985: 92).

Gambling development suggests that traditional forms of mining-camp governance, reinforced in subsequent decades that fostered booster rhetoric and independent attitudes of Gilpin County life, left local people unprepared to consider other forms of organizing, and perhaps incapable of understanding how well-entrenched their ideals were in shaping the development process. The problem was not that outsiders were responsible for keeping Gilpin County towns in a decline, but that local leadership was historically ineffective in finding new ways to bolster both local spirit and local business and government viability. Reliance on Carnival government and familiar, informal organization were inadequate for coordinating the gambling growth decisions. To outsiders, such approaches implied casualness and disorganization; although that was generally untrue, even local people were confused about how their leadership could have let them down. Boomtown governance was clearly inadequate for this contemporary situation, a conclusion that is supported by a wide variety of community interviews and was given special public acknowledgment in a 1994 editorial published in the *Weekly Register-Call*. Covering nearly two-thirds of the printed page, the editor, Charlotte Taylor (who had been in that position prior to and during gaming development) documented the human costs of gaming to the community. She wrote (May 13, 1994: 2), "We were reminded, almost daily at times, that these inconveniences would ultimately result in a better community for us all." Her final assessment, though, was that the social costs had been overwhelmingly negative.

DEVELOPMENT RHETORIC

In the process of institutionalizing gaming in Black Hawk and Central City, community impacts were expressed in both tangible and symbolic forms. Although many economic, institutional, and social impacts were manifest as visible community changes, the rhetoric of the development also had consequences that were generally more subtle and intangible in their diffusion and effects. Gaming development rhetoric had two primary features. First, sacred symbols of community were seized upon and manipulated for purposes of promoting the new gambling developments. Second, community discussion was restrained through campaign diversionary reframing practices. Persuasive efforts drew substance from the symbols of community history and landscape, though these symbols were employed differentially and selectively by gambling advocates, industry representatives, and community residents. The process corresponds to Edelman's (1988: 8) observation that "[t]he language, rituals, and objects to which people respond are not abstract ideas. If they matter at all, it is because they . . . [provide] meanings that are integral aspects of specific material and social situations."

Even prior to gaming development in Gilpin County, shared symbols drawn from the unique features of the historic and mountainous landscapes emphasized the strongly held ideals of the community and lent substance to community myths. These symbols included the natural scenery, the historic buildings in Black Hawk and Central City, opera festivals, historic cemeteries, and the saloon culture, among others. According to Flora and colleagues (1992: 66), such community symbols represent the core of values around which various groups of residents orient: "When members of the community have grown up within a common culture or have, over time, accepted a common set of values and norms, an even stronger sense of solidarity emerges. The community develops a set of sacred symbols that reflect its most strongly held values." In addition to providing a focal point for strengthening bonds among residents of a community, shared symbols also delimit the boundary between a given community and other places or people. This is as true on a grand scale as on more local terms. In Colorado, for example, the Rocky Mountains "both inspire Coloradans and separate them from the rest of the country. The mountains give Coloradans a superiority complex and encourage a sense of freedom, space, and separateness" (Cronin and Loevy 1993: 7). In local terms, the geographic isolation and historical richness of Gilpin County life separated local people from other rural and urban places, and gave special meaning to their community experiences.

From the start, gaming development was framed against a background of sacred community symbols. The imagination and memory of gold rush boomtowns, the decline of historic infrastructure, and the quality of a place left over from times past were images used by all interest groups participating in gambling campaign discussions. Gambling promoters claimed that development would improve the historic infrastructure, encourage a new boomtown, and not harm the natural features of the area. Residents, including both supporters and opponents of gambling, also invoked the same images to urge caution in protecting these significant elements of community life. Campaign rhetoric provoked nostalgia for an image of the past that celebrated individualism, a frontier spirit, and acceptance of the gambling attitude inherent in the search for gold.

Because the gaming campaign stressed primarily positive outcomes of the development and ignored negative possibilities, few local people had imagined that the towns could be transformed into single-industry casino meccas. The abstractions of the campaign led easily toward the reinterpretation of history that emerged during the subsequent gambling construction and competition periods. Local symbols were converted into marketable "currency" by gaming industry entrepreneurs, who were mostly interested in the surface images of Western frontier mining towns that might be used to entice potential visitors to the towns and casinos. The adoption of similar tactics by town governments, particularly in Central City, marks the decline of attention to historic accuracy and depth understanding in the gaming towns. Earlier claims of promoters that the "towns will die without gambling" remain unsubstantiated, but a reverse problem has now emerged. The real history of the community has become moribund under the onslaught of casino-led reinterpretations of local history.

In addition to manipulation of the sacred symbols of community life, processes of diversionary reframing influenced the structure and content of the pro-gambling campaign. Diversionary reframing tactics delimited the kinds of arguments and responses that could legitimately be made by proponents and challengers. By diverting attention from potentially sensitive issues, and reframing the debate around the qualities and integrity of persons questioning promoters' claims or making counterarguments, campaign organizers were able to control the debate and direct public attention toward issues they wished to advance. Such tactics are reasonable under certain political conditions, including situations where the outcome stakes are very high; where promoters might expect to receive substantial gains from the outcomes; where there is a need for secrecy or, at a minimum, discretion; where promoters are engaged in or motivated by greed; or where promoters know their own claims are suspect. People outside the Central City Preservation, Inc., promotional group will probably never know for sure whether that group consciously adopted diversionary reframing as a planned strategy for any of the reasons listed here, but it is clear that at least the first two conditions held true for gambling development. The stakes were very high, and local promoters (business elite and government leaders) were disproportionately likely to benefit from the institutionalization of gaming.

As a consequence of the diversionary reframing strategy, proponents successfully directed public attention toward issues organizers wished to discuss, thus avoiding other issues audiences might want to pursue. For example, by limiting critical analysis and using symbolic images that carried the emotion of community values, pro-gambling organizers improved their chances of success in the gaming campaign. The emotional rhetoric of despair used by organizers to promote gambling ("the community is dying; we cannot survive without gaming") also camouflaged and deflected attention from other relevant dimensions of the development. At least four topics related to gaming development were notable by their (intentional or unintentional) absence from community discussions: future community goals; concern about the quality of local historic buildings; objective analyses of gaming effects; and the role of the gaming industry in the development process.

At no time during the gambling campaign did organizers explicitly respond to residents' concerns about the long-term future of the community, even though such issues were brought forth at numerous community meetings.

CCPI organizers explained in interviews that although many other development options had been considered over the years, none was seen as appropriate or workable within existing community conditions. Issues such as broad community goals and impact limits did emerge once the gaming amendment had been approved, but by then, as planners and government leaders scrambled to implement the gaming proposal, it was too late. Concern about the quality of historic buildings was, in addition, an issue among only small pockets of interested residents. Historic preservation efforts were motivated primarily by community outsiders, not local residents. The stroke of genius (or the sneaky technique, depending on one's perspective) that prompted pro-gambling organizers to link gambling with historic preservation can be seen as the result of drawing on a valued community symbol and replicating, to a great extent, the campaign that produced gambling for historic preservation in Deadwood, South Dakota.

Independent data in support of promoters' claims that gambling would bring substantial economic benefits and few negative impacts were never presented; similarly, evidence challenging assertions of overwhelming positive gain was quickly dismissed as biased. Though the pro-gambling campaign drew upon the imagery of decline and imminent community death, no objective data were presented to support those claims (perhaps because, as chapter 2 demonstrated, local organizers knew that few of their claims could really be supported). The lack of evidence meant that neither promoters nor local residents knew whether gambling on the scale of Mom-and-Pop establishments was workable or reasonable. Industry representatives could have provided such information, but they could not legitimately be involved in a gambling campaign that promised a nonindustry alternative like noncasino gambling. The absence of industry representatives was also rationalized on the basis that this was a locally sponsored initiative conducted without interference from the industry. Moreover, if potential casino entrepreneurs were interested at that point, they also had good reasons not to divulge business plans that might depart radically from what CCPI organizers were proposing.

It is clear that both the issues discussed in development campaigns and the issues that do not make it onto the public platform are important indicators of the politics of legitimation surrounding community growth schemes. Although there is usually a limited set of sacred symbols in a community, the symbols are partially pliable and adaptable, assuming different interpretations and meanings for different community groups and industry newcomers. Myths that incorporate these symbols, then, provide "a bridge between the level of 'valued' reality—the 'sacred,' the unquestioned—and the level of mundane process, informed by 'problems,' at which dispute and contestation occur" (Cohen 1975: 115). Selective use of shared symbols reinforces particular community myths and allows each person to read into situations his or her own interpretations. The widespread support for the idea of "a little bit of gambling in every little business" was an example of the community appeal of frontier gambling imagery, illustrating the idea that "[p]olitical legitimisation is accomplished through the management of myths by inducing others to accept the values you impute to particular social forms" (Cohen 1975: 14). The shock and despair that resulted from the construction period of gaming development, then, reflected pain over more than the loss of old buildings: it was a collective realization of the loss of valued community myths.

EVALUATION AND PROJECTIONS

Leaders, planners, and promoters often claim that widespread community renewal and revitalization will result from tourism development activities, yet the evidence from the gaming developments in Black Hawk and Central City does not support this assertion. Arguments in favor of gaming development are primarily economic, whereas the costs are usually expressed in terms of undesirable changes to the quality of life. The gaming developments of Central City and Black Hawk confirm that there are significant economic benefits to specific groups—notably property sellers, local governments, casino entrepreneurs, and the state of Colorado. The euphoria of economic benefits, though, should not obscure the fact that there have also been substantial economic, social, cultural, and environmental costs from gaming. The naive hopes of Gilpin County residents who voted for gambling in 1990—that a few slot machines in local businesses would provide sustained community and economic development—have fallen by the wayside. As trends now show, the casino industry in Gilpin County is largely externally owned and financed, is managed by corporate organizations, and is more dependent on national cycles of profitability than on local desires. Most of the smaller casinos, particularly those established by people who had been Gilpin County residents, are now closed, because they were unable to compete in the gaming industry that emerged in the towns. Differences in capitalization influence the ability of local and external entrepreneurs to expand, take risks, provide employee benefits, and effectively market a product or service.

Even as early as the construction period, and certainly within the first year of gaming operation, the development outcomes visible in Central City and Black Hawk showed little resemblance to the images presented in the pro-gambling campaign. Although some residents made huge profits selling land or buildings, many people were adversely affected by the developments: those who rented shops, apartments, or houses in the towns; elderly citizens; people attempting to conduct business in the towns; and residents who frequented community gathering spots like cafes and saloons. In addition to the human displacements, gaming development also modified natural, historic, cultural, and physical environments that had previously supported images and symbols of the community's meaningful history.

Community impacts, including property sales, renovations, and new construction, were not limited to the preopening period. Even several years after the start of gaming, significant redevelopment beyond the casino industry has not occurred. There is still no gas station in the towns, almost all restaurants are in casinos, and the towns have been replanned around casino developments. Shops, movie theaters, and other recreation opportunities, whether for adults and children, have not appeared. If and when they do, they will likely be situated in areas that are now undeveloped county lands, because property in the commercial zones of Central City and Black Hawk is too expensive to buy or rent for interests other than gambling. Overall, the Gilpin County gaming developments show that qualitative improvements in community services tend to trail industry economic gains during at least the first half-decade of casino development. Further, negative impacts may be more likely to occur from tourism when the size and power of the industry are incompatible with the size and ability of local communities to plan and manage growth. Small, rural communities rarely have the highly skilled administrative personnel, the financial stability, or the community resources to control powerful industry ventures. Industry plans are coordinated to expected market demand and shifts, not to community wishes, and only a very savvy community can institute the requisite controls prior to initiating development processes.

The decision to allow gambling in Black Hawk and Central City was a radical solution to the problem of how to transform the two towns into economically vital communities. In this regard, it was similar to many other kinds of tourism plans that are transformed surreptitiously from an idea or development *option* to a defined *policy*. As Wheeller (1991: 94) remarked, "Many previous tourism planning policies have in fact been growth policies." In Gilpin County, the issue of how to retain a sense of community in the midst of this transformation was never resolved, and questions about the limits of growth of future casino and community developments have been unaddressed since gaming began. Moreover, symbolic issues associated with gaming development have assumed more importance in the years after Opening Day. Gaming development displaced community events and imposed added pressures on other public and private segments of community life. What was ultimately fostered in this community was acceptance of a dominant, externally controlled industry, not local development consistent with community history or imagery.

The first several years of casino gaming in Central City and Black Hawk showed an enthused initial growth spurt, followed by increasing industry competition, business reorganization that resulted in the closure of numerous small casinos, and an adjustment period characterized by the emergence of mega-casinos. This growth trajectory represents a pattern of increasing community colonization by well-financed, external casino companies that maintain substantial national and international gaming industry involvement. Their strong linkages outside the community reinforce gaming industry commitment, but provide little reason beyond economic positioning to promote community well-being. Long-term prospects for the community are thus uncertain, and long-term prospects for the Colorado gaming industry depend fundamentally on structural aspects of enterprise competition within and beyond Colorado.

The immediate future of the local community, though, is revealed in the contemporary rhetoric of casino operators and town governments. As early as December 1993, a Central City government planner forecast the future of

The construction of Harvey's casino along Gregory Gulch, just east of Central City's main business district, showed that the idea of Mom-and-Pop gambling in existing historic buildings has been entirely discarded. The only historic portion of this casino is the small, slender dark building with the steep roof (a former mine building), second from the left in front. The remainder of the casino is entirely new construction.

that town as a "destination resort" based on the construction of hotel lodging and conference facilities that were expected to deliver "long-term diversification of our economy" (*Denver Post*, Dec. 19, 1993: 1H, 8H). This prediction recalls earlier pronouncements made by gaming industry representatives about the potential for making the towns into destination resort areas. Those earlier claims had been considered outrageous by the local populace, given that the declarations emerged when gambling development was still called "gambling," not "gaming," by most local residents. The adoption and repetition of industry-sponsored imagery by a Central City leader illustrates the extent of bureaucratic slippage and gaming industry co-optation of local government that has occurred with gaming development. In addition, the repositioning of local government rhetoric reinforces the distance between what was promised in the gambling campaign and what was produced by the industry in collaboration with supporters and power brokers in the local community.

It should be obvious at this point that when gaming representatives speak about diversification, they are referring to a process of diversifying offerings within the gaming industry. Their intent is to create and incorporate hotels, entertainment complexes, convention centers, dining opportunities, and other services to expand gamblers' experiences. Local communities, though, tend to have different perspectives about diversification. Residents are more interested in services that improve the quality of life, including shops, groceries, gas and service stations, banks, laundromats, and other entertainments for children, the elderly, and families. From the community perspective, then, the development of casinos has initially narrowed rather than broadened opportunities for diverse types of services within the community. At least in the first five years of legalized Colorado gaming, residents have truly become secondary to the growth of the gaming industry, a point reinforced in a 1995 news article. The Black Hawk town manager was quoted as saying, "Our council is devoted to development," whereas the Central City town manager voiced support for a proposed $30 million southern access route to give Central City a stronger competitive advantage in gaming development and revenues (*Denver Post*, Nov. 6, 1995: 10A).

As local government leaders work to ensure the profitability of the gaming industry, thereby ensuring their own town's fiscal solvency, continued competition between Black Hawk and Central City can be expected, as can persistent efforts to develop the areas surrounding the gaming communities for employees and tourists. The spread of casinos through Gregory Gulch may eventually recreate Samuel Bowles's (1869b) view of continuous mining towns crawling up the narrow ravine. Hotel, casino, and parking complexes financed by major casino companies will likely eventually provide the centerpiece businesses around which a few small local businesses will disperse.

The further development of the casino industry will probably also place increased pressures on the local community. Many of these were never anticipated in pre-gaming days, including the probable construction of company-town-like subdivisions for casino employees, a new southern highway access route, the evolution of new attractions outside the towns, pressures to develop parcels of land in southern and mid-county areas for governmental and retail services, and a corresponding loss of rurality and remoteness. Gaming employees want to live closer to their work, and developers will eventually underwrite the construction of new housing subdivisions and strip shopping malls. Casino employees may eventually form a powerful county voting bloc, and current residents may not be able to avoid the "improvements" that will be requested by new residents. The new Gilpin County justice center, opened in 1995 and built adjacent to a well-defined housing subdivision northeast of Black Hawk, is the first indication that county government will likely attempt to develop a "campus" or service center in mid-county. As new residents move into the county, the values and images that current residents struggled to protect may disappear. Although current county residents are adamantly opposed to the proliferation of housing subdivisions, shopping strips, parking lots, or other efforts at urbanization, they are partially constrained by land use zoning decisions made years before gaming was ever considered for the Gilpin County area.

Without a southern access route directly into Central City, Black Hawk will probably retain the most profitable position in the Colorado gaming industry, as a result of its favorable location, stable casino businesses, and non-restrictive building and preservation requirements. Central City's position in the gaming industry, as well as its heritage qualities, offers an opportunity for that town to diversify its economic base with the addition of more varied tourist attractions and services, including the rediscovery of existing historical attractions that declined after gaming was introduced. Selective gaming development and enhancement of other recreational opportunities would give Central City a competitive edge in providing visitors with a richer and fuller tourist experience. Central City government leaders, though, rallying around a single goal of further developing the local gaming industry, see other options as less lucrative. Moreover, Central City's long-term debt may be a deterrent to growth options beyond casinos.

Whether one approves of gambling development or not, certain problems are likely to affect future community well-being. The historical animosity between Black Hawk and Central City, and between the towns and the county, has led to primarily competitive rather than coordinated development. As each entity attempts to further its own goals, broader community issues, such as the quality of natural resources and amenities, are likely to be ignored.

Central City's Chase Gulch water reservoir project is a first indication that development impacts will probably not be contained in the towns. County residents can only hope that the most intense future development will occur south of the gaming towns, so that the northernmost areas of Gilpin County can retain their natural resource amenities.

Undesirable effects created in the name of tourism development are currently being minimized and veiled by a new, local-government-produced rhetoric assuring residents that negative impacts are only a stage through which the community must pass on the way to widespread benefit. As this book goes to press, plans are under way among casino interests to campaign for increased betting limits in Colorado's gaming towns. Casino representatives can be expected to argue that, despite the booming business to date, their large-scale investments cannot be sustained on small betting limits when Nevada gaming opportunities are just a short plane trip away from Colorado. The competitive urges of casino entrepreneurs are now the single greatest factor in determining the future of the industry and community in Gilpin County. Deadwood, South Dakota, planner Mark Wolfe (1992) quoted a casino owner there who said, "If you don't plan your community, we'll do it for you"—but this sentiment is slightly incomplete. As the Gilpin County gaming towns can testify, even with community planning efforts, casino owners will still attempt to influence community choices by proposing apparently reasonable schemes for industry expansion, each one couched in more and more favorable economic terms that are increasingly difficult for communities to resist.

The evolution of casinos in Central City and Black Hawk represents unique forms of local economic development and symbolic production that recall earlier mining and opera establishment periods in Gilpin County. As chapter 10 will demonstrate more fully, though, one should not be deceived by the special historic circumstances of this place into thinking that gaming development is simply a harmless replication of earlier times. Arguments against the widespread and uncritical acceptance of casinos have been voiced by many, but Abt, Smith, and Christiansen (1985: 221) best summarize the patterns of change:

> [T]he evidence suggests that when casinos enter an existing resort area (whether urban or rural) the nature of the resort will change qualitatively. Whatever local appeals (climate, setting, or facilities) existed prior to the arrival of casinos will become secondary to the lure of gaming. The indigenous population will suffer some measure of displacement, and the community will undergo a substantial reorganization.... [C]asinos compete too well in a capitalistic society. Land values are inflated by speculation; skyrocketing real estate taxes prey on locals who do not sell out to speculators; and

existing institutions and recreation facilities cannot match the attraction and economic clout of the casinos.

NOTES

1. In the same way that planning consultants often found their way into permanent positions in local government, lobbyists hired by local promoters often found their way into the casino industry. Several former members of the Colorado Division of Gaming, including Roger Morris, the first executive director of that agency, left their positions and took jobs with law firms that represented casino entrepreneurs. Ms. Poundstone, after gambling was approved, became a minority stockholder in a Black Hawk casino (*Westword* 1992). Similar instances of potential conflicts of interests also occurred on local community levels as well, as former government leaders took positions in the industry.

10

BEYOND THE LITTLE KINGDOM: THE LARGER CONTEXT

We need to develop an ethic of place. It is premised on a sense of place, the recognition that our species thrives on the subtle, intangible, but soul-deep mix of landscape, smells, sounds, history, neighbors, and friends that constitute a place, a homeland. . . . An ethic of place ought to be a shared community value and ought to manifest itself in a dogged determination to treat the environment and its people as equals, to recognize both as sacred, and to insure that all members of the community not just search for but insist upon solutions that fulfill the ethic.

—Wilkinson (1992: 137–38)

Central City and Black Hawk may have been unusual and extraordinary locales in which to locate casinos, given the typical urban sites that characterized the industry when gambling was proposed in 1989 for these rural mountain towns. As events later proved, however, these two mountain towns were on the frontier of the gaming revolution in America. Although their geographic and historic situations created a specific type of development, the impacts resulting from the campaign, construction, and operation phases of gaming were not unique to these towns. Rather, the tourism developments in Central City and Black Hawk replicated and extended patterns of gaming development visible in other gaming communities across the United States.

Gaming developments in these Colorado towns also raised more general questions about the contributions of tourism in shaping desirable futures for rural communities. Many kinds of large-scale tourism developments, including ski resorts, theme parks, and retirement villages, produce growth impacts that foster similar kinds of economic, institutional, social, and cultural effects as the gaming development. From energy-resource communities in the West to ski resorts in the Northeast, company-town imagery can be applied widely to situations in which large, external corporations enter a rural community with the intent of making a profit from the natural, historic, or cultural resources characterizing that place. Corporate participation in tourism development, though, especially on the largest scales, tends to reduce the variability of

The standardization of the tourist experience is evident in the types of services provided for gamblers — in this case, a Taco Bell fast-food restaurant in a Central City casino.

rural places, diminish the number of locally owned businesses, and standardize the culture, built landscapes, and distribution systems (transportation, services, employment) supporting the community. The end result of these monopolies is that, contrary to stated goals of preserving the cultural qualities and landscape amenities that make communities unique, rural places using even diverse forms of tourism development often begin to look more and more alike.

TOURISM AND RURAL COMMUNITIES

Rural places such as Gilpin County contain small towns and significant historic or natural landscapes that have come to symbolize ideal places in our national consciousness. Though the reality may be quite different, there is a romance to the idea of living in small communities where people know one another by name and are sheltered by bucolic, beautiful landscapes. As Kunstler (1993:

185) explained, "the idea of a small town represents a whole menu of human values that the gigantism of corporate enterprise has either obliterated or mocked: an agreeable scale of human enterprise, tranquility, public safety, proximity of neighbors and markets, nearness to authentic countryside, and permanence.... The small town that Americans long for ... is really a conceptual substitute for the idea of community." In the process of seeking this sort of life, one often forgets that rural areas may also be characterized by scarce job opportunities, low wages, inadequate infrastructure or services, sparse local government revenues, and excessive amounts of wind or snow or zucchini. Many people would like to enjoy the amenities of rurality without leading rural lives, an option that is increasingly possible as people reside in rural places but commute to work in cities, shop in urban and suburban counties, or are "plugged in" via computer and satellite to urban amenities.

Declining populations and out-migration from rural areas, reduced investment in resource extraction activities, and economic instability are primary factors affecting the viability of many rural, mountain towns in the western United States. To solve these problems, many rural places now propose tourism as a community redevelopment strategy. Tourism is favored over other growth schemes because of claims that it increases economic opportunity, distributes benefits without incurring significant costs, is environmentally sensitive, and enhances local history and culture. Such long-term economic growth is supposed to be supported by community consensus; accomplished with sensitivity to local historical, cultural, and natural resources; and carry minimal negative impacts. These claims can be especially compelling for rural communities facing uncertain futures, particularly those that have a boom-and-bust history of natural resource dependence or seasonal economies.

The attractiveness of rural landscapes, and the idealized qualities of rural communities, are the valued foundations of tourism development schemes in Western mountain areas. Indeed, "[i]t is precisely [the] mosaic of natural, cultural and scenic resources that makes rural areas attractive to tourists.... Rural landscapes are becoming increasingly recognized as a functional cultural environment, a heritage resource and therefore worthy of conservation," as Swinnerton and Hinch (1994: 4, 6) pointed out. Recreation amenity resources and their supporting tourism developments have thus become the twentieth-century equivalent of gold mined from rural Western hills. Mapped over the history, culture, and scenic amenities are the tourism businesses intended to diversify the local economy. These commercial ventures come in all forms, from small, cottage crafts industries or special events like seasonal festivals, to large-scale operations such as ski area resorts, gambling casinos, or retirement or vacation home developments. The focus on economic benefits, though,

New revenues for historic preservation have been used to partially restore the Coeur d'Alene Mine structure above Central City; the Gilpin County Historical Society hopes to use it as a museum when restoration is complete. A view of the decrepit structure prior to gambling is shown in chapter 3.

masks more complicated issues related to community politics and social structure, so that "even in developed countries tourism development has not been understood as the complex social and political phenomenon it truly is. Economic considerations—short-term ones at that—have dominated policy-making" (Richter 1989: 181).

Amenity-based tourism boomtowns of the 1990s might look to history to understand how to cope with the consequences of rapid growth. Tourism projects operating under the same logic that stimulated natural resource booms of the past are likely to replicate the upheaval of those times as well. The larger the industry entering the community, the extent to which the industry is externally financed and managed, and the more the incoming industry is legislated, the less likely it is to attend to or respond primarily to local concerns. There may be important differences in the experiences of, for example, Western energy boomtowns and Western gambling boomtowns (immediate increases are seen in resident populations in energy towns, whereas tremendous increases in tourist visits are the outcome of gaming development; likewise, gaming developments are usually located in the commercial centers of towns, whereas energy extraction and processing operations are usually situated in undeveloped areas of counties). Nevertheless, there are also important similarities. If there is a truism associated with tourism development in rural areas, it is that reliance on single-industry solutions is usually an undesirable choice, as it recreates the conditions for monopoly control, reinforces boom psychology, and sets the stage for a greater degree of "bust" without the safety net of economic diversity. The repeatability of choices and issues across time and contexts frames the history of cycles of local profit and decline, and raises important questions about the viability of small, rural communities that protect valued ways of life in our society.

Increasing public and scholarly attention has recently been devoted to cases in which Western, rural, or mountain towns are "discovered" by tourists and irretrievably transformed so that neither residents nor visitors fully enjoy the amenities once valued in those places (Kariel 1989; Price 1992; Ringholz 1992; Ward 1993; Gill and Hartmann 1992). Citizens and governments everywhere desire the economic gains of vigorous tourism growth, but some communities adopt growth strategies that overwhelm the place and the abilities of local people. These types of developments often produce effects that impact all arenas of local life, including the distribution of wealth, the natural and historic environment, the stability of community relationships, and the preservation of local cultures.

The impacts of tourism development result not only from community decisions to foster growth, but also from in-migration associated with the discovery of newly defined amenity communities. Relative newcomers to rural communities are usually quite different from longer-term residents, as the split between residents of Gilpin County and the gaming towns shows. In a series of studies of Gallatin Valley, Montana, for example, Jobes (1995) found that community newcomers tended to be highly migratory, college-educated, cosmopolitan, concerned about nature but rarely active participants in outdoor recreation or local preservation efforts, and supportive of community growth initiatives. Importantly, "[f]ew [newcomers] stayed long enough to see the cumulative effect of development or to participate in planning, if they even cared" (Jobes 1995: 10). To the extent they are generalizable to other intermountain places, these conclusions have profound implications for rural Western communities whose sensitive natural, cultural, and historic resources are usually implicated in proposed growth initiatives.

The gaming developments in Gilpin County's former gold mining towns illustrate the repetitive pattern of migration and urbanization in Western rural towns. Even if gaming development is a particularly volatile form of tourism (organized as it is by national corporate interests), the gaming developments highlight the problems of amenity-based transformation of rural mountain communities. The hopefulness associated with the campaign to bring gambling to the historic towns, and the rationalization that gambling would provide sustained community revitalization in Black Hawk and Central City, was incredibly persuasive for citizens. The charming image of a few slot machines in every little business failed to acknowledge what Richter (1989: 2) identified as a basic principle of tourism, namely, "although tourism may have a frivolous carefree image, the industry is huge, intensely competitive, and has acute social consequences for nearly all societies."

GAMING TOURISM DEVELOPMENT

Gaming development has become the great social experiment of the late twentieth century. In the mid–1990s, a culture psychologically and economically fixated on betting is emerging in both rural and urban areas across the United States. Diverging from the sense of harmless fun and entertainment suggested by the 1989 proposal to develop gambling in three historic gold mining towns of Colorado, gaming is now a national industry. The gaming industry continues to show very strong growth in all markets, including land-based casinos, riverboats, and Indian reservation gaming. During 1994, Colorado ranked sixth in total amount wagered (almost $3.9 million), following Nevada (more than $96.9 million), New Jersey ($33.3 million), Mississippi (more than $17.3 million), Illinois (about $11.4 million), and Connecticut (about $4.5 million), according to *International Gaming and Wagering Business* magazine (cited in *Travel Weekly* 1995: 25). Capturing the attention and enthusiasm of media, government, and citizens across the country, riverboats, lotteries, tribal gaming, casinos, and other forms of gambling have been promoted as a way to secure the futures of communities large and small. Gambling is now seen as a routine leisure activity and a prime source of economic benefits.

The effort to make gambling publicly acceptable (and even necessary) is led primarily by two interested parties: local growth advocate coalitions and the gaming industry. Recognizing the evident business advantages of gaming development and the decline of Americans' moral objections to gambling, growth-machine advocates in towns and cities promote games of chance as options for economic improvement. Their arguments are persuasive even when the economy is not static or declining, because no one can predict when economic fortunes might take a turn for the worse. Gambling revenues are seen as immediate sources of new income and as insurance against future economic difficulties. Claims of promoters are echoed by local and state elected officials, who then function as accomplices to the growth coalitions.

Gambling proposals are appealing on this level because state governments are always searching for sources of new revenue, and gaming rhetoric promises rapid, substantial gains with little cost. These arguments set the stage for industry involvement in the development process. The industry, though, is driven by competitive and territorial urges often inconsistent with local needs or desires. As Johnston (1992: 298) explained, "what most people do is social gambling and what the gaming industry wants is commercial gambling."

The role of the state is a particularly sensitive issue in the nationwide spread of gambling. States that come to rely on the tax returns derived from gambling revenues—for education, or historic preservation, or outdoor recreation, or other social goods—may also find themselves dependent on the availability of that money. When the economic returns are overwhelming, there is a tendency to reduce general fund allocations to those services, using the gambling taxes to support the service. But when gaming revenues, and thus taxes, decline, the state is often left without adequate reserves to fund or maintain the necessary or desired level of previous services. In other words, gambling taxes give the impression that there is more money than institutions might ever use; when those funds are no longer available, there is a shortfall in provision, even for basic social programs previously funded by gambling taxes. As Goodman (1995: xiii) observed in his analysis of national trends, the spread of gambling "helps to shape a society that harvests short-term profits, while accumulating a large residue of costs for the future."

Moreover, states claim to regulate the industry for the good of citizens, but when the state receives a substantial share of revenues from gaming taxes, it becomes a tacit partner in promoting the industry. The dilemma was outlined by Abt, Smith, and Christiansen (1985: 175) in their seminal analysis of gaming in America: "[T]he public funds raised through government's extraordinary claim on gambling revenue are not derived from the creation of wealth (as they are from other taxes); they are derived from gamblers' losses, causing the economic interests of government and players to be diametrically opposed. Government, which bears the primary responsibility for the social consequences of economic activity, has a vested interest [in] the losses of a large and unprotected body of consumers." States are now financing public works on the basis of citizens' losses at gaming tables and slot machines, and as Johnston (1992: 297) points out, "to make the noblest expression of our civility, the democratic state, a partner in wagering is to encourage pathologies to enrich the states coffers, a Faustian bargain." The involvement of the state in gaming gives implicit approval to chance, risk, passivity, and electronic stimulation, rather than to what most people see as more noble virtues of thrift, hard work, community, frugality, and discipline.

It is instructive to observe that most of the current economically lucrative gaming experiments across the country are located in or near large metropolitan population centers. Gaming proponents claim that substantially increased tourism accompanies gambling opportunities, but until there is greater scientific research about tourist visitation to gaming communities, that claim will remain a hypothesis. At least in the Colorado towns, it appears that a large proportion of the visitors to gambling centers are residents of nearby metropolitan areas. The fiction that gaming stimulates regional and statewide tourism derives from the popularity of Nevada gambling resorts, which are visited by millions of tourists each year. But even Nevada is within proximity of the large metropolitan markets of California, and that state will continue to draw tourists interested in particular kinds of gaming recreation experiences. As gambling disperses across the United States, it is unlikely that tourists will form the main markets.

The experiences of Central City and Black Hawk raise grave concerns about the process and effects of transforming small, rural communities through gambling-based tourism. Economic rewards have accrued to the industry and to local, county, and state governments, but economic, social, political, environmental, and cultural costs are also a consequence of gaming development. The contemporary fortunes of the community are now so intricately bound up with the strength of industry that the community has lost the ability to act independently. The bonded indebtedness incurred by Central City is but one example of a constraining factor in that town's future choices, and as Abt, Smith, and Christiansen (1985: 213) have acknowledged, "the collective public interest is not necessarily synonymous with the interests of the institutions directly engaged in gambling or those that benefit financially from gambling revenues." In particular, residents wonder whether economic gains can compensate for lost attributes of rural mountain living, cohesiveness within community subgroups, and a sense of control over local direction.

The proliferation of gaming across the United States raises important questions about community well-being in an increasingly corporate global economy. Currently, about a dozen states allow casino and/or riverboat gambling, about two dozen have tribal gaming, and only two (Utah and Hawaii) do not allow any forms of gambling. In the past half-decade, the rapid proliferation of pro-gambling measures on state ballots across the United States has been astonishing. Gambling initiatives were listed on the ballot in ten states in 1994. Missouri residents did approve gambling initiatives in that state, but citizens in Colorado, Florida, Rhode Island, Massachusetts, Iowa, and Illinois opposed and defeated gambling measures in elections of that year. In 1995, casino gambling in Massachusetts and riverboat gambling in Indiana were also defeated. The trends suggest that, at least for the moment, Americans seem hesitant to approve the expansion of gaming. Johnston (1992: 296) warned though that "[t]he spread of commercial gaming is inevitable. By the end of this century almost every place in America where it has not already arrived will join the trend."

Industry analysts feel that opposition to the expansion of gambling may decline once states begin to see their own residents travelling to adjacent states to gamble. In addition, entities that do not allow gambling will perceive that places with gaming opportunities have unfair advantages in economic development, and so will push for legalization. The Colorado case is instructive. After Colorado voters passed Amendment 4 in 1990 to allow limited stakes gambling in Central City, Black Hawk, and Cripple Creek, fifty-six other Colorado towns, counties, airports, and reservations petitioned the state in 1992, requesting permission to develop gambling, too. Four separate amendments, proposing gambling for a total of twenty-seven towns and cities and six counties, were eventually placed on the 1992 ballot (Colorado Secretary of State 1992). In the statewide election that year, Colorado voters rejected all four constitutional amendments: Amendment 3 (to allow gambling in eleven towns, including Trinidad, and three counties); Amendment 4 (to allow gambling in fourteen "gateway" towns and three counties); Amendment 5 (to allow gambling in the town of Parachute and ban further gambling development in the state); and Amendment 9 (to allow gambling in the Lower-Downtown area of Denver and ban gambling in other urban areas). One additional gambling-related ballot measure, Referendum C, was approved by 76 percent of all voters. That referendum required a confirmatory community vote in each place that received state approval of gambling before gaming could begin.

Despite the negative outcome of the 1992 election, two new pro-gambling measures were placed on the 1994 Colorado ballot. Amendment 13, asking the voters to allow gambling in Manitou Springs, Colorado, had been promoted by a coalition of five businessmen, despite the fact that the local community had voted against gambling development in their town twice before. That amendment would also have allowed gambling in public airports across the state and would have overturned the local option vote from 1992. The measure was rejected across the state. Amendment 14, another effort to obtain gambling in Trinidad, Colorado, appeared on the ballot but was not counted (that measure was voided on technicalities prior to the election).

Because the long-term consequences of gaming activities in Central City, Black Hawk, and Cripple Creek were not yet fully understood when the 1992 and 1994 ballot measures for expansion were proposed, the eagerness of leaders and promoters in other Colorado places to seek quick-return, externally driven solutions to their own community problems was puzzling. Large-scale community projects deserve more detailed examination of their impacts over time and across contexts. This is especially true for gaming development opportunities, which tend to be promoted as if they were the final and only solution to community survival. Indeed, it is the imagined *immediacy* of the pro-gaming proposals, combined with a lack of contextual analysis, that causes concern when these proposals are put forth. In all cases of proposed Colorado gaming development with which this author is familiar, though, community leaders claimed that their towns would die without gaming, that they would personally go out of business, and that their towns planned to "do things differently" from Black Hawk and Central City. Not one, though, could explain exactly *how* they planned to do things differently.

The dangers of increased national dispersion and competition within the gaming industry are becoming apparent. In November 1995, Harrah's closed its temporary casino facility in New Orleans and stopped construction on the permanent casino there after revenue predictions declined precipitously. In conjunction with this action, the Hemmeter family, which owns both Bullwhackers Black Hawk and Bullwhackers Central City, and was a partner in the New Orleans casino project, initiated bankruptcy proceedings. Colorado analysts explain that the procedure was simply a way to protect assets, and that the Colorado casinos are under no threat. Indeed, Bullwhackers Black Hawk is continuing its expansion plans, and there have been no local layoffs. Nevertheless, the lesson is clear: local gambling issues and local industry maneuvering can no longer be understood from only a local perspective. The industry is highly interconnected, and business conditions and events in one place affect the viability of gaming businesses in another.

The findings from the Colorado gaming towns reveal general patterns evident in other casino gaming developments. Several elements of the Colorado pro-gambling campaign, for example, were similar to the campaign that brought gambling to Deadwood, South Dakota. Nickerson's (1994) newspaper content analysis of issue emergence in Deadwood found that, just as in Colorado, the debate over the merits of gaming as a local growth strategy continued well past the start of gaming operations. In addition, during the Deadwood campaign, "the way in which gaming was portrayed to the public was more positive than negative," and "the data show that very little planning was undertaken until the year gaming began" (Nickerson 1994: 63). These very same patterns were also evident in campaigns to open riverboat casinos in some states (Dimanche and Liliedahl 1995) and in Natchez, Mississippi (Miller 1995), and in Florida's proposed land-based casino developments (Liebman 1995).

Additionally, Pizam and Pokela (1985) reported, in a study of Atlantic City, that after casinos opened in 1978, the community experienced large and rapid increases in transportation and service sector employment between 1975 and 1980. As in Gilpin County, significant declines were seen in wholesale and retail trade jobs, and only a small proportion of new casino workers were local residents. The community also experienced new demands for increased public services, such as police and fire protection, social services, and new public infrastructure.

It is clear that desired community revitalization in the Gilpin County gambling towns is lagging far behind the rapid re-creation of the local business district as a single-industry gambling center, just as it is in many other gaming developments, including those of Deadwood, South Dakota (Stubbles 1990; Canedy and Zeiger 1991). In his studies of Atlantic City, Rubenstein (1984: 71) observed that the introduction of casinos produced a dependency situation in which "rapid, relatively unrestricted growth in the newly developing [gaming] sector of the tourist economy has had the effect of directing the pace of the host's redevelopment." Similarities between crime patterns in Gilpin County and Atlantic City were documented in earlier chapters of this book. On the positive side, the South Dakota and Colorado cases show that beneficial effects of gaming can accrue to traditionally underfunded community projects such as historic preservation (Jensen and Blevins 1995; Perdue, Long, and Kang 1995; Ittelson and Dutton 1995).

Colorado's third gaming town, Cripple Creek, exhibits strong similarities and some notable differences in comparison to the outcomes in Black Hawk and Central City (Kerven 1992; Catlin 1992). Located about forty miles west of Colorado Springs in Teller County, Cripple Creek was another historic gold mining town in 1860s frontier Colorado. Unlike the Gilpin County towns, though, that town has a more favorable geography and more available space for locating parking and housing developments. The potential Colorado Springs market is smaller than that of the Denver metropolitan area, so Cripple Creek has fewer large, external casino operators or corporations and more Colorado-based casino owners. The population of Cripple Creek has grown since gaming began, and the revenue gained from gaming operations has provided monies to the town treasury for streets, water, lights, and sewer improvements. But, as in the Gilpin County towns, there is an evident trend toward de-diversification, as many former retail businesses and properties have closed or been sold for casino redevelopment. There have also been rapid increases in crime, and local police forces are overloaded. Community educational and social services personnel also report more community medical, health, and social problems as a result of gaming development. The impacts are not only in the gaming communities, but are also apparent in adjacent counties and towns near gaming centers.

Similarities in findings from South Dakota, New Jersey, Nevada, Colorado, and other gaming places should serve as a warning sign to communities debating the merits of gaming as an economic development strategy. New industry strategies and rationalizations are being used to entice communities to consider and adopt gaming, and marketing techniques are becoming more sophisticated. There is, however, "a fundamental difference between allowing gambling to the extent of satisfying unstimulated demand and actively promoting gambling, using all the resources and advertising techniques of modern commercial enterprise, as though it were soap or some sort of passive entertainment. . . . There are natural limits to most consumer spending on most leisure activities . . . [but] the amount of money gamblers can spend on gambling is (at least theoretically) unlimited, and all gambling games entail (at least theoretically) the possibility of ruin" (Abt, Smith, and Christiansen 1985: 158–59). In this pervasive social movement, though, every potential consumer is targeted. For example, Las Vegas is attempting to stay ahead of other competition by recreating itself as a family entertainment center, with theme-park-like amusements for visitors of all ages.

Challenges to gambling are beginning to arise from politicians, religious leaders, journalists, scholars, and others who are reacting to the spread of problem gambling and to communities and states seemingly addicted to the quick fix of gambling dollars (Safire 1995). A national gambling commission will soon be directed to investigate the proliferation of casinos and other forms of betting and to analyze the effects of expanded gambling opportunities. As Eadington (1984: 34) noted, "The major arguments in support of the legalization of casinos in a particular jurisdiction are usually linked to potential economic benefits to be derived, and these benefits are greatest if the industry is large." So, it appears, are the drawbacks.

THE FAILURES OF PLANNING

Although some community problems related to gaming development in Colorado can be traced directly to the voracious expansion plans of the gaming industry, other problems were the result of poor organization, planning, and control by Gilpin County's rural communities. These problems reflect Hedden's (1994: 20) observation that "Westerners tend to hate planning and prize personal freedoms. Very few towns have ever thought about how much change would be acceptable, and even fewer would be willing to say 'enough' to growth." Residents and governmental leaders in both depressed and stable rural Western communities usually have noble goals about the kinds of futures they would like to enjoy, but they often have little practice in making these goals come true. Moreover, communities typified by boom-and-bust cycles are not in the habit of thinking incrementally about future visions. Developments that offer large returns are often more prized than those providing smaller, incremental, or continuing gains, and the consequences of comprehensive change are felt to be unknown or unimaginable.

The failure of many developments, including gaming and other kinds of large-scale tourism projects, to live up to the expansive claims of tourism promoters implies that there are inherent problems in tourism planning and implementation processes. The discrepancy is partially attributable to the post-hoc nature of much tourism planning, in which growth options become policies without adequate study or impact analysis. Leaders may believe that planning should be an ongoing, iterative, and evaluative process, but few communities prepare in advance for tourism; instead, they wait until a specific project is chosen. Issues such as community visions, measurable objectives, accountability requirements, designation of sacred community places, and acceptable trade-offs in community growth should be, but rarely are, considered far in advance of the selection of a particular development strategy.

The substantial recent literature about community-based tourism planning (Gill and Williams 1994; Gunn 1994; Haywood 1988; Getz 1986; Murphy 1985, 1988; and Butler 1980, among others) offers suggestions for how communities can plan in advance to resolve potential development problems. Some of the proposed strategies include using growth management tools such as appropriate design of tourism sites and regions; applying government regulatory mechanisms such as zoning or taxing schemes; and involving citizens in participatory, value-oriented, consensus planning and decision making. As Wheeller (1991: 94) noted, though, "notions of community-based approaches to tourism decision making seem fine for those communities (however defined) where there is a cohesive, established network based usually on existing economic viability. These communities . . . operating from a position of relative strength, resist unwanted, inappropriate forms of tourism." Not all rural communities have such stability, however, and those that accept dramatic changes through tourism growth may be the least likely to enjoy such conditions. Tourism scholars also promote the creation of synergistic relationships with small businesses willing to work within the bounds of scale or pace defined by the community. As the gaming developments in Black Hawk and Central City suggest, though, assumptions such as these are severely tested in rural community gaming development, because the goals of the gaming industry are often incompatible with those of small business.

When the gambling proposal was introduced in Central City and Black Hawk in 1989, comparative models of rural gaming development were limited. Deadwood, South Dakota, had only just begun operation of its casinos, and gaming operations in rural areas of Nevada were not comparable in scale to the proposed Colorado developments. In the absence of comparative models, however, state-sponsored community studies should have included assessments of potential social impacts. Instead, sponsored research was focused primarily on economic conditions and economic possibilities (a community planner, for example, once called this author requesting assistance on a study to determine "how many hotel beds we will need if gambling comes to our town"). Such booster research can hardly be called objective, but it is not unusual. As Richter (1989: 15) acknowledged, "It is far easier to tally gross receipts than to measure the net contribution or cost of a policy, tallying not only promotional and administrative costs, but also broad social and psychological costs and benefits. It is also politically appealing, containing a pro-business bias that is hard to resist and a pervasive boosterism that is common in most nations and locales." The result of such approaches is that necessary procedures for monitoring the impacts of development over time are not included in community plans, so baseline data are then unavailable for evaluating project consequences.

The complexity of evaluating tourism development impacts is evident in analysis of gaming development in Central City and Black Hawk. A historical and conceptual focus is needed, as well as detailed, simultaneous attention to different categories of impacts. Many tourism impact studies, though, suffer from an overgeneralized account of development consequences (Pearce 1989). Data are often gathered at only one or two points in time, implying incorrectly that impacts are relatively stable and persistent across development histories. As a result, the magnitude, timing, and dispersion of effects remain unknown.

The necessity for not only economic and environmental, but also social and institutional impact assessment in large-scale community development projects seems self-evident (Branch, Hooper, Thompson, and Creighton 1984; Krannich and Greider 1984; Weber and Howell 1982). Social impact assessment involves "the identification, analysis, and evaluation of the social impacts resulting from a particular event. . . . [T]he most important contribution of SIA to policy analysis comes from the ability of impact assessment to display the implications of a policy option in a form which generates focused, rational debate on the policy, and diffuses rigid, single issue attacks" (Dietz 1987: 56, 58). Social impact assessment provides the basis for comprehensive community planning and for anticipating potential effects of tourism growth. If outcomes of tourism development can be defined and evaluated more precisely, residents might be able to make more informed decisions regarding the pace, scale, and direction of community tourism growth (Leistritz, Halstead, Chase, and Murdock 1984; Keogh 1990; Choy 1991).

It is apparent, five years after the introduction of gaming in Black Hawk and Central City, that gaming development cannot be considered an effective solution for enhancing rural community sustainability. Initial analyses from the Gilpin County gaming towns show that the early years of gaming development have brought dependence on a single industry, a loss of business diversity, a polarization of community feelings, and threats to the natural and cultural environments cherished by local people. Gaming development has certainly fostered gaming industry evolution, but the communities now are remarkably different from the communities prior to gaming. The gentrification and urbanization that will likely follow in upcoming years will confirm the loss of the historic mining past in Gilpin County.

The act of turning a community into a tourist attraction or a destination resort is at odds with principles of sound community tourism planning, and is often contrary to the goals of community sustainability. Note that the emphasis here is on *community* sustainability, not *tourism* sustainability. The goal of community sustainability should be to meet the needs of the contemporary population without reducing the ability of future generations to achieve economic and social benefits (MacGregor 1993). Tourism contributes to community sustainability if the scale of development is compatible with current community size, resources, and cultures, and the growth preserves natural and cultural wealth for the future. As Burr and Walsh (1994:10) explained, "The interest in sustainable tourism development then is in protecting, using carefully and benefiting the human and cultural, as well as the natural heritage of an area, implying active participation and leadership by local people, organizations and government."

Community sustainability is a desirable ideal, but the outcomes of gaming development in Black Hawk and Central City show how easily a unique history and landscape can become simply a stage for industry operations, rather than a means for sustaining the cultural, historic, and natural environments that nourish communities of people. At the same time, some Gilpin County residents did receive personal economic benefits, and community economic benefits have accrued to local governments. Though residents exerted little control over the process of gaming development or the distribution of its impacts, the future may bring opportunities to use the economic gains to create the type of community residents desire. Such efforts will require participation and collaborative planning across the community and strength of will to overcome historical conflicts. This may be exactly the right time to encourage such activities, as there has never been a time in Gilpin County when the governments were so well funded, the internal and external pressures so well defined, and community members so focused on their shared concerns about quality of life.

Communities consistently express desires for improved economic conditions while retaining local culture, heritage, community, and place. In regard to this effort, the gaming developments in Black Hawk and Central City raise the possibility that the influence of government is in decline compared with the rise of corporate authority and morality. Though it is too early to be certain, the increasing power of the gaming industry in Central City and Black Hawk, compared with the inertia of local governments and many citizens, may indicate that there is little political will for or social commitment to a shared community future.

Under conditions such as these, governmental leaders, as guardians of the public interest, must be held accountable to accomplish the public good. This is often more easily said than done, however, because community interests may be in direct opposition to industry interests, and growth advocates may hold positions of power in the local community. Furthermore, leaders, even if nonaligned and well intentioned, may have little practical experience dealing with either large-scale community change or strong corporate investors who demand concessions as enticement to situate their operations locally. If community members do choose tourism as a growth strategy, development must be evaluated in larger political, social, economic, environmental, and cultural contexts, and over a longer time span than is normally used to evaluate tourism outcomes. Realizing that all parties in a development process have vested interests, the imposition of specific accountability standards on developers, industry representatives, and government leaders should help reduce the incidence of negative effects, and would likely reduce levels of community stress associated with development pressures. As Flora (1990: 173) wrote, "We must address policy as well as organization. In capitalist democracies, it is the role of government to make it profitable to do what is moral."

STRATEGIES FOR LOCAL CONTROL

The gaming tourism developments in Central City and Black Hawk demonstrate that economic growth is not equivalent to sustainable social, environmental, or institutional well-being. Gaming development may solve immediate problems associated with a static economy, but at the same time it stimulates extensive institutional, social, and economic restructuring in the subject community. Given the consequences of the gaming experiments in Central City and Black Hawk, and the power of the gaming industry, it is reasonable to wonder whether any small, rural community could be successful in establishing this form and scope of tourism development. The continued pressures on rural communities to seek economic gain, and the potential economic advantages of gaming development, make guidelines for gaming tourism development a necessity. What can communities do to improve or preserve their economies, values, and social and personal interests when they choose gaming tourism as the development strategy?

Many rural communities, including those in Gilpin County, have strong histories and positive values that Americans should protect and preserve. As a general rule, however, though Americans verbally support preservation of these places, financial support has come primarily from individuals or non-profit groups. Gaming development moves the concern into the public arena. The outcomes of the gaming developments in Black Hawk and Central City suggest that, no matter what the motivation to seek gaming, communities urgently need to plan not only for economic needs but also for integrating tourism into the social, economic, political, and cultural life of the community; for protecting the qualities of life residents value; for improving the special natural, historic, and cultural resources of the community; and for enhancing visitors' experiences in the community. If economic gain demands that town and county properties and heritage resources be sold to the highest bidders, that vehicles and visitors crowd the streets, and that residents perceive that they have lost their community, then it becomes difficult to argue that much besides private economic advantage has been sustained through tourism development.

Under the promise of any form of tourism development, communities must identify their valued tangible and intangible qualities, and residents must take steps to ensure that these qualities are protected in local planning and development (see Hester 1985, 1990, for examples). Goals for the future must be based on desired natural, cultural, and social environments comprising the "ethic of place" (Wilkinson 1992), not solely on desired economic growth potential. If a community fails to take charge at this stage, it is unlikely to have another chance to set the standards for acceptable local changes. Preparatory work at this stage will also help define the unique qualities that contribute to the local tourism experience. Host areas that are careful to plan for residents will also be better able to plan the special experiences visitors might enjoy.

If community members do decide that gambling is an acceptable development option, they must also discuss the desirability of different forms of gambling. Gambling proponents will attempt to limit the public discussion to ideas they wish to advance, but it is in the best interest of the community to begin to define the limits of acceptability very early in the campaign. In the

1989–1990 Colorado campaign, the idea of "a few slot machines in every little business" seemed so obvious that it precluded consideration of other possible versions of gambling. Other options, such as limiting the numbers of gaming licenses, or limiting the number of gaming devices per square foot of building space, were never publicly discussed. It is in the best interests of the community, though, to challenge gambling proponents on this point, and to assume that although gambling may be the goal, the mechanisms to produce desired forms of gambling should remain within the control of the community. As Chadbourne (1995: 5) advised, "Treat gambling as a means, not an end. You approved gambling not because you liked poker, but because you wanted to leverage economic benefits to your city."

In Black Hawk and Central City, the fanciful images of old, Western-style gambling were so subtle and persuasive that actions limiting development were never considered. As a result, the community watched while casino entrepreneurs implemented their goals of free-market, wide-open casino development. With foresight and effective planning, the community could have limited the potential impacts by deciding to limit the type of acceptable growth. Models of more limited ventures were certainly available, from the British model of pub gambling, to the Deadwood model of thirty devices per building, to the continental model of one large casino per city or resort. Certainly the more stringent development of one large casino in Central City and another in Black Hawk, with revenues going to local town and county governments and local historic restoration, would have reduced all forms of negative impacts. Mechanisms for limiting growth are available, but whether the community has the political will to enact these remains an issue. Many rural communities prefer not to restrict development, thinking instead that they are fortunate to have any sort of interest and investment in the local area. This approach is dangerous because it removes local control from the process.

Communities must be proactive in gaming development, a difficult effort for rural places where residents may be unused to collaborative action. Because local business leaders in rural communities tend also to hold local government positions, and are the ones most likely to profit from gaming development, direction must come primarily from groups of interested residents actively investing in their own community future. The goal of broad community participation must be action, not merely discussion. People feel better about themselves and their community when they talk together, but conversation without action is inadequate for effective planning. Final decisions, moreover, must not be left only to government leaders. If residents negotiate solutions directly with one another, they will begin to maximize mutual concerns over short-term individual desires, and they will begin to create the kind of livable community they desire.

In addition to an active, participatory citizenry, residents must find ways to hold their leaders accountable for development decisions. No community member will likely get all he or she wants from a development, but each should get something beneficial with the least amount of disturbance and loss. Votes in recall elections are one way, of course, to enforce accountability, but these are after-the-fact actions that tend to produce debilitating community conflict. The use of external planners and consultants is also not always a reasonable solution, as it serves to protect leaders from blame rather than ensuring accountability. A better solution may be for the community to formally establish accountability criteria early in the decision process and then to hold elected leaders to those standards.

It is impossible to divorce these issues from other political issues. The western newspaper, *High Country News*, asked the question, "Why can't officials elected on platforms of slowing growth and preserving community character get more accomplished?" (Sept. 15, 1994: 18). It proposed the answer that "the sentiment that elects pro-planning candidates is not unified by much else. . . . Real progress comes only by identifying and bringing together a wide constituency to create a voice that speaks solely on planning issues." As the gaming developments have shown, though, the manufactured conflict between planners and boosters is only a small part of the story. The presence of competing growth machines shows that there are consistent reasons why leaders, once elected, fail to respond according to the wishes of the community. Elected leaders have a vested interest in maintaining position and power, and so avoid difficult decisions that will alienate voters. They tend to take more mainstream and less ideological positions once they are elected. After their appointment, they also become more aware of the complexity of issues, and realize the limitations of the bureaucratic structures they once vowed to change (Logan and Molotch 1987).

If the gaming developments in Black Hawk and Central City are any indication, both rural community residents and leaders tend to underestimate the amount of disruption local institutions will experience with the onset of rapid growth. One of the reasons that residents feel victimized by the development process, in fact, is that the organizational structures they created suddenly begin to appear very unstable. Newcomers are hired to staff governmental offices, secretaries turn into gatekeepers with substantial power, and everyone is suddenly so burdened with work that casual interaction is an impossibility. Gilpin County residents consistently complained after gaming was established that it was impossible to telephone their local leaders, or to stop by to see them at work. A telephone call to the sheriff, for example, used to be answered by the sheriff; after gaming, operators answered phones, and the sheriff would return the call if he found a free moment—often an impossibility. Likewise, residents could no longer walk into town offices expecting to see a town or county official at a moment's notice.

The complexity of new gaming developments requires that rules be standardized, that job roles and performance be well defined, and that bureaucratic structures be obvious and consistent. What is needed is a time for organizational maturation, but this is impossible under conditions of rapid growth. Some of the frustrations of the development process are related to the fact that new systems take time to adapt, but no time is built into the development to allow communities to catch up with the demands of growth. Worse, some leaders (especially those favoring old-boy networks) seem averse to operating under more objective standards, because their personal powers are reduced. Rural communities that hope to maintain at least some measure of control over gaming development processes must nevertheless establish more formal structures as quickly as possible after approval of gaming projects. They will immediately be faced with demands for consistent policy interpretations, information dissemination, and fair treatment of all participants in the process, developers as well as residents.

Along with the institutional changes communities must make to accommodate gaming development, there are many practical tasks to be considered. Rural places must be aware of potential front-end problems, in which local budgets are stretched beyond their capability to provide monies for initial public infrastructure improvements. Even large, financially stable communities may be unable to pay the cost of improvements in advance of new revenues. Unless a large proportion of early tax dollars or development fees is tied directly to local or regional governmental causes, communities will incur unexpected debts for development early in the process and will be operating with little commitment from the incoming industry. In addition, rural communities must acknowledge that there are usually many more well-financed external investors than there are well-endowed local businesses that can enter the big-business world of casino gaming. If free-market development is allowed, especially in a small community located near a major metropolitan center, there is apt to be an influx of well-financed external investors buying local property, and a subsequent out-migration of local business owners who understand that selling their property for millions of dollars is an unbeatable deal. Even prior to adoption of gaming, increases in real estate speculation should be seen as a warning that speculators are attempting to cash in on the community's potential. If local leaders monitor these changes, and decide in advance of approval how much and what types of gaming will be allowed, they may better control the development process.

Although communities cannot always protect each individual citizen, they can attempt to protect the collective citizenry by applying casino-related impact taxes or zoning mechanisms in an attempt to contain impacts to certain local areas and prevent them from spilling over into other areas. Communities with larger, more level geographies have distinct advantages in this regard, and may be able to avoid some of the neighborhood disturbances experienced particularly by Central City residents. Communities might also dedicate some of the earliest tax monies to saving important local places, in addition to addressing immediate infrastructure needs such as roads and sewer improvements. Investing in people is as important as repairing roads or water systems, but most communities build things first, rather than building up the spirits of residents.

Small-scale tourism developments providing steady but not extravagant returns often seem to be unfashionable. Richter (1989: 195) explained that "[g]radual tourism development is far better for maintaining a balanced and diversified economy. . . . Destinations that embark on crash tourism development . . . [do] so at the expense of local control. . . . [T]he values of the host society are more likely to be respected and protected if development is phased." Gambling development can be kept small-scale if that is the desire of the community. Some mechanisms that may contribute to more local control and investment than was apparent in the Colorado cases include requiring local residency before developers open casinos, requiring citizen approval by a majority of voters on local decisions, or placing a "community culture" tax on developments so that community welfare projects receive some priority during the development process. In addition, businesses other than gaming should be encouraged with lower property tax rates. If all properties in the commercial zone are assessed at the "highest and best use" (i.e., gaming), then no other businesses will be able to afford to locate in that area. Differential zoning and taxation policies are required.

On a larger scale, Johnston (1992) proposed that states prohibit casino advertising, credit gambling opportunities, and the distribution of coupons and incentives to entice patrons into casinos. States also have the power to institute taxes and other laws that favor small, local entrepreneurs over larger companies, although casino corporations usually lobby state gaming commissions strongly against this issue. Reconsideration of the proposed 40 percent tax rate on casino revenues is a case in point. Casinos in Colorado are unlikely ever to be subjected to that taxation rate, even though voters believed that rate would be applied. If the tax rate were ever to approach that level, it is likely that some corporations would simply close their Colorado operations and move to other places with more favorable rates. Instances of this have occurred with riverboat gambling projects that simply sail away from one state when tax laws prove to be more favorable elsewhere. The Colorado land-based developments are less mobile, but capital is movable as states compete for casinos. The biggest losers in these kinds of high-stakes competitions would, of course, be the gaming towns themselves, which have mortgaged their futures on local casino success.

Chadbourne (1995: 4) explained that "gaming's ability to do good lies in: a) its ability to generate regional as opposed to local usage; and, b) the local municipalities' willingness to regulate the industry." He proposed that communities considering casino gaming coordinate local attractions to provide a unique and robust tourist area beyond casino offerings, and use gaming revenues to revitalize downtown housing and shopping. Thinking regionally, and involving other entities that can help or may be affected, will be an advantage in the long run. In Gilpin County and its gaming towns, a history of community conflict prevented government leaders from pursuing regional solutions to problems that arose prior to and during gaming development; these trends might reverse if external threats to Gilpin County's casino industry emerge. Many problems cannot be solved with isolated deterrence strategies, but only with a coordinated local and regional community development strategy.

Gaming development in the late twentieth century conveys an image of harmless entertainment and fun, but this image is manufactured by the industry that promotes the nationwide spread of casinos. Gaming is first and foremost a highly competitive business, and the largest profits accrue to the companies that successfully position themselves to enter new markets early. If local plans and regulations are not in place prior to negotiations by casino entrepreneurs, the community will find itself responding to industry demands rather than directing the dialogue about community futures. The potential for distraction is also high, as other issues are strategically moved to the forefront of discussions by interest groups. In the Colorado gaming towns, for example, much of the early discussion about gaming development was centered around warnings about the potential for prostitution and Mafia involvement in the local gaming industry. These are certainly important issues, but they were unlikely to become serious problems until the conditions for their growth were present (that is, until the gaming stakes were raised, or hotels were built in Central City and Black Hawk).

Authors writing about tourism planning often imply that tourism developments fail because residents are not well informed or do not widely participate in community meetings. Simmons (1994: 106), for example, commented that "there is evidence of a need for greater public awareness about tourism, its benefits and costs ... [and] there exists the need for a genuine sharing of information between the principal actors in planning, including the business sector, to provide the basis for informed decision making." Comments such as these permeate the tourism literature, but seem naive in the context of community tourism planning. It is not generally true that residents of a community are unable, unaware, or uninformed (though some may be unwilling to participate), and it is misleading to suggest that communities can escape the negative consequences of tourism development simply by sharing information across interest groups. Tourism development always occurs in the context of community history, politics, economics, culture, and environment. Success in gaming development, just as with any other kind of local initiative, will depend on concerned, enthusiastic involvement by residents who are dedicated to humanistic, civic goals.

GAMBLING, TOURISM, AND COMMUNITY

For residents of Black Hawk, Central City, and Gilpin County, what began as a sort of public amusement—the consideration of tourism based on recreational gambling—was transformed, after gaming development, into collective soul-searching about the nature of community. Communities are social constructions, though they are often experienced as something other than socially created. As Berger and Luckmann (1966: 60) explained, "the objectivity of the institutional world, however massive it may appear to the individual, is a humanly produced, constructed objectivity." Gilpin County residents had taken their community for granted prior to gaming development, with many residents participating only marginally in its activities. The consequences of gaming development, though, were so dramatic and far-reaching that all residents were affected. The persistence of community anger even five years past Opening Day is testimony to the uncertainties about the kind of community that had first brought, and then resulted from, gaming development.

The debate about gaming as an economic development strategy should not be framed as a growth versus no-growth dichotomy. The issue is not growth per se, but the implications of unplanned growth for contemporary and future residents, and for the place itself. On the one hand, it is both foolish and naive to expect that communities will remain static as the world around them changes. On the other hand, it is immoral to do nothing in the face of rapid change that will affect all community members, some for the better, others for the worse. One must work to support growth that is sensitive, well planned, responsive to citizens, environmentally conscious, and supportive of the future. The urgency for such attentiveness is becoming more evident as tourism development proves to have more severe consequences than previously thought. Indeed, the Archbishop of Denver, J. Francis Stafford, even focused his 1994 Thanksgiving Pastoral Letter to residents of northern Colorado on the issue of Western Slope tourism-related growth. He wrote (1994: 10), "The task . . . is not to indict any particular group or shut down the tourist resorts in an effort to return to an imagined pristine past; but to encourage growth in a direction, and at a pace, and with a variety, that serves the maximum number of people who actually live and work there in the best possible way."

Coloradans and other western residents have tended to frame debates about community growth as conflicts between the rights of individuals, on the one hand, and the pressures of bureaucratic regulation, on the other (Kemmis 1990; White 1991; Hogan 1990; Limerick 1987). Gambling was initially seen as an extension of the individualist position: local entrepreneurs would be able to pursue their dreams of an improved business climate by incorporating gambling machines into existing local businesses. After development approval, the corporate takeover of both the image and the production of gaming opportunities in Black Hawk and Central City negated many of the potential benefits to local business folk, and imposed a bureaucratic, regulatory structure on local tourism offerings. In keeping with the historic situation between the towns, and between the towns and Gilpin County, cooperation was hardly considered. Yet, cooperation would have created possibilities for more community-sensitive development. As Kemmis (1990: 123) remarked, "A politics of citizens working out the problems and the possibilities of their place directly among themselves implies a revival of the old republican notion of citizenship based upon civic virtue. . . . [It] rests upon a mutual recognition by diverse interests that they are bound to each other by their common attachment to a place."

Cooperation is at the heart of a "good community," a place where people respect and preserve what is meaningful and important from the past, resist what is detrimental or unnecessary, and choose to work together toward humanistic and civic goals. One of the strongest testimonies to the need for communities based on civic humanism is Putnam's exploration of the conditions for democratic success. Putnam (1993) explained that a civic community is characterized by at least four qualities: the active participation of citizens in public affairs; horizontal relationships of reciprocity and cooperation; helpful, respectful, and trustful citizens; and a dense network of voluntary associations that instill public-spiritedness in members. In his study of the emergence, persistence, and failure of democratic institutions across various regions of Italy, Putnam (1993: 182) concluded, "Where the . . . soil is fertile, the regions draw sustenance from regional traditions, but where the soil is poor, the new institutions are stunted." In other words, places with a tradition of civic-mindedness were likely to find ways to reinforce those virtues, and vice versa.

"Stocks of social capital, such as trust, norms, and networks, tend to be self-reinforcing and cumulative. . . . Conversely, the absence of [social capital] in the *un*civic community is also self-reinforcing" (Putnam 1993: 177).

The historical overview of Gilpin County and its gold-mining-turned-tourism-turned gambling communities illustrates Putnam's ideas. History created the circles of conflict that characterize this special place, and history also reinforced conflicts even into contemporary periods. High aspirations that gambling development would reform the economy, and thus reform the community, have not been achieved. Changing the local conditions to produce more civic-mindedness can only be done from inside the community. It depends on the willingness of people to practice civic behavior, and it may take generations to occur. Promoting conditions that foster civic consciousness means building linkages between and among neighbors, governments, the gaming industry, and other entities across the affected region. Each small step in this direction reinforces trust, public-spiritedness, equality, participation, and tolerance, producing mutual, not merely private or individual, benefits. Moreover, these patterns produce sustainable communities, as Norgaard's (1994) work on "coevolving discursive communities" predicts.

Many communities encourage tourism development because they want something from the industry, but one must ask whether the new developments will contribute to civic communities that make for quality places and people. Kemmis (1990: 118–19) framed the issue in this way:

> Places have a way of claiming people. When they claim very diverse kinds of people, then those people must eventually learn to live with each other; they must learn to inhabit their place together, which they can only do through the development of certain practices of inhabitation which both rely upon and nurture the old-fashioned civic virtues of trust, honesty, justice, toleration, cooperation, hope, and remembrance. It is through the nurturing of such virtues (and in no other way) that we might begin to reclaim that competency upon which democratic citizenship depends.

To the extent that the gaming developments in Central City and Black Hawk show the problems of gaming tourism development in contemporary society, and inform other communities about the steps required for coherent and sensitive community tourism planning, a tourism-based economy within a civic community may yet be a possibility. To the extent that the lessons from the Black Hawk and Central City gaming developments are ignored, communities that chase gambling fortunes through "wallet mining" may find themselves eventually striking only fool's gold.

REFERENCES

Throughout the text, parenthetical references to the *Weekly Register-Call* and *The Little Kingdom Come* were abbreviated as *WRC* and *LKC*, respectively. Those periodicals are listed here under their full names.

Abt, Vicki, James F. Smith, and Eugene Martin Christiansen. 1985. *The Business of Risk: Commercial Gambling in Mainstream America*. Lawrence, Kan.: University Press of Kansas.

Albanese, Jay S. 1985. The Effect of Casino Gambling on Crime. *Federal Probation* 49(2): 39–44.

Arland-Fye, Barb, and Roxanna Pellin. 1992. Riverboat Gambling: Recreational Revenue? *Parks and Recreation* 27(11): 64–66, 75.

Armitage, Susan, Elizabeth Jameson, and Joan Jensen. 1993. The New Western History: Another Perspective. *Journal of the West* 32(3): 56.

Axford, H. William. 1976. *Gilpin County Gold: Peter McFarlane 1848–1929, Mining Entrepreneur in Central City, Colorado*. Chicago: Sage Books/Swallow Press.

Bancroft, Caroline. 1943. The Elusive Figure of John H. Gregory, Discoverer of the First Gold Lode in Colorado. *The Colorado Magazine* 20(4): 121–35.

Bancroft, Caroline. 1958. *Gulch of Gold: A History of Central City, Colorado*. Denver, Colo.: Sage Books.

Barney, Libeus (1859–1860). 1959. *Letters of the Pike's Peak Gold Rush (or Early Day Letters from Auraria), Reprinted from the Bennington Banner, Vermont, 1859–1860*. San Jose, Cal.: Talisman Press.

Barthel, Diane. 1989. Historic Preservation: A Comparative Analysis. *Sociological Forum* 4(1): 87–105.

Bastin, Edson S., and James M. Hill, eds. 1917. *Economic Geology of Gilpin County and Adjacent Parts of Clear Creek and Boulder Counties, Colorado*. U.S. Department of the Interior, U.S. Geological Survey, Professional Paper No. 94. Washington, D.C.: Government Printing Office.

Bauer, William H., James L. Ozment, and John H. Willard. 1990. *Colorado Post Offices 1859–1989.* Golden, Colo.: Colorado Railroad Museum.

Bellah, Robert N., Richard Madsen, William M. Sullivan, Ann Swidler, and Steven M. Tipton. 1985. *Habits of the Heart: Individualism and Commitment in American Life.* Berkeley, Cal.: University of California Press.

Berger, Peter L., and Thomas Luckmann. 1966. *The Social Construction of Reality: A Treatise in the Sociology of Knowledge.* Garden City, N.Y.: Doubleday.

Boorstin, Daniel J. 1961. *The Image: A Guide to Pseudo-Events in America.* New York: Harper & Row.

Boulder Daily Camera. 1993. Golf: A Sure Bet? March 8: 1, 2A.

Boulder Daily Camera. 1993. Gaming Industry Eager to Jettison $5 Limit on Wagers. October 20: 6B.

Boulder Daily Camera. 1994. Boulder Firm Gambling on Biggest Casino in State. June 3: 12A.

Bowers, Karen. 1994. Laws of Chance. *Westword* (May): 18–24.

Bowles, Samuel. 1869a. *Our New West.* Hartford, Conn.: Hartford Publishing Co.

Bowles, Samuel. 1869b. *The Switzerland of America: A Summer Vacation in the Parks and Mountains of Colorado.* Springfield, Mass.: Samuel Bowles & Co.

Branch, Kristi, Douglas A. Hooper, James Thompson, and James Creighton. 1984. *Guide to Social Assessment: A Framework for Assessing Social Change.* Boulder, Colo.: Westview Press.

Brenner, Reuven, with Gabrielle A. Brenner. 1990. *Gambling and Speculation: A Theory, a History, and a Future of Some Human Decisions.* Cambridge, Mass.: Cambridge University Press.

Brown, Ralph B., H. Reed Geertsen, and Richard S. Krannich. 1989. Community Satisfaction and Social Integration in a Boomtown: A Longitudinal Analysis. *Rural Sociology* 54(4): 568–86.

Brown, Robert L. 1985. *The Great Pikes Peak Gold Rush.* Caldwell, Idaho: Caxton Printers.

Brown, Ronald C. 1979. *Hard-Rock Miners: The Intermountain West, 1860–1920.* College Station, Tex.: Texas A&M University Press.

Bruns, Don, and Patricia A. Stokowski. 1996 (forthcoming). Sustaining Opportunities to Experience Early American Landscapes. In *Nature and the Human Spirit: Toward an Expanded Land Management Ethic,* ed. B. L. Driver et al. State College, Pa.: Venture Publishing.

Burr, Steven W. 1995 (October). The Problem With Sense of Place Within a Context of Sustainable Tourism Development: A Qualitative Study. Paper presented at the Leisure Research Symposium, National Recreation and Park Association, San Antonio, Texas.

Burr, Steven W., and Jeffrey A. Walsh. 1994. A Hidden Value of Sustainable Rural Tourism. *Trends* 31(1): 9–13.

Butler, Richard. 1980. The Concept of a Tourist Area Cycle of Evolution: Implications for Management of Resources. *Canadian Geographer* 24: 5–12.

Cable, Rufus E. July 30, 1859 letter sent from Denver City to Ike N. White of Wyandott, Kansas. Reprinted in Hafen, LeRoy R., and Ann W. Hafen, eds. 1961. *Reports From Colorado: The Wildman Letters 1859–1865, With Other Related Letters and Newspaper Reports, 1859.* The Far West and the Rockies Historical Series, 1820–1875, vol. 13. Glendale, Cal.: Arthur H. Clark. Pp. 132–35.

Cady, Lew. 1994. Interviewed by Leanne Sander. Department of History, University of Colorado, Boulder. Audiotape.

Canan, Penelope, and Michael Hennessy. 1989. The Growth Machine, Tourism, and the Selling of Culture. *Sociological Perspectives* 32(2): 227–43.

Canedy, Lowell M., and Jeffrey B. Zeiger. 1991. The Social, Economic, and Environmental Costs of Tourism to a Gaming Community as Perceived by its Residents. *Journal of Travel Research* 30(2): 45–49.

Carter, Louis J. 1989. *Yesterday Was Another Day.* Black Hawk, Colo.: St. James Methodist Church.

Catlin, Linda B. 1992 (December). Reverse Alchemy: The Impact of Small-Stakes Gambling on a Colorado Gold Mining Town. Paper presented at the Annual Meeting of the American Anthropological Association, San Francisco, California.

Center for Business and Economic Forecasting, Inc. 1995. *Economic Impact of Limited Gaming in Colorado.* Denver, Colo.: Regis University.

Central City Preservation Initiative, Inc. No date. *Support Program Package.* Mimeo, 8 pp.

Chadbourne, Christopher. 1995. Gambling and Planning: Rules of Thumb. *Historic Preservation Forum* 9(4): 4–10.

Choy, Dexter J. L. 1991. Tourism Planning: The Case for "Market Failure." *Tourism Management* 12(4): 313–30.

City of Black Hawk. 1991. *General Purpose Financial Statements: Report on Examination.* Prepared by Jack Salewski, Certified Public Accountant, December 31, 1991. Idaho Springs, Colo.

City of Black Hawk. 1993. 1994 Budget: Letter to Citizens from City Manager Linda Martin. Pp. 1–8.

City of Central. 1993. 1993 Budget: Budget Message from Jack Hidahl, City Manager. Pp. 1–2.

City of Central. 1994. 1994 Budget: Budget Message from Jack Hidahl, City Manager. Pp. 1–4.

Cohen, Anthony P. 1975. *The Management of Myths: The Politics of Legitimation in a Newfoundland Community.* Manchester, England: Manchester University Press.

Cohen, Anthony P. 1985. *The Symbolic Construction of Community.* London: Routledge.

Colorado Center for Community Development. 1991. *Gilpin County Citizen Survey: Final Report.* Denver, Colo.: University of Colorado.

Colorado Department of Public Health and Environment. 1995 (July). Clear Creek Update: Clear Creek Superfund Site. Denver, Colo.: Colorado Department of Public Health and Environment.

Colorado Division of Gaming. 1993. *Gaming in Colorado: Fact Book and Abstract.* Denver, Colo.: Colorado Division of Gaming.

Colorado Division of Gaming. 1994. *Gaming in Colorado: Fact Book and Abstract.* Denver, Colo.: Colorado Division of Gaming.

Colorado Division of Gaming. 1995. *Gaming in Colorado: Fact Book and Abstract.* Denver, Colo.: Colorado Division of Gaming.

Colorado Gaming Owners Association. 1991. *Newsletter #8.* Central City, Colo. July 5, 1991. 2pp.

Colorado Racing Commission. 1949. *First Annual Report, for the Period January 1, 1949 to December 31, 1949.* Denver, Colo.: Colorado Racing Commission.

Colorado Secretary of State. 1990a. *Abstract of Votes Cast, Primary Election (August 14, 1990) and General Election (November 6, 1990).* Microfiche. Denver, Colo.

Colorado Secretary of State. 1990b. *Election Contributions Reports.* Microfiche. Denver, Colo.

Colorado Secretary of State. 1992. *Abstract of Votes Cast: General Election (November 3, 1992).* Denver, Colo.

Community Health Promotion Evaluation Program. 1989 (September). Feedback Report: Community Activation Survey, Gilpin County. Seattle, Wash.: University of Washington and Group Health Cooperative.

Community Health Promotion Evaluation Program. 1991 (September). Feedback Report: Community Activation Survey, Gilpin County. Seattle, Wash.: University of Washington and Group Health Cooperative.

Community Health Promotion Evaluation Program. 1993 (June). Feedback Report: Community Activation Survey, Gilpin County. Seattle, Wash.: University of Washington and Group Health Cooperative.

Conover, Ted. 1991. *Whiteout: Lost in Aspen.* New York: Random House.

Continuing Legal Education in Colorado, Inc. 1993 (March). *Roll of the Dice: Past, Present and Future of Colorado Gaming.* Denver, Colo.: Continuing Legal Education in Colorado, Inc.

Cortese, Charles F., and Bernie Jones. 1977. The Sociological Analysis of Boomtowns. *Western Sociological Review* 8(1): 76–90.

Cox, Terry L. 1989. *Inside the Mountains: A History of Mining Around Central City, Colorado.* Boulder, Colo.: Pruett Publishing.

Crompton, John L. 1995. Economic Impact Analysis of Sports Facilities and Events: Eleven Sources of Misapplication. *Journal of Sport Management* 9(1): 14–35.

Cronin, Thomas E., and Robert D. Loevy. 1993. *Colorado Politics and Government: Governing the Centennial State.* Lincoln, Neb.: University of Nebraska Press.

Cummings, Ronald G., William D. Schulze, and Arthur F. Mehr. 1978. Optimal Municipal Investment in Boomtowns: An Empirical Analysis. *Journal of Environmental Economics and Management* 5: 252–67.

de Chaine, Faber B. 1963. *Colorado Mountain Theatre: A History of Theatrical Festivals at Central City, Colorado, from 1932 to 1960.* Ph.D. dissertation, University of Minnesota, Department of Speech and Theatre.

DeArment, Robert K. 1982. *Knights of the Green Cloth: The Saga of the Frontier Gamblers.* Norman, Okla.: University of Oklahoma Press.

Denver City Correspondence, August 12, 1859. (From Denver City to the *Missouri Republican*). Reprinted in Hafen, LeRoy R., and Ann W. Hafen, eds. 1961. *Reports from Colorado: The Wildman Letters 1859–1865, With Other Related Letters and Newspaper Reports, 1859.* The Far West and the Rockies Historical Series, 1820–1875, vol. 13, 147–50. Glendale, Cal.: Arthur H. Clark.

Denver City Correspondence, August 28, 1859. (From Mountain City, Gregory Diggings, to the *Missouri Republican*). Reprinted in Hafen, LeRoy R., and Ann W. Hafen, eds. 1961. *Reports from Colorado: The Wildman Letters 1859–1865, With Other Related Letters and Newspaper Reports, 1859.* The Far West and the Rockies Historical Series, 1820–1875, vol. 13, 162–68. Glendale, Cal.: Arthur H. Clark.

Denver Post. 1992. Eager Gamblers a Deadly Element on Crowded Road. June 15: 1, 2B.

Denver Post. 1992. Developers: Bias Plagues Central City. June 22: 1, 2B.

Denver Post. 1992. Casino Moratorium to Continue. June 25: 1, 5B.

Denver Post. 1992. Cop Who Vanished in '89 Gets Police Job. July 18: 1, 4B.

Denver Post. 1992. Central City Alderman Center of 'Tip Off' Probe. August 28: 1, 23A.

Denver Post. 1992. Gaming-Site Misdeals Bring Owners Jackpots. November 4: 1, 5C.

Denver Post. 1992. Casino Moratorium Backers Targeted. November 30: 1, 8A.

Denver Post. 1992. Two Survive Recall Vote in Central City. December 2: 1B.

Denver Post. 1993. Central City Banks on New Hotels. December 19: 1, 8H.

Denver Post. 1993. Harrah's Comes to Colorado, Takes Stake in Two Casinos. December 22: 1C.

Denver Post. 1994. Casino Shut Down by State. February 18: 1, 4B.

Denver Post. 1994. Gambling Calling the Shots: With Casinos, Towns Have Bull by the Tail. November 27: 1C.

Denver Post. 1995. Bus Crash Kills 2, Hurts 42. August 28: 1, 8A.

Denver Post. 1995. Danger on Roads to Riches: Alcohol-Related Crashes Up 79% After Casinos Open. August 30: 1, 24A.

Denver Post. 1995. Harvey's Plans Parking Garage in Central City. October 18: 4B, 5B.

Denver Post. 1995. Gaming Towns Doubt Benefits. November 6: 1, 10A.

Dietz, Thomas. 1987. Theory and Method in Social Impact Assessment. *Sociological Quarterly* 57(1): 54–69.

Dimanche, Frédéric, and Ellen Liliedahl. 1995 (June). The Impacts of Gambling and Related Tourism Development on a Mississippi Urban Area: A Case Study. Paper presented at the 26th Annual Travel and Tourism Research Association Conference. Acapulco, Mexico.

Ditmer, Joanne. 1992. Central City: Gambling and Opera Can Coexist. *Denver Post.* July 12: *Contemporary Magazine* 3.

Dombrink, John, and William N. Thompson. 1990. *The Last Resort: Success and Failure in Campaigns for Casinos.* Reno, Nev.: University of Nevada Press.

Dorset, Phyllis F. 1970. *The New Eldorado: The Story of Colorado's Gold and Silver Rushes.* New York: Macmillan.

Dürrenmatt, Friedrich. 1962. *The Visit.* Translated by Patrick Bowles. New York: Grove Press.

Eadington, William R., ed. 1976. *Gambling and Society: Interdisciplinary Studies on the Subject of Gambling.* Springfield, Ill.: Charles C. Thomas.

Eadington, William R. 1984. The Casino Gaming Industry: A Study of Political Economy. *Annals of the American Academy of Political and Social Science* 474(July): 23–35.

Eadington, William R., and James H. Frey. 1984. Preface: Gambling Views from the Social Sciences. *Annals of the American Academy of Political and Social Science* 474(July): 9–11.

Eco, Umberto. 1986. *Travels in Hyperreality.* William Weaver, trans. San Diego, Cal.: Harcourt Brace Jovanovich.

Edelman, Murray. 1988. *Constructing the Political Spectacle.* Chicago: University of Chicago Press.

Erikson, Kai T. 1976. *Everything in Its Path: Destruction of Community in the Buffalo Creek Flood.* New York: Simon and Schuster.

Etulain, Richard W. 1993. The New Western Historiography and the New Western History: Continuity and Change. *Journal of the West* 32(4): 34.

Fabian, Ann. 1990. *Card Sharks, Dream Books, and Bucket Shops: Gambling in 19th Century America.* Ithaca, N.Y.: Cornell University Press.

Faithfull, Emily. 1884. Glimpses of Glory. In *Chronicles of Colorado.* 1984. Edited by Frederick R. Rinehart, 102–17. Boulder, Colo.: Roberts Rinehart.

Fifth Session of the Legislative Assembly, Territory of Colorado. 1866. An Act to Suppress Gambling and Gambling Houses. *General Laws* 56–60. Central City, Colo.: David B. Collier, Miners' Register Office.

Findlay, John M. 1986. *People of Chance: Gambling in American Society from Jamestown to Las Vegas.* New York: Oxford University Press.

First Session of the Legislative Assembly, Territory of Colorado. 1861. An Act Concerning Licenses. *General Laws,* § 8, p. 70. Denver, Colo.: Thomas Gibson, Colorado Republican and Herald Office.

First Session of the Legislative Assembly, Territory of Colorado. 1861. Offenses Against the Public Morality, Health and Police. *Practice of Law,* Division 10: § 112, p. 313. Denver, Colo.: Thomas Gibson, Colorado Republican and Herald Office.

Fischer, Claude S. 1982. *To Dwell Among Friends: Personal Networks in Town and City.* Chicago: University of Chicago Press.

Fitchen, Janet M. 1991. *Endangered Spaces, Enduring Places: Change, Identity, and Survival in Rural America.* Boulder, Colo.: Westview Press.

Flora, Cornelia B. 1990. Presidential Address: Rural Peoples in a Global Economy. *Rural Sociology* 55(2): 157–77.

Flora, Cornelia B., Jan L. Flora, Jacqueline D. Spears, and Louis Swanson, with Mark B. Lapping and Mark L. Weinberg. 1992. *Rural Communities: Legacy and Change.* Boulder, Colo.: Westview Press.

Fossett, Frank. 1879. *Colorado: Its Gold and Silver Mines, Farms and Stock Ranges, and Health and Pleasure Resorts.* New York: C.G. Crawford.

Fourth Session of the Legislative Assembly, Territory of Colorado. 1865. A Bill for and Act Limiting the Operation of an Act Entitled An Act to Suppress Gambling and Gambling Houses. *General Laws,* p. 72. Denver, Colo.: Byers and Dailey, Printers.

Freudenburg, William R. 1992. Addictive Economies: Extractive Industries and Vulnerable Localities in a Changing World Economy. *Rural Sociology* 57(3): 305–32.

Freudenburg, William R., and Robert Gramling. 1992. Community Impacts of Technological Change: Toward a Longitudinal Perspective. *Social Forces* 70(4): 937–55.

Freudenburg, William R., and Robert Gramling. 1994a. Bureaucratic Slippage and Failures of Agency Vigilance: The Case of the Environmental Studies Program. *Social Problems* 41(2): 214–39.

Freudenburg, William R., and Robert Gramling. 1994b. Mid-Range Theory and Cutting Edge Sociology: A Call for Cumulation. In *Environment, Technology, and Society.* Newsletter of the Section on Environment and Technology, American Sociological Association 76(Summer): 1–7.

Freudenburg, William R., and Robert Gramling. 1994c. *Oil in Troubled Waters: Perceptions, Politics, and the Battle Over Offshore Drilling.* Albany, N.Y.: State University of New York Press.

Freudenburg, William R., and Robert E. Jones. 1991. Criminal Behavior and Rapid Community Growth: Examining the Evidence. *Rural Sociology* 56(4): 619–45.

Frey, James H. 1984. Gambling: A Sociological Review. *Annals of the American Academy of Political and Social Science* 474(July): 107–21.

Friedman, Joseph, Simon Hakim, and J. Weinblatt. 1989. Casino Gambling as a "Growth Pole" Strategy and Its Effect on Crime. *Journal of Regional Science* 29(4): 615–23.

Gale, Richard P. 1986. Sociological Theory and the Differential Distribution of Impacts in Rural Resource Development Projects. In *Differential Social Impacts of Rural Resource Development.* Edited by Pamela D. Elkind-Savatsky, 37–59. Boulder, Colo.: Westview Press.

Garrison, A. F. July 4th, 1859 letter from Gregory's Diggings, Kansas Territory, sent to L. R. Smoot of Leavenworth, Kansas. Reprinted in Hafen, LeRoy R., and Ann W. Hafen, eds. 1961. *Reports from Colorado: The Wildman Letters 1859–1865, With Other Related Letters and Newspaper Reports, 1859.* The Far West and the Rockies Historical Series, 1820–1875, vol. 13, 108–10. Glendale, Cal.: Arthur H. Clark.

Gephart, Robert P. 1993. The Textual Approach: Risk and Blame in Disaster Sensemaking. *Academy of Management Journal* 36(6): 1465–1514.

Gern, Jesse W. 1960. Colorado Mountain Theatre: History of Theatre at Central City, 1859–1885. Ph.D. dissertation, vol. 1. Ohio State University: Department of Speech.

Getz, Donald. 1986. Models in Tourism Planning: Towards Integration of Theory and Practice. *Tourism Management* 7(1): 21–32.

Gill, Alison, and Rudi Hartmann, eds. 1992. *Mountain Resort Development.* Proceedings of the Vail Conference, April 18–21, 1991. Centre for Tourism Policy and Research, Simon Fraser University, Burnaby, British Columbia.

Gill, Alison, and Peter Williams. 1994. Managing Growth in Mountain Tourism Communities. *Tourism Management* 15(3): 212–20.

Gilpin County Advocate. 1990. The Boom is Back for Gilpin. November 8: 1, 3.

The Gilpin Gazette. 1993 (April). More than Mountains at Miner's Mesa. 1(1): 2.

Goodman, Robert. 1995. *The Luck Business: The Devastating Consequences and Broken Promises of America's Gambling Explosion.* New York: Free Press.

Goudy, Willis J. 1990. Community Attachment in a Rural Region. *Rural Sociology* 55(2): 178–98.

Gower, Calvin W. 1965. Gold Rush Governments. *Colorado Magazine* 42(2): 114–32.

Granruth, Alan. 1991. *A Guide to Downtown Central City, Colorado.* Black Hawk, Colo.: Author.

Granruth, Alan. 1994. Interviewed by Leanne Sander. Department of History, University of Colorado, Boulder. Audiotape.

Greeley, Horace. 1860. *An Overland Journey, from New York to San Francisco, in the Summer of 1859.* New York: C. M. Saxton, Barker, & Co.

Greeley, Horace, Albert D. Richardson, and Henry Villard. Report of June 9, 1859, from Gregory's Diggings, near Clear creek [sic] in the Rocky mountains [sic]. In Hafen, LeRoy R., ed. 1941. *Colorado Gold Rush: Contemporary Letters and Reports, 1858–1859.* The Southwest Historical Series, vol. 10, 376–82. Glendale, Cal.: Arthur H. Clark.

Greeley, Horace, Albert D. Richardson, and Henry Villard. June 11, 1859. Printed originally in the *Rocky Mountain News.* In *Early Records of Gilpin County, Colorado: 1859–1861.* 1920. Edited by Thomas M. Marshall, 10. Denver, Colo.: W. F. Robinson.

Greenberg, Joanne. 1986. *Simple Gifts.* New York: Henry Holt.

Greenwood, Davydd J. 1989. Culture by the Pound: An Anthropological Perspective on Tourism as Cultural Commoditization. In *Hosts and Guests: The Anthropology of Tourism.* Edited by Valene L. Smith, 171–85. Philadelphia: University of Pennsylvania Press.

Greider, Thomas, and Lorraine Garkovich. 1994. Landscapes: The Social Construction of Nature and the Environment. *Rural Sociology* 59(1): 1–24.

Gressley, Gene M., ed. 1994. *Old West/New West: Quo Vadis?* Worland, Wy.: High Plains Publishing.

Grimes, Ross. 1992. Letter to the Colorado Gaming Commission. July 28. Photocopy.

Gulliford, Andrew. 1989. *Boomtown Blues: Colorado Oil Shale, 1885–1985*. Niwot, Colo.: University Press of Colorado.

Gunn, Clare A. 1994. *Tourism Planning: Basics, Concepts, Cases*. New York: Taylor and Francis.

Gunn, John. 1989. Enquiring Minds Read It in *The Little Kingdom Come. Peak to Peak Magazine*, May-June: 27–30.

Hafen, LeRoy R., ed. 1941. *Pike's Peak Gold Rush Guidebooks of 1859*. The Southwest Historical Series, vol. 9. Glendale, Cal.: Arthur H. Clark.

Hafen, LeRoy R., ed. (1942) 1974. *Overland Routes to the Gold Fields, 1859, from Contemporary Diaries*. Philadelphia: Porcupine Press.

Hafen, LeRoy R., and Ann W. Hafen, eds. 1961. *Reports from Colorado: The Wildman Letters 1859–1865, With Other Related Letters and Newspaper Reports, 1859*. The Far West and the Rockies Historical Series, 1820–1875, vol. 13. Glendale, Cal.: Arthur H. Clark.

Hakim, Simon, and Andrew J. Buck. 1989. Do Casinos Enhance Crime? *Journal of Criminal Justice* 17(5): 409–16.

Halaas, David F. 1981. *Boom Town Newspapers: Journalism on the Rocky Mountain Mining Frontier, 1859–1881*. Albuquerque, N.M.: University of New Mexico Press.

Hall, C. Michael. 1994. *Tourism and Politics: Policy, Power and Place*. New York: John Wiley & Sons.

Halliday, Brett. 1943. *Murder Wears a Mummers Mask*. New York: Books, Inc.

Hartmann, Rudi. Forthcoming. Of Booms, Busts, and Winning Streaks: Geographical Factors for Casino Development in Two Colorado Mountain Towns. In *Casino Gambling in America: Origins, Trends, and Impacts*. Edited by Klaus J. Meyer-Arendt and Rudi Hartmann. Philadelphia: University of Pennsylvania Press.

Haywood, K. Michael. 1988. Responsible and Responsive Tourism Planning in the Community. *Tourism Management* 9(2): 105–18.

Hedden, Bill. 1994. Towns Angling for Tourism Should Beware of the Great White Shark. *High Country News*. 26(16) (September 5): 20.

Hester, Randolph T. 1985. Subconscious Landscapes of the Heart. *Small Town* 2(3): 10–22.

Hester, Randolph T. 1990. The Sacred Structure in Small Towns: A Return to Manteo, North Carolina. *Small Town* 20(4): 5–21.

Hidahl, Jack. 1994. Interviewed by Leanne Sander. Department of History, University of Colorado, Boulder. Audiotape.

High Country News. 1994. How to Get Involved and Push the Process. 26(16) (September 5): 18.

Hoffmeister, H. A. 1940. Central City Mining Area. *Economic Geography* 16(1): 96–104.

Hogan, Richard. 1990. *Class and Community in Frontier Colorado*. Lawrence, Kan.: University Press of Kansas.

Hollenback, Frank R. 1961. *Central City and Black Hawk, Colorado: Then and Now*. Denver, Colo.: Sage Books.

Ittelson, Ellen, and Ron Dutton. 1995. Lessons and Challenges of Gambling and Historic Preservation. *Historic Preservation Forum* 9(4): 11–19.

Janes, Robert W. 1958. A Technique for Describing Community Structure through Newspaper Analysis. *Social Forces* 37(2): 102–9.

Janowitz, Morris. 1967. *The Community Press in an Urban Society.* Chicago: The University of Chicago Press.

Jensen, Katherine, and Audie Blevins. 1995. Gambling on the Lure of Historic Preservation: Community Transformation in Rocky Mountain Mining Towns. *Journal of the Community Development Society* 26(1): 71–92.

Jewett, M. M. November 18, 1858 Letter from Auraria. In *Colorado Gold Rush: Contemporary Letters and Reports, 1858–1859.* 1941. Edited by LeRoy R. Hafen. The Southwest Historical Series, vol. 10, 163–64. Glendale, Cal.: Arthur H. Clark.

Jobes, Patrick C. 1995. Migration in the West: A Gallatin Valley, Montana, Case Study. *The Western Planner* 16(3): 10–13.

Johnson, Charles A. 1992. *Opera in the Rockies: A History of the Central City Opera House Association, 1932–1992.* Denver, Colo.: Central City Opera House Association.

Johnson, Charlie H., Jr. 1980. *The Central City Opera House: A 100 Year History.* Colorado Springs, Colo.: Little London Press.

Johnston, David. 1992. *Temples of Chance: How America Inc. Bought Out Murder Inc. to Win Control of the Casino Business.* New York: Doubleday.

Johnstone, Barbara. 1990. *Stories, Community, and Place: Narratives from Middle America.* Bloomington, Ind.: Indiana University Press.

Jones, Bernie. 1991. Personal correspondence. July 18, 1991.

Kariel, Herbert G. 1989. Tourism and Development: Perplexity or Panacea? *Journal of Travel Research* 28(1): 2–6.

Kemmis, Daniel. 1990. *Community and the Politics of Place.* Norman, Okla: University of Oklahoma Press.

Kemp, Donald C. 1949. *Colorado's Little Kingdom.* Golden, Colo.: Sage Books.

Keogh, Brian. 1990. Public Participation in Community Tourism Planning. *Annals of Tourism Research.* 17(3): 449–65.

Kerouac, Jack. 1955. *On the Road.* New York: Viking Press.

Kerven, Anne. 1992. Gambling on Colorado. *Colorado Business Magazine* 19(9): 32–41.

King, Joseph E. 1977. *A Mine to Make a Mine: Financing the Colorado Mining Industry, 1859–1902.* College Station, Tex.: Texas A&M University Press.

Kisling, Jack. 1992. They Don't Make 'Em Like They Used To. *Denver Post.* July 14: 7B.

Kramer, Kathryn. 1990. *Siren Song.* New York: Dell.

Krannich, Richard S., and Thomas Greider. 1984. Personal Well-Being in Rapid Growth and Stable Communities: Multiple Indicators and Contrasting Results. *Rural Sociology* 49(4): 541–52.

Krannich, Richard S., Thomas Greider, and Ronald L. Little. 1985. Rapid Growth and Fear of Crime: A Four-Community Comparison. *Rural Sociology* 50(2): 193–209.

Krannich, Richard S., and Craig R. Humphrey. 1983. Local Mobilization and Community Growth: Toward an Assessment of the Growth Machine Hypothesis. *Rural Sociology* 48(1): 60–81.

Kunstler, James H. 1993. *The Geography of Nowhere: The Rise and Decline of America's Man-Made Landscape.* New York: Simon and Schuster.

Lamm, Richard D. 1994. Personal interview. December 19, 1994. Denver, Colorado.

Leistritz, F. Larry, John M. Halstead, Robert A. Chase, and Steven H. Murdock. 1984. A Systems Approach for Impact Management: Program Design and Implementation Considerations. In *Resource Communities: A Decade of Disruption.* Edited by Don D. Detomasi and John W. Gartrell, 137–52. Boulder, Colo.: Westview Press.

Leistritz, F. Larry, and Steven H. Murdock. 1981. *The Socioeconomic Impact of Resource Development: Methods for Assessment.* Boulder, Colo.: Westview Press.

Lesieur, Henry R. 1977. *The Chase: Career of the Compulsive Gambler.* Garden City, N.Y.: Anchor Books.

Leyendecker, Liston E. 1992. *Palace Car Prince: A Biography of George Mortimer Pullman.* Niwot, Colo.: University Press of Colorado.

Liebman, Nancy. 1995. Three Strikes, You're Out. *Historic Preservation Forum* 9(4): 28–34.

Lillydahl, Jane H., and Elizabeth W. Moen. 1983. Planning, Managing, and Financing Growth and Decline in Energy Resource Communities: A Case of Western Colorado. *Journal of Energy and the Environment* 8(2): 211–29.

Limerick, Patricia N. 1987. *The Legacy of Conquest: The Unbroken Past of the American West.* New York: W.W. Norton.

Limited Gaming Act. Proclaimed by the Governor, January 1991. Colo. Const. Art. 18, § 9.

The Lincoln Company. 1992. *Contiguous County Gaming Impact Study: Interim Report of August 3, 1992.* Prepared for the Colorado Division of Gaming. Vol. 2: Research. Littleton, Colo.

The Little Kingdom Come. 1990 (February 16). It's Not All Black & White, But It Sure Is Green: An Analysis of the Heavy-handed Enforcement of DUI Laws in Gilpin County. 10(4, 5): 2.

The Little Kingdom Come. 1991 (February 1). What's Wrong With Our Town Meetings? 10(10): 7.

The Little Kingdom Come. 1991 (October 18). Bell Fruit or Bell Canto, It's All The Same. 11(5): 1.

The Little Kingdom Come. 1991 (October 18). It's good! It's bad! It's big! It's here! WALLET MINING! 11(5): 1.

The Little Kingdom Come. 1993 (June 16). Sidebar to Gold Coin Twinkieized. 12(2): 1.

The Little Kingdom Come. 1995 (August 4). Black Hawk: Now You See It. Now You Don't. 13(3): 1.

The Little Kingdom Come. 1995 (December 12). The *LKC* Ran This Story in our August Issue: This Man is a Liar. 13(4): 6.

Logan, John R., and Harvey L. Molotch. 1987. *Urban Fortunes: The Political Economy of Place.* Berkeley, Cal.: University of California Press.

Long, Patrick T. 1995. Casino Gaming in the United States: 1994 Status and Implications. *Tourism Management* 16(3): 189–97.

Long, Patrick T., Jo Clark, and Derek Liston. 1994. *Win, Lose, or Draw? Gambling With America's Small Towns.* Washington, D.C.: The Aspen Institute.

Longstreet, Stephen. 1977. *Win or Lose: A Social History of Gambling in America.* Indianapolis, Ind.: Bobbs-Merrill.

Luloff, A. E., and Donald G. Hodges. 1992. Attitudes and Bureaucrats: Assessing the Representativeness of Local Officials in New Hampshire. *Rural Sociology* 57(3): 381–95.

MacCannell, Dean. 1976. *The Tourist: A New Theory of the Leisure Class.* New York: Schocken Books.

MacGregor, James R. 1993. Sustainable Tourism Development. In *Encyclopedia of Hospitality and Tourism.* Edited by Mahmood A. Khan, Michael D. Olson, and Turgut Var, 781–89. New York: Van Nostrand Reinhold.

Madrigal, Robert. 1995. Residents' Perceptions and the Role of Government. *Annals of Tourism Research* 22(1): 86–102.

Marks, Paula M. 1994. *Precious Dust: The American Gold Rush Era, 1848–1900.* New York: William Morrow.

Marshall, Thomas M., ed. 1920. *Early Records of Gilpin County, Colorado: 1859–1861.* Denver, Colo.: W. F. Robinson Ptg. Co.

Mathieson, Alister, and Geoffrey Wall. 1982. *Tourism: Economic, Physical, and Social Impacts.* New York: John Wiley & Sons.

Mestrovic, Stjepan G. 1994. *The Balkanization of the West: The Confluence of Postmodernism and Postcommunism.* London: Routledge.

Milier, Mary Warren. 1995. Gambling Doesn't Pay in Historic Natchez. *Historic Preservation Forum* 9(4): 40–47.

Minnesota Tourism Center. 1991. *A Training Guide for Rural Tourism Development.* Minneapolis, Minn.: Minnesota Extension Service, University of Minnesota.

Molotch, Harvey L. 1976. The City as a Growth Machine: Toward a Political Economy of Place. *American Journal of Sociology* 82(2): 309–32.

Motz, Annabelle B. 1981. Toward Assessing Social Impacts: The Diachronic Analysis of Newspaper Contents. In *Methodology of Social Impact Assessment.* Edited by Kurt Finsterbusch, 273–83. Stroudsburg, Pa.: Hutchinson Ross.

Motz, Annabelle B. 1983. Historical Documents. In *Social Impact Assessment Methods.* Edited by Kurt Finsterbusch, Lynn G. Llewellyn, and C. P. Wolf, 111–25. Beverly Hills, Cal.: Sage Publications.

Murdock, Steven H., and F. Larry Leistritz. 1979. *Energy Development in the Western United States: Impact on Rural Areas.* New York: Praeger.

Murphy, Peter E. 1983. Tourism as Community Industry: An Ecological Model of Tourism Development. *Tourism Management* 4(3): 180–93.

Murphy, Peter E. 1985. *Tourism: A Community Approach.* New York: Routledge.

Murphy, Peter E. 1988. Community Driven Tourism Planning. *Tourism Management* 9(2): 96–104.

Nash, Gerald D. 1993. Point of View: One Hundred Years of Western History. *Journal of the West* 32(1): 3–4.

National Park Service. 1990 (April). *National Register of Historic Places Registration Form: Updated and Revised Survey of Properties in the Central City-Black Hawk National Historic Landmark District.* Denver, Colo.: Rocky Mountain Regional Office, USDI. 71 pp. mimeo.

Nevadaville miner, writing to *Rocky Mountain News.* November 26, 1860. P. 2: From Nevada. In *Early Records of Gilpin County, Colorado: 1859–1861.* 1920. Edited by Thomas M. Marshall, 137. Denver, Colo.: W. F. Robinson Ptg. Co.

Nickerson, Norma P. 1994. Tourism and Gambling Content Analysis. *Annals of Tourism Research* 22(1): 53–66.

Norgaard, Richard B. 1994. *Development Betrayed: The End of Progress and a Coevolutionary Revisioning of the Future.* London: Routledge.

Patterson, E. H. N. 1859. The Platte River Route: Diary of E. H. N. Patterson. In *Overland Routes to the Gold Fields, 1859, from Contemporary Diaries.* 1974. Edited by LeRoy R. Hafen, 591–97. Philadelphia: Porcupine Press.

Pearce, Douglas. 1989. *Tourist Development.* New York: John Wiley & Sons.

Perdue, Richard R., Patrick T. Long, and Yong S. Kang. 1995. Resident Support for Gambling as a Tourism Development Strategy. *Journal of Travel Research* 34(2): 3–11.

Perrigo, Lynn I. 1934. *The Little Kingdom: A Record Chiefly of Central City in the Early Days.* Boulder, Colo. Mimeo.

Perrigo, Lynn I. 1936. *A Social History of Central City, Colorado, 1859–1900.* Ph.D. dissertation. University of Colorado: Department of History.

Pettem, Silvia. 1980. *Red Rocks to Riches: Gold Mining in Boulder County Then and Now.* Boulder, Colo.: Stonehenge Books.

Pizam, Abraham, and Julianne Pokela. 1985. The Perceived Impacts of Casino Gambling on a Community. *Annals of Tourism Research* 12(2): 147–65.

Powers, Ron. 1986. *White Town Drowsing.* Boston: Atlantic Monthly Press.

Preister, Kevin. 1987. Issue-Centered Social Impact Assessment. In *Anthropological Praxis: Translating Knowledge into Action.* Edited by Robert M. Wulff and Shirley J. Fiske, 39–55. Boulder, Colo.: Westview Press.

Price, Martin F. 1992. Patterns of the Development of Tourism in Mountain Environments. *GeoJournal* 27(1): 87–96.

Putnam, Robert D. 1993. *Making Democracy Work: Civic Traditions in Modern Italy.* Princeton, N.J.: Princeton University Press.

Ransome, F. L. 1917. Preface. *Economic Geology of Gilpin County and Adjacent Parts of Clear Creek and Boulder Counties, Colorado.* Edited by Edson S. Bastin and James M. Hill. U.S. Department of the Interior, U.S. Geological Survey, Professional Paper No. 94. Washington, D.C.: Government Printing Office.

Ray & Associates, Inc. 1975. *Comprehensive Planning Documents, City of Central, Colorado.* Boulder, Colo. Vol. 1: Goals and Objectives; Vol. 2: Environmental Resource Inventory and Analysis; Vol. 3: Socio-Economic Characteristics and Housing Inventory; Vol. 4: Historic Preservation Plan; Vol. 5: Water Utility Master Plan.

Relph, Edward. 1976. *Place and Placelessness.* London: Pion Limited.

Richardson, Albert D. 1873. *Beyond the Mississippi: From the Great River to the Great Ocean; Life and Adventure on the Prairies, Mountains, and Pacific Coast.* Hartford, Conn.: American Publishing.

Richardson, Sarah L. 1991. *Colorado Community Tourism Action Guide.* University of Colorado: Colorado Center for Community Development (Denver, Colo.), and Center for Recreation and Tourism Development (Boulder, Colo.).

Richter, Linda K. 1989. *The Politics of Tourism in Asia.* Honolulu, Haw.: University of Hawaii Press.

Ringholz, Raye C. 1992. *Little Town Blues: Voices From the Changing West.* Salt Lake City, Utah: Peregrine Smith Books.

Rocky Mountain News. 1992. Casino Plans a Mountain Extravaganza. May 10: 7C.

Rocky Mountain News. 1992. Black Hawk Ex-mayor Laments Gambling. August 1: 55.

Rocky Mountain News. 1992. Central City Casino Shut; 32 Lose Jobs. September 2: 37.

Rocky Mountain News. 1992. State's Biggest Casino Planned for Black Hawk. September 24: 52.

Rocky Mountain News. 1992. Casino Owners Try to Stop Rapid Expansion of Colorado Gaming. September 27: 120.

Rocky Mountain News. 1992. Tax Burden Shifts to Big Casinos. September 30: 10.

Rocky Mountain News. 1992. Highest Casino Tax Puts Colorado at Disadvantage, Nevada Prof Says. September 30: 49.

Rocky Mountain News. 1993. Denver Inc.: Late Entry. April 27: 51A.

Roehl, Wesley S. 1994. Gambling as a Tourist Attraction: Trends and Issues for the 21st Century. In *Tourism: The State of the Art.* Edited by A. V. Seaton, 156–68. Chichester, U.K.: John Wiley & Sons.

Rosecrance, John. 1988. *Gambling Without Guilt: The Legitimation of an American Pastime.* Pacific Grove, Cal.: Brooks/Cole Publishing.

Rubenstein, Joseph. 1984. Casino Gambling in Atlantic City: Issues of Development and Redevelopment. *Annals of the American Academy of Political and Social Science* 474(July): 61–71.

Ryden, Kent C. 1993. *Mapping the Invisible Landscape: Folklore, Writing, and the Sense of Place.* Iowa City, Iowa: University of Iowa Press.

Rystrom, Kenneth. 1991. Editorial Pages Critique. *Grassroots Editor* 31(1): 6–9.

Safire, William. 1995. New Evil Empire. *New York Times.* September 28: A17.

Sayre, Hal. 1929. Early Central City Theatricals and Other Reminiscences. *Colorado Magazine* 5(2): 47–53.

Shibutani, Tamotsu. 1986. *Social Processes: An Introduction to Sociology.* Berkeley, Cal.: University of California Press.

Simmons, David G. 1994. Community Participation in Tourism Planning. *Tourism Management* 15(2): 98–108.

Smith, Duane A. 1973. *Horace Tabor: His Life and the Legend.* Boulder, Colo.: Colorado Associated University Press.

Smith, Mary J. 1988. *Contemporary Communication Research Methods.* Belmont, Cal.: Wadsworth Publishing.

Smith, Valene L., ed. 1989. *Hosts and Guests: The Anthropology of Tourism.* Philadelphia: University of Pennsylvania Press.

Spencer, Elma D. R. 1966. *Green Russell and Gold.* Austin, Tex.: University of Texas Press.

Stafford, J. Francis. 1994. The Heights of the Mountains Are His. Pastoral Letter from the Archbishop of Denver to the People of God of Northern Colorado on Western Slope Growth. Thanksgiving Day, November 24.

Stamm, Keith R. 1985. *Newspaper Use and Community Ties: Toward a Dynamic Theory.* Norwood, N.J.: Ablex Publishing.

Stegner, Wallace E. 1992. *Where the Bluebird Sings to the Lemonade Springs: Living and Writing in the West.* New York: Random House.

Stokowski, Patricia A. 1992. The Colorado Gambling Boom: An Experiment in Rural Community Development. *Small Town* 22(6): 12–19.

Stokowski, Patricia A. 1993a (July). *Report of Research Findings: Planning Project for Gilpin County Public Library*. Gilpin County, Colo.

Stokowski, Patricia A. 1993b. Undesirable Lag Effects in Tourist Destination Development: A Colorado Case Study. *Journal of Travel Research* 32(2): 35–41.

Stokowski, Patricia A. 1996. Crime Patterns and Gaming Development in Rural Colorado. *Journal of Travel Research* 34(3): 63–69.

Stout, E. P. October 30, 1858 Letter from Cherry creek [sic], published in the *Omaha Nebraskian*. In *Colorado Gold Rush: Contemporary Letters and Reports, 1858–1859*. 1941. Edited by LeRoy R. Hafen. The Southwest Historical Series, vol. 10, 140–43. Glendale, Cal.: Arthur H. Clark.

Stubbles, Russell. 1990. The Deadwood Tradition: Putting Gambling Before Planning in South Dakota. *Small Town* 20(3) (November–December): 20–27.

Swinnerton, Guy S., and Thomas D. Hinch. 1994. Sustainable Rural Tourism: Principles and Practices. *Trends* 31(1): 4–8.

Third Session of the Legislative Assembly, Territory of Colorado. 1864. An Act to Suppress Gambling and Gambling Houses. *General Laws*, 96–98. Denver: Byers and Dailey, Printers.

Tierney, Luke, D. C. Oakes, and Stephen W. Smith. 1859. *History of the Gold Discoveries on the South Platte River, to Which is Appended A Guide of the Route*. In *Pike's Peak Gold Rush Guidebooks of 1859*. 1941. Edited by LeRoy R. Hafen. The Southwest Historical Series, vol. 9, 89–145. Glendale, Cal.: Arthur H. Clark.

Travel Weekly. 1995. Spotlight on Gaming: U.S. Casino Wagering. July 24: 25.

Tuan, Yi-Fu. 1977. *Space and Place: The Perspective of Meaning*. Minneapolis, Minn.: University of Minnesota Press.

Turner, Louis, and John Ash. 1975. *The Golden Hordes: International Tourism and the Pleasure Periphery*. London: Constable.

Urry, John. 1990. *The Tourist Gaze: Leisure and Travel in Contemporary Societies*. London: Sage Publications.

U.S. Department of Commerce. 1994. *County and City Data Book*. Washington, D.C.: Government Printing Office.

van den Berghe, Pierre. 1993. Cultural Impacts of Tourism. In *Encyclopedia of Hospitality and Tourism*. Edited by Mahmood A. Khan, Michael D. Olson, and Turgut Var, 619–28. New York: Van Nostrand Reinhold.

Voynick, Stephen M. 1992. *Colorado Gold: From the Pikes Peak Rush to the Present*. Missoula, Mont.: Mountain Press Publishing.

Walden, Spencer N. 1991. Developments. *Limited Stakes Gaming Review* 1(1): 2–3.

Walden, Spencer N. 1992. Developments. *Limited Stakes Gaming Review* 1(5): 2.

Ward, Martha C. 1993. *The Hidden Life of Tirol*. Prospect Heights, Ill.: Waveland Press.

Watson, Robert. 1989. Just Like Clockwork. *Grassroots Editor* 30(3): 10, 14.

Webb, Eugene J., Donald T. Campbell, Richard D. Schwartz, and Lee Sechrest. 1966. *Unobtrusive Measures: Nonreactive Research in the Social Sciences*. Chicago: Rand McNally College Publishing.

Weber, Bruce A., and Robert E. Howell. 1982. *Coping With Rapid Growth in Rural Communities.* Boulder, Colo.: Westview Press.

Weekly Register-Call. 1989. Efforts Again Underway to Legalize Gambling in Central City. September 8: 1.

Weekly Register-Call. 1989. Black Hawk Considers the Idea of Gambling. September 15: 1.

Weekly Register-Call. 1989. Want Ads. November 3: 7.

Weekly Register-Call. 1989. Group Will Promote Gambling in Central City. November 10: 1.

Weekly Register-Call. 1989. Readers Forum; letter by Bob Brusco, Chairman, Public Relations Committee, CCPI. December 8: 2.

Weekly Register-Call. 1989. Readers Forum; letter by Lary Brown, Central City. December 29: 2.

Weekly Register-Call. 1990. Gambling Idea Starts Land Rush in Area. January 26: 1.

Weekly Register-Call. 1990. Local Plan Unlike Deadwood. March 2: 1.

Weekly Register-Call. 1990. The Real Facts Behind the Limited Gaming Proposal. April 6: 2.

Weekly Register-Call. 1990. Gambling Would Stimulate Economy (column by State Senator Sally Hopper). April 13: 2.

Weekly Register-Call. 1990. New Tokens Promote Gambling. August 3: 3.

Weekly Register-Call. 1990. Voters Will Decide Gambling. August 24: 1.

Weekly Register-Call. 1990. Gambling Creates Controversy. August 31: 1.

Weekly Register-Call. 1990. PIC Picks Poundstone to Promote Gambling. September 28: 1.

Weekly Register-Call. 1990. Gambling Proponents Speak Out at Meeting. October 5: 1.

Weekly Register-Call. 1990. DiBenedetto Issues Challenge to Poundstone to Hold Public Debates on Gambling Question. October 5: 2.

Weekly Register-Call. 1990. Publishers Corner: William C. Russell. October 19: 2.

Weekly Register-Call. 1991. Are Central's Streets and Walkways Hazardous to Health? June 14: 1.

Weekly Register-Call. 1991. Jewelers to Relocate. July 12: 8.

Weekly Register-Call. 1991. They Paved Paradise, Put Up a Parking Lot. July 19: 2.

Weekly Register-Call. 1991. The Time for Special Consideration Is Over. August 23: 2.

Weekly Register-Call. 1991. Mobile Homes Shouldn't Be Allowed in Subdivisions. September 20: 2.

Weekly Register-Call. 1991. Forced Resignations Will Cause a Leadership Vacuum (letter by Stephen P. Grogan, Executive Director, Colorado Gaming Owners Association). September 27: 2.

Weekly Register-Call. 1991. Central's Docket Too Crowded, Says Rogers. December 13: 3.

Weekly Register-Call. 1992. Kwik Mart Collapses During Construction—City Says Pull It Down. March 6: 1.

Weekly Register-Call. 1992. Want Ads. March 13: 5.

Weekly Register-Call. 1992. City Government Doesn't Want to Hear From Us. July 10: 2.

Weekly Register-Call. 1992. Big Fish, Little Pond: Where's the Accountability? July 31: 2.

Weekly Register-Call. 1992. Short Cut Leads to Long Night. September 11: 1.

Weekly Register-Call. 1992. Turning Back the Pages, 30 Years Ago: October 5, 1962. October 2: 3.

Weekly Register-Call. 1992. Raising Money for Jail a Frustrating Task. December 25: 1.

Weekly Register-Call. 1993. The Gold Coin is More Than a Bar, It's a Community Scrapbook of Shared Memories. June 25: 3.

Weekly Register-Call. 1993. Central Considers Naming Stahl to Staff. September 3: 1.

Weekly Register-Call. 1993. Who Is Accountable? September 10: 2.

Weekly Register-Call. 1993. Central City Needs Change. September 17: 2.

Weekly Register-Call. 1994. Trust Must Be Earned. February 4: 2.

Weekly Register-Call. 1994. Remember When They Told Us that Limited Stakes Gaming Would Benefit Us All? May 13: 2.

Weekly Register-Call. 1994. Commissioners Say No to Recreation Special Tax District. August 5: 1.

Weekly Register-Call. 1994a. Casino Association Disagrees with MAB Marketing Strategy. November 25: 1.

Weekly Register-Call. 1994b. Shady Ladies Promote Central City by Celebrating Role of Women in Old West. November 25: 1.

Weekly Register-Call. 1994. There Is a Lack of Communication. December 9: 2.

Weekly Register-Call. 1995. Is It Time to Secede from Gilpin County? January 25: 2.

Weekly Register-Call. 1995. Pine Street—Valet or Residential Parking? March 10: 1.

Weekly Register-Call. 1995. Lou Bunch Day: 20 Years of Taking to the Streets. June 16: 4–5.

Weekly Register-Call. 1995. Better Pay Attention to What's Happening—The Rules May Be Changing. July 21: 2.

Weekly Register-Call. 1995. Central City Budget Cut 2.5 Percent from 1995, Marketing Board, Inc. Dissolved. December 15: 1.

Wellman, Barry. 1979. The Community Question: The Intimate Networks of East Yorkers. *American Journal of Sociology* 84: 1201–31.

Westword. 1992. Place Your Bets. October 28-November 3: 14–26.

Wheeller, Brian. 1991. Tourism's Troubled Times: Responsible Tourism Is Not the Answer. *Tourism Management* 12(2): 91–96.

White, Richard. 1991. *It's Your Misfortune and None of My Own: A History of the American West.* Norman, Okla.: University of Oklahoma Press.

White, Stephen. 1993. *Private Practices.* New York: Viking.

Wilkinson, Charles F. 1992. *The Eagle Bird: Mapping a New West.* New York: Pantheon Books.

Willits, Fern K., Robert C. Bealer, and Vincent L. Timbers. 1990. Popular Images of Rurality: Data from a Pennsylvania Survey. *Rural Sociology* 55(4): 559–78.

Wolfe, Mark. 1992. Remarks at the Colorado Gaming and Community Development Forum. Lakewood, Colorado, May 29.

Working, D. W. 1927. Some Forgotten Pioneer Newspapers. *Colorado Magazine* 4(3): 93–100.

Yearbook of the State of Colorado. 1918. Denver, Colo.: State Board of Immigration.

Young, Allen. 1993. *Opera in Central City.* Denver, Colo.: Author.

Young, Frank C. 1903. *Echoes from Arcadia.* Denver, Colo.: Author.

INDEX

Note: Citations in **boldface** refer to material in photographs and tables.